INQUIRY INTO INQUIRIES

Essays in Social Theory

INQUIRY INTO INQUIRIES

Essays in Social Theory

by

ARTHUR F. BENTLEY

Edited and with an Introduction by

Sidney Ratner

THE BEACON PRESS · BOSTON

Copyright 1954
Sidney Ratner

Library of Congress Catalog Card Number: 54-6165
Printed in U.S.A.

Acknowledgment is made to the following journals for permission to reprint material in this book: *Journal of Philosophy* for " Situational *vs.* Psychological Theories of Behavior," " Some Logical Considerations Concerning Professor Lewis's ' Mind,' " and " The Factual Space and Time of Behavior "; *Journal of Psychology* for " The Jamesian Datum "; *Philosophy of Science* for " The Positive and the Logical," " Physicists and Fairies," and " The Human Skin "; *Psychological Review* for " Observable Behaviors "; and *Science* for " Kennetic Inquiry."

The *Faust* quotation for the Epilogue was suggested by Richard W. Taylor, " Arthur F. Bentley's Political Science," *The Western Political Quarterly,* Vol. 5, June 1952, p. 214.

Valuable counsel was given by Dr. F. P. Kilpatrick on the essay " The Fiction of ' Retinal Image ' " and by Julius Altman on the selection of various essays in this volume.

Contents

Foreword	vii
Introduction by Sidney Ratner	ix
1. Knowledge and Society	3
2. Remarks on Method in the Study of Society	27
3. A Sociological Critique of Behaviorism	31
4. New Ways and Old to Talk About Men	37
5. Sociology and Mathematics	53
6. The Positive and the Logical	101
7. Physicists and Fairies	113
8. Situational *vs.* Psychological Theories of Behavior	141
9. Observable Behaviors	175
10. The Human Skin: Philosophy's Last Line of Defense	195
11. Some Logical Considerations Concerning Professor Lewis's "Mind"	212
12. The Factual Space and Time of Behavior	214
13. Memoranda on a Program of Research into Language	223
14. The Jamesian Datum	230
15. The Fiction of "Retinal Image"	268
16. Logic and Logical Behavior	286
17. An Aid to Puzzled Critics	320
18. Carnap's "Truth" *vs.* Kaufmann's "True"	325
19. Muscle-Structured Psychology	335
20. Kennetic Inquiry	337
Epilogue	355
Arthur F. Bentley: A Bibliography	357
Index of Names	359
Subject Index	362

Foreword

Yielding to the wishes of friends, perhaps too readily, I am including in this book certain papers that are far from finished in form, and one at least that is not checked and tested in content. My excuse is that completion is beyond my present competence. These imperfect papers nevertheless exhibit significant trends in modern research. Since my work is in growth without pretense of final achievement, this may be as it should be. Let us wish for the best.

A. F. B.

September, 1953

Introduction

By Sidney Ratner

The essays brought together in this volume examine basic problems in the natural and social sciences and in the theory of knowing and the known. Many of the essays have come to be regarded as classics since their first appearance in technical journals, but are difficult for the general reader to obtain. About a third of this volume consists of essays never before published. Thus within the compass of one volume, the reader can discover for himself the continuity and growth in Dr. Bentley's inquiries from " Knowledge and Society " (1910) to the present. The cumulative impact of these essays rivals that of such works as John Dewey's *Philosophy and Civilization* and William James's *Essays in Radical Empiricism*.

Dissenting opinions will be forthcoming from the champions of the views that Bentley seeks to disestablish. But his opponents will have to study this volume carefully if there is to be any effective point-counterpoint discussion. Bentley is an opponent worthy of any reader's best steel. He has gone down to bedrock in examining the evidence on disputed issues, he *knows* what he doesn't take stock in, and he advances his alternative proposals only after the most scrupulous and incisive consideration of their warranted assertibility.

Arthur F. Bentley has spent most of his life in scientific inquiry, and at the age of eighty-three displays an active interest in scientific progress and world affairs equal to that of men decades younger. He was born in Freeport, Illinois, on October 16, 1870, the son of a small-town banker, a man of unusual ability and intellectual candor. Bentley received his early education in the schools of the Midwest (Freeport, Illinois, and Grand Island, Nebraska). After going for little more than a year to York College, Nebraska, and the University of Denver, he interrupted his college education for reasons of health and worked for several years in his father's bank. At the age of twenty he entered Johns Hopkins University, attracted by the reputation of Richard T. Ely, and with economics as his major interest. Although Ely left Hopkins for Wisconsin, Bentley stayed at Hopkins, did the three-year course in two, and was graduated in 1892 with high honors and an A.B. degree. The next three years he devoted to graduate work in economics and sociology, the first and third year at Johns Hopkins, the middle year at the Universities of Berlin and Freiburg im Breisgau. During his years of graduate study at Hopkins, as Bentley himself has put it, " there was no faculty in economics, only a bright young instructor or two in a few lecture courses from the outer world. . . . Sociology was just at that time a-borning in America and in France, with companionate chirps from spots of Germany and Austria." His aim was to " find out how to fit the marginal utilities of Carl Menger into a fully behavioral sociology." But, because of the curtailment of his European studies by the depression of 1893, Bentley did not study with Menger in Vienna. He never fulfilled his aims for economics. Instead, he developed his own reconstruction of the logic of the social sciences, with applications made first to history, political science, sociology, psychology; further developments embraced mathematics, the natural sciences, and formal logic.

The first published work of Bentley was a substantial thesis written at Hopkins in 1892-93, *The Condition of the Western Farmer as Illustrated by the Economic History of a Nebraska Township*. Written shortly after Bentley received his A.B., it surpasses most doctoral dissertations published today in thoroughness of research and maturity of analysis. In 1896 he presented for his doctoral dissertation at Johns Hopkins an essay entitled " The Units of Investigation in the Social Sciences." This stressed the human mind as a central point for all study of social phenomena, and reflected mentalistic or psychical formulations then current which Bentley later came to discard completely.

Within a few years Bentley developed a new method of approach that became basic to all his future work. This new point of view grew out of his sensitivity to the work of groups represented by such persons as Simmel in Germany, Gumplowicz in Austria, Durkheim in France, and Dewey in America. Seminars with Simmel at Berlin in 1892-93, and with John Dewey at Chicago in 1895-96, also stimulated Bentley to rethink his basic positions.

After a brief fling at college teaching in 1895-96 as a docent in sociology at the University of Chicago, Bentley went into newspaper work, first as a reporter, then as an editorial writer, on the Chicago *Times-Herald* and *Record-Herald*. This newspaper work brought Bentley from the intellectual world of the University into direct contact with the bustling turbulence of Chicago and workaday America. With the material of politics that he himself observed directly, or by way of the first-hand observations of others coming over his editorial desk, and with the aid of the scientific publications available in the Crerar Library close by his newspaper headquarters, Bentley made the notable inquiry into political behavior embodied in his first *magnum opus,* published in 1908, *The Process of Government.*

Today this book is recognized as one of the great classics in the field of political science, not only for America, but for the world at large. Yet, when it was first published, and for almost twenty years thereafter, it shared the fate of most classics: of being cited, but not read widely. In the 1930's and '40's the book was rediscovered and hailed as a work of genius by increasing numbers of scholars. The heart of this book is Bentley's demonstration that the raw material or the real stuff of government can be found " only in the actually performed legislating-administering-adjudicating activities of the nation and in the streams and currents of activity that gather among the people and rush into these spheres." Bentley developed with great power an analysis of " group interests," an analysis which became the basis for the intensive work later done on pressure groups by Beard, Holcombe, Odegard, and Herring, among others. But Bentley characterizes " group interests " in terms of the multiple activities and objectives of human beings in contrast to the more static and limited " interest groups " of conventional contemporary political science.

After retiring from newspaper work in 1910, and establishing himself at Paoli, Indiana, Bentley did not publish another book until 1926. His activities in private business affairs and during World War I cut into his writing. After the war, he wrote a book on the American business and political scene, *Makers, Users, and Masters,* that unfortunately has remained unpublished. Then he launched an inquiry into a reconstruction of social theory as affected by Einstein's methods of viewing space and time as integral phases of the events experienced and studied by human beings. Bentley's aim in his treatise *Relativity in Man and Society* was to prove that every statement about society is relative to the conditions of its origin and use, and that sociological frames of reference, comparable to those used by physicists, can be established for handling social facts. He argued that interpretations of society in terms of atomistic personalities are nothing more than examples of the use of one such reference frame, with no special validity beyond the success of its application. Bentley presented an alternative frame of reference which stressed cross-sectional observation. This approach developed the group-activity analysis he had set forth eighteen years before in *The Process of Government,* but was still formulated with too heavy an emphasis upon social phenomena as things in opposition to the then prevalent emphasis upon individual phenomena. Bentley later constructed a more adequate approach in terms of full postulational procedure.

During the six years after the publication of *Relativity in Man and Society,* Bentley was extremely active. He developed further the ideas he had set forth in his earlier books, he presented certain new positions with great force and effectiveness in articles published in England, France, and Germany, and he carried on his powerful exploration of the problem of meaning and postulate in science, with particular reference to mathematics, in his work the *Linguistic Analysis of Mathematics.* He was impressed with the difficulties and paradoxes with which mathematical realists like the early Bertrand Russell and his rivals in the establishment of "logical foundations for mathematics" became involved. Convinced by Hilbert's work that the way out of paradox was the establishment of a mathematical consistency in its own mathematical right, Bentley sought to establish a firm construction for the language through which mathematical symbols are developed, communicated, and interpreted.

Though some professional mathematicians criticized various formulations made by Bentley on the subject, his book had a notable impact upon John Dewey. It stimulated consideration of certain issues by P. W. Bridgman and Leon Chwistek, two noted authorities on scientific method. A close examination of Dewey's great treatise *Logic: The Theory of Inquiry* (1938) reveals Bentley's profound influence. He aided Dewey in analyzing the nature of mathematics. Bentley helped to clarify the way in which both the new and the traditional schools of formal logic imposed upon scientific inquiry meanings imported from regions beyond those covered in actual empirical scientific researches. Bentley also enabled Dewey to make more precise his contention that modern logicians assume uncritically obsolete psychological constructions.

In Bentley's own developmental history, the *Linguistic Analysis of Mathematics* represents an advance in his basic construction: the overspecialized way of presenting the social group in the cross-sectional approach to human behavior in his earlier writings is replaced by the observational-postulational system set forth in this and all his later volumes.

In 1936 Bentley published in *Behavior, Knowledge, Fact* the most fully rounded presentation of his ideas on effective techniques for studying human behavior. His central problem was: What is social fact? His answer was expounded in terms of a closely knit theoretical structure which determined what is *fact* for science in terms of the techniques and procedures of science itself. His basic requirement was direct observability in space-time of every presentation or description of behavior as valid scientific fact. He rejected any description of social behavior which was not as definitely under the control of observation as are the descriptions employed by physics and the biological sciences.

In line with this criterion of observability was his espousal of the new "objective" psychologies growing out of the work of psychologists with such varied backgrounds as John Dewey, J. R. Kantor, Albert P. Weiss, and Madison Bentley. With the tools of analysis developed in this volume, Bentley was able to secure a presentation and description of language as observable social fact. He demonstrated that no language appears as such unless it is itself a *communication* in which both transmitting and receiving men, and their physical media of communication, are participant. Through an elaborate analysis of the different types of communication, he gave social scientists technical constructs that should be fruitful in developing the theory of communication. He also showed the necessity of a behavioral space-time for an adequate inquiry into the conveyance of meanings, in place of the Newtonian or the Einsteinian constructions of space and time.

The great contributions made in *Behavior, Knowledge, Fact* were acknowledged by such sociologists as George Lundberg. The historic importance of the book for philosophy stems from the influence it had upon John Dewey. Reinforcing the stimulus which the *Linguistic Analysis of Mathematics* had given him earlier, it helped Dewey clarify his ideas on the autonomy of logic and on the extent to which logical systems had been based on ideas drawn from fields outside that of logic. Moreover, Dewey benefited from Bentley's elucidation of the space-time component of every scientific statement of fact.

Between 1936 and 1949, Bentley published many important articles, most of which have become a permanent part of the literature of their fields and have been included in this volume. These essays fall into several groups. One attacks certain basic errors in the logical structure of the movement called Logical Positivism or Logical Empiricism. Another criticizes the mentalistic colorations of P. W. Bridgman and other theoretical physicists. A third develops situational theories of human behavior as against psychological. A fourth presents firm constructions for studying observable human behavior in space-time.

In 1949 Bentley published with John Dewey their epoch-making book *Knowing and the Known*, which is based upon a group of previously published essays that center on the need for a re-examination and reformulation of key words and constructions in contemporary logic. This volume represents the confluence of Dewey's and Bentley's thinking, and presents the most explicit revision and explication to date of many of the leading constructions in Dewey's *Logic: The Theory of Inquiry* and Bentley's *Be-*

havior, Knowledge, Fact. This 1949 volume was an historic event insofar as it gave a new turn to the movement to place man and his "higher" faculties within nature instead of outside and over it. The naturalistic approach to human intelligence, which Darwin, James, Peirce, and Dewey fostered in different ways, here received a notable exposition and extension.

From the beginning of his career, Bentley has been passionately concerned with language reforms that would clear away the mass of confusions and fictions that prevent human beings from perceiving the processes in nature and in society that science is capable of revealing. This concern inspired him to join with Dewey in developing sets of leading words " capable of firm use in the discussion of ' knowings ' and ' existings ' in that specialized region of research called the theory of knowledge." Dewey and Bentley also developed and presented cogently an approach which they called " transactional," and which they considered the most advantageous method of analyzing phenomena in process. Their guiding principle is best expressed in Charles S. Peirce's statement that " the woof and warp of all thought and all research is symbols . . . so that it is wrong to say that a good language is *important* to good thought, merely; for it is of the essence of it." To Bentley, as to Dewey, one central task is to make others see " language, with all its speakings and writings, as man-himself-in-action-dealing-with-things." In *Knowing and the Known,* they most clearly reject the still fashionable isolation of " real " objects from " minds," of " words " from the speaker, of " knowings " from the " known." They set down the following postulations to be faced and organized for behavioral (social and individual) research: (1) The Cosmos: as system or field of factual inquiry; (2) Organisms: as cosmic components; (3) Men: as organisms; (4) Behavings of men: as organic-environmental events; (5) Knowings (including the knowings of the cosmos and its postulation): as such organic-environmental behavings.

Dewey and Bentley place in the center of their approach the viewing of physical nature and human society from the transactional as against the inter-actional or self-actional point of view. The three levels of the organization and presentation of inquiry may be most compactly characterized and contrasted as follows: " *Self-action:* where things are viewed as acting under their own powers. *Inter-action:* where thing is balanced against thing in causal interconnection. *Trans-action:* where systems of descriptions and naming are employed to deal with aspects and phases of action, without final attribution to ' elements ' or other presumptively detachable or independent ' entities,' ' essences,' or ' realities,' and without isolation of presumptively detachable ' relations ' from such detachable 'elements.'" Clerk Maxwell in his famous little volume *Matter and Motion* (1877) had significantly used the word "transaction." Dewey had found the word advantageous in some of his earlier writings. John R. Commons had applied it forcefully and with increasing power for a special range of economics. But the most articulate statement and justification for the use of the word "transaction" in the contemporary social science field is to be found in Dewey and Bentley's *Knowing and the Known*. To scientific inquiries in all fields, the central constructions of this work offer the bases for further advances in accurate specification and exact symbolization.

Other investigations of Dr. Bentley's, which he had carried on without putting the results into print, can now fortunately be made accessible in this volume. One of these hitherto unpublished studies presents a penetrating analysis of the knowing-activity as a social process. Another such study presents a devastating attack upon the fiction of "retinal images." A third states the case for abandoning the convention of localizing behavioral facts along strings of neurons and for locating such behavior (in a somewhat similar sense) in areas of muscle. A fourth explains to puzzled critics of *Knowing and the Known* what the objectives of Dewey and Bentley in that work were. Bentley's interest in developing an adequate theory of language is also represented in an essay on a program of research into language which he wrote in 1941 as an introductory lecture before the Columbia University Philosophy Department's Seminar on Language. This elicited high praise for its attack upon the doctrine of some formal logicians and semanticists that language can be best analyzed in isolation from the context of its use and users.

To Bentley, most symbolic logicians, as he once put it in an unpublished talk in 1938, "are so confident that they are thinking that they never attempt to find out what that thinking may itself appear to be in competent description. Ask that question and all logic stops at once." This view of formal logic Bentley developed in two of his hitherto unpublished papers, written in the later 1940's. One explores the meaning of the terms "true" and "truth" as used by two important contemporary logicians. The other presents a fresh approach to the much-debated subject of "Logic and Logical Behavior" by interpreting the work of logicians on a naturalistic basis, namely, what their behavior means as observable events in space-time. Although this essay was only three-quarters finished when Bentley, for reasons of health, had to suspend work on it, it breaks new ground, and carries forward Dewey's and Bentley's reconstruction of logic as a theory of scientific inquiry.

In 1950 Bentley published an article, "Kennetic Inquiry," which is a remarkable restatement of the central approaches and constructions of Bentley's life work, with far-ranging applications to major problems and examples of procedures allied to the transactional approach as given in *Knowing and the Known*. This essay elicited highly laudatory responses from leading figures in research in diverse domains of science. It rightly crowns this volume.

The influence of Bentley's inquiries and writings is steadily growing. The central problems, constructions, and procedures that he has formulated and developed during the past half-century are in accord with the methods of the natural sciences, and have stimulated some of the most constructive work being done in the social sciences. These methods and constructions are a major contribution to the clarification of evolutionary naturalism and experimental logic. Darwin had brought first animal life, and then human life, into a space-time framework where hypotheses could be tested concerning the continuity between different forms and levels of life. Yet since his time few have attempted to work out a *thoroughly* consistent explication and application of the evolutionary approach to all forms and phases of life, especially to the linguistic, logical, scientific, and other social phases of human activities. In these latter fields Bentley's work, building upon that of Peirce, James, and Dewey, has been notable for its range and penetration.

Even dissenters from Bentley's conclusions will not remain untouched by the abrasive force of his skepticism toward conventional views. At the age of eighty-three, Bentley retains the intellectual verve for which he is noted. He sees much that remains to be done on basic problems in the theory of knowing and the known, and refuses to regard his own work as the last word. His lifelong inquiry into inquiry provides the liberating tools which will aid others in making further advances in the varied domains that he has cultivated with such zeal and distinction.

INQUIRY INTO INQUIRIES

Essays in Social Theory

CHAPTER ONE

Knowledge and Society*

I

IN WHAT SENSE DOES AN "INDIVIDUAL MAN" HAVE
EXISTENCE FOR SCIENCE?

Some people who use such terms as "individual," "individual man," "human individual," "person," or again "I" or "you," understand by them only labels for problems of great difficulty. They recognize the practical usefulness of the terms, but they would be far from giving them sharp definition, either intellectually or emotionally.

Others, when they use such terms, believe they are talking with almost the maximum of definiteness, and even when they eschew verbal definition they hold that their feeling for individual existence is fundamental as truth. Such are, of course, in the great majority. It is here that many elaborate discussions of the problems of individuality are based on a naïve acceptance of the substance of the matter discussed.

The query which forms the title to this section will give no offense to persons of the former class. For the benefit of the latter, permit the preliminary remark that it is not the vital experience of pulsating human life that is drawn in question here, but only the adequacy of certain ready-made conceptions of the "individual" as being the bearer, or content, or — we may even say — the fact, of that life. And also this further remark that not any mystical absorption of the individual in a "higher reality" is intended, not any question of ultimate values, but only the values of observation by eye and ear under the regulation of experience — in short, of science.

Let us begin by considering what a speculative fog arises from the use of ordinary conceptions of the individual. Man, in this way so far from being the measure of all things, comes much nearer being the origin of all speculative evil. Dogmatically assumed in one or another sense, the term

---

* MS essay, dated October 25, 1910; marked "first draft." Not further developed, but important for viewpoint consistently adhered to during course of later growth.

"individual" nevertheless remains always illusive, undefined, instable in meaning; and therein lies the difficulty.

What a difference, for example, it would make with the vast literature of immortality, could the disputants agree fully in advance as to exactly what they mean by the individual man of which they are predicating or denying immortality. The split is not merely between those on the one hand who hold that the individual is really a soul which will ultimately cast off its crippled clay carcase, and those on the other hand who have abandoned the double entities of soul and body; the split is within the ranks of the latter themselves. Many is the man of scientific training or supple thought who, having substituted "mind" for "soul," and having followed in all their sinuosity the parallelisms of nerve and feeling, still asks: "For what do 'I' exist, beyond this complex of mortal doings?" and "Will not 'I' live on and understand the meanings after physical death?" The "I" of these questioners is, if they are pressed, their "love-of-music," their "struggle-for-bread," their "joy-in-small-beer," their "worry-over-the-day's-work," and other contents of action and emotion. Much would be simplified in discussing the place of the person after death if, first of all, the person before death were defined so that a preliminary understanding was reached in regard to him by the disputants; if for example an exact estimate of the completeness of the "I-loving-music," fused with the "I-struggling-for-bread," and the other "I-doings" and "I-feelings" as a description of the "I" itself, could be reached.

But it is not life after bodily death that is here to be discussed, but life before bodily death. It is a question of the existence of the individual man, not in any metaphysical sense of existence, but in the sense of asking whether there is any such thing as an "individual" who acts all along the line of pre-scientific and scientific investigation in the way he would have to act if he existed with the independence, or so to speak with the "individuality," assumed to him by expressed definition and by unexpressed environing meanings. Let no quibble of skepticism be raised over this questioning of the existence of the individual. Should he find reason for holding that he does not exist in the sense indicated, there will in that fact be no derogation from the reality of what does exist. On the contrary, there will be increased recognition of reality. For the individual can be banished only by showing a plus of existence, not by alleging a minus. If the individual falls it will be because the real life of men, when it is widely enough investigated, proves too rich for him, not because it proves too poverty-stricken.

Now there is one sphere in which the term "individual man" answers — almost — all that is expected of it. That is the sphere of everyday life.

When I go down the street and meet my friend John Smith, and we walk along together, he answers for all practical purposes to what I mean when I talk about an individual man. He has a certain name, a certain form, certain members, certain types of reaction, and I can deal with him on certain definite lines, because I find him acting himself on definite formed lines. I said " for all practical purposes," but that is perhaps going too far. Even " John Smith " is apt to be erratic at times and get outside the boundaries of my " individual " understanding, while as for the Toms, the Dicks, and the Harrys, they give me greater difficulties, each in his degree.

Nevertheless, no one wants to deny that in the multifarious events of practical everyday life, as man meets man, each is for the other an individual sufficient more or less unto himself, and that that point of view, manner of speech, theory, interpretation, what you will, works satisfactorily enough in the progress and development of those multifarious affairs.

Admitting now in the individual man this measure of individuality, let us see what his position is when the biologist, or more specifically the physiologist, begins to investigate him. The physiologist is interested in space relations. If the movements which he studies cannot always be followed in their course in space, they have at least their initial and terminal stages in spatial forms. It would seem that the physiologist's definition of an individual, whatever else it might contain, would of necessity fix definite spatial limits for him. This, however, it cannot do. However spatially isolated the individual appears at a crude glance, the more minutely he is examined, the more are his boundary lines found to melt into those of his environment, the more frequently are functions found which work through both individual and environment so that it cannot be told where the one ceases and the other begins, leaving by the way products near the limits which can hardly be said to be either the one or the other. So the physiologist comes to study with increasing interest all that is taking place under his view without becoming too dogmatic as to just what the " individual " is. Nor does the individual fare better when genetic problems are investigated, for by the germ cells are parents and offspring connected into one great life, and within " the individual " many successive individual phases are found strung together in the course of a life.

So in these vital sciences the individual may be referred to for convenience in making the cruder distinctions, always remembering that where the convenience ends, there the individual ends in any way in which scientific dependence can be placed on him.

The everyday man is able to treat the vagueness of physical boundaries which the physiologist detects as merely one of the curiosities of science. The fact makes no difference to him. But, unfortunately for him and his condition of satisfied sureness, there is a vagueness of boundary to be detected in the individual when he is examined at points which are much more closely in contact with his everyday experience. And this vagueness is so marked and so important that when it has once been investigated and the positive aspects of the phenomena are involved, we may expect to see even the sureness of the everyday man somewhat affected. That, however, is not a matter of immediate present prospect.

This new vagueness is to be found in the active life of the individual, that very active life which the everyday man has to do with. It appears as soon as the interest in the doings of John Smith ceases to be an interest that arises out of immediate dealings with him. It develops both when we dissect the active life of John Smith in order to examine it in its parts, and when we broaden out that active life by considering it in close contact with the active lives of other people, beginning perhaps with wife, child, brother, passing to business partner, fellow sectarian, fellow partisan, and ending with fellow citizen and fellow man.

Let it be clearly held in mind, as we proceed to examine the appearance of such vagueness, that we are dealing with the activity of the individual, with all his movements and expressions and interactions with other people. We are disregarding him as so much matter, and considering him as motion. We are disregarding even the motions that physiology studies and are considering only his " doings " as a person. Take the individual as an organ; then we are studying that organ's functions. All of which is highly arbitrary, but at the same time of high temporary use as providing us with a scaffolding to hold up our subjectmatter of study while we work upon it.

First as to the dissecting of the active individual. When we begin this we are in the realm of physiology. The first step, however, is not toward vagueness but toward stiffening the individual's outlines. The " soul " and " faculty " psychology appears. All the individual's actions are referred to his thinkings, feelings, and willings, and these are referred to faculties of his soul. Neat enough — but too neat. Its trouble is that it won't work under continued investigations. It is merely a matter of the history of psychology that the faculties break up, and that in one way or another the bounds of the individual are transcended. Perhaps an " absolute " is set up into which all individual souls are swallowed (though remaining undigested). Perhaps epistemology tries its hand at mediating between knower and known. Perhaps an investigation of the development of consciousness in the individual shows that an outer world is clearly present before the conscious individuality appears. Perhaps a functional psychology appears which traces all the developed phenomena of individual action out of a stimulus or tension which is not so much individual or non-individual as it is an undifferentiated reality in these respects. At any rate the sharply outlined individual which at first appears when this course is followed proves promptly to be spectral, and whatever positive characteristics are later found in the facts are, whatever else they may be, at least not definitely limited properties of a definitely limited individual.

Next as to the broadening out of the active individual by considering him in his interactions with others. Suppose we find John Smith in the possession of a formulated bit of scientific knowledge. We say he learned it at school — from the newspapers — by reading such and such a late contribution to the literature of the science. If we went into the metaphysics of how much a bit of knowledge could pass from one sharply defined individual mind to another similar sharply defined individual mind we would get into a slough of despond. It would be the same slough into which Zeno's questions about the fixed points and motion between them led unwary disputants. Its answer indeed would have to be the same answer, the *solvitur ambulando,* the answer, namely, that not the points are the realities in terms of which motion must be explained, but that the motion is the reality and that the points are merely marked off within it. But without troubling ourselves with the metaphysics, if we disown for the moment our preconceived notion as to the individual's definiteness, which of course we have to do in order to bring this question of the existence of the individual before us as a vital topic of investigation, we soon see that the " bit of knowledge " as such (i.e., defined as such) has greater definiteness — or, if one will, greater individuality — than the individual's accepting it in its formulated state and carrying and repeating it. This statement, remember, must be held strictly to what it is, a preliminary statement of a phenomenon under observation, without further implications one way or the other.

Or again, suppose we are observing a riot, a lynching, or a popular demonstration in honor of some returning Admiral Dewey. The observer and student soon becomes so impressed with the unity of feeling and action in the mass of the crowd that he begins to write treatises on the " mob mind." He gives practically, in short, a greater individuality (for the purposes of the moment) to the whole mob-act, than to the individual part-acts. Other students of men in society find it necessary to transcend the individual by positing a " social will " with its own high-grade individuality.

Further illustrations hardly seem necessary. We have seen — just as a matter of the way men make observations when they once break off from the limited practical judgments of man in interaction with man — and in whatever of two contrasted ways they push their observations — that the limits, the boundaries, of the individual become vague. We see this entirely without regard to the special theories the observers build up positively, and utterly disregardless likewise of the extent to which they carry criticism back upon their old definition of the individual. They can retain that definition, they can abandon it, or they can add to its hierarchy of other individualities; and they can be right or they can be wrong; the fact remains that their eyes have noted transitions of functions, that the boundaries of individuality have become vague in the acting individual, much as the boundaries of physiological function at a similar issue become vague for the biologist.

Now this vagueness in the individual man in his function of " doing things " has an analogy in positive aspects to the physiological vagueness. In neither case is the vagueness empty or meaningless. In both cases the difficulty arises because of a " plus of meaning," to repeat a phrase used before. The society, the group, the mob, even the isolated fact of formal knowledge, seem too rich to enclose in any one individual or in any addition of such individuals, one to another. Our task then becomes to look at this richness directly and see what we can make of it, abstracting from the question of individuality or non-individuality, at least until we can get a sufficiently concrete grasp of it to enable us to return to that question of individuality with some prospect of contributing toward the setting of the meanings better to rights.

So far as this positive quality has yet appeared in this article, it may be described merely as a lapping over of the edges of individual " doings." That is, we find " doings " which seem to run across several " individuals." Our " bit of knowledge " and our " mob mind " are in point. This " lapping over " has been credited phenomenally with a greater individuality than the individuals who bore it, so far as their relation to the immediate events of observation are concerned.

The statement in terms of such a " lapping over," that it is itself hard fact and not merely some constructed " relation," is consistent so far as it goes with an interpretation in terms of " over-individuals " such as social wills, or with the functional interpretation that I myself am inclined to give. It is not consistent with an interpretation that posits definite, fixed individuals, and lets what has just been called the " real lapping over " appear merely as a fictional glare on a fictional sky. As to these interpretations, however, nothing is in question for the moment. We proceed to go into more detail as to the positiveness of this lapping over by considering various instances of it.

Picture to yourself now the moving (i.e., acting) society in this state of reality. There it is. The hands of " one man " move, or his lips move or his pen moves. The motion lies straight across " other men." The action " is " the action of the two or three or thousand as one. It is the real thing. The actions are not " epiphenomena " to the " men, body or soul things," but are the living fact.

Suppose now we want to dissect this mass, not into channels of activity, but into individuals. We would cut through a thousand channels at a thousand points, and we would say " all that lies within these section lines is the individual ' A ' "; " all that lies within such and such other section lines is individual ' B ' "; and so forth. We can picture the whole society so cut into individuals. But we cannot do it without arresting for the moment the whole action, that is, the whole life, of our society. We cannot do it without " staining " our tissue. We cannot do it without finding that our product is morphological in the least helpful way; it is " dead," " stained," and capable of observation under the form of individuality, but with no good evidence that this form of individuality is the morphological form best to be chosen for knowledge of the living society.

The " individual " so cut out will readily be seen to be very different from the naïve " individual " assumed prior to a grasp of the reality of social action for science. The latter individual is somehow assumed to be " the whole thing " underlying the shadowy social world. The former is a real piece of the actual social whole. The latter is thoroughly illegitimate. The former is legitimate as fact, but without evidence as yet of its utility for science.

Let us now glance backward over the results thus far.

We have found that in the actual doings of men the boundaries of an " individual," by whatever method he is defined, are transcended; and that this transcending is itself action of positive immediate reality.

We have therefore found that in order to study the phenomena of men in society we must take all stress off " individuals," careless for the time whether we have to do with individuals at all or not, and intent only on the real material of our study.

The implication of this may perhaps be brought out into high light by casting a few illustrative shadow pictures on the screen.

First of these pictures shall be that of society, that is, the doings of men in masses, under the theory which makes individual men naïvely accepted as the real existences which are to be investigated. Truly, " society " on such a basis is a shadow. It has form, but it is too tenuous even to permit a cobweb to be used in metaphor for it. The cobweb in comparison is grossly material. The men are seen. All acts of each man are " his acts " and his only. All these acts of all the men fit together into a great system. The system is what it interests us to study. And yet the system is forever elusive, forever a shadow, because the sum of the definitely limited individuals constitutes all reality. The metaphysical system of Leibnitz parallels the position of some scientists here. For Leibnitz the individual was real. Hence (Leibnitz being an uncompromising thinker) — monads. The monads went through their marvelously interesting careers, retaining forever their independence as monads. Hence — cosmic evolution, without interaction. But, all formed one great system of evolution. Hence — harmony by act of God. The everyday man who envisages a world of individual souls, reigned over by God, may at any rate be on good terms with logic. But the man who — whatever he may believe of the existence of God — at any rate leaves God out of scientific interpretations and yet keeps individual minds in all their individuality — for him little sympathy or respect can be felt. His individuals are either too little or too much: his society is next to nothing at all.

For a next shadow picture, let us put upon the screen the " social will," " social consciousness," or any one of the varied group or class " minds " of which we hear from time to time. By means of these constructions a certain recognition of reality is given to the activity which transcends the boundaries of the individual. But it is not satisfactory, for logically it forces us into the difficulties inherent in a hierarchy of individualities; while beyond this it fails to do justice to much of the activity which transcends individual boundaries without being necessarily personified in the " social mind." It gives different grades of reality, and does not get all the action in one common field.

A final picture, still of shadows, is that " society " which so commonly in modern investigations is opposed concretely to the individual. Starting from the standpoint of an individual, it can readily be seen how a " society " is placed in opposition to him. There is the reality of the social activity. The individual who is part of it, being postulated concretely in advance, appears to be impelled by it as concretely and definitely as a ball struck by a mallet is propelled along the grass. This fact being strongly seized, leads to a system in which the " influences of society upon the individual " are discussed. " Society " here means manifestly " other men." By the same token the conception is faulty, for the real social activity which we want to investigate includes not merely " other men," but " all the men." We do not want to oppose " A " to a " society " consisting of " B–Z "; nor " B " to a " society " consisting of " A " joined with " C–Z," and so on, but we want to understand directly the workings of the society which is " A–Z " with no left-over individuals.

Turn our attention now for the moment from the individual to society. We might ask a question similar to that of the title of this section: " Is there such a thing as a society?" or otherwise put: "In what sense does a society have existence for science?"

On the basis of the preceding discussions society is clearly the totality of the organized doings, or activities, or, more simply still, actions, of the animal group under consideration. But action must be taken, not as stripped bare of meanings, but as including the full richness of meanings which have been observed by men who talk of " individualities," and then more. The upholders of " individuality " have no private title to the richness of social meanings, simply because they adhere to one special interpretation of them. They have no right to exclude other observers from the study of that richness.

Again this action, of which society is the totality, is the same as movement, motion. But not the bare abstract motion of the physicist, nor yet the more complex motion of the chemist and physiologist, but motion in the full richness of the elaborate processes in which we observe it, motion which is work.

As function society can be so stated, with no residuum of " matter " left over, save as from the standpoint of the particular study, the simpler motions of other studies are called matter. But society as a whole can also be stated as matter. Unless both statements can be made our work is manifestly faulty. And just as the motion, the activity, of the banded men of society has involved much of the environment, working it up in appropriate forms, and working then with and through it, so looked upon as matter society must be defined as the total mass of the men and the assimilated non-human things (animal, vegetable, and mineral, to use the old terms). In terms of men alone society cannot be stated.

But now, just as " individual " is not exactly an apt word to describe those sections of social activity which were earlier in this paper mentioned as being scientifically possible for consideration as individuals, so society is an almost impossible term for use in any scientific study that wishes to be exact. Into this term every man will read his own type of meanings; above all, the whole background of meanings that place society in some sort of concrete opposition to individuals will be present; and they will be fatal to exact ascription of scientific meaning.

My friend Mr. M. A. Lane, feeling this difficulty strongly, has suggested a sort of terminology derived throughout from Greek roots which will have sufficient elasticity to meet the needs of future investigations, and which therefore will be comparable to physiological terminology in the work it can do and the aid it can lend investigation. The initial term that of course suggests itself is *symbios,* life in common. (The fact that symbiosis is already a biological term is not a deterrent, because of the limited nature of the phenomenon the biologist uses it to designate.) Combine with this *taxis,* arrangement, and the final *osis,* and we get symbiotaxiosis, which may be used as a general term for the totality of the ordering or arrangement of social life. A symbiotaxium would be any society Symbiotaxiplasm, or more simply taxioplasm, would be the mass of men (or, alternatively, any associated animals) and assimilated things which forms the society, regarded as matter. Symbiotaxis would be the social process or function, regarded as such. The effectiveness of such a terminology ought not to be difficult to see. For example, there is no word existing to designate exactly the mass of material things which have been taken up by socially organized men and incorporated in their common life: matter that is transformed into clothes, food, tools, playthings, etc. But any science of organized human life needs to know very early in its career something about the qualities and laws for such incorporated matter, and without a term to designate it as such it can make no progress in that direction. (Could one more strikingly illustrate the undeveloped status of our knowledge of social life?) By the aid of Mr. Lane's terminological suggestion one can readily fix the exact matter for study. His tentative terms are homoplasm for the human constituents of a symbiotaxium, and heteroplasm for the non-human constituents. Similarly for the " individual " in any aspect in which we define him a term can be developed, and so for any type of group relation.

The study of symbiotaxiosis, taken as we have taken it, would rest in physiology, much as physiology rests in chemistry, without dogmatism, but making the best of the hypothesis.

Now to summarize our results and to answer the question whether an individual exists (in what sense he has existence for science).

That human life in societies set in the cosmos exists is our datum, and of course not at all in question either here or anywhere else within the limits of science.

That the " individual " is a common manner of statement for a certain phase of the great social-in-cosmos activity is also to be admitted, and not to be challenged in and for its practical purposes.

That there is (" is " being not metaphysically existential, but the practical " is " of working life) an individual man crudely cut off in space, we admit. But physiology transcends his boundaries the more frequently, the more thorough are its investigations.

That there is an individual man crudely marked off in time, we also admit. But genetic biology transcends his limits in every study of the germ cell and the egg.

That there is an individual man crudely marked off in society, which is action, which is movement, we also admit. The study of social life forces us, more and more consciously, however, to transcend his limits.

But even the coincidence of all three, we hold, does not make more than a crude individuality. It answers the needs of everyday life. It does not answer the needs of scientific study. For this latter end we dare not take naïvely our individuals as we find them defined in everyday life. According as is our problem, so we must discriminate in the analysis of our material.

Finally this remark. It is no answer to anything that has been written to say: " I feel that I am a person." That men so feel is not denied. But there is nothing more notoriously unreliable than such feelings as the basis for research. Their own use, that of hypothesis for careful test, is usually ruined by the stiffened obstinacy which they tend to take on. It is as it was with Shakespeare. When he dealt with virtue or vice it was with something absolute, unquestionable. A woman's virtue was an almost physical thing. Characters revolved around these fixed points of virtue or vice. Today one must go far to find a person who holds to such fixity of virtues with no accompaniment of discriminating analysis of conduct. But the person, the individual man, is commonly held today with similar fixed naïveté. A similar progress must be made toward enriching the meaning of the term person, as has already been made with the terms for the virtues and for vices, and with the terms virtue and vice themselves.[1]

II

THE PERSISTENT IN KNOWLEDGE

The problem of knowledge, whether we take it in formal logic, in epistemology, or in modern instrumental logic, has found statement in a great variety of ways, differing greatly in character. Most of these statements have been exceedingly abstract, in the sense that they have sought a maximum rigidity of the terminology employed and have aimed to derive solutions by the aid of the fixed terms. At stages at which the problem has sharply altered its nature, of course, the pressure of the environing and underlying problems has shown itself in more fluid terminology and greater vitality of investigation, and in this respect the problem of knowledge has at such times been more concrete. That it was very concrete for Socrates, by way of example, everyone knows.

That the present is such a time we know. The problem of knowledge comes close home to us; is vital rather than verbal. To the conquest of

[1] See the references to Ribot *et al.* in J. M. Baldwin, " La logique de l'action," *Revue de Métaphysique et de Morale, XVIII* (juillet et novembre, 1910), pp. 441–57, pp. 776–94.

the field of the evolution of life by Darwin and his scientific successors it is that this is due.[2] Science has before it as a matter of direct investigation " minds " which are not only found embedded in an organized, environing world (that world including both the organism that bears the mind, and the organism's own environment) but which are seen to have evolved in that world and which are seen to function in it and nowhere else. On the other hand, having abandoned its first crude guess of inert minds and energetic matter, science finds itself more and more closely facing a world to investigate which it can allege to exist, and which it can give reality to, only as it is known to and tested by those very " minds " which are comprehended in it. It is the problem of a world existing only in mind and yet of mind existing only in the world — existence in both cases meaning the practical, functioning, investigable quality; it is this problem, so concretely put, which is the very essence of the problem of knowledge today. To the discussion in this form we shall attain in due time. Meantime for the moment our task is to avail ourselves of the possibilities of a more fluid terminology toward getting at the heart of the conflicts between the technical theories of knowledge in the light of this recognized scientific (and therefore practical) problem of knowledge.

Let us begin by getting at this problem in a preliminary way from different points of view, taking snapshots of it, as it were.

Evolution is a process which in the practical working hands of the scientist has neither beginning nor end. True, one can construct an initial or terminal situation, but such a construction will be only a by-product, not a necessary part of the scientific work. The tests and proofs of evolution are all found within a process that is in motion from and presumably prior to the point where we take it up, to and presumably beyond the point where we drop it. Now knowledge, i.e., the body of knowledge that we possess, is also in evolution, and this evolution is not a mere addition of new elements to old elements but a continual transformation. Taken as we find it in society, this body of knowledge upon which the generations are at work has neither beginning nor end, but must be studied always and only in motion. True, we can construct a picture of a knowledgeless initial status, and one of a full-knowledge terminal status, but these again are by-products, metaphysical in nature, and not of any importance for the real knowing which we study. The new pragmatisms are all of them energized by this evolutionary setting, and that even when they do their work most definitely in terms of individual men taken as their units.

Again — it is specially characteristic of the age in which we are living

[2] Compare John Dewey, *The Influence of Darwin on Philosophy* (New York, 1910), pp. 1–19.

that so many large bodies of knowledge have been reconstructed that most investigators are accustomed to accept this reconstructability as inevitable in their most cherished bodies of truth. This attitude is almost as current now as the companion attitude that no knowledge can fully be accepted save on experimental proof. Whereas once the Ptolemaic astronomy was held as stating the facts, and later the Copernican, now it is more and more recognized that both systems stated gave statement to the facts, but with different degrees of clumsiness, with different degrees of completeness. Simon Newcomb was accustomed to assuring his students that the Ptolemaic system would suffice for calculating eclipses as well as the Copernican, though with much more involved and awkward procedure.[3] And what has once been reconstructed may be reconstructed again. Now in the midst of all this reconstruction men are no less positive than before in the assertion of their practical knowledge, but they are vastly less dogmatic in the assertion of any final, absolute, or, we may say, unalterable, knowledge. Men "know," but they no longer are so certain that their knowledge will not be rearranged. A man may believe that his knowledge or some part of it will hold good permanently, but he feels compelled to recognize this as his "belief" in a sense distinct from "knowledge." One knows, but one does not know that the knowledge will not reconstruct itself later. To know that the knowing would never need reconstruction would be to transcend the knowledge of actual practical life, or (if one prefers a slightly different point of approach) it would be to assert that the limit of the knowing procedure has been attained — the limit toward which all former knowing has been but a gradual approximation.

The concrete knowledge problem of the day, as pictured in the preceding illustrations, brings out for discussion as the central characteristic of knowledge, so it seems to me, the characteristic of persistency in what we know. We have seen that our knowledge is by scientists today regarded as not outside of the cosmos, not outside of the process of its own construction and reconstruction, and, further, that while it forms a real structural body of knowledge, yet it is continually changing or at least to be regarded as susceptible of change and transformation. The persistency characteristic is clear whether we consider knowledge more on its structural or more on its transformation side. One can use the term persistency without dragging in implications in favor of one philosophical system or another which decide the question in advance. If idealists and realists are assumed to be two mutually exclusive camps, the idealist will certainly not deny the characteristic of persistency in knowledge, nor surely will the realist. Either

---

[3] George B. Halstead, "The Unverifiable Hypotheses of Science," *Monist*, XX (October, 1910), pp. 563–73, at p. 567.

would choose some different term more suited to his needs. Both can recognize what is meant by this term. If, then, the term persistency satisfactorily describes a dominant feature of the material which is to be studied, it is a useful term for our purposes.

The persistent in knowledge is what some of the opponents of pragmatism refer to when they assert that truths are " found," not " made," as the pragmatists may declare. It is what W. B. Pillsbury in his *Psychology of Reasoning* calls the " accepted potentiality of recall," and again " the accepted capacity for reinstatement." It is what E. B. McGilvary in recent controversial articles describes as Experience, in opposition to mere experience.

Now, as I indicated a few pages back, the problem before us at this immediate moment is not to come to terms concretely with the problem of knowledge, but to locate by the aid of that problem in its crude statement the central issue around which recent technical investigations and disputes over the knowledge problem revolve. This central point is that called the characteristic of persistency in knowledge. The great dispute of the day is, of course, that between the various evolutionary thinkers, roughly labeled pragmatists, including Dewey, James, Schiller, and probably also Bergson on the one side (with J. M. Baldwin affiliated in more respects than he is opposed), and their enraged idealist and obstinate realist opponents on the other.

It is the defect of the pragmatists up to this time that they (whatever they have actually proved) have not satisfied their opponents that their theories and proofs give due consideration to the element of persistency in knowledge. That is a mere statement of matter of fact about the controversy. It is the defect of their opponents of the realist persuasion (and here, now, I assert merely my own conviction) that in their overemphasis of the persistency characteristic they go to such an extent that they get outside the problem of knowledge altogether, and outside at the same time all question of knowledge, passing into an assertion of a belief in the characteristics of a future knowledge, which, so far as we can see at the present moment, is inevitably doomed by its very terms to remain a belief — if it does not perchance fall back to the state of an hypothesis not even carrying belief with it — and, at that, a belief of a type which parades ostentatiously its lack of the knowledge characteristics. As for the idealist opponents of the pragmatists, they seem really in such a state of confusion that they do not accomplish anything for their side unless they commit the very vice of the realists, with the added vice that on the top of its " belief " they build a second-degree belief that the position they hold is still the idealistic position in the old sense in which idealism is opposed to realism.

III

THE "SOCIETY" OF THE MODERN LOGICIANS

In the preceding section we have given critical examination to the quarrel of pragmatists and anti-pragmatists in the endeavor to locate the underlying fact which, variously interpreted, gives cause to the quarrel. In this section we shall study in a somewhat similar way the concept "society" as it enters into modern logical investigations, endeavoring to bring clearly before the attention the material of science which can be seen through the disputes; in this we shall be carrying forward in a more positive manner the positions taken in the first section in regard to the individual. In the section that is to follow the present one, we shall endeavor to bring our facts as to society and facts as to knowledge together into a consistent theory of knowledge as a practical affair of scientific investigation.

By all means the best approach to this question can be obtained, so it seems to me, through the writings of J. M. Baldwin and John Dewey, especially the former. I would not, it may well be believed, go so far as Pillsbury, who thinks that these two writers have said about all there is to say on society in its bearings on the intellectual life. (See the Preface to his *Psychology of Reasoning*.) On the contrary, they seem to me to point well the need of something more to say. Baldwin is the more significant, because, having gone very far with his important special studies in showing the effect of social influences on the individual, he still retains a concept of society as something opposed to particular individuals, and because the later development of his thought has tended to stiffen this opposition and work out all its implications. Dewey, in contrast, has recognized a much broader concept of society and has felt its value, but has not, to my knowledge, worked out in any detail its bearings on the theory of knowledge. While he has imparted the same feeling or sense for society to various of his followers, the situation still remains so vague that some of them can still work with his method and yet derogate society as such to a place of phantoms in contrast with the reality of individuals.

Before, however, examining either of these authors let us mention just a few opinions drawn from recent controversial literature by way of orientation.

We find occasionally so extreme a statement as that of Warner Fite [4] that when one comes down to close thought nothing to be called " the so-

---

[4] "The Exaggeration of the Social," *Journal of Philosophy, Psychology, & Scientfic Methods*, IV (July 18, 1907), pp. 393-96.

cial" exists. He defines everything as individual, postulates reality of the individual, and then when he hears people talking of the social, retorts: " Be careful. Your social is simply a mass of individuals. You are merely using a lazy man's term to save yourself the need of keeping the real individuals in mind." Among the pragmatists we find Schiller (an adherent of " personal idealism ") sneering at the use of the term social, and we find James rarely taking it into account, and much more inclined to discuss temperaments than society: temperaments being for him as elsewhere the product of a direct study of the individual which is assumed to explain the same facts that other people analyze on the social side. H. W. Stuart, one of Dewey's school, in his contribution to the 1903 *Studies in Logical Theory* edited by Dewey, tells us that " the socially current object " is an abstraction and that the only " concrete object " is the individual's construction.

As illustrations of the view that accepts the social concretely and then opposes it with more or less attributed importance to the individual we may note Pillsbury, who treats " the social " similarly to the way in which he treats " action " (thereby misunderstanding Dewey's position) as merely one among many stimuli to the intellect. Josiah Royce also, where he deals with the world of description, uses the social in a very concrete form. Dewey himself reduces the social to this concrete condition, as for example where he speaks of " values, aesthetic, social or ethical " [5]; and in the detailed studies of Dewey and Tuft's *Ethics*, this attitude repeatedly appears and is, indeed, the continuing attitude of the work.

Having traced the incompleteness of the work of these two writers, obstinate in the first, fluid in the second, we come again to an effort at more positive statement of symbiotaxis (dropping the term society immediately, as is essential if any ground is to be won).

It is a commonplace of recent ethical investigations that nowhere can egoism be found sharply distinct from altruism; nowhere can a situation be detected which is all one, and not at all the other. As Royce puts it: There is no conscious egoism without social reference.[6]

What now is this underlying fact in which both egoism and altruism get their meanings? Is it some phantom, some shadow of academic disputants, or is it the hardest kind of fact? Certainly the latter.

Again, as Georg Simmel brilliantly has shown, there is no conflict without an underlying unity. Only in a common matrix can conflict arise. The wolf fighting with the pack over the too-limited quarry is as much sym-

---

[5] Dewey, *Logical Conditions of a Scientific Treatment of Morality*, Decennial Publications of the University of Chicago, 1st ser., vol. 3, pt. 2 (Chicago, 1903), p. 20.

[6] *Studies of Good and Evil* (New York, 1906), p. 203.

biotactic as when previously with the pack it was running down the prey. Is this common basis a shadow or a reality of scientific study? Most certainly real.

Leadership and its following are no longer being regarded as distinct things of different classes, but as a vigorous living functioning, with differentiation, indeed, but only in the form of division of labor and extrusion of tools. Are we to regard all the vigorous life as elusive shadow, and only the leader and the led defined apart from one another as real? Again certainly no.

And again, the self cannot be conceived of as apart from other selves. (For one among many references, see Royce, *Studies of Good and Evil*, 205, thesis 1.) Is this mutual conditioning of self and other selves merely some shadowy abstract ghostly relation, or is it the vital fact? It is most assuredly the latter.

In all such cases as these the symbiotaxis is what is scientifically real, scientifically capable of study and development under the student's hands. The symbiotaxis is, to use such a picture, the cloth in which a pattern appears, a pattern of self and other selves, of leadership and its following, of conflicting individuals, of egoism and altruism. Brilliantly attractive to the eye as the pattern may be, it is yet but the pattern in the cloth.

Royce and Baldwin build up ego and non-ego out of a previous undifferentiated world. When they have built it up they drop that previous undifferentiated world and regard the ego and non-ego and other egos as the real facts for examination. But these latter are but phases, modifications, slight superficial renderings of what was there before them and what persists in great bulk beneath their pattern and coloring. You can't leave the undifferentiated as something to drop out altogether, as a merely curious early stage. You have got to reckon with it all along.

Baldwin and W. M. Urban give their hands away in their evolutionary arrangements, which are always personal, with a pre-personal and a post-personal stage.

By some the social is taken as a limit, or rather the individual is a limit within a continuum (R. P. Baker–C. S. Peirce). This is a conception needed in mathematics, etc. I am engaged in descriptive work, and my individual is a very complex thing, whether taken popularly, or cut out of the cloth (as described in Section I of this paper). I am trying to pick out the lines along which we should move toward a limit, and not trying to approach any limit now. Moreover, it would be better to say the hypothetical limit is to be called an individual than that a given individual is a limit.

IV

SOCIETY AND THE PERSISTENT IN KNOWLEDGE

Our task now is to take the Dewey theory of knowledge as arising at crises of action and broaden it out, so that it will be explicitly stated in terms of more than individual lives; to take at the same time the facts as to a society's concrete influence upon the individual in the knowledge field, and deepen them till the concepts individual and society merge in symbiotaxis; and to discover in the joint procedure whether the characteristic of persistency in knowledge does not stand forth in a guise that is realistic so long as it is a realism of knowledge that is in question, and that at the same time is idealistic in so far as it is a system of knowledge. The claim that will be made is not dogmatically that the difference between the two philosophic creeds has been effaced, but merely that here in this world of man — including evolution as we now comprehend it — the essential facts of the problem ("facts" in the Dewey sense) as they are advanced by the two opposed sides are all given recognition, which is adequate so far as present knowledge goes; leaving to new advances in description of the cosmos the production of new conflicts and new solutions.

Professor Dewey plunges into the logical problem not by positing an external world and a more or less formal observer, but by taking an observing life in the midst of its observations and examining it. He has to start with something thoroughly alive. That life is a process of adjustment and readjustment is a commonplace, the phrase serving sufficiently well to indicate the fact-problem, without committing oneself to any of its special implications when "adjustment with an environment" is meant. At critical points in this life, points of the need of readjustment, sensations and feelings appear; with increasing complexity of readjustment we have perceptions, then successively elaborate plans, and established truths, all of these terms being taken as fluid, that is, as indications of stages in one development.

If now we did all that we might wish to do with this problem of knowledge, we would needs go back to the simplest situations in which what we know as sensations appear and ask ourselves whether these concerned one organism and specified isolated bits of environment close to it in space. I may make my guess that something very much wider than this is involved in the simplest sensation of the simplest animal form, and that the living organism can even here only be interpreted in the mass, not in the isolated individual; but my guess would be a bare guess. I have no elaborated proof to offer, and consequently no claim to a hearing in any place where the standards we call scientific are in vogue; and the place of such standards, I am free to confess, is the only place in which I care for a hearing. When it is a matter of perceptions we are somewhat better off, for much of the technique of planning and truth enters into perceptions. But even here we cannot wisely make our beginning. If my very perception of the house I see across the street is symbiotactic through and through, I cannot hope to convince people of a positively contradictory opinion of the truth, because I cannot as yet mass the facts at the right place for the assault. We are compelled to begin where we have the greatest accumulations of symbiotactic phenomena at our service for examination, and this of course is among the most complex phenomena of argument. Professor Dewey himself puts his stress at a corresponding point, although not under as strong compulsion to it as we shall be. He does not aim so much at showing that perception arises at tangled points in action, as that it is at such points that the split between ideas and facts occurs with all its resultant consequences as developed in the functional theory of knowledge.

Now the situations on which Dewey most dwells in his studies are those of a living observer in crises in which other observers are involved, if at all, only as " facts " for the given observer whose knowing process is being examined. A typical situation of this kind is " the man lost in the woods " finding his way out, or any situation in which a man deals with his " physical environment." But such a situation is really highly abstract, if my contentions are correct. In the first place it is not a typical knowledge situation in the sense of being the common or ordinary case; the cases in which many people are involved symbiotactically are that. In the second place I know of no case of that kind which can be found in which symbiotaxis is not involved, if not explicitly, at least tacitly. There may be such cases, but I would want to be shown them clearly, and likewise have their importance shown before considering them as such. The " man lost in the woods " has of course his tree-lore, his ground-lore, his weather-lore, and much other lore, all symbiotactic, in play meeting his problem.

Let us call the above-described knowledge case in which abstraction is made from all symbiotaxis, the " isolated knowledge crisis," calling it thus not because we intend to use it ourselves, but simply so as to be able to indicate briefly the kind of case used in other discussion. Some investigators are content to assume that the isolated case is the typical phenomenon of knowledge, and they reach the social facts from it through some such mechanical device as imitation. This, however, is not Dewey's position at all. Of him I have merely said that he habitually uses the isolated case as his material, recognizing, as I think, its symbiotaxis, but not passing on to discuss it symbiotactically. The failure to progress takes revenge on Dewey occasionally when we find him and his followers as a practical matter in special cases treating the social elements as mere stimuli to the individual observer. Just as Pillsbury misunderstands Dewey when he speaks of " action " as merely one of the stimuli (and society as another), so Dewey himself falls at times practically for the moment into the treatment of society as one of the stimuli.

Society, however, if it means anything at all, means stuff of the same fiber as Dewey's " action." No more can it be one stimulus among many, than that " action " can be. When we use symbiotaxis in place of the term society we do it, as has been said, for the sole purpose of getting this exactness in meaning and not falling into the difficulties of the " one of the stimuli " attitude.

With this much achieved it should not be so difficult to broaden Dewey's concept of action into our concept of symbiotaxis. The action must be taken as real, the lapping over of the action of one life upon another must be taken as real; the action across these many lives must be taken as real. The symbiotaxis is achieved.

But this broadening of the action concept can be accomplished only in connection with a corresponding deepening of the society concept along lines already indicated. We must here specify the points as they affect knowledge. Not only is the symbiotactic knowledge crisis the typical one, we have said, but even in the case of the apparently isolated crisis, the background tacitly accepted is symbiotactic. Consider some of the elements of this background.

Suppose an absent-minded man walks into a blind alley and suddenly becomes aware of the blocking of his path. He is at a knowledge crisis of the isolated type, and one much simpler than when we suppose a man lost in the woods. He is in contact with the fence so far as his nose is concerned, with the ground so far as his feet are concerned. But this fence is not a " fact " with no other meanings than those of physical wood. It is symbiotactic — i.e., material taken up into a symbiotactic meaning. The man could easily jump over it, but it does not carry that meaning to him. By the same token the ground under his feet is symbiotactic — a path to be followed backward, not forward. The action that ensues is not that of an " individual man," any more than a bit of a tide movement in the ocean is the separately initiated motion of a particular drop of water. It is symbiotactic. Nor is it true that all these " social " facts appear objectively to the man determining his action as factors additional to the objective fence. In short, neither a statement of the situation in terms of habit (which Dewey would use to include them), nor in terms of an objective society, is satisfactory. The statement must be symbiotactic. We must recognize here a formed portion of a symbiotaxium including the human plasm and the non-human plasm (equally formed), the whole in active function just for what it is.

A slight effort will show how easy it is to restate Dewey's theory of knowledge on this basis, without doing injustice to any part of it, but, on the contrary, increasing its scope and causing it to answer objectors who heretofore have not been satisfied as to its actually showing the technique of durable knowledge.

Our individual man, facing a crisis in which " facts " prove unworkable and " ideas " arise in opposition to them, meets and solves the problem and works through to new and better-adjusted " facts " just as Dewey describes the process, save that he works not as an " individual man " but as taxioplasm. It is not a question whether at exactly the same moment some other man is facing the same problem and solving it the same identical way, any more than in a corresponding case in physiology at an identical moment identical cells were acting identically. Not uniformity but variety is characteristic of life. But the living function, the organic bond, is none the less observable; it " is " none the less the fact for science. It is not a question of the influence of anything " social " upon anything " individual." It is a question merely of the process as one through and through; a question of the whole cloth in which the patterns appear.

We have then a reconstruction of old facts into new and better-equilibrated facts. When the process is complete our result is nothing that can be called " subjective " or " solipsistic " in the evil sense as against individual functioning. It is a result which has symbiotactic value; and what we mean by symbiotactic value will prove, in the end, to be what the realists mean by objectivity so far as the realists remain within the boundaries of the problem of knowledge. This does not mean that every decision by an individual is symbiotactically true, any more than Dewey's theory means that every chance hypothesis of the individual is true. Dewey makes every hypothesis real, but lets truth apply to the tested result. The tested result that works symbiotactically is the truth.

It is apparent from recent discussions that truth is too limited a word to cover all the phenomena that need to be recognized. The pragmatist has argued at times that whatever is satisfying is true. He has made a good case, and at the same time he has left himself open to be sneered at by certain types of opponents. Yet the matter disentangles itself readily in terms of the symbiotactic theory. A typical case is that, let us say, of one of Frazer's grain gods. This god is real and his teaching is true in terms of the life of the group of his worshipers. For he symbolizes the planting and the harvest; his worship stimulates agricultural virtue. In some metaphysical sense of " is," it is true that the god is not, does not exist; but that is an infinitely small sense compared with the sense of truth in the group defined. It is irrelevant, incompetent, and immaterial, though true in its way. But for men living today this god is not real nor his doctrine true. We have our lives otherwise arranged, our values otherwise symbolized. We have different truth, and yet no truer truth. Now the absolutist, the realist, the idealist, and their like should be last of all men to stand too positively on the truth of today; yet that is just what they do in such criticisms of the pragmatist as have been referred to. By the test of the truth of today the truth of four thousand years ago is false. But *quis custodiet ipsos custodes?*, who will verify our truth by the test of the truth of four thousand years hence? Surely not the anti-pragmatist of today. He is not big enough for that. There is indeed a scientific truth which may be opposed to the kind of realistic truths we have just mentioned. This scientific truth generalizes itself more successfully to cover the past and future, by not merely rejecting the past, but by remaking the past within itself, reinterpreting that past and predicting the future. Nevertheless the Ptolemaic system as Newcomb characterized it in a reference a few pages back may well be remembered for the kind of truth it still retains.

Proceeding to a more detailed working out symbiotactically, we must deal with discussion groups and organization groups as in *The Process of Government*. How every phase of discussion grouping has symbiotactic reference, representativeness, meaning, must be shown.

We come then to a definition of truth in terms both of taxioplasm and taxis. It is borne by the living society, and functionally it has meaning, values for groups, values as a limit for all groups, and as a further limit for all groups for all time, time being understood of course with reference to the present physiological constitution of the homoplasm as still existent.

We shall find that in the taxioplasm develop the subject and object, but these are merely representative of taxioplasmic values (symbiotic values). We do not have subject and object replacing what went before, but merely organizing it, providing nuclei, leadership.

We comprehend now how truths are neither found nor made, but how they are both found and made in society, according as you look at them from a localized spot or with a broader perspective.

We may find the puzzle of realism and nominalism solved, though hardly more than Dewey has already solved it, and it is a good thing to keep away from. Our statement of the solution would be in terms of socially meaningful action. Dewey's answer is on the " going " basis after style of answers to Zeno.

We come back to realism, which is Deweyism plus a structural fixity in knowledge (I am talking of the younger realists of this decade), but this structural fixity I give to the full extent of its knowledge value symbiotactically.

We return to a status of world in the mind, yet mind in the world. We solve it by symbiotaxis. The world is in the mind socially taken as action (symbiotaxis). The symbiotaxium constructs the world — knowledge — i.e., it " is " that world. The world (knowledge) includes mind (mind as psychological technique).

V

KNOWLEDGE AND THE COSMOS

I am willing to admit the weakness of the theory of knowledge herein set out in one respect. This weakness lies, however, not in what it is, but in what it is not. Its trouble is that it does not go far enough. I can join in the aspirations of those who wish to go further. I can welcome any work they do to widen the theory. For myself I can simply say it is not I who have done the work. Mere aspirations are not criticisms. The real criticism of this theory must come through the construction of the one that in its actual working out goes further; one, in other words, that shows knowledge as a function not merely of symbioplasm, but of the cosmos in its aspects of the greatest symbiotic phenomena.

What this all comes to is that when we come down to bottom facts, we find that although we have explained much that was ignored or that remained troublesome in knowledge, we have not found in the symbiotaxium a worked-out answer for the making and finding of the bottom facts of physical existence as they present themselves. This bottom fact of existence does, it is true, rest deeper than the knowledge phenomena we have investigated. It may be that we have really carried the knowledge study the whole way that it can go, short of deepening it to the sensation study which includes the feeling and the nerve. Therein rest the roots of the whole interpretation. It is not at all impossible that the advance of knowledge will at no far distant date place us where we can restate the whole knowledge and life situation in such terms.

Finally, critics who approach from the opposite side, from the side of the older theories of knowledge, based on splits between facts and ideas such as Dewey has brushed off the boards, or even on the more modest realism and idealisms of the post-Dewey type, are not at liberty to stick to their old presuppositions and jump clear over this theory to bring the ultimate nerve-feeling duality into use as an argument on their behalf. If they want to get finally to that problem, they may use this theory for a ladder, or they may build a better ladder, but they may not destroy this ladder and ladders as imperfect under the avowal of their intention to lift themselves to their goal by their bootstraps. They may not disregard the facts that this theory strives to reconstruct. Their way forward most certainly lies straight through these facts, not in devious byways which avoid them altogether.

[The conclusions that Bentley reached in this exploratory analysis are set down in the following series of statements, which should be regarded, not as final, definitive formulations, but as guide-posts to further inquiries. These theses originally were intended to be published as a preface or abstract to the essay when Bentley planned to revise the essay and send it to a periodical like the *Journal of Philosophy* for publication. Editor.]

THESES

I. In What Sense Does an " Individual Man " Have Existence for Science?
- (a) The individual is transcended as to his boundaries by physiology in space, by genetic biology in time, and by social studies in action (i.e., in society).
- (b) He is so transcended only because the material under study is too rich to be handled by the individual under his old definition.
- (c) As action, the happenings of men in society have the same immediate reality, as contrasted with postulated individuals, that motion has as contrasted with fixed points in its path.

II. The Persistent in Knowledge
- (a) The pragmatists have not satisfied their opponents that they do justice to the persistent in knowledge.
- (b) Their opponents overemphasize persistency to such an extent that they no longer deal with knowledge.

III. Society as Modern Logic Handles It
- (a) Baldwin opposes a concrete society to the individual.
- (b) Dewey has not this fault; potentially he allows fully for society; actually he has not worked out a statement in terms of action that is social.

IV. Society and the Persistent in Knowledge
- (a) Knowledge is of the very texture of society.
- (b) It is the process not of society opposed to the individual, but of symbiotaxis.

V. Knowledge and the Cosmos
Knowledge is, no doubt, of the very texture of the cosmos; and when a serious attempt is made to prove it, by working out all the connections, no one will be better pleased than I.

CHAPTER TWO

Remarks on Method in the Study of Society*

Current psychological and philosophical terms, from souls to larynges, are attempts at fixating the verbal values of practical talk, the form of fixation being the " thing," a form from which science flees. In science, as today developed, such terms as " gold " or " the moon " are merely indications of problems; and the trend, so far from being toward their heightened specification as things, is toward the blending of all their indicated processes into the wider processes of scientific experience.

Sociology deals with material things and with analogous psychic things, but until it passes beyond these in their approximate values as things, and goes through them into their full processes, it can hardly qualify itself for the term " science " in the recent sense in which the word is used above. Not fixation of things, but processing, is what it must seek.

The other sciences, except psychology, need not bother much with the process of experience; their field is in a content of experience. Psychology works inside a process of experience, assuming an environment. It is the peculiarity of sociology that it must deal with great procedures that work through the experiencing process.

Sociology has had its struggles to locate a social thing in addition to various material and psychic things; but in that way does not lie science for it. It must cut through the bifurcations, subject-object among them, if it is to do its work. In the social aspect it must find, not an added type of thing, but the clue to unification and to analysis of process in the unified material. It may approach this problem in disregard of the techniques of all theologies, philosophies, and psychologies for the very reason that the tests and goals of those systems of approach are to be found within its own material.

This problem must be solved, to the extent at least of a working scheme,

* From *American Journal of Sociology*, Vol. XXXII, No. 3 (November, 1926), pp. 456–60.

before any advance whatever may be considered as having been made toward a statement of the process of social living with values comparable to those of other contemporary sciences.

The following remarks can hardly be of interest to any investigators who regard the problem as one merely curious or incidental in character; or to any who satisfy themselves in retaining " things " as their material with some unifying hypothesis as a sop to their minds; or to any who by reason of their dominating practical goals do not feel the need of cutting under those goals themselves. They are intended only for investigators who refuse to regard themselves as making progress at all until they can deal with a knowing-known direct, instead of with the hypothesized interactions of some knowing thing and some thing known.

Of method much is written. With method little is done.

Roundabout ways of satisfying self, or others, that something is — or may, or should, be — as one wants it, are legion.

But for knowledge upon which all may agree good eyesight and accurate words are alone required.

Visibility and language are the conditions of science — they are its substance.

Nor are they in the end separate. As instrumentalities they coalesce.

Visibility has been low in the social sciences. Facts have presented themselves borne in the personalities, the individualities, of men. Through these personalities we have tried to look — as through a glass, darkly.

Terminology has been poor in the social sciences, drawn as it has been from the language of everyday life — from the vocabularies of the manipulation of one man by another.

But not the point of view of one toward another is what we seek, rather the very processing itself of the ones-with-others. The everyday language has been a hindrance, not capable of purification.

A generation ago the atom was a hypothesis. Chemists still assumed that bare-eye reports, or magnified eye-reports, were the known facts. Today the electron is not a hypothesis, in the older sense, but — thanks to Millikan — rather in the class of things seen, and vision has become instrumental in new ways.

Then, spectroscopic vision was in its infancy. Today, the spectroscope reports as accurately on hundred-thousand-light-year intervals as the keen-sighted woodsman on what moves in the tree-tops. This is not to make a creed of the electron; it is only to refuse to make a creed of the squirrel in the tree-top.

Then, mathematics was a thin-air dweller: abstract, unreal, but helpful when not mere curiosity. Today, mathematics is the language of physics, an aid to the vision of physics, and the recorder of that vision. Mathematically stated vision is physics.

The method of social science is likewise vision and statement, both processes instrumental.

Quantity and quality in social science consist in how much and how well we can see, and in how much and how well we can tell what we see. For "how well" understand "how coherently." Quantity and quality both are to be found in the extent to which our observations and reports of observations fit together fluidly, flexibly, coherently — every observation, every statement of every worker, ready promptly to destroy itself in accordance with the ever-changing requirements of all the other observations, all the other statements, in the system, the whole system of social science.

Social science, as I have said, has long been looking at the facts of men's social living through personality. It has been reporting these facts largely in individual point-of-view language, that is, in psychological terms. It has been assuming that psychological terms indicated psychological existences — a naïve assumption. True, indeed, but true like a nymph in a tree trunk.[1] It has been assuming that personality was a resting-point for social fact, a starting-point for social interpretation.

Sweep it away. That is the first of the two points of method which I wish to emphasize.

Sweep what away? Not the personality-in-the-body, nymph-in-the-tree idea, feeling, belief. That idea-feeling-belief is very lovely, very true, very useful — in its own time and place.

Sweep away only the naïve assumption that that is *the* method to see and record facts in social science.

Reduce, then, the personality system of seeing and recording to the position of one among many possible systems [2] of seeing and recording.

Try the other systems, and see which gives the most complete, the most coherent, delivery.

The personality form of statement is a good form for domestic quarrels, but a bad form for theories of crime and punishment. It is nice for hero-worshipers, illusion for Buddha, bedrock for Western theology, multiplicity-in-unity for psychoanalysis, hypothesis for the philosopher, and the most uncertain thing in the world to its closest students.

[1] Spirit occupancy of a tree is of course a true statement of tree life if that is the best system of expression the observer commands in which to make his reports.
[2] For such systems the phrase "verbal frames of reference" is probably more satisfactory. See my book *Relativity in Man and Society*.

Incidentally it is accepted datum to most sociologies. Almost certainly it ought not to be.[3]

The president signs the bill with the treasured pen. His act is physical and personal and social. It is prospectively capable of complete statement as physical, of complete statement as personal, of complete statement as social.

Under present technique, we know the physical statement of presidential pen-pushing cannot be perfected to our satisfaction.

The personal statement we know to be confused. The literature of the confusion is in evidence.

The social[4] statement, not as complement or supplement to physical or personal, but as alternative, in its own right, for complete observation and description, is steadily advancing in power.

The yield for this social form of observation and statement in the immediate future will depend apparently not so much on whether we can command the words to report its observations as upon how far we can make the effort successful to see full facts under its form. One grits one's teeth over it; sometimes one gnashes them. But words are both the material and the tools of social study. We must see through them before we use them.

Therefore we come to the second of the two points in regard to method which I desire here to make.

It is entirely hopeless to expect a satisfactory technical sociological statement to develop in any one existing language.

It is equally hopeless to expect any worker to make real progress unless he controls several languages, at the very least, in their symbolic values.

One-language terms drag in the absolute, make the worker himself an absolute, and therefore wreck him and his work.

Multiple-language terms shimmer. They compel knowledge.

---

[3] "There is also the feeling that any adding in of 'conscious' factors which cannot be measured and do not obey the same laws as the rest of nature must play havoc with all hopes of satisfactory explanations: and this feeling is justified" (C. K. Ogden, *The Meaning of Psychology*, p. 166). This passage refers to psychological, not to sociological, investigations, but is nevertheless pertinent.

[4] The word "social" is arbitrary here. "X" would do as well. Every adult student in this field knows there's the rub.

CHAPTER THREE

A Sociological Critique of Behaviorism*

In a recent article in the *Archiv für systematische Philosophie und Soziologie,* Professor John B. Watson, pioneer and foremost advocate of Behaviorism in the United States, ably presents his case for a psychology dealing wholly with what can be observed, and held closely in line with what he asserts to be the procedure of other natural sciences. He expressly insists that he is not proposing a mere laboratory procedure, but that his method does now, or ultimately will, cover and control the scientific study of all the behavior, all the reactions, of men, including those more complicated reactions " labeled social."

Psychologists will criticize his position from their various points of view, and I do not wish to encroach upon their field. I propose instead to examine Watson's work from a sociological point of view, and in especial to ask: (1) whether that which he defines as " observation " of facts is really an adequate significant scientific observation, or, instead, merely a limited provisional observation, useful in simple cases but not extending significantly to " the more complicated reactions labeled social "; and (2) whether his procedure is or is not actually in line with that of other natural sciences as he asserts it to be. I shall undertake this examination, not from a standpoint in opposition to that of Watson psychologically, but instead with a full willingness to regard his system as useful and adequate within the ranges in which he has actually thus far used it. I shall go with him as far as I can, and ask merely how the case stands when one must perforce go further.

The leading assertions of the article in question are:

1. All behavior can be observed, like the phenomena of all other natural sciences (but consciousness has never been observed).

2. All behaviorist observation can be presented in the form S-R, i.e., stimulus-response.

3. Physico-chemical studies, neuro-physiological studies, and behaviorist

---

* From *Archiv für systematische Philosophie und Soziologie,* Bd. 31, Heft 3-4, 1928, pp. 234-40.

studies, taken together, cover the full field of investigation of human reactions.

4. In general, " the behaviorist does not admit for a moment that any human reaction cannot be described in such terms."

5. In the study of the more complicated reactions, one may substitute the " situation " for the " stimulus," without departing from behaviorist technique (this position being presented not so much as definitive assertion, but instead rather as assured assumption).

6. Social situations are to be studied and analyzed as stimuli to individual " human animals " (this, again, appearing rather as corollary to assertions 3 and 4 above, than as definitive balanced assertion in its own right).

Whatever else in these positions may cry for examination by psychologists from their respective points of view, the point that cries to me sociologically for examination is the identification of situation with stimulus in social ranges: an examination to be made under the test of actual social observation of the scientific type.

The remarks that follow may assume a wholehearted agreement with Watson in the following points:

1. The rejection of all terms dealing with consciousness or mentality in any of its technical forms, and the refusal to use categories arising from terms of this type for any scientific purpose.

2. In especial the rejection of instinct as a point of interpretative departure either in psychology or in sociology.

3. Acceptance of his theories of conditioning and of transfer within the range in which he actually has employed them.

4. His criticism of the psychoanalytic approach.

5. His interpretation of the talking and thinking procedures in the physical organism, summed up in the words: " We think and plan with the whole body."

But this agreement of approach, although it goes far, will stop short of accepting his wider theoretical position. Rejected are the claims to comprehensiveness (though not the practical value in limited ranges) which he makes for the following points:

1. His treatment of the " situation " as merely a complex of stimuli.

2. The assertion, with which he concludes the article before us, that " words are the conditioned (C)S substitutes for the world of objects and acts."

3. His assertion that all human reactions may for scientific purposes be adequately described in terms of his formula; and his belief that after the physico-chemical and the neuro-physiological studies, the behaviorist (i.e., stimulus-reaction) study is all that remains to be made.

Let us examine first, through simple illustration, the kind of phenomena a sociologist is compelled to analyze; and after that let us try to determine what the requirements are for knowledge in such fields.

Admitted that analysis into stimulus and reaction can be easily and profitably carried through in animal behavior, in infant life, and in such adult behavior as admits significant specific description under ordinary three-dimensional space categories, the query is: how does this analysis succeed when the behavior is much more complex and when the space description fails to yield the necessary scientific significance?

"A man may fire a gun." This is a reaction that Watson can examine under an S-R formula. But, after all, the fact that a clearly grammatical set of six words is presented us is no guarantee that we have been given a scientifically significant description. A man may fire a gun at a king; or at a bird; or at a target; or into the air for the firing's sake. Are these merely four qualifications of one clearly defined act, or do we have here four descriptions of typically different character, despite the fact that each of the four contains the six identical words: "A man may fire a gun"? Evidently the four are sharply separate sociological descriptions, and not merely sub-classes of one description, so far as sociological significance goes. And evidently it would be easy to set down lists of reactions pages long, all sociologically different despite the fact that each included the words: "A man may fire a gun." But this is only the first stage in our difficulty in defining the reaction. Take "firing a gun at a king"; it may mean a king in his personal, domestic, or private functions; a king as one who performs some offensive kingly act; a king as representative of a particular existing government; or a king as a representative of any government. One may have to drop down through stage after stage of description before he gets the reaction he is after so specified that it has scientific significance.

Turn to the side of stimulus. The stimulus for the firing of the gun at the king may be given as hunger, as personal abuse, as the abuse of a relative or friend, or as any abuse humanitarianly grasped; it may be given as a racial factor, as a disease factor, or as the man's membership in some group, whether organized closely as a society, or loosely held together as a doctrine; again, a thousand more descriptions are possible.

But I hardly need to point out that when we give exact description to the stimulus and exact description to the reaction under such circumstances as these, we find in the end we do not have separate descriptions of stimulus on the one side and reactions on the other, but only one single description covering stimulus and reaction both. The whole happening is in space and time, but it is in social space and social time; and the effort which Watson's procedure requires in order to get the necessary exactness for his formula, proves to be possible only when it can be made in the kind of space and time mechanics use, which in our field strips off inevitably most of the significance of what is presented for study. I offer no opinion as to how far the behaviorist analysis into stimulus and reaction can be profitably carried under the procedure of a discipline called psychology; but I am certain that under the procedure of a discipline called sociology, this analysis results in the end in talking about just nothing at all.

The behaviorist will misinterpret the statements I have just made, and it is desirable for me to show just why and how. He will admit that description can be made along the lines I have indicated, but he will hold that they are preliminary or superficial in the sense generally conveyed when the term " historical " is used in opposition to the term " scientific." He will make this misinterpretation and criticism, not on the basis of sociological investigation he has actually made himself, but upon the basis of the fixed advance construction he uses as frame for his investigation: viz, the individual man. The behaviorist, in short, although he rejects the terms of individual consciousness from his descriptions, still retains the individual behavoristic agent as the basis, the seat, and the frame for all his experiments and reports.

To him in this respect the sociological attitude is in flat opposition. For sociology it is the behaviorist's description with its analysis into stimulus and reaction which appears as preliminary and superficial. For sociology it is the well-worked-out description across both stimulus and reaction, taken in social space and in social time, which must be regarded as direct observation essential for the interpretative purposes of science. Such description I have studied under the style of " cross-sectional " in my books *The Process of Government* and *Relativity in Man and Society*. And I hold that the really valuable results of sociological investigation for the last two generations are given us adequately in this form, and that we do not need the frameworks, whether behavioristic or not, so commonly and so elaborately built under them with pretense of sustaining them.

So much for the detail of sociological analysis. Turn now to a consideration of the general requirements of scientific analysis in this field.

Philosophy has always faced the problem involved in the following preliminary description: there is a world (objective) spread out, of which we in our physical bodies are a part; but this world is spread out in some sense " by " or " before " or " within " us (subjective), or as in knowledge: a problem recurrently appearing in terms of unity or disparateness. Recent sociological analyses of men of many races and ages have yielded wide data as to the possible extensions and limitations of meaning for the term " us," but the problem remains as acute as ever.

Now when sociology settles down to its task, under scientific tests and standards, it is working in a field in which this same preliminary description of subjective and objective presents itself and cannot be avoided, since the sociological field is the very field of acting, knowing men in groupal life. A sociology which starts with a firm philosophical postulate upon this point cannot be scientific, because the one essential scientific requirement is admission of the weakness of postulates and determination to secure all postulates as provisional from within the field of study, and never to be accepted as fixed from without. A behaviorism which flatly ignores the presence of this problem in sociological descriptions cannot hope to be scientific: not only, as I have shown in the preceding discussion, because it never gets its full problems stated to itself; but further, because its very act of ignoring is the equivalent of a fixed initial philosophical postulation.

The physical sciences have been increasingly successful in making their studies within the range of the objective statement; but in the process the objective statement has transformed itself into something that is neither objective nor subjective, but rather to be described as " operational." The physical language, mathematics, and especially differentials, becomes the physical world. The effective work of physics is all within the operational field: barring on the one side some surviving adhesions to matter, or perhaps to ether, and occasionally to Newtonian space and time as " existences ": and barring on the other hand the Cantorian mathematics and Russell's interpretations of it, resting in a philosophical distinction between cardinal and ordinal numbers, and apparently near to the point of eliminating itself. The operational characteristic is that every bit of physical knowledge, whether presented as concept or as world-fact, offers itself freely for transformation by the tests of the systematized, coherent, self-controlling range of developed operations.

Behaviorism is an effort to study psychological facts taken as animal reactions, within the objective field; but it antedates in its approach the operational position. That is nothing against it in its experimental and laboratory work. So long as stimulus and reaction can be adequately defined for the purpose at hand in the older, or mechanical, space and time forms, well and good. But when behaviorism claims to be able to cover all " those reactions called social " by the same technique that it uses for simplified animal or child studies: when it claims to control the analysis of that very society, which, as one of its characteristics, is the bearer of space and time, under standards of one of the limited sets of space and time forms which society creates and uses: then it is beyond its proper range and beyond its effective powers. In this field its analysis of stimulus and reaction is crude, with at most a preliminary value, and barren of important results. The " situation " cannot be analyzed into stimuli and reactions under the dominant form of spatially isolated individual human bodies, except for the crudest preliminary purposes. For broader studies the situations themselves must be allowed to present themselves in full temporal and spatial phenomenality for operational analysis, let the results come as they may.

CHAPTER FOUR

New Ways and Old to Talk About Men*

I

From the reader of this essay I beg a simple and kindly, nay even an unsophisticated, consideration. I shall discuss ways of talking about men; and from time immemorial, ways of talking about men have been the broideries of human trouble.

It is not that I shall concern myself with racial hates, religious scorns, industrial loathings, or other hostile ways in which men in masses regard one another; it is rather with ways of speech about individuals, and very technical ways at that, ways of speech about individuality or personality as such. The need of a kindly approach is nevertheless just as great, for this field involves immortality and the mortal, minds and bodies, ideas and realities, powers and capacities, intelligences, geniuses, and originalities — in short, an entanglement of speculations, beliefs, and faiths, concerning which prejudices may be as deep and arguments as bitter, though issues rarely so bloody, as in other and more immediately practical fields of human struggle.

Kindliness? yes: all serious effort to disentangle involved problems, no matter how faulty, deserves that. But what of a request for a simple, an unsophisticated, a naïve, consideration? I should like to write a preface on the importance of being naïve when one starts to study the life of men in society — the importance of being so extremely naïve that all the professionally wise men of the world will laugh one to scorn: how it is because of the very plague of the age-old wise, with their brains a-spin, that one must become as a simple child if one wishes to learn of society: how the spider-webs of the wise must be torn, if the little one is ever to spread his wings. But instead of arguing in a preface, I shall exemplify in the essay. I shall be naïve. You may judge of the import.

This naïveté will be signalized by its attitude toward intellectual sophistication, for it will regard all sophistication and all intellectualism as

* From *The Sociological Review*, Vol. XXI, No. 3 (October, 1929), pp. 300–314.

merely a passing aspect or phase of the social life of men at such and such a time and such and such a place. The wisdom of absolutes, realities, verities, facts, will be regarded as present before us in society, but not as potentially the master of knowledge or of life. Yes, even " facts " must lose their sophisticated claim to dominance. My naïveté will regard everything as fact, even a wrong theory: and will admit no claim to independent actuality for any fact whatever as opposed to any non-fact whatever. But how indeed can a sociologist do other, when the world and life and mind are all his jumbled field? This openness to all presentation, all phenomena, all description, I shall choose to regard, for the purposes of this paper, as scientific; and I shall uphold it for our subjectmatter, not with the thought we of our science-proud generation are finally telling the world the truth about itself; but instead with the frank admission that while our new science now seems the most useful frame for our knowledge, nevertheless that very science may well be looked down upon by future generations with much the same condescension that the wise of today show for the animisms of the savage.

II

The *soul*, the *mind*, the *body, life, society:* these in their ramifications of terminology are all ways of talking about men. As such we shall examine them.

The soul is a way of speech about men, and indeed not merely one way but many ways. Some souls present themselves with beginnings, but no endings; others with no more a beginning than an ending. Some are rigid and awful; others merge gently with Deity in mystic union. Some anticipate physical torments or blisses; others foresee spiritual joys or sufferings. We never can tell. Souls are ways of speech. We may believe, but belief is a way of speech. Are souls facts or not facts? Fact is a way of speech: and no well-assured way at that, since the dogmatism of fact is often the most dangerous dogmatism of all. Indeed, to assert either that soul is fact or that it is not fact, is to attempt to specify the more certain by the less certain. Nothing is less certain than " fact " in that sense in which it claims to dominate knowledge: the sense of " fact as such." The physicist can differentiate fact from non-fact tentatively for certain specified purposes, but no longer may he claim to be the interpreter par excellence of fact; too bitterly has he been taught his lesson over and over again in the last generation. The practical man or the theologian may make fact-assertions about soul, but both the theologian and the practical man, along with the souls and the ideas about souls in their thousandfold variations, are all parts of the field of sociology: all alike facts-fragmentary, facts-claimant, but none facts-dominant.

Consciousness, mind, is a second way of speech about men. It is that way of speech, I take it, in which soul is inspected in its earthly surroundings in the durations of a lifetime. It is that way which is used when investigators wish to inspect those same human problems, otherwise talked of as soul, apart from the particular purposes and stresses commonly brought acutely to attention when the term soul itself is used. Mind is taken as the man himself, as character, as individuality, as personality. With mind goes a family of terms of psychic or mental character, for which it stands as symbol, or synthesis or locus. Sometimes mind is taken broadly to cover all of personality: sometimes more narrowly for only a portion of it, as when, for example, to consciousness is annexed the subconscious. It is characteristic of Mind that it and its terms are used as though directly offset against Matter, as phenomenon of correlate standing, provisionally or permanently, in varying degrees. With soul this was not so much the case, for to soul and its problems, matter was at most transitory, and always insignificant except perhaps as experience or as trial for soul in its earthly career.

The body that is correlated with mind is itself merely another way of speech about men — the third way; and under the naïve approach of this paper it has no independent claims to fact value of higher degree than have the preceding ways of speech, those of soul and of mind.

Life is a fourth way of speech about men. Life, as distinguished from body, at times presents itself as a special vitalistic way of speech with values of its own intermediate between the mind way and the body way. At other times body and life tend to fuse into one type of speech; and in this respect some real progress toward harmonization and reorganization has been given us by the physical and biological sciences. The way of speech in terms of life stretches out, it is true, to include animal and vegetable phenomena beyond the phenomena of human beings, and the way of speech in terms of body stretches still further, passing into the regions of the inanimate; but in this lies no radical distinction from the other ways of speech, for we shall find that there is also some stretching in our understanding of individual mind as it runs across the field of the social. All the ways of speech stretch, and stretch confusedly, not coherently: that is indeed the great difficulty with them all for the would-be scientific investigator. " Life " as fixed " fact " has no separate and firm definition upon which all workers can rely, any more than has mind or soul; and it is coming more and more to be realized that the same is true of body, that it is indeed only by delimitation in an arbitrary Euclidean space that the limits of a single body, a single organism, may be specified. Sunlight and interstellar rays are in the body processes, and if they are there in full operational value, then the Euclidean boundaries of the single body are assuredly arbitrary, mere terms of convenience for certain practical purposes and nothing more.

Up to two generations ago these four ways of speech, the ways of soul, of mind, of life, and of body, all of them operating in a background of posited realities, truths, or actualities, provided the full working equipment of the philosopher, psychologist, economist, and political scientist. It was out of this equipment that was produced all that structure of wisdom which now at least temporarily must be disregarded and cast to one side, if one wishes to make progress in understanding. The defect in it all was that one additional great range of fact had not yet been clearly identified, that one additional great way of speech about men, the social way, had not yet appeared. It is from the observations of Sir Henry Maine and Le Play, and from the generalizations of Comte, that this later development can best be dated.

Society is a way of speech about men. I emphasize. Discussion of men in social terms is today just as direct, just as immediate, just as inevitable, just as fully implied in whatever investigation we make, as in discussion in terms of life or mind or body. Was it not with social eyes that Le Play looked out upon the world? Is this not the value of " regional " in regional studies? Does not the very existence of such a title as *The Sociological Review* imply it? Does not the formula Place-Work-Folk use it directly in preference to the older speech forms? When we use the term " institution " what have we but such a direct description, no matter how desperate our struggles may be to formulate in terms of one or more of the older systems of speech exactly what it is which we are attempting to describe? " Institution " cannot be expressed adequately in terms of soul, nor of body, nor of individual life, nor of mind or personality. It needs its own language. And in this field it is that the language of mind reaches out beyond the ranges of individual minds in some mysterious way, much as the ranges of body and life language run beyond the individual man in their respective fields.

The great problem before sociology is the reconciliation of these various speech forms as technical tools of investigation; and with them of course the reconciliation of any others that may appear. This is sociology's primary scientific concern. The scientific approach I have chosen to regard as being that of openness to all phenomenal presentation. It is the willingness to let every fact-claimant have its chance, the stern determination to let no fact, however firmly it may pretend to be established, dominate rigidly and finally the study of other facts. The great scientific technique is, of course, mathematics, and mathematics is nothing but language with the insistent requirement of maximum definiteness of meaning in all terms used and in the manner of their use. Every great stage in the progress of science is marked by new definiteness of terms, and some of the greatest stages have been signalized by what at first sight appeared to be merely a slight variation of old values for fundamental words. Even where the terms used are not given mathematical formulation this requirement of definiteness is vital; indeed, sometimes more vital outside of such formulation than within it. If this be the case, then surely sociology will continue to have difficulties with its claim to scientific standing until it can make sound progress toward the reconciliation, the functional co-ordination, of its five conflicting and confused speech forms.

III

Of these five ways of talking about men, those of soul, of mind, of life, of body, and of society, I shall examine three: namely, life, mind, and society. I shall omit consideration of soul, partly because certain of its claims to absoluteness run beyond scientific technique, and partly because all that part of its field which may be scientifically treated falls within the language of mind. I shall omit body, considered as matter, inert, quiescent, because the established sciences are ever more centering on active processes, operations, events, to such extent that their discoveries are tending to become fully expressible in operational terms without need of any rigid substratum of inertness to bear them. Light and electricity parted early from the old field of matter, and electrons and the newer gravitational studies have completed the divorce. I have no single word of opposition to offer to discussions in terms of either soul or matter, except that they are no longer pertinent to the particular purposes of the present examination.

The examination is into ways of speech; but it is not terminological in the old sense of an attempt to establish whether or not a particular expression is adequate for a particular fact taken as apart from the expression. It assumes that facts as facts are not definitely known until they are definitely expressed; it assumes that the expressive values of a particular term are never definite except as we take them in the full system of expression to which the term belongs; it therefore proceeds to inquire into the nature of the conflict that exists between the three great ways of speaking that have been named, in the belief that if these expressive systems can be rid of internal confusions and can be harmonized, a richer comprehension of their fact values will immediately follow.

Let us select for first consideration the relations of the two ways of speech that run in terms of mind and of living body. The attitude of the man in the street is something as follows: " I am a person, and I have a body. My body I regard as materially spread out in space. But I, the person, am not material in that sense and I am not spread out in space so that I can be measured by the aid of a rule. Just what I am I do not pretend to understand any too clearly; but I am sure that I am mind, I am a person, I am I, and not mere matter, despite the fact that my personality stays close by my body while I live, and that I cannot get rid of my body during life. Though I reside in my body I myself am other than that body." Here now in the face of this situation enters the older wisdom. On this basis, taken as presented fact, the older metaphysical, philosophical, and epistemological theories have been constructed to explain the relations of mind and body and outer world: and on the same basis appear the newer psychological, physiological, and neuro-psychological theories. Under the present approach we discard all of these theories for the simple reason that none of them make any substantial progress toward reconciling the two systems of language, the systems of mind and of body. Whether as monisms, dualisms, or parallelisms: whether as correlating particular ideas with particular brain cells, idea systems with neurological systems, or personalities with single organisms: their effort at harmonization is not by direct treatment of the values of the terms in the two systems, but by the construction of speculative theories of a connective nature: speculative by this very test that harmonization, co-ordination, functioning, of terms is not secured.

Take next the mental and social ways of speech, and the constructions offered to connect them. Philosophers of the absolute and their apprentices have offered us Social Wills and Social Consciousnesses in which the mental as individual wholly disappears. Other experimenters have suggested to us Social Minds set over against individual minds as different and apart from them. Neither form of construction has satisfied investigators. The former distills most of the current values out of the mental, and leaves the bodily form of speech unassimilated. The latter merely adds to the difficulties that formerly existed.

Finally, consider the social and bodily ways of speech when brought into combination. Here truly the confusion is at its worst, and the need of better technique of expression becomes clamorous. Describe an institution, say Parliament, in purely bodily language and you have nothing.

Describe it as a sum of individuals, or in some peculiar way as a sum of aspects of individuals, and you may perhaps have a speculative interpretation, but you leave out its social immediacy. You get nothing of its trends in durations, nothing of its complex interactions with other institutions.

In contrast with all such constructions and interpretative systems, let me illustrate again from Le Play. When he roamed the world studying men in society, did he bother with metaphysics? Not at all. True, he had a set scheme of world and man provided by his religion, but he did not let it control and formulate his observations. He saw the people regionally at work. He sensed their experiences in large durations of time, not as instantaneous acts of dogmatic will. He used his scientifically trained eye and mind for their observation, and he made his reports. He took the same simple naïve direct attitude toward the combined facts of mind and body and society that I am advocating here. His followers have made that attitude continuously more systematic and profitable.[1] Mr. Branford has helped to develop the analysis of societies in terms of Place, Work, and Folk; and twenty-five years ago in an American sociological publication, when contrasting " objective, determinist, or geographical " studies with " subjective, psychological, or libertarian," he wrote: " These two approaches are just opposite sides of a hill that has to be traversed on the way to sociology." What did Professor Geddes do when he wrote *The Charting of Life?* Quite frankly to the " everyday material acts of life " he added its " everyday mental facts." Now I shall not come out at the place Professor Geddes came out. I intend to treat those two kinds of facts, not as certainties, but as mere provisional everyday descriptions. I shall attempt to show that there is little value beyond that of a practical rule of thumb in the everyday separation between them. I shall try to determine a way of speech that will cover them both, and with them the social facts as well. But, different as my form of statement may appear from his, I am in full sympathy both with his starting-points and with his view of social phenomena in the outcome, though not with his way of telling it. It is an interesting fact that British sociologists have in general been much less inclined to spend time on speculative connective structures than have their fellows of other countries; and whether they are to be congratulated or their case deplored I can hardly say. To their credit is that they have conserved their powers to apply in fields in which they could make substantial direct progress; to their debit is the fact that when they do introduce speculative interpretation the results are sometimes peculiarly atrocious, as was evidenced when McDougall was transplanted to

[1] I refer, of course, to his scientific followers, not to the school of social reform bearing his name.

America by his effort to fit himself into the prevailing scheme of things through the setting up of a working mechanism of society in terms of instincts. McDougall went about it just as though instincts were little concrete " things " which could be picked with forceps out of human life, and made to work like gears in a machine, on a concealed postulate that when you had found the gears you understood the machine, and under the great embarrassment that every month when you looked your gears over anew you saw, or thought you saw, a different set. Professor Geddes, on the other hand, while he talks in terms of the material, the psychic, the extended psychic or social, and finally the objectified socially psychic, giving us Place-Work-Folk, Sense-Experience-Feeling, (Com)Emotion-Ideation-Imagination, EthoPolity-Synergy-Achievement, never is found picking out a master reality like an instinct to explain anything else. He keeps a simple operational purport throughout. He never gets away from the spirit of his two starting formulas: that of life,

$$\frac{EfO}{OfE},$$

and that of Society,

$$\frac{PWF}{FWP},$$

which to my mind are as sound as anyone could want them, providing the terms are all in one general field of knowledge, and none of them mysterious strangers from abroad.

IV

Now, in our attempt to function with the three speech types, mind, body, and society, our first effort must be to locate any terms used in all of them which shift in meaning as between them. Having for our immediate purpose divested ourselves of the realities of soul, and of the actualities of inert matter, and confined ourselves to going operations, to events, to happenings, this effort is simplified. We manifestly have first of all to examine space and time, not in the sense of some assumed actual space or actual time, but in the sense of the terms as we use them to portray the spatial and temporal characteristics of our physical, mental, and social phenomena.

Time is a term which covers two very different kinds of situation, one that of instantaneity, the other that of durations. Instantaneity is a very doubtful term full of implications of reality, of existence, and only by courtesy or confusion an affair of time at all. Duration, however, is an affair of measurement by clocks and nothing else. Space, in the sense of spatial extension, is, like time, an affair of measurements — of measurement, however, by yardsticks or light rays, instead of by clocks. Apart from this definite value of mensuration, the term space is even more vicious in its implications than is the term time when instantaneity is confused with durations; for in current usage the term space serves to drag in a cloud of obscure suggestions which may mean anything or nothing, and which certainly means hardly ever the same thing to any two men. We shall confine ourselves to the definite meanings, to the measurable value of extensions and durations, in order to see what import they have for our three ways of speech about men.

The mental, the physical, and the social ways of speech all offer us phenomena in the durations of time. But as for extensions in space, it is only the physical way of speech that carries exact spatial values in the sense of measurability. Mental phenomena, indeed, get their very mental specialization in speech from the fact that they cannot thus be taken as directly measurable spatially. The social phenomena appear under this test as a confused mass of the measurable and the non-measurable, the spatial and the non-spatial.

Holding to the standard of measurability, we may now characterize the first two types of speech as follows. The way of speech in terms of mind is that collection of words which is taken as capable of measurement in time but not as capable of measurement in space. The way of speech in terms of body is that collection which is taken as capable of both spatial and temporal measurement. The latter we may, by this test, call temporal-spatial, and the former temporal–non-spatial, whether as terms or as phenomena.

Given this much of definiteness in dealing with language, our next procedure will be to examine into the respective values of the terms individual and social. Since individuality or personality comes out to approximate clearness of expression only in the temporal–non-spatial terminology, we shall approach the problem first of all in that particular terminology, limiting ourselves precisely to it. To examine we must select some situation which clearly has both individual and social values, which is institutional, and yet which is not so complexly institutional as to be beyond the possibility of direct analysis by the aid of such technical powers as we now possess. We may not start dogmatically with some definition of an individual as we assume to know him in advance, nor with some socially defined construct as if we knew it in advance as fact; but instead, we must just naïvely and simply take a situation that presents itself to us as both social and individual to see what we can get out of it.

Let us start with Jack-loving-Jill as temporal–non-spatial presentation.

It is clearly social whatever the term may mean, since both Jack and Jill are involved; and it is clearly institutional, since the manner of their involvement — this being the described phenomenon we are to study — varies greatly in different ages, among different peoples, and under different circumstances, ranging from cavemen lovers to cicisbeos, and from Victorian families to the ritualistic concupiscence of the East. And it is clearly individual, for in it Jack-in-love preens himself in full glory. Our problem now is to differentiate the pure individuality of Jack out of this full Jack-loving-Jill situation: we must get rid of Jill while still retaining love-in-Jack, or Jack-in-love, or just simply Jack, whatever you choose to call it. And we must do this, remember, without dragging in any elements from the temporal-spatial terminology, but holding ourselves closely at all times within the ranges of the temporal–non-spatial.

This project cannot be successfully carried through.[2] Analyze as carefully as you will, we can never succeed in locating Jack-in-love without his Jill. You may knock Jack down physically, you may sentence him to jail from the bench, or consign him to Heaven or Hell from the pulpit, but that will not get rid of the Jill-ness in the particular situation, the Jack-loving-Jill we have been studying, in the terminology in which we are taking it. The common manner of doing it, or rather of pretending to do it, is to assume Jack as an instantaneously real existence, and then to describe all of his social relations as somewhat less vividly real experiences in a durational world. But we, remember, are proceeding without the right to make any such assumptions. Before us we have Jack-loving-Jill, and that is a phenomenon in durations of time. If we try shortening those durations from the month, or day, or hour, or minute we have chosen to start with, and if we proceed downward to split seconds, we never discover Jack without his Jill or his Jill-substitute or his Jill-like content, until we translate him into the instantaneous; but to translate him in that way is to take him out of duration, out of measurable time, and into some field of absolute existence with which we have no concern. Or we may proceed in the opposite direction, increasing durations into enormous periods, into infinities, and pretend to construct an immortal Jack; but that again is outside the range of our chosen terminology, the temporal–non-spatial. If we try the immediate present, we are no better off, for that again is only instantaneity in another form.

---

[2] An extended theoretical discussion of the argument that follows in terms of postulates, definitions, and theses, will be found in the article " Individual and Social: Terms and Facts," *Revue Internationale de Sociologie*. A brief indication of the form of approach in contrast to the dogmatic attitude of Behaviorism, which limits us to stimuli and reactions, has appeared in the article " A Sociological Critique of Behaviorism," *Archiv für systematische Philosophie und Soziologie*, Bd. 31, Heft 3–4, 1928.

V

It will be evident to anyone who analyzes the preceding argument that I have been endeavoring to work in continuities. For such procedure I feel no need of apology. All that continuity implies is " tracing transitions," and there should be nothing shocking in a paraphrase such as: *Societas non facit saltum.* In the physical field of study if an arrow is now at A and later at B, we feel that we can only deal with it as arrow and as event if we can follow its path, or if we can assume a type of path we have experience in following under circumstances that indicate that such a path has been used. When the path disappears, either knowledge disappears, or else knowledge is greatly enriched by the discovery of new types of paths. In our sociological field I refuse to take a magic leap outside of continuities from the Jack-loving-Jill to the Jack-in-himself; though I am perfectly willing to make the transition whenever anyone can show me a path. For the present I am merely asserting that I do not find such path myself.

There exists in mathematics a procedure known as determining limits, and if, now, one examines the argument with the theory of limits in mind, it is immediately evident that such descriptions as love-in-Jack or Jack-in-love have the general appearance of limits, in the technical sense, to the full Jack-loving-Jill situation; and if this be true of those descriptions, it is also true of the description Jack-himself.

Again in mathematical analysis there is a device known as deleting the domain by which one gets rid of unmanageable limits and proceeds without any apparent sacrifice of efficiency, indeed with greatly heightened efficiency, since this device is used only where otherwise one could not proceed rationally at all. In sociological investigation, when one centers one's attention on the technique ordinarily in use with respect to mind and matter, it is certainly clear that there is no such thing as rational procedure at all under the old speech confusions; and, because of this long-continuing irrationality, it is my conviction that the time has come when sociologists must delete the domain, and eliminate the unmanageable instantaneous Jack so far as their technical purposes and procedures go. This should be done, not for a moment with the idea that we are asserting ultimate truth, nor indeed with the idea that we are asserting any kind of truth at all, but merely as a technique by which we can handle the full richness of the social situations without sacrificing anything of the equally rich knowledge of individuality which has been conveyed heretofore in the temporal–non-spatial terminology.

No one need be terrorized by this suggestion. However great the restraint one puts upon oneself technically in this respect, one may still give Jack all the aesthetic, religious, emotional, or absolute values he will, outside of and beyond the technical procedure. Moreover, within the procedure itself individuality and personality in sound descriptive forms are retained for technical use, under which each Jack is given his own specification in the full individual-social field by the use of limiting statements of a type that can be successfully manipulated in a field of continuities. I regret that from consideration of space I cannot here develop this simple and practical construction.

The results thus far reached may be formulated somewhat as follows: If we agree to regard as spatial and temporal only that which is measurable or taken as capable of measurement, then if we examine those ways of speech about men which are taken as measurable in time but not in space, we find that we cannot draw a dogmatic line anywhere as between the individual and the social in the durational presentations before us, though we are still able to discuss each individual effectively as an empirically isolated portion of the whole combined social-individual presentation.

VI

If now I have perhaps succeeded in presenting the first step toward the reconciliation of speech forms without too repellant an aspect, I fear that when the same manner of examination is continued further, the next result will cause universal horripilation. To get over the shock and to allay the bristling as soon as possible, I shall formulate this result at once as follows: Under our defined meanings for spatial and temporal in terms of measurements the terminological distinction between the spatial and the non-spatial forms of description breaks down, just as the distinction between the individual and the social broke down in the temporal–non-spatial terminology; the social Jack proves to be no longer non-spatial in description, but instead to be as fully and vitally spatial as any other phenomena; and all three ways of speech, those of life, of mind, and of society — once we have escaped the limbo of the old vague meanings of space and time — fuse into one common form of expression, in which not so much as one single shading of the sound workable values of the old ways of speech has been lost. The social Jack I propose to show to be a spatial Jack, not however in the sense of some obscure dead space opposed to some equally obscure fixed reality of mind, but in a fused functioning living world of comprehensive experience.

To aid us in this step, let us substitute for the term temporal-spatial the term durational-extensional, which is exactly what we have defined temporal-spatial to be; and for the term temporal–non-spatial the term durational–non-extensional. The question before us will then be: Do we anywhere find phenomena which are durational but not extensional, as we search all the phenomena of man's spiritual and mental life, refusing to take these phenomena as instantaneous realities but holding always to them instead as measurable durations in which the social aspect up to the last instantaneous limit clings tight to the individual aspect? The answer is, No. Jack-loving-Jill is spread out in space in much the same sense as the phenomena of thermodynamics or of electricity or of light rays. You cannot handle any of these phenomena under three Euclidean dimensions, isolated, absolute, dominant, but in truth you cannot handle anything whatever completely under such a frame. When you make use of that frame you find it covering them for what it is worth: and, I may add, for no more than it is worth, there or anywhere else. For (Jill) in Jack-loving-Jill you may substitute (Jill)′ or (Jill)″; for (Jack) you may substitute (Jack)′ or (Jack)″; for (loving) you may substitute (loving)′ or (loving)″; these last may be hatings or honorings or whatsoever else, as focus of study changes — Jack-craving-to-stand-for-Parliament, Jack-trying-to-reform-the-world. You may take the stone age in Europe, or the Assyrian empire, or Renaissance art, or modern peace ideals: in every case the object under discussion is composed of social men and is describable in measurable extensions and durations. You may take Jack in his most sublimated spiritual or mental descriptions: in every case the terms are durationally meaningless without their social values, and those social values spread out in durations and extensions.

VII

Thousands of objections may be raised against talking about men and society in this way; at least I have pried into so many objections that I suspect they can be raised by thousands. But I find none valid as against the purposes of the scientists who study events by the use of frank hypotheses, and who loathe one thing and one alone, dogmatism. When an objection appears, first is to consider whether it is raised for a purpose or under an influence radically different from that which here rules. If the purposes, the assumptions, are the same, one can argue the objection. If they are different, argument of the objection itself must be postponed until one decides whether the new purposes, the new assumptions, are the more desirable. Unless these purposes and assumptions show comparable aims and equal or greater desirability, the objections are out of court so far as the present discussion goes. One court of last resort in such issues which formerly had dogmatic authority is now closed, so far as our generation with its given range of power and authority is concerned. There is no appeal to Fact. The critic may no longer fall back upon his own declaration of Fact as the basis of his criticism; all his facts and all ours, except as they develop values in a co-ordinated system of science, are assumptions; to all the dictum *solvitur ambulando* today applies.

Not from its power of disputation, but from its ability to do useful work, will the suggested technique of speech receive its test. Without appeal to authority or disputation whatever, anyone can make the test and determine for himself, first what his own purposes really are, and, second, providing those purposes be of the type here in mind, whether this technique of speech is comprehensive and helpful. He has but to take whatever bit of social structure he chooses, whether it be religious or aesthetic, economic or political, or otherwise social, and seek the richest possible description, analysis, and re-description he can find for it: under, of course, the one requirement that he starts with it as presented in durations of time, and that he holds to durations until he can through his own investigation and analysis escape from them: under, in other words, the requirement, that he do not set up in advance existent mind and existent body, held apart by mystic barriers in a space-fog, as verbal masters of his study, but that he consent to learn of mind and body, of space and time, from the study itself.

For his guidance I offer two warnings: or, perhaps more courteously, for his consideration I present two suggestions.

When an investigator uses the separated forms of speech, those of mind and of body as I have described them at the beginning of this paper, and holds them apart as different realms, his common way of bridging between them is to give Jack's mind pseudo-localization in Jack's body. I say pseudo-localization because actual or normal localization involves measurement, and the attribution of non-spatial mind to spatial body must be done without possibility of measurement in any sense which connects the terms of the two systems together on a measurable basis.[3] Such pseudo-localization is a mere assumption of a connection which, it is anticipated, will be somehow understood when the spatial fog clears up. The first suggestion for consideration is this: has such pseudo-localization any value whatever for our studies, if we determine to use with some definite meaning, with any definite meaning whatever, the terms space and time?

The other suggestion has to do with the current construct of a " single " organism — in this special case, the individual body of Jack — taken as

---

[3] The measurements of psychological laboratories are manifestly not in point here, any more than are those of I.Q. scales.

living in the world: a problem of which mention was made earlier in this paper. Jack, the anatomical organism, is the outgrowth of germ cells from parents and uncounted ancestors; better said, he is the present durational aspect of the age-long history of those cells: he contains within himself germs of countless descendants, due to appear as aspects of the same history in later generations. Jack, the physiological organism, has sunlight and star-rays in his very living, the very explosion of atoms on the sun is working in him always; and space and time for this light and for these rays and electrons are not what space and time once seemed to be. Jack, the individual, may go to jail, and we can glibly say for practical purposes what body is restrained within what four walls; but jail walls and laws and the conducts of Jack, his comrades, and his rulers, are aspects of age-long durations and of territorially broad extensions of place and work and folk. The " singleness " of Jack, whether body or mind or socius, is a singleness merely in a frame of Euclidean space, a frame we now know to be not a frame of facts apart from speech, but a frame of speech about facts, whatever facts may be. The warning is: take heed to your steps, that you fall not into the pit of Euclid, the pit the common toiler digs with Euclid's tool in which to store his humble mind's belongings.

VIII

If, now, by taking definite meanings for space and time — and those meanings, I may add, the very ones which alone for physics and mathematics and the efficient sciences have sound values for their working portrayals of the world — if, now, it is practicable in this way to harmonize our various speech forms about men into one working system, then an immediate benefit of the very greatest importance will result in connection with the use of that very essential term, environment. I do not know a more maddening term in the whole range of sociological writing than this very word, environment. It is often troublesome enough in the biological sciences, but in sociology it is disgraceful beyond measure. Observe what this one term is made to cover: first spatial environments to spatial phenomena (matter to matter); next, spatial environments to non-spatial phenomena (the world to the mental man); then, non-spatial individual environments to non-spatial individual phenomena (persons to each other); again, non-spatial social environments to non-spatial individual phenomena (society to the person); and with these, so many other variations of situation, in terms of races, groups, and institutions, that coherence, valid meaning, disappears entirely. Could any set of situations, taken in the ways in which they are currently expressed, be more radically different from one another in values than these? And yet it is daily practice for writers flaunting the banner of science — science whose very definition is the humble desire to be exact — to use this one single term with the rankest inexactness for all these various situations. If the old ways of speech about men are to be kept separate and distinct, then assuredly the various environmental situations must be analyzed and held separate from the very start, even if, to accomplish it, one has to begin his work again from the bottom and do it all over. But if the harmonization of speech-ways which has been suggested can establish itself, then we shall have before us one continuity of phenomena in which we may, from time to time, for each specific purpose that arises, isolate organisms or individuals or groups or institutions, name and define them, and by that very procedure define their environments, so that study can intelligently be made. First, isolation, assumed to be of fact, and definition, assumed to be of words — but the two always obverse and reverse of the same social mirror: then search for recurrences, and controlled experiments wherever possible: these are the procedures of knowledge. Words are the tools, the technique, of sociology. The word as tool has power. If the word fails us, if we close our eyes to its failure but still support ourselves on its dogmatism, then and then only are we lost.

CHAPTER FIVE

Sociology and Mathematics*

I

THE COMMON PROBLEM OF ANALYSIS

When a paper is offered upon the subject of sociology and mathematics, one may reasonably expect it to discuss those many mathematical techniques which have so usefully been taken over by the social sciences, such as series, graphs, correlations, probabilities, and other statistical methods; or, if not these, then those mathematical constructions of demand, price, money, and competition which are known as pure economics. We shall have here, however, no concern with any of these topics.

Such mathematical techniques and constructions require, before they can be put to use, the provision by the social sciences of the statistical data, or, alternatively, of the postulational elements, with which they are to deal. These data and postulational elements in their turn require, before they can be assembled, or before they can be given precision, an analysis of the general situation to be investigated, and the determination of a scheme of classification. Mathematical techniques contribute nothing directly to the analysis; and the wider values of the results secured through the techniques are always dependent upon the adequacy of the antecedent classifications and postulatory fixations which the analysis has furnished,[1] though it is of course true that work of this kind may often stimulate a return to the preliminary procedures of analysis.

Sociology is much more than a manipulation of data assumed as factually well established and adequately provided for its use. Mathematics is much more than a compendium of technical devices.

Mathematics is itself the great science of rigorous analysis; and to

* From *The Sociological Review*, Vol. XXIII, No. 2 (July, 1931), pp. 85–107; No. 3 (October, 1931), pp. 149–72.

[1] In making this statement I have directly in mind the present status of mathematical technique as exhibited, for example, by Griffith C. Evans in his *Mathematical Introduction to Economics*, 1930, and by Irving Fisher, in his Willard Gibbs' lecture, "The Application of Mathematics to the Social Sciences," *Bulletin of the American Mathematical Society*, April, 1930. For an appraisal of the important work of Professor Evans, see Part II, Section 6, of this chapter.

mathematics in this sense its own techniques are rather the by-products of its development than the living body of the science itself.

The social sciences are the very ones among all departments of knowledge today in which the need of deeper and more far-reaching analysis is most keenly felt. Indeed, whether we have now, or in the future will have, a true science of sociology, is the same question as to ask whether the existing analyses of social situations are, or whether the future analyses will be, adequate for the wider generalizations which we require for our social studies and for our social work.

The field of the social materials and theories which need better analysis, and its relation to the science of mathematics which is the possessor of maximum power of analysis, is the subject of attention in Part I of the present paper; and it is the possibilities for mutual interaction between the two which I wish here briefly and tentatively to develop.

I identify first of all a region of difficulty and obscurity which is common both to sociology and to mathematics.

Despite all of its great successes in many wide fields, and despite the maximum power which it possesses, mathematics has not yet finished its work of analysis for its own most general field. It has fully consistent constructions for its three great branches taken separately, for its Arithmetics and Algebras, for its Geometries, and for its special discipline of Analysis; but while it has offered many tentative — and some dogmatic — constructions to bring these three departments into consistent system with one another, it has secured as yet no generally acknowledged success. In Algebra and Arithmetic it long ago broke down the obstacles that seemed insuperable with respect to minus quantities, incommensurables, and imaginaries: it has passed onward to ideal numbers, has established algorithmic consistency, and has differentiated many types of algebras with their corresponding arithmetics. In Geometry, after destroying by deeper analysis the realism of the Euclidean parallels, it has gained enormous consistent development in many forms, metrical and non-metrical. In Analysis, which was itself created by Newton and Leibnitz under the influence of the wider analytic search to handle the phenomena of transitions, the long struggles over infinitesimals culminated, with Weierstrass, in consistency of statement of its procedures in the form of limits. But in the effort to bring all three departments together, despite the great logical system of Russell-Whitehead, despite the twenty-year struggle of Hilbert to establish *Widerspruchsfreiheit* in a construction of *Zeichen als Objekte,* and despite numerous minor experiments such as that of Brouwer, the paradoxes and the basic uncertainties still remain in every program of consistent construction for the general field.

These mathematical difficulties center around the mathematical values

Sociology and Mathematics 55

of the common, everyday words: " one," " some," " many," " any," " all," and " none "; and this is just another way of saying that they involve the problems of consistency, in the interior of the mathematical field, with respect to those issues much more pompously known as the finite and the infinite, the continuous and the discrete.

If, now, we take the above list of common words, the " one " and the " any," the " some " and the " all," and carry it over into our region of sociological investigation, we have at once a set of sign-boards for our most difficult problems of scientific organization — the issues of individual, of group, and of society, in all of their various linguistic expressions, whether psychological, physiological, or biological, or whether, indeed, immediately and directly sociological. A moment's pause will further make it clear that that other manner of phrasing in terms of finite and infinite, of continuous and discrete, is also involved for society: not, of course, in the more specifically arithmetical or geometrical usages, but in the vital characteristics of the analysis. Whenever, for example, we use such a phrase as " social ideals " we are struggling to express a continuity of social procedure across a discreteness of individual men; whenever we use the generalized term " society " we are involving something of an infinite in comparison with a finiteness of the individual.

It is true that this identity of problem centering around the presentations [2] " one " and " some " and " all " in mathematics and in sociology is not often emphasized, perhaps indeed is not generally recognized. It is concealed from view beneath a very prevalent attitude and distinction under which mathematics is regarded as " abstract " in the extreme, while social presentations, by contrast, are regarded in their characteristic of immediate experience and behavior as the most vitally " concrete " of all. If one accepts such a distinction of abstract and concrete as basically sound or true, and if, along with this, he regards the abstractness as implying a certain " unreality," while on the contrary the personal and social experiences seem to him to have the truest and fullest " reality," then he of course sees the problems of the two fields as of entirely different nature. But the distinction abstract-concrete is far from possessing theoretical rigor, whether in psychology and logic, [3] or in practical and scientific life; it is

---

[2] I shall make frequent use of the word "presentations," employing it as the most nearly neutral term I can find, in place of such terms as phenomena, appearances, expressions, to indicate any portion of our experiential-linguistic materials of investigation. Where the term phenomena is used for convenience of phrasing in the text, it is to be understood in this sense.

[3] The attitude of this paper toward " logic " is that it is a specialized and limited technique of language. Such a status for logic may be suspected from the fact that, however dependable it has been in limited ranges, it has invariably in wider generalizations led to paradox. The demonstration of its limitations has been given by the mathematical research of the past generation. Mathematics has used logic more rigorously than has any other department of knowledge, and finally it has reached problems in which logic, for it, is in

far from being a firm basis of classification within knowledge; and, beyond this, the implications of " reality " and " unreality " are even less secure in their meaning. Given any such uncertainty in these basic forms of discrimination, then the comparison and correlation of the problems of " one " and " some " and " all " in these two regions, mathematical and sociological, becomes at once of the greatest importance; and the way is open for an inquiry as to whether any light may be thrown by the situation in one of the regions upon that in the other.

In mathematics the pertinent problems of such investigation have come to be called by the special name " foundation theory "; and the interpretative constructions thereunder make use of three general terms, or names, or categories, which designate three kinds of materials or presentations found most important in the study: these three being Things (or Objects), Relations, and Operations. Mere mention of these words involves a cloud of discussion, logical, metaphysical, philosophical, psychological, epistemological. We shall disregard all this discussion as though it simply did not exist, and shall confine ourselves to examining what these three kinds of materials include as presentations within the body of mathematical knowledge itself, and to bringing them into system within that particular body of knowledge.

The mathematical Thing — which is, of course, to be taken as " abstract " in the extreme values of whatever it is that the word " abstract " indicates or implies — is any separate or distinct presentation used as a fixed base or reference for further development. It may be the natural number, such as $1, 2, 3 \ldots n$; it may be a line-segment or solid; it may be a group, a vector, or a tensor.

The mathematical Relation appears in such simple forms as odd, even, or prime; it covers geometrical propositions; and it rises to include the " great relational certainties " of mathematics; so that in the end it may come to mean even the structure of mathematics itself.

The mathematical Operation is everywhere present. Plus and times are operations,[4] and arithmetic is operational clear through to the most complex operators of infinite series. Algebra is throughout operational. In

---

complete collapse. Hilbert and Ackermann have shown fully in their *Grundzüge der Theoretischen Logik* (1928) that if logic is to handle mathematical " fact," it must operate upon various levels or *" Stufen "* which as between themselves lack logical coherence. Hilbert's proposed construction of consistency, his *Widerspruchsfreiheit*, rests in a broader linguistic development. So also, though in a different way, does the construction of semantic consistency used in this paper. Reference should also be made to Russell's theory of types, and to Brouwer's proposed limitation of one of the Aristotelian canons.

[4] Whitehead, indeed, in his useful little book, *An Introduction to Mathematics*, p. 81, said, with regard to these, that the operational interpretation was the only one that would everywhere hold, a remark which we need not here attempt to bring into adjustment with *Principia Mathematica*.

the geometries, no matter how strenuously the relational structure is emphasized, there remain always the operational procedures; all use of translations and rotations, all appeal, frankly or implicitly, to motion, and, in general, all that has to do with congruence, is operational. Differential and integral calculus have been the cause of much worried speculation over many generations, due to the fact that they appear so wholly operational in their nature, and so little concerned with fixations or relations of Thing, that the discomfort of the theorist becomes acute.

In their constructions the mathematical foundation theories choose, now one, now the other, of these three categories or presentations, as basis: the logical systems pick, in effect, the Relation as fundamental; Hilbert chooses the Thing, or Object; while Brouwer (under the influence of Kronecker and Poincaré) made an effort, especially in the earlier stages of his development, to use the Operation. It is by the aid of these terms that the foundation theories present constructions to handle the difficulties of " one " and of " some " and of " all." But what is most strikingly significant is that none of these systems has brought forth a consistent and thorough interpretation of the terms Thing, Relation, and Operation themselves, with respect to one another, definitely within their mathematical development. They have taken over the terms as they have found them in conventional extraneous (and very questionable) uses, and they have applied them to mathematical phenomena, but they have not as yet subjected them to direct and exhaustive mathematical analysis under the standards of mathematical consistency itself.[5] They are straining to this end, but have not as yet gained it. The deficiency is all the more notable since the most important of these systems all aim to establish forms of consistency which will reach far beyond the specific mathematical field, and which will, if established, dominate the development of all knowledge whatsoever.

If we now turn once more from mathematics to sociology, we shall recognize, just as in the case of " one," " some," and " all," that these three presentations, Thing, Relation, and Operation, are similarly essential, directly or by implicit use, to all our sociological constructions, and are similarly lacking as yet in thorough internal analysis. In other words, what these three terms really *mean* with respect to one another, and what they are, or turn out to *be* in the consistencies of language, will in the end be criterion for such sociological success or failure as we may secure. That the situation is still very obscure in this respect will be admitted, I think, by all sociologists, except those, probably, who develop their work from

[5] The obstacles which have operated to hinder progress, and the reorganization of postulatory materials which is needed, are discussed at length in my monograph, *Symbol and Meaning in Mathematics*, shortly to be published. [It appeared in 1932 as *Linguistic Analysis of Mathematics*.]

some dogmatic Absolute, or those others who use an equally dogmatic biologically individual basis. We have had sociologies of Things, both men-things and society-things, sociologies of Relation between men-things, and very much sociological development on an Operational basis. Whether the group is itself a Thing for sociology, whether it is a Relation between men-things, or whether it is a social Operation, and in what sense it is any or all of these, is just our most fundamental problem of analysis.

My own conclusion has been that terms of these three types in sociology must be taken in system with one another, so that their meanings may be understood, not through some dogmatic superimposed definition, but in their actual scientific-sociological organization; and in especial that this is crucial for the terms "individual" and "society," so that each of these terms is in a very significant sense a limiting expression in the development of the other.[6]

Applying this method of approach to the mathematical constructions of Thing, Relation, and Operation, and remembering further that mathematics itself is a social procedure and production, it is possible to generalize mathematical analysis in a manner which may be called Semantic, since thereby the meanings of all of its terms are brought into linguistic (and, in the limit, into symbolic) system with one another.[7] This yields a construction in mathematical consistency in which we find (a) that Relations present themselves sometimes as Things and sometimes as Operations, and this to such extent that they may be regarded as reducible to these other two forms, though always with the right to hold them separate for a time in some special branch of study as desired; and (b) that any particular presentation has the possibility of appearing either as Thing or as Operation with respect to other presentations, which then in their

---

[6] See "New Ways and Old to Talk about Men," *The Sociological Review*, October, 1929: "L'individuel et le social: les termes et les faits," *Revue Internationale de Sociologie*, mai-juin, 1929: and the development in Part II of the present chapter.

[7] Professor Geddes has called my attention to the writings of Lady Victoria Welby and to her theory of Significs. While the values with which she was concerned and her goals of investigation were very different from mine, I find pleasure in acknowledging a great similarity of attitude, which will be very clearly evident in such citations as the following from her book, *What Is Meaning?*: "All systems inevitably concentrate in Significance as their essential value as well as test: and thus Significs alone gives us the power of inter-translation"; "Significs gives us the right to postulate Man as in a true sense the expression of the world"; "The true answers to our most vital Whys can only come through a long stern searching discipline of unanswered question"; "We must look forward to the substitution of the Significian for the Metaphysician"; and, with respect to a particular detail of construction: "Infinity merely thinks away space, as Eternity does time." I could cite passages from her writings in regard to mind and psychology which would be even more significant of sympathy in approach, but I omit them, since her much desired Significs has made so little progress in the world in general, that among the many possible specialized readings of the language she uses, the wrong ones would be much more commonly taken than those her context itself indicates.

Sociology and Mathematics 59

turn appear respectively as either Operation or as Thing with respect to the one first taken. This means, for example, that the 1, 2, 3 of mathematics are not to be taken for algorithmic mathematical purposes as " realities " in any sense " external " to it, but as developments of its operational system of equations in the full spirit of Poincaré's induction; that the axiom constructions of geometry become wholly systemic, each within itself, without specialized foundation in either separated Thing, separated Relation, or separated Operation, the forms in which we commonly find them; that calculus no longer needs futile struggles to pin it to realistic bases, but operates in its own semantic right; and that all of these three divisions of mathematics gain systemic organization with one another free from inconsistency or conflict.

A construction of this kind, when once developed for mathematics, becomes in turn of the greatest aid to more thorough analysis in sociology, since it widens and generalizes the suggested systemic treatment of Thing and Operation in the special cases of man, of group, and of society, and provides new technical aids for dealing with those special fixations of social Thing which, however important they may have been in the past, and however useful they remain for special purposes in the present, have become hurtful when too rigidly adopted in general sociological theory.[8] The value of this construction will be shown in the second part of this paper through an investigation of the problem of space in sociology; and, no matter how far this investigation may fall short of completeness at its present stage, it will most plainly be made manifest that we have here to do with a great complex of problems submissive to sociological analysis, and not to be arbitrarily brushed aside by the insistence on some conventional " idea " of space, nor by the rigid application of some space offered by a physical science. We shall find not only spaces which are taken as " external " to the individual or to society, but also spaces which are peculiarly social, and, so to speak, " internal " to society itself:[9] those separations, distributions, and mensurations of men, groups, institutions, yielded by social observation itself; and we shall find no assurance that any one of these spaces, whether " internal " or " external," is dogmatically " thing " or " fact " to which all others must adapt themselves.

---

[8] This semantic construction, or method, is not, of course, confined to mathematics and sociology. To be valid for these it must be capable of use in handling the problems of fact and theory in physics, which, just at the present day, with corpuscle and radiation in conflict, are especially acute: and it must likewise furnish helpful aid for biology and psychology: since in all of these departments of knowledge the issues of " one," of " many " and of " all," of " thing," of " relation " and of " operation " are ever intruding. Into the problems of these other sciences we fortunately have no need of entering here.

[9] For a discussion of " external " and " internal " see the last paragraphs of Part II, Section 5, following.

Before attacking these problems let us consider a somewhat different characterization of the semantic point of approach from that above: this time especially with reference to the term "fact," a term which is necessary for use in all our studies, and which must be given a meaning free from misinterpretation. The semantic approach may be generalized by saying that it is a determination to secure full consistency of expression in and through language, *before* attributing realistic value or assigning basic factual reference to any of the particular terms which the language of the investigation includes. It is an approach which permits, for special purposes and at special times, the isolation of any of these particular terms, and the attribution to them of factual value for the special study undertaken, but which does not permit the attribution to any term whatever of basic factual value for the general purposes of all knowledge — not, at any rate, under the particular stage of ignorance in which we exist today. It asserts that so long and so far as inconsistencies and paradoxes remain in the linguistic expression, just so long and so far the realistic attributions are uncertain, and, being uncertain, are unjustified. This approach does not interfere with the right of any person to make any realistic constructions which he desires, and it enters no objection whatever against the making of them. It merely insists on radical severance between procedures in terms of realisms, and its own type of work which proceeds through integrity of expression. On its own side it fully recognizes, employs, and cannot get along without, specifications of fact, but it makes these specifications cautiously for the particular purposes in hand, not dogmatically as in control of knowledge in general.[10]

If we inspect the prevalent uses of the term "fact" and of that "factuality" which it is supposed to present, we may spread them out in a sort of linguistic spectrum. In the middle ranges of this spectrum we will put the various shadings and degrees of fact in its sense of practical dependability for whatever it is in the way of investigation or work upon which we may be engaged. To the left hand we may throw the increasingly dogmatic renderings or understandings of factuality, running to extreme realisms or absolutisms of meaning at the far left end. To the right hand we may throw the more cautious and hypothetical renderings of factuality, ranging onward to full postulatory construction, with those of mathematical fact at the far right end, where we find the permanent dependability of 1, 2, 3, the invariance of *pi*, the certain outcome of the sum of two naturals, or the value of the sum of two angles of a Euclidean plane triangle. Astonishingly enough, we observe the maximum human

---

[10] See also the final paragraphs of Part II, Section 3.

vigor in assertion of factuality at the extreme left, but the greatest certainty in the employment of factuality at the extreme right. At the extreme left, moreover, is the least consistency of language; at the extreme right, the greatest consistency of language, which here takes the form of full symbolic expression.

The identity of problem in the use of the term " fact " in the above organization with that of the term " thing " in a system of things, relations, and operations, is sufficiently evident. For our purposes in this paper, the term " fact " must be read without realistic values, its range of meaning must be limited within the context of its use, and its claims to dominance in knowledge must be held in subordination to the linguistic consistency of its use.

II

MATHEMATICAL AND SOCIOLOGICAL SPACES

A generation ago any discussion in the field we now approach would have used the term " space " directly in confrontation with the term " society," and would not have introduced the plural form " spaces." Such a phrasing would have signified that the discussion concerned itself with space and with society as though they were two fundamental facts to be brought into relation.

Today various spaces are used in the physical sciences, while behind them is a great array of mathematical spaces upon which the physical sciences draw for aid.

What import this situation may have for sociology is here to be examined.

1. *The Terminologies of Space*

Spaces are before us for examination in systems of words, among which words the highly specialized " symbols " of mathematics and physics are to be included. If there are several spaces under consideration we keep them distinct to our attention by differentiations of the systems of words used for them. Such systems of words we may be permitted to call terminologies. Each space, or each presentation of space (for in our plan of study we have no dogmatic primary severance between the two, whatever form of construction may ultimately be developed), has therefore its own terminology; and each such space-terminology is to be understood as including all its own special modulations of ordinary language, as, for example, its special application of the verb " to be," an application which is clearly very different in a physical space from a social space, and very different in a mathematical space from either of the others. If we wish to decide whether any two spaces are "the same" or "not the same," we must do it then not by personal dictum, but by full analysis of the space-terminologies; and our final decision must involve an understanding of what we mean by "the same" as well as what we mean by the spaces we are comparing.

We may inspect five such terminologies which are important to us here, and we may name them vulgar space, mathematical space, physical space, social space, and sociological space.[11]

By vulgar space [12] we shall understand any system of space which is expressed and accepted by the people of any specified social time and social place [13] as "external" to them, and as the physical locus in which they find themselves; and which is embodied in their current meanings of pertinent words, and taken in account in their own understanding of their own practical life. It carries always a conventional implication of, or dogmatic insistence upon, its factuality: which implication or insistence is here taken as part of the terminology, and in especial as the range of meaning of the verb " to be " as this verb is employed within it.

By mathematical space we shall understand the various constructions in full symbolic form which mathematicians have developed, beginning historically with Euclidean space, passing thence into the non-Euclidean spaces, and including the still more recent topological spaces.

By physical spaces we shall understand those mathematical spaces which at any given social time and social place are taken by physicists as best organizing the results of physical and astronomical observation and experiment. For an earlier generation, Newtonian space was the sole member of this group, but Newtonian space now appears as one member among many.[14]

By social spaces we shall understand those discretenesses and continuities, those separations and distributions and purely social mensurations, which are found among men outspread in societies.

By sociological spaces we shall understand theoretical constructions which, with respect to social spaces, hold a position comparable to that of mathematical spaces with respect to physical spaces.

It will be observed that the form of phrasing used to describe the social

---

[11] If anyone insists that "actual space" should also be investigated, he may add it as a special terminology of its own under that name, and proceed to its treatment.

[12] The word vulgar is to be read with its older English values.

[13] For social time and social place see Section 5, following.

[14] Geographical space, especially as taken in system with geological time, might be subsumed under the physical terminologies, or added as a special terminology itself. It is, however, common meeting ground of vulgar, physical, and social spaces, deeply rooted in these last named, and will be allowed to receive interpretation and valuation through these others.

and sociological spaces differs sharply from that used to describe the physical and mathematical spaces. This difference corresponds to the difference in degree of development of these two types of investigation at the present time: the physical and mathematical spaces having fact and theory in close technical organization, the social and sociological spaces resting rather in crude description and tentative construction.

One may isolate a special region within any one of these space terminologies for detached study, as, for example, within mathematics, an Euclidean space; or one may study the system of each terminology by itself; but in the full extent of scientific development across generations, it is evident that efforts must and will be made to bring them all into consistent interpretation with one another; and that this again will involve clarification of the uses of the verb " to be " in its most general scientific meanings for all of them, as distinct from either its practical involvements or its philosophical pretenses.

2. *The Circle of Interpretation*

Two great trends or directions of investigation will be at once remarked when we make the beginnings of an effort to examine all of these space terminologies and bring them into organization.

On the one side, the physical and mathematical spaces are forms of knowledge; but knowledge itself is manifestly a social development, a process or a product according as you take it; and therefore the entire development of physics and mathematics falls within the scope of the most general sociological study.

On the other side, any sociology that we may establish will manifestly be conditioned by physics and mathematics, because it itself is a part of knowledge, and the physics and mathematics are more richly and securely established parts of that knowledge than it is. Sociological development will be conditioned by the physical spaces in so far as these latter become firmly established as forms of basic physical fact. It will be conditioned by the mathematical spaces in so far as these latter in their most highly generalized or " abstract " presentations furnish patterns for sociological space constructions.

We have here a circle in scientific research which we may as well recognize for what it is.[15] It is not a vicious circle of logic, involving its con-

---

[15] For a descriptive expression akin to the theoretical position here asserted (but not at all involving its authors in any imperfection of my present generalization) see Geddes and Thomson, *Biology,* p. 139: " Our vast dream-Palace of the Life-Science is next seen to shrink, and shrink again — at length into a tiny sphere — the unit-cell of knowledge, yet packed with all its hereditics: for it is now the microcosm of mind, within the Macrocosm of Nature. Yet again this process reverses: for the human Mind is ever extending anew, and cannot cease to grow, towards the ever-fuller ensphering of Nature which is the aim of science." Compare also in specific application, *Ibid.,* pp. 178–9; 237–8; 242.

clusion in its premises, but a situation before us for investigation, demanding maximum clarity and consistency of analysis. We can break the circle by a dictum, but we break progress in knowledge at the same time. As between the two complementary trends in our work, the two " directions " within it, we are free to choose which we will, and to work with our choice, but we have no power to place either such choice in full control of all knowledge. Using the general construction for linguistic knowledge set up in Part I of this paper, we have in the present situation merely to say that we may take either set of presentations as basic " fact " or " thing," and work operatively into the interpretation of the other set. If dominance of the one over the other is ultimately to be established, there is no manifestation of it in knowledge as yet.

3. *Vulgar Space*

If, on the one side, the physical and mathematical spaces are proper starting-points for the study of social and sociological spaces: while, on the other side, sociology is a proper starting-point for the investigation of physics and mathematics as knowledge: what, now, are we to say of that other terminology of space which we have listed above, namely, vulgar space? Involved is the question as to whether such a vulgar space furnishes some criterion by which the physical, mathematical, social, and sociological spaces are to be tested, or some goal of interpretation toward which the sciences dealing with these latter must strive.

A vulgar space has been defined as any system of space popularly characterized and accepted at some specific social time and social place as an " actual," " external " space. The inquiry which first presents itself is whether we can identify many such vulgar spaces or only a single one in our field of study. We know, of course, that there are many popular forms of description for space, and our question, more loosely phrased, is one as to whether the human race possesses and uses one sole " external " space construction which is its true vulgar space, and with respect to which all the expressions of particular social times and social places are but adumbrations; or whether, on the contrary, it is more accurate, and scientifically more useful, to say that these forms of expression fall into groups identified by particular social times and social places, each of which groups is before us as a distinct vulgar space. Since none of these varying space expressions has as yet attained consistency, and since all of them still involve paradoxes, such an inquiry must incidentally face the question as to whether these inconsistencies and paradoxes are of any deep significance, or whether they are to be disregarded as mere quibbles of language, which are certain to be disentangled by human ingenuity in due course of time.

The vulgar space which first comes to mind, indeed the sole vulgar space of which most readers will think of their own accord, is that which has been prevalent for the last two hundred years. It is a vulgar space which has close affiliations in its terminological development with Newtonian physical space and with Euclidean geometry. It makes use by implication (and, at times, explicitly) of Euclidean straight lines, of infinite line extension, and of three " real " dimensions, as characteristics of an " actual " space, which it regards as basic frame for stellar systems, earth, life, and mind. Herein it sees " fact," and it bothers not at all with the paradoxes of continuity and infinity, or at most regards them as a pastime; and, while it " locates " the vivid psychic life of men and society in this frame, it cannot develop the " psychic " under its spatial terminology; but, quite to the contrary, resists vehemently any project of extending that terminology, including such items as foot-rules, over the psychic life; satisfying itself in the meantime with ancillary constructions which it calls " theological " or " philosophical." None of this interferes, however, with its own factuality of belief and realism of expression.

Let us now separate the realism from the terminological construction; or, more exactly, since the realistic reference is itself a feature of the vulgar terminology, let us give attention to the terminology as itself specifically comprising its own internal realistic reference and assertion; and let us set off to one side, as not in any way concerning us here, any desire of our own to pass judgment upon the realism on the basis of further realistic tests or procedures. We may signalize this specialization of attitude by describing the prevalent vulgar space as an " externalized " space, instead of speaking of it either as " external " or as " realistically external." [16]

Let us first ask ourselves whether the prevalent vulgar space as above described is the sole or exclusive vulgar space of the present age, or whether it has rivals among the populations of today. To answer even such an apparently easy question, involving only first-hand description, and to answer it with any degree of precision, will require, however, much better scientific technique than we today possess. It will require not only such initial constructions of social and sociological spaces as are discussed in Sections 4 and 5 following, but a considerable degree of advancement in the

---

[16] For further development of precision among terms of this type see Section 5, following. For aught I know or care the prevalent vulgar space of the present day may be the true, ultimate, eternal, and absolute representation of " reality "; though considering the rival vulgar spaces of the past, the probable rivals of the future, and its own internal inconsistencies, such an outcome would be a most striking coincidence. The problem of " reality " is simply not our problem in this paper, which is the more humble one of investigating the linguistic consistencies — the knowledge — that we have of various space presentations, among which this particular vulgar space appears before us as one.

use of them. The best we can do with our present equipment is to point out that philosophers belong to our existing populations, as members or elements, and that they in their various ways envisage things very differently; so also do physicists engaged in the more recent developments of their science and so also at the far extreme do the depressed and unlettered elements of the population, among which there are great numbers of men who have never had such a construction as that of straight lines in infinite extension brought before their attention, and who inspect all that is about them concretely in masses of experience without the use of any such generalized form; while still beyond these are the outlying primitive populations maintaining tribal tradition in various forms. A guiding clue to a measured statement of fact with regard to all this complicated presentment is lacking to us, and we will pass it by, letting its issues be subsumed under those of the historical-evolutionary series next to be considered.

Looking backward over history we find similar variations; and many ethnologists and sociologists have described space systems used by primitive peoples which are sharply different from our own vulgar space. In especial Durkheim has emphasized some of these in discussing the objective social origin of what he calls "categories"; and we shall return in a moment to the consideration of some of the direct predecessors of our present vulgar space.

Inspecting pre-human or collateral evolutionary lines, we find indications of still more variant spatial presentations. The space of a dog is commonly described, under the best approximations of study, as a running flat space, with strong smell orientations, in contrast with the human three-dimensional space with slight smell orientations. Behind these, moreover, are insect spaces, taken to be in all probability specifically smell-spaces, with slight accompanying visual orientation; and behind these again we may suspect in still lower forms of life radiant space orientation, wholly lacking in specific sense differentiation.

Here are phenomena which can manifestly be brought into array, on a provisional level, with the series of human vulgar spaces in one long evolutionary line. Let us put them in such array, merely for the purposes of preliminary study, without at this stage presuming to imply for a moment that such an array is the best structural array, or phenomenally the most "fundamental." It may still turn out to be true, despite the indications of this array, that all the human vulgar spaces can be reduced to adumbrations of one characteristically human space presentation, and more particularly to a space which takes physiological or psychological interpretation. Such a reduction would divide our phenomena into two groups on such a basis that the separation of the groups might have more import for our investigation than the similarities which caused us to establish the array. We shall return to a consideration of the physiological and psychological space problem later. Here I wish to stress merely this one observation that if such a reduction is made, then the exact point at which the human space differentiates from the non-human or pre-human becomes of great significance, since once such a differentiation has been identified by the scientist as critical then all the human vulgar spaces must hold together for him in one coherent group or sub-group, the characteristics of which must be entirely clear and unmistakable in contrast with the non-human space constructions. Under the array which I have set up, we have, on the contrary, no requirement of such a sharp point of severance; we can content ourselves with the full evolutionary-historical series, and if by chance we find a more radical differentiation, or what seems to us to be a more radical differentiation, as between certain members of the human series than we find as between the most primitive human and the pre-human members, we are not thrown into complete disorder and compelled to begin all over again from the ground up.

Keeping this point well in mind, we turn now to a consideration of evidence which we can examine with a much firmer hand, and with more exact critical decision. It has to do with the rise or appearance in society of exactly that vulgar space which we have called the prevalent vulgar space of the present time, namely, the presentation of an external world in a form in general popular accord with Newtonian physics and Euclidean geometry. It is a common view that what Euclid did for the geometry of the things around him, and what Newton did for celestial and global space, was merely to bring out " theoretically," " abstractly," or " scientifically," the " truth " of what was crudely known to all men in a vulgar way. Is this view correct? If it is correct, we have preliminary evidence in favor of one sole " human " vulgar space, to which all other vulgar spaces of society can be reduced. If it is not correct, then we have instead evidence for the view that there exist and have existed in society many vulgar spaces not reducible to a single space.

We may depend here for guidance on the development by Albert Einstein in his lecture at Nottingham University, June 7, 1930,[17] in which he discussed geometrical and physical spaces and space-time. For the Greeks, he pointed out, geometry was a science of rigid bodies; the material bodies were " things "; space was not a " thing," but solely a " relation " between such bodies. This status lasted long, so that even when Descartes set up his co-ordinates, these co-ordinates did not present a separate factuality of

---

[17] *Nature,* June 14, 1930, p. 897; *Science,* June 13, 1930, p. 608.

space, but solely a generalized relationship. It was not until Newton, we are told, that space as itself a " thing " was introduced into physics, taking its place, along with the absolute Newtonian time, as another " thing " additional to the matter-things.

Einstein, of course, had no thought of vulgar spaces in this discussion. But when he shows the appearance of Newtonian space as a " thing " (or, in other words, for the uses we are making of it, as an identifiably separate " fact ") at a definite date in scientific history; when the space-thing that then appeared is so closely comparable with the vulgar space of today that the latter may readily be regarded as its non-technical analogue in colloquial expression; when the pre-Newtonian scientific space had no reference to anything similar to our present vulgar space, but was instead only a thin, technical relationship between bodies (the term " relation " having here precisely the value of " not-thing "); when an evolutionary-historical series of other space presentations can be shown behind our present vulgar space; then we have a strong case for regarding our present " externalized " vulgar space as depending in some way upon Newtonian scientific space, possibly in some sense as its by-product; and we have more evidence for the reduction of our present vulgar space to the position of one space among many. In this background it is perhaps possible, but hardly probable, and certainly not to be presumed — when we consider the close relationships in development and interaction between scientific knowledge, common media of language, and practical work and living — that what we have called the prevalent vulgar space of today, with its Newtonian affiliations, was, in its essence, and with mere unimportant differences of expression, the factual vulgar space of earlier ages, running back not merely to the Greeks, but vastly further to that stage in evolution at which differentia between the human and the pre-human are introduced. It is much more probable, and certainly the proper presumption upon the basis of the showing above, that our prevalent vulgar space, inclusive of its " externalized " reference and its pretense of " actuality," is merely one social form among the many which need to be taken into account by sociology.

To have a presumption of this kind, however, does not settle the matter by any means, even though it adds its strength to the array in the evolutionary-historical series that has been set forth above. We have still to take into account the status of that specifically " human " physiological or psychological space referred to before as a possible criterion of procedure. To settle the issues herein involved, investigations will be necessary which will run into the widest fields, and which will doubtless require long periods of time before they are completed. Such investigations, however, will be worthless unless they are undertaken upon an impartial and unbiased basis: a basis which does not simply accept the frame of interpretation set up by the psychologies and physiologies of today as though it were safely and certainly " fundamental," but which inquires into the derivation and range of usefulness of that very frame itself: so that a greater breadth of interpretation can be secured. Here only a few indications of the problems at issue can be given.

A central point of investigation is the extent to which the prevalent vulgar space, itself having Euclidean-Newtonian origins, has entered into and conditioned the construction of both the psychologies and the physiologies, which psychologies and physiologies in their turn are appealed to as authority for upholding this particular vulgar space as the sole true " human " space itself.

All our psychology as a science is post-Newtonian, and we know very well how Kant was conditioned by Newton, and how Locke developed in that type of intellectual environment we call Newtonian.[18] Much light is thrown upon the situation by recent philological-philosophical exhibits of the development and transformation stages of our modern " inner " psychic terminology from the very objective and " external " Greek and Latin beginnings.[19]

When we turn to physiology, which is so freely used in guaranteeing the foundations of a specifically " human " space, we find that this science is itself constructed in a Newtonian space form, to which it dogmatically holds, and to which it is confident that it will in the end reduce all its theory; despite the fact that its own inner aspects of organization — all that which it means by " life " itself — have never yet been given a consistent Newtonian statement; so that today the vitalisms and mechanistic structures of the biological sciences still struggle with one another as speculations and as temperamental attitudes and beliefs, rather than as true components of a family of scientific procedures.

Here now we have indications that even the physiological, the psycho-

---

[18] We have here a problem of "social times" much richer in meaning than "clock times." Einstein, holding to geometry and to physics and to space as "thing," can use Newton's date in the calendar to fix his reference. The sociologist does not inspect solely the "Newton" and the "date," but must use much more subtly the developmental time and procedure of the society itself.

[19] See, for example, O. O. Norris, "A Behaviourist Account of Intelligence," and "A Behaviourist Account of Consciousness," *The Journal of Philosophy*, XXV, p. 700, and XXVI, p. 29, p. 57, for the development of such terms as "intelligence" from sources of picking and choosing; of "consciousness" from orientations of knowing; of "quality" from objectivity of kinds; and, on the Germanic side, of "meaning" from pointing. The whole "psychic" terminology, with all its implication and reference, is a development within language, always inconsistent, hardly of fundamental or permanent import, and much more probably a transitional phenomenon, despite some hundreds of years, or a thousand or two, of history.

logical, the sensuous, the "accepted human" space is a construction of and within linguistic knowledge; and that therefore it loses its right to regard itself as established "foundation" fact authorized to control and dominate the development of other reaches of knowledge in all that concerns their space presentations.

I say we have indications, and I mean just exactly that, and nothing more. I do not regard the case as proven by any means; indeed, what we have here is the kind of issue which will most probably be resolved in the end, not by a decision in favor of one side or the other, but by an entirely different and deeper construction which will interpret both. But merely to possess such indications in the strength that they have, is to cause us to pass far beyond the naïve view that in any conventional current space we have a direct reference to "reality." And this not only makes it possible for us, but it makes it our duty, to pursue investigations from both points of view. Take away the naïve identification of the physiological or psychological "human" space with the prevalent vulgar space regarded as its best approximation in ordinary language, and at once that prevalent vulgar space falls to the position we have assigned it, of one vulgar space among many. Incidentally, it becomes at once clear that the paradoxes of this vulgar space can no longer be disregarded as something which, we may take it for granted, will be resolved or smoothed away in due time, but that they are standing challenges against the use of the prevalent vulgar space for generalized or dogmatic purposes until they have been cleared away, or until a construction is substituted which does not drag them in with it.

We now revert to the question suggested in the first paragraph of this section as to whether the prevalent vulgar space, or indeed any vulgar space, furnishes some criterion by which the physical, mathematical, social, and sociological spaces are to be tested, or some goal toward which the sciences which deal with these latter must strive. Postponing to the next section that part of this inquiry which concerns physical and mathematical spaces, we consider here merely the purported right of this vulgar space to dominance over sociological construction. To this question we have no dogmatic answer. What the ultimate outcome in knowledge will be does not concern us, but only the present situation of investigation in which our requirement is that of the highest efficiency. As for this intermediate problem of scientific investigation, it might well be the case that even after the prevalent vulgar space had been reduced to the status of one social formation among many, it would still remain the best kind of space for sociological construction. Here, however, there is a great accumulation of evidence that it wholly fails to perform its service. During the last two generations there has been huge development in the way of enlarging the picture of the social part of the " contents " of space. What we call institutions comprise a great part of our sociological materials, and though we take these institutions as if located and evolved in a spatial world, we simply cannot give them any spatial construction of the Newtonian or vulgar kinds whatever. All that vague field called " social psychology," which is treated as though in some sense " external " to the individual, is nevertheless not " external " in the sense of the vulgar space. For all of these materials, and, in general, for all of sociology, some better space form than the vulgar space is required, if consistency is to be reached. Constructions of society have been attempted as a relation, as an operation, and as a thing; none of them has been satisfactory, and the reason is that all of them have been erected in a conventional, an inadequate, and — so far as the problems in hand are directly concerned — a fictitious space.

The answer then is that the prevalent vulgar space furnishes neither criterion nor goal for sociology, and that it can only hamper sociological construction where it insists on dominating it.[20] This answer requires, however, two forms of qualification. The first is that the prevalent vulgar space is unquestionably the most convenient frame for the accumulation of first-hand sociological data, and for much of the provisional classification of data. The second is that if sociology adopts for its most general construction some different spatial frame, some frame specially devised by and within itself for its own purposes, then it must also at the same time devise adequate technical methods for transforming reports under its own frame into reports under the vulgar frame, and vice versa. It must be able to transform from one set of linguistic co-ordinates to the other, somewhat as mathematics makes transformations within its own field. This is a requirement which will receive further attention in a later section of this paper.

It may perhaps help in the appraisal of the above conclusion to consider the issue in the form of the query: " Is space a fact? " a query which, more fully expressed, becomes: " Is space, either in the form we have called the prevalent vulgar space, or in the form we have called the physiological or psychological ' human ' space, a fact? " This query, now, on the basis of the remarks about fact at the end of Part I, must be subdivided into two. On one side, one asks: " Is space, as it stands, or in itself, or for all general basic purposes of knowledge, a fact? " On the other side, one asks: " Is such space a basic fact for sociology? " We disregard the first form of the

---

[20] This attitude does not destroy the vulgar space as " fact " within its own range, but reinterprets it under the construction of local point-of-view discussed in Section 5, following.

query as entirely beyond our province, and consider only the second. Here we can appraise our answer by considering what it is that is meant by a basic fact, not merely for sociology, but for any kind of science. We note two contrasted attitudes which men habitually take as to science. One attitude is that science deals with facts; the other is that science is the system of the discovery of fact. Conflict between the two attitudes arises only when science in its process of discovery brings about the displacement of data which, under the first attitude, had been accepted as basic fact. Such conflicts have been innumerable in the history of the development of knowledge, and will doubtless continue. There is nothing radically new in the present situation. Always there are vehement upholders of the basic nature of the old " facts "; always there is violent resistance to rearrangement in terms of new " facts "; and for that matter no prejudice need be implied either in behalf of the " old " or the " new," since either may well prove to be inferior to the other, or even " wrong." Consider the situation of a sociology which perhaps existed under Ptolemaic astronomy and Ptolemaic space; what would have been its attitude toward a reorganization of itself in terms of Copernican astronomy, or, later on, Newtonian space? We do not need to guess; it is sufficient to substitute for such a sociology another comparable form of interpretation of human life, namely a theology, and we at once know the answer.

Turning to the physical sciences, the atom, forty years ago, was a speculation, an hypothesis: in the course of a lifetime we have seen it pass through two other stages, first becoming firmly established as basic fact, then being transformed into a derivative or appearance of basic facts, which now in their turn are inspected as basic. Just today physics, facing the conflicting results of the Compton and the Davisson-Germer experiments, is uncertain whether to regard the corpuscle or the ray, or neither, or both, as basic facts. Physicists may writhe as they feel what is in their hands, but they do not deeply worry; they trust to the development of their knowledge itself to bring them their answers. Newtonian space in physics has taken its turn in transformation, and has become approximation to better formulations in space-time; and now it may be that the vulgar form of the Newtonian space may have to yield its claim to the basic fact for social studies. Indeed, as vulgar form itself, it has no certainty of continuing on into coming generations; and the steady spread of variant attitudes among physicists and mathematicians, not merely as technical devices, but as ways of looking at the world around them, is a fair warrant that it will not.

4. *Mathematical and Physical Spaces as Social*

Our discussion of vulgar space systems has gone just far enough to destroy the illusion that the particular way in which men in any given age look upon the factuality of space — including the way in which our own age looks upon it — is final and conclusive for the general purposes of investigation. The reader who regards " space " as one certain and definite existence, who regards the individual " mind " as another certain and definite existence which makes definite individual contact with that " space," and who regards all of his language and knowledge structures as mere incidental approximations to the " truth " about it, will have difficulty in following the further argument; for his are just the propositions with respect to which we have now shattered the dogmatic claims. For such a reader any " success " which the science of physics attains or may hope to attain will be tested in the end by the way in which it upholds his own peculiar space presentation; just as any " success " which he will attribute to the sciences of psychology or sociology will be measured by similar standards. Such, very certainly, is not our attitude and criterion here.

We have next to consider the mathematical and physical spaces as social developments and constructions, and to bring them, so inspected, into relation, first to vulgar space, and then to a science of sociology. Here we make use of the first of the two trends or directions of investigation which we identified in Section 2, preceding: that, namely, which regards mathematics and physics, and all of their content and reference and delivery, as part of knowledge, and this knowledge as social process or product; [21] and which undertakes to appraise these sciences from this point of approach.

Now, so far as the mathematical spaces are concerned, a word will suffice. The popular attitude makes mathematics " abstract " in the extreme as contrasted with the " concrete " parts of knowledge; and, however weak this distinction theoretically is, it serves as a label to place the mathematical spaces under investigation as knowledge and from the sociological approach. Both from this popular point of view, which differentiates the subjectmatters of science, and from our own differentiation of attitudes of approach, the mathematical spaces therefore appear as social processes or products. We may postpone any further consideration of them until we return in a later section to an examination of the manner in which they may be helpful to sociological space construction.

---

[21] The distinction between process and product need not concern us in this paper. Where desirable, it is of course to be set up and understood semantically, on the basis of the postulatory choice of a basic " fact " or " thing " for a particular purpose of inquiry.

With respect to the physical spaces we must, however, ask several questions. In what sense are they submissive to the control of vulgar space? In what sense are they social procedures or products? In what sense do they condition sociology or furnish it background and basis?

We may begin by making further use of Einstein's discussion of space in his Nottingham address, previously cited. After Newton had established space as a separate thing, he tells us, the next great stage in development did not appear until Maxwell formulated his electromagnetic equations. These seemed to require the introduction of a new basic " thing," namely ether, having a behavior different from that of the space of matter. When special relativity appeared, space and time were consolidated into one " thing," space-time, the four-dimensional continuum. Ether now gradually became unnecessary and tended to be dropped from the list of " things." With the interpretation of gravitation in space-time under general relativity, and with Einstein's efforts, and the many others that are being made, to establish a general " field-theory " to incorporate not only electromagnetic phenomena but also corpuscular phenomena, it is Einstein's expectation, his " pious hope," that space-time will survive as the sole " thing " of physics.

What we have to take into account is not any specific feature of this development, nor any specific future change in it which may appear, but the significance which any such development whatever has for sociological investigation. We are shown first the old space-matter-thing, then a certain not-space-matter-thing, which seemed necessary in addition, and finally the space-time thing which has consolidated part of the materials and which, it is hoped, may consolidate all of them.[22] These are shown to us in course of construction, evolution, discovery — however one may prefer to describe it — in knowledge and society. Their evolution is in mathematical patterns. They are not holding to any control by the prevalent vulgar space with its factual externalization of Newtonian origin, and with its recognitional psychology. They involve intricate psychological or psychological-type problems of their own. Construction, externalization, and recognition are all involved together within them. They are not fly-by-nights of knowledge; but are instead of the most fundamental reference and importance. Their psychological intricacy cannot be brushed away

---

[22] To appraise them we must remember to take the realism out of Einstein's term " thing," and consider it as a systemic specification within knowledge, always with the possibility that what is " thing " from one point of attack may prove to be operation from some other point of attack; so that the space-time construction may be an operative factor, without affecting its scientific value; just as Cartesian co-ordinates, set up by Descartes as relational exhibits, and treated by Einstein as factual specifications, may themselves in the end appear as operational symbols in full linguistic knowledge.

by any dictum of old dogma. Nevertheless their psychological aspects are not being handled by the psychologists, and we may even be justified in suspecting that the present psychological science as a development of the Newtonian era is not capable of handling them. Nor are these problems being handled by the physicists who have their own work to do. Nevertheless the presence of the problems is open, it cannot be denied, and in the end they must be seriously faced. All of this is to say that the current physical spaces are constructions and problems within knowledge. To call them " abstract " in some sense not so " abstract " as mathematical spaces, but more " abstract " than vulgar space, does not settle the problem by any means; it merely labels it.

Suppose, now, that in the development of observation and experiment some one, or possibly more than one, of the physical spaces is accepted as a standard construction for physics over a longer or shorter period of time: a period, let us say, long enough so that young men grow up into it, and do not witness signs of deterioration or destruction within it during their working lives. Will such a space, perhaps conventionally externalized and accompanied by a new specimen of vulgar space, furnish the positive and inevitable world-form under which a sociology must be constructed?

The answer must be two-directioned, as all general expressions of so wide a nature should be. Dogmatically such a physical construction cannot be the unquestioned basis for sociology, since it will be a form of knowledge, and that knowledge will be itself a social development; and the province of the sociology will include all of the social. But, on the other hand, it may prove to be so richly a form of construction for the social that it will be entitled to appear as basic in all sociological construction. Just at the present day, if there is a direct method of valuing the existing experimental physical space-constructions, and of applying them with certain fertility to sociological construction, I am not aware of it.

The indirect import of the present transitional stage for sociology is, however, very great. Physics has definitely rejected the prevalent vulgar space, so far as the latter may make claim to dominate physical construction. Truer it would be to say, of course, that however much this present vulgar space may have seemed to be the actuality behind Newtonian physical space, it never influenced the latter at all, but that the influencing was in fact entirely the other way around. It can hardly be urged, if this is true, that the new physical spaces will ever be " externalized " into the pattern of the present vulgar space. We are therefore set free by the new developments of physics from any sense of compulsion to take over the Newtonian frame as our necessary sociological frame; and we are given incentive as sociologists to work out our own salvation by the study of all space forms, whether externalized or internal to the society, whether of Newtonian or of other derivation.

The two following sections of this paper will discuss, first the factuality of the immediate presentation of social space, and then the manner in which mathematics can furnish models and aids for the sociological formulation of such factual social space. The one requirement for both of these branches of discussion is that we force ourselves to honest and thorough analysis of what our meaning is when we describe any of those phenomena which we call social — an organized institution, a language form, a law, a convention, a creed — in terms of direct fact and as itself a " thing " before our examination. The need of clarity here is all-pervasive in sociological investigation. It is just as vital when we speak of a social environment to a person, as when we speak of society as itself a subject, or as itself our subjectmatter. Without this clarity, our foundations are throughout confusion.

5. *Social Space as Fact*

We have now achieved a certain freedom for sociological investigation. What value that freedom may have for us depends on what use we may be able to make of it.

Are our social phenomena spatial? Is their spatial form a peculiarly social space? If it is, in what way does this social space differ from a Newtonian or vulgar space? Is it narrower and more specialized, or is it broader, richer, and more comprehensive? Is this social space a " fact? " If it is a fact, how are we to organize it in connection with other facts, social and physical?

The manner of approach [23] may be summarized from the preceding development, thus:

---

[23] For a comparable development in physiology one may examine Dr. Alexis Carrel's article " The New Cytology " (*Science,* March 20, 1931) reporting on work done in the laboratories of The Rockefeller Institute for Medical Research. Dr. Carrel makes time a direct dimension of his study of cells and tissues. Cells he describes as " in physiological continuity with their environment "; " cells and environment form a whole "; " structure and function are two aspects of the same thing "; " a tissue is an enduring thing, its functional and structural conditions become modified from moment to moment," so that " time enters as a part into the constitution of a tissue "; " to study it at only one instant of the duration is almost meaningless." In contrast with the old method which " only reaches the mental constructs that were considered as being the anatomical elements," Dr. Carrel proposes the study of " a system of cells-environment, of which the structural, functional, physical, physico-chemical and chemical conditions are considered in time as well as in space." Cells " never live in isolated units, but in colony formations of various types." Relations between mediums and growth energy of cells have been identified. Cells which are apparently morphologically identical prove to belong to different races characterized by differences in their nutritional properties. The food requirements are as fundamental as the morphological properties. Different cell types are also defined by the manner in

We find no scientific justification for setting up any part or parts of our materials as certainly "fact," with respect to which other parts hold the place of "pure theory."

We find no scientific justification for assuming that whatever it is that we emphasize at some particular stage of our development as basic fact will permanently hold that position; since fact and theory are seen developing together in knowledge.

We find no scientific justification for assuming, at the present imperfect stage of our knowledge, that we can pick any one fact or structure of fact as best even for all present purposes.

We do find, instead, full justification for proceeding first with one set or system of facts, and then with another, to discover which gives us the richest results.

We find this approach valid, whether we start with the physical sciences and physical facts and work toward the social, taken as within the physical and as seen through it; or whether we start with the social sciences and social facts and work towards the physical, taken as within and as seen through the social.

In especial the entire problem as to what is to be taken as "thing," and what as behavior, activity, or operation of "thing" in society, is to be approached in this way.

If, now, in accordance with the older usage, we start by selecting as our basic fact or thing a physical world in Newtonian space and chronological time, with "life" evolving out of it, and with "higher mentality" evolving in that "life," we come in the end to the phenomena of society, the social "relations" or social "operations" which it is our special task to investigate and interpret. Already with "life," and in still greater degree with "mentality," science has been unable to frame what it takes

---

which they modify their environments: "each tissue or organ certainly manufactures in some measure its own medium, which, in its turn, acts on the cells."

The methodological aspect of these citations is manifestly in close correspondence with the positions taken in the present paper. The differences in the contemporary situation of investigation as between physiology and sociology should, however, be noted: (a) the physiologist can proceed experimentally step by step from his older formulations to his newer; (b) his methodological considerations may therefore appear as incidental results of his procedure rather than as its postulational basis; (c) the sociologist has before him physical, psychical, and institutional forms of expression which are vastly more defective than even the older physiological abstraction of staining and slides; (d) the sociologist is therefore driven to much stronger immediate emphasis upon methodological postulation in order to break the barriers and gain position from which to make headway. The difference in the degree of emphasis upon the methodological considerations is, however, only a transitional difference in the stage of development of the investigation. There is no more dogma in the one case than in the other, and no more limitation in the one case than in the other. If sociology is at an apparent disadvantage in this respect, it has in another respect a great advantage. Physiology has reached a stage at which it must use most laborious and expensive techniques if it is to proceed. Sociology, however, once it gains an adequate linguistic frame for handling all of its materials in a single system of postulatory research, will find itself in much more direct interior contact and with closer powers of appraisal for the materials of research which it requires.

to be their essential characteristics by the use of its Newtonian formulas, so that it has come to regard and describe them as non-spatial or " inner " in contrast with the spatial " outer "; and if it has with some slight appearance of success brought the vital and the mental into connection in a common " inner," it is then faced with the social, which insists on presenting itself as a new variety of " outer." In the earlier papers cited above, I have argued that even under the approach through a space of physical mensurations, the spatiality of the psychic and of the social must be recognized if consistency in development is to be secured.

Here in contrast with the above historical approach we shall start from the other end, and shall select as our basic fact or " thing " all that which we mean by the social, as directly envisaged. This is very different indeed from selecting a defined and limited product called society under the preceding type of approach.[24] We do this, *not* as if we knew or could know in advance precisely what the terms " social " and " society " mean, but rather with these words as labels for a field of investigation. We have this society before us in the form of men and their activities and all that those activities involve. This includes the knowledge factors that are in the men and in their activities and their society. It also includes the factual references or implications, and the realisms and externalizations of their knowledge. It does not solve the epistemological problems of knowledge and the factual basis of knowledge. Neither does it evade them. It approaches them the other way around. Instead of inspecting a factual world with a knowledge factor floating in it, it inspects a living procedure of knowledge-experience-contact, with the stress for knowledge not on its

---

[24] A comparable approach in psychology will be found in J. R. Kantor's *Principles of Psychology* (2 vols., 1924, 1926: see also his *An Outline of Social Psychology*, 1929). Professor Kantor sets before himself a primary descriptive presentation of individual behavior in precisely the spirit in which I set before myself a primary descriptive presentation of social situations. His fact of observation, which he names the " segment of behavior," is always human activity, and it always exhibits the coupled characteristics of stimulus and response, each functional to the other. Therefore, while he is a student of behavior and of nothing but behavior, he is not a behaviorist in the sense of those who reduce their phenomena to physiological by-products, any more than he is an anti-behaviorist in the sense of the " inner-consciousness " psychologies. His behaviorism is " objective," in that it starts with direct and immediate description of phenomena; it is " organismic " in that its locus is the whole reacting organism in its full environment. Since Professor Kantor concentrates his attention on the conduct of individuals taken individually, and uses historically or biographically the individualistic approach, while I concentrate mine on the conduct of individuals taken in groupal activity, and use historically or biographically the sociological approach, our respective constructions show marked superficial differences in their treatment of society. These differences are so sharp that criticism under any of the ancient philosophical-psychological standards might make them appear to be radically opposed to each other. They are nevertheless differences of borderland results, rather than of basic understanding, and they are differences of that very type by means of which scientific advance may be secured. The combination of the two forms of approach, on a common basis of observation, offers, I believe, prospect of important gains in knowledge in this inadequately developed field.

exactness but on its indicativeness. It yields a single great system of research, trending toward the incorporation of all fact, in contrast with the extreme mechanistic or "outer-fact" systems which trend to take over and subordinate the interpretation of all knowledge and society. One advantage it has which we may immediately note is that within its own range of work it gets rid of the dogmatic inner-outer split which has been ruinous to the older approach.

The social, so inspected, is most certainly spatial. It is not spatial in either a formal Newtonian sense, or a naïve vulgar sense; but for that matter it may be that nothing is spatial in exactly those senses, since the term "space" has widened far beyond those limited meanings. It has separations and distributions, it has discretenesses and continuities, and it has its own comparisons and mensurations. Its space is a peculiarly social space, for it is not under the control of any other space erected as though external to it; and indeed those purported external spaces are themselves capable of presentation as social constructions, whether or not in the end they or any one of them may furnish the deepest and most substantial form for sociological theory itself.

Let us now use the word "institution" to designate descriptively some special complex of the social situation, understanding that we are observing it with our sociological eyes directly, and not merely constructing a semblance of it under some pre-established theory. For illustration, let us consider the institution money. If we apply to it Newtonian, vulgar, or, let us say, geographical space, that space will describe coins, bills, checks, tills and depositaries, but it will formulate almost nothing of our social meaning. Yet the institution is spread out socially, it is socially spatial in every part of its description. Its social spatiality is so interwoven with its very sociality as to be inseparable. The money procedures have continuity throughout society, a continuity which a Newtonian form will not yield for it; but which, on the other hand, the Newtonian form cannot break, since this latter space simply does not reach to it at all.

Do not think that anything is added to, or changed in, the widespread functional phenomena of money when we call them spatial. The word "space" as applied to them gives a form under which they can be observed and investigated. Moreover, it gives a form which, we shall proceed to argue, covers every part of the phenomena and every bit of material which is needed for their interpretation just as fully as the Newtonian space form covers all mechanical phenomena, and in much the same sense.[25] That is our purpose here, and that is the purpose of all scientific

---

[25] The terms "form" and "thing" may both be applied to space without radical distinction of meaning. The semantic interpretation is applicable to this as to other word-couples.

investigation — to get, namely, all the phenomena involved under interpretative construction in system, in one system, in a full system.

Suppose we take for illustration, in place of such a wide-flung institution as money, one more closely organized, say a Tariff Reform League. This now has its own spatial spread running into Parliament, into various trades and business organizations, into investors' and consumers' circles, and into activities more vaguely specified as those of the common welfare. It connects with the Government, with the permanent offices of administration, and with the legislation of the future. It can be followed through under the same social spatial form until it connects with every citizen of the nation in which it is found, and, outward from the particular nation, without any break in its spatial form, into the entire world phenomena of industry and trade, and into all the living of all of the societies of the globe. Under this spatial form we can bring all the linguistic, argumentative, and, hence, theorizing activities of societies and of society; under it we can bring the utilizable physical earth, its mines and fields and power resources, entering in the forms of experience and knowledge, extensive or slight, with no radical cleft between the knowledge elements as to whether they are accurate statements or vague indications and implications of experience; with no radical cleft as to whether that experience is verbalized-psychic or physiological-vital.

Under this social spatial form we lay off our phenomena into divisions and patterns which seem best suited to their description and interpretation. Suppose we take for special consideration such an element as is indicated by the common expression " idea " or " theory." Here we do not find a mysterious and unregulated stranger from some foreign region, but we have before us a linguistic structure spatially spread out, and representative of other spatially spread-out factors in our more general study. We have this special element in a common field or system with the rest of our materials. We identify our socially spatial discretenesses in many forms, one perhaps being as between two Tariff Reform Leagues with opposing policies. We follow through the continuities underlying these surface separations. If we take two nations with rival commercial interests as the discretenesses, we have still the continuities beneath offered by the specifically human social industrial organization of the present era. Our greatest need in all sociological investigation is mensuration, the weighing of conflicting or co-operating needs, powers, capacities, interests, purposes; here under a common social spatial form we have at last the possibility of such comparative estimations, on a basis upon which they may in the end be checked and verified.

What we call the individual man becomes now, under this inspection, one special discreteness among many. Perhaps he is the most important of them all. Perhaps he is not. Investigation alone will establish. More probably he is the most important for certain ranges of study, and the less important, even the least important, for other ranges. Full knowledge of these ranges is still far in the future. But in one respect at least we already have the individual presentation under control. Recent physical investigations have distinguished local times, and similarly local spaces, from the more general form of space-time. In the individual's reaction within his social world we have distinctly a phenomenon of this type. We may use the term point-of-view for the individual's presentation of himself to the world and of the world to him. This individual presentation is distinctly a local point-of-view within the full social situation; even the " wisest " man in the long temporal and wide spatial reach of society is but a dot within it. So taken, we have at once the basis for a reconstruction of the language that we must inevitably adopt out of everyday life and use as tool for our sociological investigation. That language, both in its practical forms and in its physiological and psychological adaptations, has been developed under this individual, local point-of-view. It is tied to it, and carries its imperfections forward with it. In physiology it is already notoriously imperfect. In psychology it is perhaps wholly bad, and certainly so largely bad that the greatest precautions must always be taken when it is used.

And, further, our individual-discrete in the general social space proves at once — indeed, we may say it has shown itself from the earliest of sociological investigations onward — to be itself a complex, tied in its various parts into a thousand other groupal or institutional social discretenesses. The process of contacts and influencings in and among the physiological-psychological persons may, under a constructive separation of process and content, be called the " pure " functional psychology. The " content " phases are all social, historical, evolutionary, cosmic, down to the last specifications of feeling or sensation. We thus have in the social space our region of psychological investigation ready for clarification and development. In this space we have neither the individual appearing " in his own right," nor the institutional appearing " in its own right," but we have the phrasing " in his, or its, own right " canceling out on both sides; and we are free to take either aspect as " fact " and as base from which to investigate the other.

When we have become able to use the term " social space " as a direct expression of the general form of social procedures, we must be prepared to find many social spaces which must be analyzed and interpreted with respect to one another. Let us consider the description " specified social place" as I have used it in connection with "specified social time"[26] in the definitions of vulgar spaces and physical spaces in Section 1. Both of these terms are very much richer and more real from the interpretative sociological view — if not from the dogmatic vulgar view — than are geographical place and calendar time. These latter are but clues to the true social times and social places; they are constructions of society to aid it in carrying on its work, and they derive from social experience as that covers and includes all physical nature. They are very useful for the special studies of physics, though their usefulness was found in the end to have bounds; they are very practical from the local point-of-view within the range of a man's physical movements and lifetime; they are useful and practical indeed in much wider ranges than these latter, but with notoriously decreasing usefulness and meaning the further they are carried, whether in finite or in infinite extensions. To refer again to Newton and the space-thing, as Einstein has characterized it, we do not now have to connect the appearance of the latter in knowledge with a certain calendar date in the life of a certain man in England. It is not gauged by a clock moment or a parish boundary. It has its rise in the life of Newton and of many men around and before Newton, and the calendar gives only a crude clue to the description. We do not have to wonder how it was that the "same" thing or something similar appeared elsewhere, or before or after; but we can identify this transition as fact in society, taking either the scientific or the vulgar development for primary examination as "thing," and letting it itself — along with other presentations similarly investigated — be a measure of social times and social places, with the clock time and the geography as convenient aids to, but not certainly reliable frames for, our knowledge of what happened. We may express this also by saying that the important, the interesting, the vital aspect of this social development and of any other is not the calendar date, nor the geographical locus; and that these latter are but incidental formulations of the real social times and places. Social speeds are not clock speeds; social expansions are not held firmly to national or physical boundaries; however well the clock speeds and the boundary measurements may be read over upon them for whatever they are worth.

[26] A development for the term "social time" in its relation to "clock time" or "calendar time" or the generalized "geological time" within which evolution on the earth is assumed to be framed, would run parallel to that for social space, and would be an important component of a general sociological construction. It lies beyond the special purpose of this paper, and I content myself here with recommending for serious and protracted study by all believers in the stability of dogmatic one-way calendar time as the basis of sociological theory the following shrewd inquiry by the physicist Percy W. Bridgman in his *Logic of Modern Physics*, p. 78: "It is amusing to try to discover what is the precise meaning in terms of operations of a statement like this: 'It is true that Darius the Mede arose at 6.30 on the morning of his thirtieth birthday.'"

We have now presented social space as a "fact" of society which is broader, richer, and more comprehensive than the narrower physical space constructions. We have illustrated this in the case of phenomena of the type commonly called institutions, we have shown how the full procedure of the individual member of society can be assimilated under this spatial form, and we have given concrete meaning to the term "social places," and along with that to the term "social times," in the society. Much other illustration will readily suggest itself, such as caste and class, the phenomena indicated by such phrases as "the working-class mind" or "the capitalist mind," or by religious and racial antipathies: though of course in our presentation such words as "mind" and "antipathy" which arise from the local point-of-view are deprived of their pretense to explanatory value, and are taken as mere indicative names for situations in the social space.

In all of this description, barring the express construction of social space as fact, I have used a manner of envisaging social phenomena which is common to all of the sociologies. It is the "objectification" of social situations for study; and without such objectifications, implicit or explicit, there would be no sociology unless as a minor subdivision under psychology or physiology. What is essential in the present description is not the term "space" itself as here used, but the extension of the social objectification, the social envisagement, so as to bring the full range of study into one system or field. Nevertheless, the term "space" is the proper term for scientific use today, though it would not have been the proper term a hundred years ago. Its definite applicability is of course the purpose of this entire essay to show.[27]

The obstacle to its acceptance, and the understanding of the present development, lies in the implications of externality and internality in

[27] The reader may test this construction on the basis of his personal experience and methods of work by preparing a list of customary forms of description, and examining these for completeness and consistency. Suppose he takes for consideration the presentation of The Government as an institution. He will note the possibility of its investigation under various linguistic frames, including, among others, the following: (1) a construction, under one of the sharper forms of behaviorism, of atomistic stimulus and reaction; (2) the vaguer descriptive stimulus-reaction treatment of some popular modification of behaviorism; (3) a construction of personalities, types, temperaments, and motives: (4) an objectivation as social; (5) an expressly postulated social space. There is apparently no objection to the use of any of these frames. The problem is, how well do they do their work, how well do they serve the more general purposes of knowledge? Ask now in what sense the Government "exists," or is a "fact," at a time at which all of its ministers are asleep. This is a crude, almost childish, form of inquiry, but from its very crudity one can readily advance to the more significant formulations of the issue. Is the government the separated responses of its members? Is it a bundle of personal psychologies? Or is it a social continuity? The best answer will not be the one that best fits current conventions of language, nor the one that most strongly insists on its own "truth" or "reality," but instead the one that is most efficient and comprehensive for purposes of investigation.

common language, in psychological theory, and more particularly in the phraseology of that which we have discussed as " vulgar space." Into this region of difficulty we must now enter with greater detail.

We have before us social spaces as fact. We have also before us linguistic procedures in this social space which present a physical or natural space as if outside of, external to, or prior to, all society, and which thereby proclaim this physical space as basic fact, with respect to which the social spaces are mere incidental descriptions, relations, or products. How are we to handle this conflict?

To begin with, of course, it is handled by scientific hypothesis. Without interfering with the basic physical hypothesis for its own uses, I have simply shown reasons for, and asked the privilege to employ, a different hypothesis for other uses. The solution therefore will be given solely within the limits of this different hypothesis. The linguistic systems, passing from a presumptive stage of early naïve word-thing confusion, through the Socratic, Platonic, Aristotelian development, settled down to a two-thousand-year-long status in which it was assumed that it was possible to identify and establish basic terms which directly presented or represented basic facts. But this system and all of its included systems of meanings are social procedures or products. All the fact-thing references and all the externalizations it includes are socially developed and require sociological examination. We have then merely to make a provisional, interior, sociological distinction between spatial attributions " external " to all that men do and are, and the attributions of spatiality to the socially spread-out men themselves. Whether now the externalized spaces are to be interpreted in terms of the social spaces, or whether the latter are to be interpreted in terms of the former, becomes a problem for long investigation and careful appraisal, not for dogmatic determination in advance. The way is left open here for either outcome, but the study is made under the first of the two constructions.

Beyond this particular case, the very distinctions " internal " and " external " in any and all of their generalizations are socially produced, and seen in social variations, transformations, and developments across the ages. It is the crudest of errors to assume for the general purposes of all investigation that the particular form these distinctions most commonly take today is the ripe fruit of knowledge and bound to survive for all future ages. This present common form does not belong at all to the Greek point-of-view. It has had various intervening forms. Taken in psychological rendering, in which the human mind is the " inner " and the physical world is the " outer," the apparent consistency of these terms broke down with the very beginnings of sociology; for even in these beginnings, situations were clear which were " outer " to the individual " inner," and yet not parts of the physical " outer." The paradoxes remain unsolved by psychology as a science, and they are accentuated by the recent developments in the region of radiation and electrons by the science of physics. In their present confused state they have no right, either directly or by implication, to presume dictation to the experimental development of sociological knowledge. Practically we may always use " inner " and " outer " as we need them, if we keep in mind primarily our hypothetical construction of one great system or field of investigation which includes them both. To a special presentation, a particular discreteness, brought before us for study, we may identify its inner characteristics and contrast them with that which is outer to the particular presentation. In all such cases the linguistic value of the terms must be read in accordance with the full context, including its full postulation, and not dogmatically. In geometry such terms are freely used without miscomprehension; and in connection with them two forms of boundary have been found necessary in point set theories, the boundary which closes a construction, and the boundary which limits it without belonging to it. We are faced no doubt with even more complex situations in sociology, but the attack must be by refinement of precision, not by confused dictum.

If one inspects the various theoretical sociologies with reference to the use of the spatial form, one will find many approximations to a presentation of social space, whether the term space itself is definitely employed or not, and even where that term is " defined " in sharp contrast to the manner in which it is used here. Simmel, for example, writing twenty-five years ago, used the term space (*Raum*) expressly for " fact " in three Euclidean dimensions, and regarded space as a non-active form under which all social process was before us. Nevertheless, it was just this nonactive space (with its peculiar characteristics that each particular locality within it is so fully set off by itself that it cannot be called " the same as " any other locality, and that it cannot be grouped in a collection for which a plural noun-form can be used) that made possible for other objects the presentation of a plurality of fully identical samples.[28] He set up as criterion for the establishment of a science of sociology as distinct from the special social sciences the practicability of the identification of common forms of socialization, recurring in all departments of social life,

[28] *Soziologie*, pp. 460–462.

and consequently recurring in each of the separate social sciences. He distinguished thus, sociological form [29] from the psychological contents of the special social sciences, as an abstraction justifying separate and peculiarly sociological study. Under the expansion which the term "space" has taken since the date of Simmel's writing, it is clear that his whole presentation of social activity and process is itself spatial in this wider sense, so that his many brilliant interpretations of social phenomena are ready for use in full social spatial organization. So for him it was not the geographical boundaries or the area in square miles that identified an empire, but the nexus of social interactions by means of which the area and the boundaries took form.

In America where sociological interpretation presents itself so largely as "psychological" — in other words, where crudely snatched morsels of society are detached under individualized forms of language, and naïvely regarded as individually "psychic" — the trend is to degrade the consistency of whatever social spatial presentations come to be recognized. Some theorists, introducing the term "social distance," see substantially nothing but characteristics of remoteness between inner psychic states of persons realistically taken. Others, affected by the ecological developments of biology, attempt its reproduction in sociology, but soon find themselves with nothing more than an external geographical frame within which they attempt to localize various psychological characteristics or behavioristic situations.

Very different is the development of Regional Sociology, originating with Geddes and carried forward by Mukerjee. Mukerjee presents "the idea of the region as an intricate network of interrelations," in which "man is part of the processes by which the balance of the region is maintained or shifted." [30] If one reads this language postulationally in full functional value it yields a fair statement of social space-time in the sense in which I have used it. If, however, one stresses the term "part" realistically as if separate "parts" could be fully identified,[31] it yields either a descriptive approach to the position here taken, or else a sharp deviation from it, depending upon the degree of dogmatism with which

---

[29] A recent criticism of Simmel, published in a series issued by one of the greater universities, proposes to "refute" him by declaring, first, that forms cannot be isolated from contents, and second, that he actually used much psychological material in his social interpretations. Such complete miscomprehension is just one more evidence of the vital need of deeper linguistic and factual analysis in this field. Simmel's distinction of form and content is in contrast with the suggestion in this paper that content may best be considered as sociological, with process as psychological; but either construction is a permissible postulation for experimental development under semantic approach.

[30] "The Regional Balance of Man," *American Journal of Sociology*, November, 1930.

[31] For the difficulties of part and whole, see end of Section 6, following.

the " part " isolations are stressed. Mukerjee's latest expressions record a distinct advance over the positions taken by him in his book *Regional Sociology*, [32] where he specifies as components of his construction, first, the intertwining of social, economic, and political life, second, Professor Geddes' development of Le Play's scheme of Place, Work, and Folk, and third, the application of social anthropology and collective psychology, these materials not yet appearing as well fused in his thought.

The status of sociology as Professor Geddes sets it forth in his well-known organization of the materials into three great groups, bound together functionally in time and space, furnishes, I may perhaps venture to say, the one essential scientific background within which such a construction of social space as is here proposed may be attempted.[33] The differences are those of stage of investigation and of immediate purpose, not of attitude of approach. Comparisons are not easy or exact, but one may perhaps think of a full descriptive presentation of the organized knowledge of the heavens in contrast with the work of astronomical physics, or of the more general syntheses of biology in contrast with the full physiological-chemical-electrical-radiational investigations of that science; but this only as though in each case we had obverse and reverse aspects of the same field, each aspect aiding the other, and neither having assurance of priority so far as the future of knowledge is concerned. The heart of the matter is the full functional comprehension. More and more does it appear, as one follows this route, that when one sets up a certain specification of organism and a certain other specification of environment to it, he must be prepared soon to find these specifications inadequate, and to carry his analysis further by breaking down his first forms, not in the sense of showing them to be wrong, but rather in the sense of showing them to be incomplete approximations instead of primarily established factual isolations. It is just one attempt under this background and in this direction that I have to offer in this paper. In the next section I shall consider some of the possibilities in the use of co-ordinates for social knowledge, and the relatively " concrete " scheme Place, Work, Folk undoubtedly provides a very useful set of co-ordinates for such purposes: but when Professor Thomson, adopting Professor Geddes' scheme, compares it with Descartes' mathematical co-ordinates and with " Darwin's biological co-ordinates," and rigidly insists that " the sociological co-ordinates *must* remain Folk, Work, and Place, and the *whole* of sociological inquiry *must* be in that framework " [34] he distinctly outruns the

[32] Pp. 235–6 (1926).
[33] See the citations in a footnote to Section 2 preceding.
[34] *What Is Man?*, p. 135 (italics mine).

type of statement that is theoretically permissible, considering what we know of the historical development of human knowledge, and considering the future possibilities we are permitted even now to envisage.

Turning to recent German sociology, the development of L. von Wiese is the one most fully in accord with what is here attempted. Taking his initiative from Simmel's presentation of forms of socialization, as do all of the more important recent German sociologists, Wiese stresses as fundamental the immediate and direct observation of a realm of social facts. This is his "*soziale Optik*," vital to his entire work. Differing from the present approach, however, he co-ordinates the social realm with the physical and psychical realms; accepting these latter as he finds them in their respective lines of scientific investigation; and demanding only for the social its full right to its own independent investigation, on a par with the others. In this social realm he finds possibilities of measuring and counting; and these not as mere borrowings from other sciences, but as peculiarly social techniques. It is these possibilities that justify a separate science of sociology; and because of them he asserts the existence of a peculiarly social space, "*den sozialen Raum.*" He defends this construction of social space strongly against attack, without however proceeding to a fully functional analysis of it in system with physical space and with the psychical space presentations.[35] The physical space therefore appears in his interpretation as an outlying or indirect "cause" of happenings in social space, and not as an intimately involved region of the full sociological investigation. Wiese's program is for the most complete possible study of the social system, the social space, in its own terms, with incidental drawing upon the physical and the psychical when and as needed. His work has yielded what is in my view the most important systematic sociology that we thus far possess; and the argument with respect to it here is merely that further generalization is practicable and essential for increased efficiency. Wiese's own insistence on the importance of homogeneous procedure is just the basis for such further generalization.

6. *Sociological Spaces as Mathematical*

Assume now that we have before us society in its own spatial form, so that either we directly sense it (as some of us can) in its factual spatiality, or else (as others of us may) we recognize in varying degrees the possible or practical helpfulness of such a construction in investigation. Our next question will concern the manner of analysis of social spaces, and in

---

[35] *Allgemeine Soziologie:* Teil II, *Gebildelehre;* pp. 10–11; p. 44.

especial the suggestion and aid which the existing form of mathematical analysis may give to sociological procedure. Only the briefest sketch of some of the possibilities may here be attempted.

In order to protect the procedure from misinterpretation I shall first indicate the way *not* to envisage it. The two following figures are to be regarded as merely schematic and illustrative, and not in any sense attempts at theoretical completeness.

THE WAY *NOT* TO PROCEED

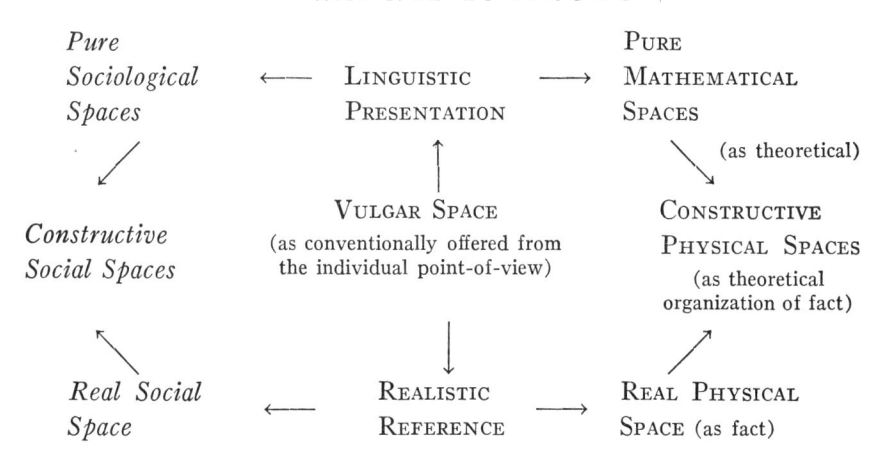

Pure Sociological Spaces	←— LINGUISTIC PRESENTATION —→	PURE MATHEMATICAL SPACES
↙	↑	↘ (as theoretical)
Constructive Social Spaces	VULGAR SPACE (as conventionally offered from the individual point-of-view)	CONSTRUCTIVE PHYSICAL SPACES (as theoretical organization of fact)
↖	↓	↗
Real Social Space	←— REALISTIC REFERENCE —→	REAL PHYSICAL SPACE (as fact)

The right-hand capitalized terms exhibit the existing scientific organization on the physical side. The left-hand italicized terms represent a presumable replica on the social side. No such replica is here sought. The right-hand construction is shot through with speculative difficulties. The left-hand construction would be no better. Each of the arrows indicates an epistemological or psychological difficulty, concerning which we may say that none of the theoretical interpretations offered us " make sense " at all. To the right-hand construction, taken for itself, any sociological interpretation, or any attempt at one, is folly; and indeed to it " society " as a term or presentation becomes little more than a linguistic crudity or malady which is greatly in need of curative treatment. To the left-hand construction, presumably, the physical world as a presentation would itself be a somewhat similar type of malady. Both physical world and social men require however scientific investigation and interpretation, and a construction of rival abnormalities is distinctly not one which promises to be helpful.

In place of this consider the following, similarly schematic, figure in which the speculative difficulty of the arrows is absorbed into the field of technical or scientific-hypothetical procedure under the control of standards of linguistic consistency.

A HINT AT PROCEDURE

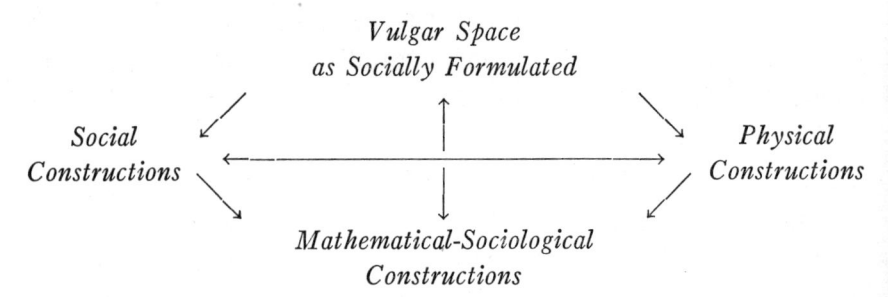

Vulgar Space
as Socially Formulated

Social   *Physical*
Constructions ⟵——————⟶ *Constructions*

Mathematical-Sociological
Constructions

  The arrows here indicate merely that in our problems of interpretation we seek consistency of expression and connection by developments in every direction, and from any starting point, and are not bound down by any dogmatic or conventional realisms of mind and matter with respect to which we are the more strenuously assertive the less we have delved into them. The ranges of fact, experience, knowledge, and language are all included, and we slide our interpretations around and among them in whatever way may seem desirable in order best to make them fit together in system, always holding to consistency of development as our highest guide.

  Our social phenomena are before us both in time and in space, and we may freely assume, unless and until some other status is actually shown us, that they are never before us in the one without the other. If we have exhibited social space as a fact, and indicated how a corresponding development for social time as fact may also be made, we are ready now to combine the two in social space-time as fact. We do this without any dependence on any realistic presentation of physical space-time as fact, without any direct use of any physical space-time, and without consideration of any of the speculation which has accompanied the development of physics in the last twenty years. If realisms of fact are sought they are undoubtedly much easier in the social range than in the physical, but the matter of ease or difficulty is merely one of breaking through conventional uses of language, and of no further importance. We are in no way interested in the realistic developments, but solely in the possibility of dimensional development in sociology analogous to that dimensional development in mathematics which, as one of its special instances, has combined geometrically a time dimension with three space dimensions or more.

In this social space-time we set forward the individual men, the groups and institutions, and the societies or society, as components of one system; and we have already noted their various discretenesses and continuities and possibilities of social mensuration as space-like characteristics. This space is of course extremely complex, and when one seeks mathematical aid in dealing with it, it is not in a geometry of greatly specialized type like the Euclidean that one may expect to find it. Nevertheless, even an Euclidean geometry has characteristics comparable to it which it is worth while to display.

The essential in the development of Euclidean geometry was the systematization into one linguistic and symbolic system of all the necessary elements.[36] The area, the solid, and the line segment, were organized under the same degree, or presumably the same degree, of " abstraction " with that of the point, and of unlimited space extension. It is just such common linguistic organization of individual, group, and society which is necessary in the construction of sociology. In this background we may note, as an analogy and not more, a correspondence in presentation between, first, the area, solid, and line segment of the Euclidean system and the groups and institutions of the sociological system; next, between the unlimited space extension of the one and the socially infinite extension in social space-time of the other; and, finally, between the point of the one system and the individual personal participation or activity of the other. What the investigation seeks in the one system is full detailed knowledge of such configurations as triangle, circle, sphere, icosahedron, conics; and what it seeks in the other is similar knowledge of the social configurations, the groups and institutions and other phenomena to which more technical names may be applied. From this approach the operative constructions which the one uses are point and infinite space, and those which the other may comparably use are individual and society.

This is suggested merely as an analogy, but it is an analogy of the helpful kind, so far as it reaches. The " individual " so taken is of course not the impacted, solidified, concrete " soul " or " living mentality " or " personality," but the activity-point in social participation. There is a different form of analogy which is used in current psychological interpretation where the individual is made the reality and the society a mere relationship. This is an analogy with the realistically taken Euclidean

[36] Or, more precisely, of what passed at the time as all the necessary elements. We know now that not only was there a confusion in the axiom of parallels, but, further, that various operative elements were forced into the background and remained a region of uncertainty. Any use whatever of such a term as " all," considering a " future " for the human race and the possibilities in the development of knowledge, must allow for similar fringes of uncertainty.

point — a form in which the latter is very frequently taken, despite all protestation. It may even be suspected that the person as "unit" in practical life, in psychology and in some sociologies, has been constructed in large measure under the influence of the presence in knowledge of this kind of geometrical point; this latter form of analogy, or of derivation, if it is derivation, is both crude and vicious and has never yet been submissive to consistent development.

In the present approach, if we take some institution, let us say for example the family, what we mean by the "family" is not a census count of detached unitary individuals of variant age and sex, but a certain nexus of activity, a certain form of activity, a certain social situation, which we can hold before us and inspect as a phenomenon or fact, or thing, for the purposes of our study. It is of course true that every bit of this activity is capable of statement in terms of individual lives. If we so desire we are entirely free to state it in this latter way, but when we do, we do not put before us the "family" as a specific phenomenon or social "thing" at all: and long experience has shown that in this case we get nowhere with our desired scientific analysis. We find that we require the social form of statement also. But this social form of statement never yields us the family as a "thing" which we are enabled to regard as external to the individuals who compose it, in the way in which we are perhaps able to regard a wooden tool as external after the man who made it had laid it aside. The family is a thing which, as "thing," is composed of individual participations in, of, and as, activity. When so taken, and only when so taken, the individual participation may be regarded as a point-like participation of the social configuration, the family, in the social space. And the whole construction involves and requires that joint organization of thing, relation, and operation in one common system which was discussed in Part I, and which was established as semantic under special postulation appropriate thereto.[37] So that, if any particular projects require a different construction of thing, we are free to take either the society as a whole or the individual as a person for our basic thing, from which to develop other phases of the system. This again is just what the axiom-makers of geometry have done, using alternatively relations, things, and operations for their basic points of approach; sometimes taking points, sometimes motion, sometimes line-segment, sometimes sphere, sometimes order, sometimes inclusion, more often selections and combinations of these for theoretical basis of attack.

Now the Euclidean geometry was the development of a special local

[37] This construction also of course requires a comparable presentation of the individual physical body as in system in its environmental and evolutionary setting.

Sociology and Mathematics

point-of-view in the sense in which we have previously used that term. This local point-of-view was that presenting the surrounding objects or bodies in a way which was readily basic to a relationship geometry of three dimensions and parallel straights, the whole situation being linguistically set up, and linguistically characterized as " real," with the geometry, itself linguistic, taken as correspondingly or representatively realistic, no matter in what way its propositions were specially called " abstract." In these realistic characterizations this situation and its included geometry may be compared with the prevailing local point-of-view as to human beings which takes the individual mentality, despite the fact that it is always before us in its full socialized imprint, as "real " — as an " inner " real — and depends upon it psychologically to dominate all description and construction. The geometries of mathematics have long passed beyond the stage of such one-way abstraction, of such one-type realistic presentation. The historical steps in the transition are well known. The realism was taken out of the parallel axiom and certain non-Euclidean geometries were constructed, but that was only one of the details of the development. Long before this, the Cartesian co-ordinates had appeared and facilitated functional interaction and co-operative development with algebra. Riemann discovered new cases of non-Euclidean geometry, and secured a new generalization for them all, while also originating the investigation of analysis situs. Möbius set up " elementary-related " configurations, and identified among them the one-sided surfaces. Grassmann proceeded n-dimensionally. Gibbs gave the vector its strong form for the use of physics by the aid of Grassmann space, establishing it fully as a mathematical " object " in its own right. These, along with many other innovations, including the appearance of the newer non-Riemannian geometries, have made geometry a possible form for all physical knowledge, so that finally we arrive at the present stage of search for some unified field theory. All of this greatly widened procedure, and all of its possibilities of further extension, are at the service of sociology, the instant that sociology can grasp its full field of materials in postulatory unified system for its work of investigation. The popular phrase " qualitative," as applied to certain of these geometries, in contrast with the older " quantitative " geometry, while of no direct linguistic value itself, is indicative of their possible scope.

Using the labels " abstract " and " concrete " for what little they are worth, we may inspect the presentations of discrete material things as concrete, the Newtonian physical space as a first abstraction, to which a concreteness or realness of its own came to be assigned, and the Euclidean geometry (although historically of earlier appearance than the Newtonian space) as a further abstraction. Using the presentation of discrete psychic men as concrete, we may similarly regard social space as an abstraction to which concreteness or realness may be assigned, and a possible formal development of this space in sociological space-configurations as a further abstraction.[38] Our proposition now is that the many geometries arising out of the primary Euclidean construction have so far generalized themselves that they have the promise of applicability to sociological work. Such an inspection, however, cancels the terms abstract and concrete, grasps all the developments which we have before us in one general linguistic-theoretical form, and seeks wholly consistency of interpretation, leading over from the first to the second diagrammatic scheme shown at the beginning of this section.

In this background we may examine the value of the constructions of dimensions and co-ordinates for sociology. It is common for sociologists to say that society is a many-dimensioned field. What the social dimensions are, or more properly what the most important social dimensions are for any specialized line of investigation, is our sociological problem in general. The search for precision in their analysis and use is the sociological space problem. Dimensions in this sense, though not under that name, have long been sought. A sociology setting forth individual, family, and state as basis for its interpretation uses, in effect, these three presentations as dimensions. Sociologies using basic human desires or instincts, or in a more elementary form depending on temperaments, take these factors for dimensions; they do not call them dimensions because they take them realistically, concretely, as forces or agents; but for us, seeing such materials as abstractions, and crude preliminary abstractions at that, they have the dimensional meaning. A theological system in terms of Deity and souls is dimensional, with variations in its additions of principles of Good and Evil, and of cosmic setting. Systems of Law of Nature, personal liberty systems, even school histories biased by national pride, have dimensional setting in this sense; and so also such fantastic devices as the " Nordic " for the organization of social knowledge.

The term co-ordinates describes a kind of instrument of precision for the study of dimensions and configurations. In a realistic background

[38] One may compare Carrel's remark in the article elsewhere cited that the cells and tissues of the older histology are abstractions, and that what the new cytology proposes is a truer abstraction. This manner of seeing, when applied to our own problem, spreads the label " abstract " over material things, and psychic men as well as over interpretative constructions of them. Carrel's insistence on the return to close observation of the " concrete event which a tissue is " is paralleled for sociology by a similar return to observation of the full complex of man-society-nature as the sole " concrete " for its reference.

of mind and nature with a dogmatic rendering of abstract and concrete, and a pervading vagueness as to what language is and does in such a setting, the co-ordinates of geometry have nothing to do with sociology. In the full linguistic setting and under the semantic search for consistency covering mathematics, physics, and the social sciences as well, systems of co-ordinates may be aimed at in social spaces with exactly the meaning and value they have in mathematics. For co-ordinates in society we may choose one, or two, or several structural lines which we obtain by analysis, or hope we are obtaining. We must then establish them by definitions in which all the elements are confined closely within one system of expression and study. The procedure might be somewhat as follows. In a given region of social space-time, say Europe-America from the consolidation of nations in Europe to the present day, select some characteristic which can be held to close definition as a first co-ordinate; then select some other for a second, and lay off a two-dimensional study, seeking whatever patterns may be found. Suppose for a clue to a first co-ordinate we take the term " cruelty." We inspect not a psychic quality, since no such quality ever has been defined in such a way that a man can be found who is wholly or purely cruel by its terms. We inspect instead social manifestations which under some psychological scheme might be attributed to some instinct or attribute of cruelty, but we inspect them as though the alleged instinct or attribute were itself an abstraction and a poor one at that, and we undertake in place of it our own form of abstraction. We analyze, finding cases in which one man inflicts physical pain directly upon another man; cases in which one man, say a ruler, inflicts pain through an agent, his gaoler, or executioner; and other cases of a still indirect nature as where an employer, paying starvation wages, inflicts pain on his employees. In all this, exact definition for the immediate purpose of even the term " physical pain " must also be sought. We may find other cases where the pain takes less and less a " physical " description, and more and more a " mental " description. Selecting one such definition, or combining several into a wider definition, we may establish spatial and temporal transitions in amount or intensity: and thus have a kind of social co-ordinate. For a second co-ordinate one may work similarly in terms of wealth, industrial organization, church membership, or religious intensity. One has then two lines of guidance through the social space-time, and may begin to establish configurations, or clarify configurations taken as found in ordinary vague discussion. In all of this one enters no field strange to sociology. What one does is to grasp all of his materials in one system, one social form, strip off irrelevancies, confine his procedure to postulation, and seek precision.

He gains accuracy in factual control, but sacrifices dogmatic insistence on validities.

Supposing now that upon the basis of numerous such studies as that suggested above we have established a number of dimensional lines for the organization of our social knowledge. The desire will be always with us to bring them into higher synthesis, and search will be made for correspondences, and, in especial, for characteristics common to the configurations which appear under different dimensional organizations. Here we will begin to work in a field which in a humble, tentative way is comparable to that of geometrical transformation. In geometry invariance under transformation is the highest assurance of firm texture of investigation. The very remoteness of sociological study from such firmness of texture is a reason why it must be characterized as sociological, and not as itself mathematical, no matter how well the mathematical precedents may aid it. Again, we have nothing before us that the sociologies have not already attempted, but we have the problems stripped down for closer interpretative study.

One special case of such sociological transformation between co-ordinates may be considered. It is that already indicated in Section 3 as necessary between descriptions in terms of vulgar space and alternative descriptions in terms of social space. The ordinary language of description, in which the raw materials of our sociological studies come to us, may be said to have as its dimensions Newtonian space, clock or calendar time, and the individual mind or person. The last of these is taken as an activity in contrast with the other two, which are regarded as comparatively inert; and the inadequacies and inefficiencies in its use have been repeatedly emphasized. Here we merely accept it as before us in current language, and as the main tool of that language for orientation of its reports in our particular field. Treating it in this way as one system of expression among many, as merely one possible set of sociological dimensions instead of as true and solid expression of reality, the development of a method of transformation from one type of expression to the other presents no difficulty. The essential is, as always, the stripping off of the crude realisms, and the substitution of consistency of expression as standard and guide; the abandonment of the superstitious belief in the magic power of conventional words as revealers of reality, and the substitution of the cold requirement that the " magic " either transform itself into full consistency of meaning or quit the field altogether.

On this basis we may now introduce numerical factors, much as geometry introduces them, for what they are worth. They are worth a very great deal to geometry, despite the fact that general mathematical analysis has not yet solved its own foundation problem as to just how the discrete number is to be interpreted in terms of the continuity point. Mathematics inserts a dictum to this effect, and the same can be done in the sociological study of social spaces. If one wishes, for example, to use census returns or other enumerations of estimates gathered under a Newtonian space form, one may apply them for what they are worth, for whatever value they may have in the presentation. In general the Newtonian space presentations may be brought over into constructions of social spaces as aspects of the system instead of as fixed exterior conditions.

I suspect now that a reader who has his footings in the older natural science and the older philosophy and psychology will make indignant protest to the effect that while the talk is about space and geometry the illustrations are all drawn from " activity," which he takes to be a category of wholly different nature. The immediate response to such a criticism is: " Consider the vector." I shall try, however, to make the situation clearer by a brief analysis of one of the most difficult problems in the range of scientific consistency, the problem, namely, of whole and part.

An individual is in one sense " part " of society; social life is, in another sense, " part " of individual life. In the first sense no man can say what the " whole " of society is; in the second sense no man can say what the " whole " of individual life is. The very terminology of parts and wholes is, in these applications, shot through with inconsistency. It has a certain reasonableness in middle ranges, as where we say that a judge is part of a court, or a court part of a government, but it has no consistency at all in generalization.

But do we have anywhere at all in the field of knowledge an interpretation of part-whole which is throughout consistent? It is very much to be doubted. Part-whole is just another way of characterizing those problems of mathematical foundations which were discussed in Part I of this paper in terms of finite-infinite, discrete-continuous, one and all, thing, relation, and operation. In mathematics, if anywhere, we should find consistency of meaning, and in mathematics exactly it is that the problems of consistency have become most desperate.

" Quantity " would at first sight seem a dependable tool for a construction of part-whole; but quantity proved so useless that it has long since been discarded by mathematicians for any of their more general purposes.[39] In a system of natural numbers, 1, 2, 3 . . . n, we have a system

[39] Russell, *Introduction to Mathematical Philosophy*, p. 195; Weyl, *Philosophie der Mathematik und Naturwissenschaft*, p. 50.

of specific defined parts, and of constructed relational wholes, so long as we hold to finites; the moment we proceed to the infinite whole of natural numbers, we have a confusion. Quite to the contrary with geometrical areas: here we take a presentation that we regard as a whole, and we can readily subdivide it finitely into parts, but when we proceed to the infinite subdivision our point-like part is a new order of presentation, and not a consistent part of such a whole as the kind we started with. When the mathematicians, as the result of the introduction of Alephs and Omegas by Cantor, were forced to closer consideration, they developed various logical interpretations, the *Mengen* and the *Elemente* of the Germans, the classes or sets and the members of the English. The result is seen in Russell's paradoxes of types, in Hilbert's *Stufen*, and in various dubious expedients and compromises such as Brouwer's private and peculiar version of the excluded middle and Fraenkel's *Beschränktheitsaxiom*.

If we pass to the part-whole problem of animal life, we find it in terms of anatomy and of physiological chemistry on the one side, and of vitalism on the other; and the issue is still a highly speculative and temperamental one for biologists, nowhere approaching scientific precision in its treatment. In the social field we must expect our part-whole problem to be still more complex and difficult. We so find it; but, further than that, we find that it is a problem which can in no way be evaded, if our investigations are to secure any consistency whatever. We cannot proceed in physical terms. We cannot proceed in terms of pure individual psychology. We must face our situations in their direct part-whole presentations. Much more intricate than the problems of mind in body are the problems of sovereignty in government, of government in society, and of society in men. To handle them we must carry our constructions backward and forward, so as to include and interpret at the same time the many other part-whole situations of the many other investigations and sciences which are themselves social developments. The mathematics of sociological investigation must therefore be a mathematics of social activities, and not of some rigid presentation of society or of individual man, and of physical and psychical nature, as separately identifiable facts or parts.

An important work in one of the more highly developed fields of sociological investigation, namely, pure economics, may serve to exhibit very clearly the possibilities in the construction of sociological spaces, although it is far from the thought of its author to recognize any such possibilities; his attitude being rather that he and his fellow mathematicians and economists have succeeded in isolating a region of sound knowledge, a region which should be carefully kept clear from all the vague strivings and yearnings known to him as sociology. This is Professor Griffith C. Evans' book *Mathematical Introduction to Economics.*

Professor Evans does not make his start with any assumed characteristics of human beings, nor with any dogma of society. Instead he sets before himself certain presentations, such as commodity, cost, quantity, and unit of time, and examines them under certain defined hypotheses for three central economic situations, namely, monopoly, association, and competition. He secures for his investigation certain dimensions, namely, money-value and time, and for each commodity a dimension of that commodity, quantity: and sets up the heuristic principle that under these dimensions laws may be written invariant to a change of units. He at once gets rid of " wealth " in the sense of a total of material things, and of " pleasure " in the sense of a possible psychical maximum. Neither the pleasure nor the material things are dimensional to his study, and both may be passed over. In other words, what he in effect does is to take direct " social " presentations as his material of investigation and as his basis of study, and to discard entirely, as lacking significance for his purposes, all of the physical, and also all of the psychical, forms of characterization. He thus develops formulas for situations concerning taxation, tariffs, rent, foreign exchange, interest, the equation of exchange, and price indices, directly within the range of his chosen data and dimensions. It is not until two-thirds of his book has been written that he pauses to ask questions concerning " general concepts and methods," and when he does come to such questions in his Chapter X, his essential observations are: Do not hope to gain generalization by creating complication; seek it instead by examining the limitations of the various theories, by clarifying assumptions, and by the systematic separation of different economic situations. To stress " bases " or " springs " of economic action, he points out, leads to attempts to organize them through unification, and unification under any such term as " pleasure " amounts simply to canceling them out of the investigation altogether. With this once clear he offers a brilliant discussion of utility in fully social terms; and only upon this basis, and as a very special case, does he examine marginal utility and the conditions of exchange between two individuals. His more general theory, in which he makes use of functionals, very significantly studies economic systems in compartments, with that compartment or set of compartments relating to money as one of the most important.

In all of this we find Professor Evans working within the frame of an economic space-time, and in a way that fully accords with the approach set up in this paper; and in such construction and development he represents not some peculiar aberration of theory but the consistent forward advance of pure economics. We do not, however, find him recognizing that what he is doing in economics is exactly what must be done in all departments of sociology, nor that the economic space-time which he uses is just one particular specification of a much more general system of sociological space-times. All sociological investigation that is outside of his own field he is content to relegate to practitioners of a wholly different kind of inquiry, in which the discarded " springs of action," " pleasures," " mass psychology," and other psychological presentations may be manipulated in any desired way, for all he knows or cares. But economics is social, and so also are all the other investigations of society, and what proves the efficient treatment in the one will most probably prove an efficient treatment in the others, regardless of the extent to which it, at any particular stage, may be advanced. As it is, Professor Evans leaves his economic construction as though it may possibly be, and indeed very probably is, a pure or absolute human system; although the very thing that his construction next needs is a setting in the wider reaches of social space-time, within which the chosen postulational procedure which establishes his particular economic space-time may be identified. That means the determination of wider social dimensions with respect to which his own dimensions may be organized by further extension of the very methodological approach which he himself uses. In all of such work, the discovery of fact, the development of theory, and the consideration of method, are phases of one procedure; and if that procedure takes now one direction, now another; if it passes back and forth inspecting the psychical from the physical point of view, the physical from the psychical, and both from the social; if it goes in a circle, that circle is one of full consistency of expression, not the vicious circle raised by the implicit realisms of the ancient logic.

CHAPTER SIX

The Positive and the Logical*

One is tempted to look upon the positive and the logical somewhat as one looks upon the quick and the dead. Yet the issue is hardly that sharp. Viability has strange possibilities and varied forms, and must often be appraised with an eye directed as much toward the environment as toward the claimant organism. Stretching the application of the world "viable" to complexes of behavior such as the philosophies and theories of knowledge, we may ask: Is the combination of the positive and the logical in logical positivism viable? And is this logical positivism itself as it stands either positive or logical?

These are interesting questions and no doubt endlessly debatable, though I have no thought whatever of entering the lists of the disputants. I find, however, that a certain amount of light can be thrown upon them by a method as elementary and as humble as that which a high-school student is taught to employ in his first contacts with microscope and bug. We shall try such a method, jot down certain observations in our notebook, and study our reports as they come, with no pretense to deep or soulful understanding.

Logical positivism is an activity or behavior of certain men who call themselves logical positivists;[1] it is their highly characteristic behavior in the region of their most active interest. The logical positivists are alive, and the viability of their theory is dependent upon their continuing life and activity and upon that of such successors as they may have. We may ask whether men of their manner of thought and action are on the way to enjoy successful and widening participation in the great human activities of knowing and of interpreting the known. We may ask whether their behaviors are of a type fitted to maintain themselves in the kinds of environments we may anticipate for their immediate future.

* From *Philosophy of Science*, Vol. III, No. 4 (October, 1936), pp. 472–85.
[1] Logical Positivism is the name most widely current, and it has been approved by Carnap, although he himself more commonly speaks of Logical Analysis and of Physicalism. Other current namings are The New Positivism, Philosophic Analysis, [Logical Empiricism], and Logic of Science.

The material that I shall here examine is limited to five contributions to *Philosophy of Science* by Carnap, Feigl, and Blumberg.[2] The inquiry itself is one phase of a wider inquiry undertaken to appraise the present status of the interpretation of science, for which the file of this magazine offered an appropriate assemblage of materials. Various strange situations were found, involving often astonishing abuses of words, even in papers purporting to deal with symbolic logic. Among these the procedures of Carnap and his associates present but a single illustration.

Taking our materials, i.e., the papers above described, just as they come, I apply two tests which I make as simple and as little exacting as possible in the hope that they will not exceed what any reasonable man will think may be required in any serious discussion of science and of knowledge.

Logical. If a procedure is to be regarded as logical, its advocate may not within the limits of any one essay declare a proposition to be fundamental, use it as such, and then later on casually introduce a protecting clause to the effect that the proposition itself may of course be defective or perhaps even false. Nor, when he makes an assertion, may he follow this later within the same essay by its contradictory, without explaining the transition.

Positive. If a procedure is to be regarded as positive, it must employ materials of investigation and adopt attitudes of inquiry comparable to those used by the successful sciences of our era — the ones we most generally recognize and describe as positive with respect to the form of the knowledge they offer. It may not merely steal the use of a popular name. It must, in particular, exclude the use of all fairies, spooks, and spirits, whether fair or foul.

Lethal. Where a construction shows itself defective by both tests, and where, moreover, the defects of the first type can be directly traced to improper procedures of the second type, we may fairly regard the whole construction as an inadequate form of human behavior, lethal in its type, and doomed to disappear.

It may as well be stated at once that the evil spirit we shall find at work in the selected papers before us is one that manifests itself in the use of the word " concept." The " concept " as our logical positivists employ it proclaims a reserved right on their part to " really mean " something different from what they say. Their " concepts " may thus be taken as marking gaps, or holes, in their language — places where

[2] R. Carnap, " On the Character of Philosophic Problems " (I, 5), " Meaning, Assertion and Proposal " (I, 359); H. Feigl, " The Logical Character of the Principle of Induction " (I, 20), " Logical Analysis of the Psychophysical Problem: a Contribution of the New Positivism " (I, 420); A. E. Blumberg, " The Nature of Philosophic Analysis " (II, 1).

words fail and where the expounder waves a magic wand to assure us nevertheless that all is well.

As to the status more generally of this word " concept," we may remind ourselves that it derives from the old language of " consciousness " and " mind," and that all formal definitions of it are in terms of some " mental " that is a " not-physical." Its peculiarity is that it is in common daily use by men who have long since abandoned all belief in any such " mental "; they take it for granted, apparently without once asking themselves what expressly it is that they are talking about. They face some kind of a " factual " situation; they find the word " concept " not only convenient but eminently respectable; they proceed to use it. The result is that " concept " becomes a weasel word in philosophy's service far more efficient in deception than any word the amateurs of the political party platforms have evolved. One can find it with as many as half a dozen distinguishable applications in a single paper. While indicating sometimes a " bit of consciousness," or " a thought," or an assumption of " precise meaning," at other times it can be directly replaced in the text by the word " word " itself. It may offer any desired combination of, or stage of transition between, " mind " and " word." It may cover sentence, proposition, theory, or doctrine. The part it plays for logical positivists is therefore not unique, but merely symptomatic of a disease of language, widespread in our era.

The purpose of *Philosophy of Science* as announced by the editor in his introductory statement (I, 1) [3] was to aid in the clarification of philosophy and science, and perhaps in their unification through such typical projects as " the examination of fundamental concepts [4] and presuppositions in the light of the positive results of science, systematic doubt of the positive results, and a thoroughgoing analysis and critique of logic and of language." Upon all of these questions Carnap and his associates have had much to say, and Carnap's paper " On the Character of Philosophic Problems " was well indicated for the leading place in the first issue. It was Carnap's emphatic assertion, his main thesis, that by " purely formal procedure " the logic of science can " finally arrive at the answering " of all connotative questions (I, 9). This " connotative " of Carnap's (in the German, *inhaltliche*) covers all issues of what we most generally describe as " meanings," since he places the *inhaltliche* in sharp opposition to the *formale*, and expressly defines the latter as covering the study of

---

[3] References in the text are to volume and page of *Philosophy of Science*.

[4] " Concept," of course, may be honorably used. In the present instance it stands for " that which is written about philosophy and science," while the " fundamental " and the " presuppositions " serve to concentrate attention on those regions of the wide field that seem of greatest significance for purposes of clarification and unification.

symbols and propositions "*without reference to the meaning*" (I, 9). In plain everyday language Carnap asserts that all questions of meaning can be answered without reference to meaning; or, in more erudite language, that a symbolic procedure stripped of all implications of meaning will be humanity's final resort for solving all problems of the import of knowledge.

Remember now that we are to examine only the materials immediately on the table before us. If we do this in a highly " formal " way, Carnap certainly should not be the man to object. It does not matter to us what Carnap writes elsewhere nor how he may modify his construction from year to year; our only concern is the integrity of the particular specimen of work before us. It is as if the boy in the laboratory studying the bug should disregard all speculation as to its place in Nature's Mighty Scheme, and confine himself to such simple observations as how well its wings are fastened to its body, and whether its alimentary canal is open at both ends.

We begin by applying our first simple test, which we labeled with the word "logical." And here we can follow a lead already taken in the pages of the magazine by John Dewey. Dewey read Carnap's paper and at once asked him certain pointed questions which, to anyone interested in the simpler "facts of life," have devastating import (I, 237). Carnap gave no sign of attention either to facts or import, but instead spun the web of his reply (I, 359) in a manner much nearer the medieval than the modern. Since questions and answers with accompanying page citations are directly available to all readers who have this magazine in hand, I may be permitted to paraphrase and condense.

Dewey first cited Carnap's assertion that by "purely formal procedure" the logic of science can "finally arrive" at the answering of all *inhaltliche* questions. He then set side by side with it three of Carnap's further statements as follows: mathematical meanings derive from empirical considerations; statements of fact are synthetic [5] (that is, neither analytic nor contradictory, but involving definite truth or falsity); the very selection of a linguistic form on which to rely (such as *formale* or *inhaltliche* itself) requires an empirical decision.

Dewey was very gentle and considerate in his comment. He merely said that Carnap's position " it not clear to me beyond a certain point." But he proceeded to show that among Carnap's tabulated illustrations,

---

[5] Carnap gives his distinction between "analytic" and "synthetic" on p. 53 of *Philosophy and Logical Syntax*, 1935, a small book covering more fully the ground of his two contributions to *Philosophy of Science*. "The terms," he says, "have already been used in traditional philosophy; they are especially important in the philosophy of Kant; *but up till now they have not been exactly defined*" (italics mine).

seventeen in number, the *formale* expressions were apt to be the ones with precision of " meaning," while their *inhaltliche* alternatives were too often either meaningless or just vaguely ambitious. And beyond that he was surprised to find Carnap, at the end of his paper, after having built entirely on a severance of *formale* from *inhaltliche,* calmly remarking that there was nothing fundamental at all about his distinction between the two approaches.

Carnap in reply admitted a lack of clarity in his fifteen-page essay. He said this was because " concepts " were necessary which were far too technical for use in any such place. Even in personally addressing Dewey he was compelled to fall back upon descriptions which he admitted to be " somewhat inexact." He " distinguished " three sorts of sentences — " real object-sentences," " pseudo-object-sentences," and " syntactical sentences ": the first of which deal with " extra-lingual objects " (elsewhere called " empirical matter "), the second " deal seemingly " with them (although actually with " the lingual signs of those objects "), while the third " deal with lingual expressions." He assured Dewey that the whole distinction between *formale* and *inhaltliche* concerned only those sentences " which deal with language," as though that were extenuation enough for factual falsity.

We have here an authoritative sample of Carnap's " logical analysis." The question is whether it is entitled to be called " positive " ? More particularly we may ask: Does the array of sorts of sentences which Carnap " distinguishes " offer us a *positive* classification of linguistic materials in any sound sense of the word " positive "? How far can we outline " operations " or establish " facts " to correspond? How far can we so much as attempt this?

The first difficulty we find lies in the criteria of classification, one sort of sentence being identified with respect to language, another with respect to what *is* not-language, and a third with respect to what *seems to be* not-language. We have here " sentences," " objects," and " seemings " used for tests in classifying sentences themselves, and we may expect much confusion in the search for applicable " operations."

Next to attract attention is the peculiarity of the hyphenation. Order the groups as follows: syntactical sentences, real object-sentences, pseudo-object-sentences.[6] Observe this closely. You will find that it would

[6] This manner of hyphenation is not accident or error in hurried magazine publication; it is repeated in the book just cited, p. 61 (table and accompanying text). A typical effort to throw light on the " pseudo-object-sentences " is as follows: " We may call the quality of being a thing-designation a *parallel syntactical quality* to the quality of being a thing " *(Ibid.,* p. 62). The objection here is not nearly so much to the highly formal terminology Carnap uses, as it is to the heavy burden he imposes on the wholly informal term " quality."

take several pages to bring out all the issues the hyphens evade. The "syntactical" is not balanced against the "object" in a first stage of classification, nor the "real" against the "pseudo" in a second stage; it is not even clear which stage has precedence; no "genus" can be identified for the three "species." The hyphens are disingenuous; they are Ethiopians — "conceptual" Ethiopians, so to speak — in the linguistic woodpile. They mark, not classification, but casuistry.

So much for the "syntax" of Carnap's procedure. Inspect it now rather for its "content." He fails to show that his test, i.e., what the sentences are "about," is dominant for his problem; other important possibilities for ordering are available, but we may pass this over. Most troublesome is the fact that he posits his "real object-sentences" and his "syntactical sentences" in such conceptual purity that it would be difficult for him (personally I would say impossible) ever to exhibit a specimen of either. All the interest of inquiry lies in the intermediate territory, and here the procedure is deliberately that of facing both ways. The reader will note (a) that instead of clearing the presentations from the difficulties of the "seeming" and the "actual," this complexity is expressly maintained; (b) that the phrase "material mode of speech" is here applied because of its verbal suggestion of empirical matter on the one side and of formal mode on the other; and (c) that the parallelism of "being a thing" with "being a thing-sign" is another bit of prestidigitation between matter and mode. In effect Carnap arranges a logical keyboard to be played by both hands in the pious wish that in time the right hand may come to "know" what the left hand is doing. Right hand plays language-language with a permitted shift from a formal to a material mode. Left hand plays thing-language with a set of pseudo-thing variations. The organ stop marked "parallel syntactical quality," when pulled out at the right moment by the right man, is supposed to make "logical analysis" become "positive."

One further conflict in Carnap's statements may be noted, though its nature is much like what has preceded. In connection with his assertion that all science is language in the sense of a system of propositions (I, 8, 14), he maintains that language is a "calculus" and that its formal rules of procedure are "mechanical operations" (I, 10). Then later he remarks that "mere calculating about" is not enough (I, 19). Without the first attitude he could not set up his main thesis, nor undertake his proposed sentence-classification. Without the second he could get nowhere after setting his thesis up. The status is this: A certain "parallelism" of ancient lineage is disclaimed and expelled. Later, however, hobbled and veiled, it is admitted through the back door. We are told that this does not matter, for now it is fully under linguistic control. " The distinguishing of the formal and the material modes of speech concerns only those sentences which deal with language " (I, 360). There it is justified, there it rules, there it characterizes " logical analysis "; otherwise, incidentally, it is false.[7]

Carnap, of course, himself sees unity and coherence in all this; and we must seek the locus of his confidence. But first observe how powerful that confidence is. Dewey had asked him a further question, one concerning the distinction he had set up between " assertions " and " proposals." He could not answer this question, but he assured Dewey nevertheless that the distinction was sound, and that his criterion could be applied, " true or false," to any sentence, " provided of course the sentence S_1 as well as the whole connection to which it belongs is given in a perfectly correct and complete form " (I, 360). Here is a requirement which a disciple may no doubt accept, but which to the ordinary inquirer midway in the passage of our lives may perhaps seem an ideal just a shade too bright and good. Nevertheless it exhibits Carnap's reliance, his typical reliance, in all his work.

Proceed, Carnap tells us in effect, with an infinite series of regressive " meanings," being very careful at every stage to strip yourself of factual or experiential debasement; make every " meaning " a " symbol," and purify the symbol so thoroughly of all meaning that you become sure it has " no meaning at all "; then in the end you will secure final and complete control of all " meanings " and of all knowledge. He casts this " proposal," this device, up against the logical sky in the form of a huge calculating machine. He does not, however, assert it to be independent and absolute perpetual motion. It has to be produced in some way, and it evidently has some kind of an operator. What operator? His operator is in plain view, even though its head is buried in the verbal sands. It is what in mathematical analogy we may call the " point-soul," or in physical analogy the " particle-mind." [8] It is that from which everything starts and to which everything comes back, the limit of all possible statement. From it arise the verbal flights through which knowledge is to be acquired and appraised. In it lie the attributes of truth on which Carnap relies even when all his words and sentences prove false. It alone is

[7] Compare Blumberg's blunt assertion (II, 3): "There are two basic groups: assertions of syntax and assertions of fact. This dichotomy follows from the nature of language."

[8] The " asperities of a marriage between Empiricism and Solipsism " are noted by the translator of Carnap's essay " The Unity of Science," p. 12.

the authority whereby the logician may dare to soar above all those situations which currently we regard as experientially factual or as approximations to fact.

This operator of Carnap's possesses a tool — a magic tool — the "concept." The "concept" does everything the operator wants it to do. When he wishes, the concept garbs itself as a "word"; then the system deals with "language." When he wishes otherwise, then the concept transforms itself into "meaning," and the system runs far away from the "language" of its primary confession of faith. By means of the "concept," itself a word, every word is empowered to take shifting values — concept, meaning, symbol, proposition, language, science, even "no meaning at all." The intention of the "concept" is pure, and everything must come home in the end to roost on the wrist of its master, the point-soul; then why bother with minor temporary inconsistencies, or tests, or practical "operations" en route? [9]

Carnap and his followers take advantage, nevertheless, of whatever opportunity opens to associate their procedure with Bridgman's operations; at times they draw support from him, at others they allot him approval as an earnest seeker, though of the lower caste of science.[10] Bridgman makes "concept" his keyword and brings in a credo of the solipsistic self like a refrain to his writing. The difference between Bridgman and the logical positivists is, nevertheless, almost antipodal. What Bridgman *does* with concept and self is to bring them under harsh control by physical operations of the most advanced laboratory type. What the logical positivist *does* with them is to run to them for help whenever he gets into trouble.

Point-souls of the type Carnap uses are largely discredited in more recent psychological and sociological inquiry, and they are wholly discredited by the *phenomenon* of Gestalt; but they are so deeply embedded in the German language with its terminologies of *Geist* and *Seele*, *Ver-*

[9] Matter-of-fact examination of Carnap's "concepts" of *Inhalt*, *Gehalt*, and *Folgerung* will give other interesting examples of evasiveness in conceptual procedure. *Folgerung* is said to be "quite different" from material implication, since the latter depends only on truth-values while the former "is not quite determined by the truth-values" (I, 11). *Gehalt* is "a purely formal concept"; nevertheless it "corresponds completely to what we mean when we (in a vague manner) are accustomed to speak of the 'meaning' (*Inhalt*) of a proposition" (I, 12–13). Carnap's creed of conceptual infallibility has been expressed by him as follows: "Die Begriffe sollen aus gewissen Grundbegriffen stufenweise abgeleitet, 'konstituiert' werden, so dass sich ein Stammbaum der Begriffe ergibt, in dem jeder Begriff seinen bestimmten Platz findet." (*Der logische Aufbau der Welt*, 1928, p. 1.)

[10] *See* Feigl, I, 20; I, 424. Compare also two papers in *Journal of Philosophy*, 1931, one by Blumberg and Feigl, p. 281, and one by Blumberg and Boas, p. 544. In the latter we are told that Bridgman calls his theory of meaning "operationalism," that it is "a technique for building concepts," and that as such it "can be shown to be a special case" of logical positivism. For these writers it is "definition" which "formulates operations."

nunft and *Verstand,* that linguistically they dominate there beyond all suggestion of observational search or test. Even the experimental work of Gestalt is most often construed in one or other of their forms; even the Marxian is still bound. Carnap is of their inner faith. The last stronghold of such point-souls is in logic, and there the issue will be fought out. What concerns us of course is no question of "reality," whether such souls actually "exist" or not being of no direct importance. We are concerned strictly with the phenomena before us, namely, those linguistic behaviors in which point-souls whether by direct assertion or implicit use are prominent factors.

We have one more astonishing observation to make with regard to this point-soul of Carnap's as it actually performs. As itself concept and bearer of concepts, and as sole point of ultimate reference, it refuses to remain a point. It splits. It becomes a two-faculty soul of a type so ancient and elsewhere so discredited that it is astounding to find it surviving and strongly entrenched in a recent logic. The proposition about the "two languages" which the logical positivists make and all their distinctions of data and constructs arise in this way. Our own discussion has covered this situation in a different linguistic form, and it will be enough here to give footnote reference to other comments upon it in the pages of *Philosophy of Science*.[11]

If we take Carnap's *formale* and *inhaltliche* out of the rigid "conceptual" forms in which he propounds and contrasts them, and if we examine them in everyday life where although Carnap recognizes their union he has no "logical" use for it, we find our separations of them all temporary and provisional, and the return always necessary to their combined behavioral process. We forever strive to formalize our expressions as fully as we can, and to succeed we must limit. But also we strive forever to give our expression as rich, as complete, as factual a reference as we can. And here each success means a new destruction of

---

[11] Schilpp accuses the logical positivists of refusing to permit any analysis of the concept of the "given," even though it is fundamental in their construction, and even though the analysis of fundamental concepts is declared by them to be the sole legitimate work of philosophy. "The 'given,'" he says, "is the point where the logical positivists turn mystics" (II, 129). Weinberg (II, 387) from a different behavioral base, with wholly different objectives, and by the use of professionally logical techniques, attacks a similar problem in the case of Wittgenstein's logical simples; this criticism is pertinent since Wittgenstein's attempted rigor is the historical source from which the degeneracy of logical positivism stems. Stevens (III, 100), speaking for psychologists, finds the dichotomy between data and constructs artificial. Malisoff (II, 339) notes the "black magic" in the "intersubjective" of the positivists (for a case of its use, see Feigl, I, 433 ff). Kattsoff finds Carnap's construction "misleading and doomed to failure" (III, 70) though this is mainly on the ground that it is a two-valued logic. Other comments will be found at I, 325, 331, 482; II, 256, 273, 295, 364; III, 124.

the old "conceptual" identifications; it means the widening and organizing and systematizing of our knowledge. Carnap has every right to make his split, and to make it as sharp and rigid as he can. But this is the right to postulate and to test. He cannot expect to convince the world by fiat or by spiritist appeal or by glowing picture of ultimate ideal success. He must work within the stream of knowledge and within that portion of the stream within which we find ourselves today. It is this which can and will guarantee factual orientation on the one hand and heightened consistency of expression on the other — the two hand in hand.

The papers of Feigl and Blumberg are strikingly similar to Carnap in the characteristics we have been considering. Feigl's logical positivism results in verbal anarchy. Blumberg surpasses him by expressly recognizing that such is the outcome, while at the same time holding as firmly as ever to the basic principles of the creed.

Feigl proposes to exhibit " the strict identity of the 'mental' life with certain processes in the 'physical' world " and to show that this is " not a matter of belief . . . but a truth capable of logical demonstration " (I, 420). His confidence is so great that he declares (I, 444) that if his analysis leaves any riddle unsolved " then it is an insoluble one that cannot be expressed as a significant question in any logically legitimate language." His procedure, he says, will be by way of " a metaphysically neutral logical analysis of fundamental concepts " (I, 420). He uses an " epistemological subject "; he declares this to be a necessity for logic since it is the only source of answer to the question: " How do we justify our factual assertions? " (I, 428); nevertheless he protests vehemently all the time that it is a fiction.[12] He disclaims all dogma that makes such a subject " individual," but he says that in use it inevitably becomes " individual," and that in no other form is it possible. If this is " solipsistic," says Feigl, it is " only in the *methodological* sense, which is metaphysically strictly neutral " (I, 429). In other words Feigl exorcises metaphysics, but goes right ahead with " fundamental concepts," " epistemological subjects," isolated " individuals," and whatever else he wishes, all under the name of " logic " and of " method." He gets rid of some of the spoiled chicks of metaphysics, and makes a great virtue of it, but he builds a gilded temple over the metaphysical incubator, and proclaims a priestly rule in the name of the logical and of the positive.

In various other ways the dangers of the " conceptual " procedure are

---

[12] Another case in which Feigl deliberately adopts a fiction as a " necessity " for logic is that of " form " and " content " (I, 440). This, he says, is a radical dualism, it is the only radical dualism he acknowledges, and it is a " very important but nevertheless artificial philosophical abstraction."

The Positive and the Logical

demonstrated in Feigl's pages.[13] He begins, for example, by declaring " perceptions, thoughts, desires, dreams " to be " empirical existences " — data that all trained people can agree upon under the very same tests that are applied to " tables, trees, people, stars. . . ." etc. (I, 423). He winds up by turning the " physical " and the " mental " into two separate " symbolic systems," " universes of discourse, characterized by their logical syntax " (I, 442). In the course of his development for these " two languages," both under the aegis of a " language about languages," he arrives at the following sentences which we may cite without further comment:

" The physical language is *retranslatable* into the language of data " (I, 430).
" The physical language is not only translatable into the language of data but also vice versa " (I, 435).
" Mutual translatability means nothing but identity of structure " (I, 436).
" The two languages have incompatible syntaxes . . . they are structurally completely disparate " (I, 439).

Blumberg uses the title " Philosophic Analysis " for his form of logical positivism. I will set down its characteristics as literally as I can in the immediate terms of its presentation. He tells us that we must say " verify " (but if we do not like to say " verify," then we may say " confirm "; II, 4). If we " confirm," however, we must be prepared to admit all factual statements as " at least theoretically capable of verification," which means that such statements must permit themselves to be " completely translated " into " atomic propositions " (but if we do not believe in " atomic propositions," then we may " take the terms ' simple,' ' ultimate,' ' basic,' and ' atomic ' in a relative and not an absolute sense "; II, 5).[14] Proceeding thus he quickly finds " true definition " and " correct usage " in close quarters, but it is wholly wrong to attempt to equate them; instead we may carefully say: " The analysis which yields the definition will be *correct* if the definition does actually render the usage examined " (II, 7). All this, however, is merely " description " and philosophers must rise to " prescription," though when they get there they

---

[13] In another paper Feigl comparably handles " the principle of induction " of which he says " as long as there is knowledge . . . it will be its inescapable guiding maxim " (I, 28). One may note as characteristic his frequent assertions of what *must be,* as, pp. 26-7, for the " ground floor of knowledge," for atomic propositions, and for the possibility of psychology; his certainty that the principle of induction is to be explained by a frequency theory of probability, even though the latter is not yet achieved (I, 25); and his many struggles to reformulate Bridgman's " operations " through un-Bridgmanlike terms such as prescript, prescriptive rule, regulative maxim and the principle of a procedure (I, 20, 27).

[14] Blumberg's statement (II, 5) as to what " completely analyzed " would mean in a relativistic sense " at-a-given-level-of-atomicity " makes good collateral reading. Interesting also is the way " sign," " signify," and " significance " are used (II, 4).

have nothing to rely on except " considerations of utility, convenience, and aesthetic value " (II, 7); nevertheless they may in the end come to " speak of *the* meaning of a sign, *the* correct analysis of an assertion." While all this is " difficult in practice " it is " simple in theory " and will finally result in a substitution of the " concrete, practical " for the " vague, exalted, mystical " (II, 8).

The above somewhat astonishing outcome of " philosophic analysis " flows professedly from " the nature of language " which involves a " fundamental distinction " (II, 3) between statements of syntax and statements of fact. The parentage of this linguistic base itself is in point-soul and concept. Blumberg does not use the word " concept "[15] in his paper, and abstention here, unless it is a minor treachery, is always a favorable sign. His stress is heavy on the behaviorally phrased inquiry: " In what ways do people use a certain sign? " His outcome is close to immolating point-soul and concept alike, and by that test we may say that it offers something that a normal scientific investigator would regard as a fair, even though still crude, starting point for his inquiry. One may even anticipate on his own showing that he, or some other inquirer in similar state, will soon strip off the apparatus of logical positivism in order to undertake direct and positive investigation.

It is hardly necessary for me to say that with the great objectives of the logical positivists — the expulsion of metaphysics, and the development of a linguistic frame for appraisal and organization — I am in the fullest sympathy. What is criticized in the present paper is solely some of the detail of workmanship.

---

[15] He uses " notion " once, and otherwise distributes the work of the word among " term," " assertion," " sign," " meaning," " usage " and " definition."

CHAPTER SEVEN

Physicists and Fairies*

John Jay Chapman to William James: "You said something about a *concept*. Now what is a concept? ... *Are you sure that there is such a thing?* If ... the story of one of these concepts were brought before you, would you not ... quench and dissipate it, and show it to be a mere mist and vagary and never-twice-alike will o' the wisp? ... I can just imagine your polite 'not proven.' ... But when you get on your tripod, you go puffing out these things at the top of the smokestack in perfect unconcern." (*Harper's Monthly Magazine*, December, 1936, p. 52)

William James to John Jay Chapman: "A certain witness at a poisoning case was asked how the corpse looked. 'Pleasant like and foaming at the mouth' was the reply. A good description of you describing philosophy. ... There are concepts, anyhow." (*Letters of William James*, II, 321)

I

Fairies

When the layman reads a book or two of popularized physics and then moves solemnly forth, as occasionally happens, to expound some comprehensive doctrine purporting to be built directly out of the materials he has picked up, the type of comment which the physicist will make is plain enough in advance. But why does it so rarely occur to the physicist that others may think of his epistemologizing much what he is sure to think of their quantizing?

The odds for intelligent statement are all in favor of the outsider and against the physicist. Physics offers the world a large amount of firm knowledge. But the philosophical and psychological sectors of inquiry have nothing of that kind to offer. They are at best in a Copernican, perhaps rather in a Ptolemaic, stage; their keenest investigators know this, and from time to time we find one or another of them breathing the hope that now at last his science is attaining some measure of Galilean directness and simplicity.[1]

The objection is not at all to either physicist or psychologist going into the other's territory, nor to his using as best he can what he finds

* From *Philosophy of Science*, Vol. V, No. 2 (April, 1938) pp. 132-65.
[1] Thus: J. R. Kantor, *Principles of Psychology*, 1924, vol. I, p. xvi; Kurt Lewin, "The Conflict between Aristotelian and Galilean Modes of Thought in Psychology," *J. Gen. Psychol.*, 1931, vol. 5, 141-177.

there. The two fields of work are drawing closer, problems of increasing difficulty are arising, and aid from many sources is needed. The risk is great, but the forays into surrounding fields are apt rather to increase in the near future than to decline. What needs criticism is rather a gullibility in accepting without factual check materials that are tricky enough in the hands of their primary users; and a solemnity in taking a dogmatic stand upon issues which are so obscure, even to the philosophers, psychologists, and logicians who debate them, that these gentry themselves rarely profess to understand one another when their arguments run to a finish.

Psychology — at least the kind of psychology that the physicist is most apt to get his fingers on — deals mostly with fairies, sprites, and spooks. Some of our psychologists, rhetorically speaking, are born fairy-minded, others lapse into it, while still others have fairy-mindedness thrust upon them; it is almost a necessity for their academic and professional survival.[2] I have not the slightest objection to a dainty Titania or a merry Till Eulenspiegel when the time is ripe, but these stodgy spooks that parade the field of modern inquiry in solemn pomp are another matter altogether. They are reminiscent of the mercury of the philosophers which purported to be the soul or essence of ordinary mercury, of vitreous earths, and of volatile principles; they are somewhat less reputable than was, in its day, phlogiston, the principle of inflammability — not fire itself, but that principle of fire by which combustible bodies burned.

The particular spook I propose to examine in this paper is the concept. This is the one that physicists take so confidingly and regularly, as if by common assent, into their households.[3] The "whence and what art thou?" they do not ask; the "execrable shape" they do not suspect. They never seek to get a specimen in hand. The traditional philosophical and psychological abracadabra suffices to compel their belief. A word or two will be said later about the metaphysical pit from which the concept was first hoisted, but in the meantime the interchange between Chapman and James placed at the head of this essay will suffice for a warning that all the sailing is not so plain.

[2] The psychologists often try to camouflage their fairies. The physicist usually takes his in primitive forms. The difference, however, is not great.

[3] Those who have only casual acquaintance with the word "concept" will be surprised both at the extent and at the chaos of its use. Among twenty-two contributors to two issues of *Philosophy of Science* in 1936, eighteen used the word from one to forty times each. Of the others, one used a still cruder word as substitute, two had very short contributions, and only one was notable for abstention. Classifications of its application or "meaning," based on a wider study of contributions, gave (a) slipshod, (b) impressionistic, (c) dishonestly evasive, (d) honestly hesitant, and (e), in the very rare case, cautiously constructive with respect to "postulate" and "theory." Logicians were the worst offenders, exhibiting at times incoherences of so criminal a type that, in comparison, the exhibits to be offered later in this paper drop to the level of petty misdemeanors.

II

Facts

Physics deals with facts. Fact, conversely, is what physics establishes. Thus our physical knowledge stands securely as our soundest knowledge. These statements, separately or together, in one manner of emphasis or another, have long stood firm for the range of our inquiries into " nature."

Modern relativity and the quantum have brought difficulties; but the very difficulties are invigorating; they enable us to inspect more closely than ever before the issues of " factuality " itself. These issues display themselves in three historical stages, all of which, of course, have correlates at hand contemporaneously for our examination. The first is that in which ordinary perceptions under ordinary descriptions, such as rising suns, flowing waters, and smashing stones, are taken as basically factual; the second is that in which, upon a framework of superfactual space and time, the Newtonian lengths, durations, and masses, and the velocities, accelerations, and forces take rank as the most assured " facts " of the universe; the third, finally, is the very recent stage in which the great superfact itself is brought back to its original dependence upon observer or observing mechanism, and in which, more annoyingly still, determinate positions and momentums, when jointly sought, demand capacities from the observer greater than he is able, under sound rules of workmanship, fully to provide.

I spare the reader expansion of these statements or even any attempt at precision for them, and content myself with remarking, (a) that in the first stage the " fact " was always " experienced fact " so far as the individual observer was concerned, however rigorously " externalized " it was in its description, and that it always involved the tacit assumption that the individual experiencer was a good center for the universe and a good guarantor of actualities, however trivial he might be otherwise; (b) that, in the second stage, the grandiose absolutism was merely a provisional isolation of certain phases of the experienced fact in order to get better working control of other phases; and (c) that, in the third stage, not only do the reputed absolutes again find their way back into ordinary life from whence they came, but the earlier rigidities of externalization are themselves dissolved, and this with no harm to the virility of the " facts " — *teste* the study progress the photon makes into domestic service.

Much excited discussion is natural in such a situation as this, with epistemological optimisms and epistemological pessimisms entering a new phase of their ancient war. Such discussions arise, however, in the narrow background of the conventions of the generation, and I confess to little worry over them or their outcomes. I have read a book, and I know that the excited armies of words march up the hill and then march down again, and that the pillars of the temple do not fall. The fact-finders in person look tolerantly on, and their work proceeds unhampered when the time is ripe.

What concerns us here is solely the manner in which physicists reach out for psychological aid — and the type of aid or hindrance that they get — in this new situation which introduces a human variable, or a variable that seems and may possibly prove to be human, into their equations. We shall seek a display of what is taking place in physical interpretation, with close confinement to actual pages written by actual physicists. The inadequacy and weakness of the daemons which the physicist summons to his aid can in this way most clearly appear. This procedure seems unkind to the particular physicists chosen for exhibit. Perhaps they will feel no need of solace, but if they do, they can find it in the fact that they are chosen not on their own account but because they are typical of many others, and because they hold the most prominent place in the particular locus in which I have sought my immediate materials, namely, the pages of *Philosophy of Science*. Understand, then, that my sole purpose here is to show what the fairies do to the physicist when they get at him.

III

Bridgman

So far as my observation goes, there is just one recent physicist who, in extended endeavors to interpret the status of the new knowledge, has in any sense dealt " factually " with the phenomena which he employs from the region of — or better said, from the vocabulary of — the " mental." He is the one who has shown the least yearning for " mental " support, and the least dependence on it, which is probably a sufficient reason for the degree of " factual " success he has had. Even in the case of this man, who is, of course, Percy W. Bridgman — the early Bridgman of the *Dimensional Analysis* (1922) and of *The Logic of Modern Physics* (1927) — he has been so steadily worked on by the Brethren of the Hobgoblin that in his latest book, *The Nature of Physical Theory* (1936), one finds it difficult at times to keep the bold scheme of his criticism and construction free from the fuzzy clouds surrounding. His early work identified and described the " haze " in ordinary observation more efficiently than anyone else had ever done. There he was dealing with the "human" as he found it; but the added degrees of needless obscurity in the later work are not the "human" that he finds, but an intrusion of "bad human talk" that should be got rid of — indeed an intrusion of the very type of bad talking that he had so successfully attacked in earlier work through his displays of meaningless questions and concepts.

What Bridgman did in his early work was to say in effect: "Space and time are right here in my laboratory just as much as they are off at the far ends of the universe. Einstein has destroyed the old self-subsistent space and time I grew up to know. If such a thing as this can happen to the space and time that is right under my hands, then what tests do I have for the validity of my other physical knowledge, and what assurance for its permanency?" Bridgman thus generalized the issues of relativity, and later of the quantum, with respect to himself as observer and operator, in a way that Einstein himself not only has not done, but has rigidly refused to consider as of physical importance.

Bridgman was a worker with high pressures. What he did, he did with his hands. What he talked about, he wanted to talk about competently. This much of bias, if that is what it should be called, we may allege against him from the start. His method in getting his answers was very simple. He just pushed away all the rubbish he found around him without any feeling of awe for it at all; he made fresh, direct observations of the way physicists actually work; and he asked the kind of questions the worker in the laboratory wants, and needs, to have answered.[4] Then he established procedures for answering with a minimum attention to spooks of any kind. In doing this he gave "Empiricism" a modernized dress, both physically and psychologically, and set up programs which are deeply influencing psychologists as well as physicists, and which by all the signs will grow greatly in influence in the future, if their main lines can be kept clear of distortion.[5]

---

[4] See a review of Bridgman's latest book by Karl Darrow in the *Review of Scientific Instruments,* 1936, p. 374, for a physicist's opinion of Bridgman's critical procedures closely akin to that which I here assume.

[5] In the pages of *Philosophy of Science,* and without any effort at a complete survey, I have noted about a score of writers naming him, or taking positive orientation towards his operational procedure. The chaos of appraisal is astonishing. The opposition of Margenau and Lindsay will be examined later in the text, and Malisoff's extended criticism will be referred to. Among psychologists, Tolman (II, 364) lists Bridgman as a "logical positivist" and proposes to parallel in psychology the good job Bridgman and his associates have done for physics; Stevens, however (III, 93, 100), casts out the logical positivists, but retains Bridgman, and is inspired to exhibit a psychological operation, namely "discrimination," which will be at one and the same time the foundation of psychology and of "operationism" as well. Among physicists, Bender (I, 259, 265-6) accepts the operational view, but sees a possible differentiated place for the "configurational." Northrop (III, 230), discussing probability in quantum mechanics with the aid of 43

The wide attention Bridgman has received is in part due to the appeal of his terminology, and more to the fact that he was early in his special field of criticism. His matter-of-fact procedure had the effect of providing his very empiricism itself with an empirical origin, so to speak, which was in sharp contrast with the highly rationalized empiricisms of the preceding generations.[6] This characteristic of his work, particularly as it is exhibited in the psychological range, is the one which he himself styles " naïve "; yet it must be regarded as immeasurably superior to the " sophistication " he manifestly feels he has attained in his later work. This early " naïve " approach we are now to examine, keeping always in mind that we are not now interested in his own beliefs or professions of faith — of which a further word later — but solely in his actual practice with hand and pen.

Psychologically what Bridgman did was to make use of the behaving physicist just as he found him in the special case of " himself in his laboratory " — a living, breathing, working organism, dated to his nation and generation, trained to his profession, and set at a definite position in a long historical line of scientific advance. Bridgman opened his eyes and took the man he saw — himself — and put him to work " performing operations " and " having concepts." He made little effort to adapt his views to what the well-tailored mind is supposed to be thinking in this generation; he made inquiries, it is true, but found no nutriment in what was offered him, and let it lie. In this early development he made no use at all of the ancient psychological man, possessor of a " mental " faculty, nor of the pseudo-man's successor, a brain, or musculature, or neural or vascular system, or perhaps a " whole-organism " presented as a

---

" concepts " in 17 pages, and with no attempt whatever to indicate what a concept may be, assigns what little plausibility he is willing to admit for the " operational theory " to the manner in which its proponents hide the fundamental distinctions. Reiser (I, 199, II, 1118) holds that an operational theory of concepts merely limits the range of application of terms. Feigl (I, 20, 424) rates Bridgman as an enlightened mind; Benjamin (I, 232) thinks Bridgman's " operational definition " is " simply an act of thought "; Norris (III, 286–7) generalizes all logic as " operational." Other references or comments are by Wheeler (III, 53), Rosenzweig (IV, 105), Frank (II, 210–11), Carnap (IV, 38), and Gruen (III, 331–3). An inspection of the first fifty papers in the magazine showed sympathy and antagonism about equally divided. The opportuneness of Bridgman's discussion is shown not only in the wide adoption of his specialized word " operational," but by the way various philosophers and logicians seek affiliation with him, by the way certain psychologists and biologists pattern after him, and above all by the vigor with which rationalists of all schools unite to belittle him.

[6] Space cannot be taken in this paper to discuss Bridgman's *Dimensional Analysis*, but no appraisal of his main theory is well grounded which does not build directly from this work. The word " concept " does not appear in it at all, and the word " operation " only in the early chapters and in a special technical application. The objective throughout is, however, to expel the mysticism, and allot the physical dimensions a sound operational status.

gnomic[7] " plus " to the organism proper. Neither did he use the faculty-man's ancient rival, the idea-kaleidoscope, nor this fellow's recent successor, the mechanist's gearing of reflexes.

To develop his interpretation Bridgman adopted the two key-words with which everyone today is acquainted, " concept " and " operation." What the world has to be thankful for and in my judgment will long appreciatively acknowledge is that instead of hunting up meticulous definitions for these words, and then doing his best to degrade himself to the level of his definitions, Bridgman shook the words out like two signal flags, and planted them, one on each side, to mark out the territories that must be taken into account.[8]

The word " operation " indicates the thing-happening, a specific case of the physical fact as it is taken up by Bridgman for interpretative inquiry. The word " concept " indicates any specific case of the presence or registration of the fact-as-known. In a way, then, but not at all in any of the ordinary ways, " operation " represents the empirical, and " concept " the rational element of the older disputations. The great difference is that the two are not split apart, detached; they are stresses in the one common situation of man-experiencing-fact. And right here is the point at which the primary Bridgman " feel " for his problem is sympathetic, physically and psychologically, to the great requirements of the undertaking.

" Operation " is certainly in the range of things-sensed, but it is with equal certainty in the range of things-planned; and it is planned-things in the specialized forms they have attained as the outcome of long human experience and history. It is experiment and it is fact, and it is technique for getting at fact; it is nature itself passing through the laboratory, but it is nature channelized in apparatus, with the laboratory itself as the sum-total of the apparatus at work in the channeling. Operation is thus experience with empirical emphasis, but it is not at all the ancient and absurd " passive " receptivity assigned in theory to fictive " senses," nor does it consist of the equally ancient and absurd isolations of fragmentary experiences alleged to be " facts." What Bridgman put to work in the laboratory was not a robot; neither was it a medicine-man; it was the physicist at work with his hands — himself a phase of the on-going natural process. He put him there with the clear-eyed recognition that where hands are at work, there head is at work also — a simple factual observation that our " mentalists " never can tolerate.

[7] Take either " gnome " you prefer as base for this adjective.
[8] In this he is at the far pole from the " logical " positivists who claim affiliation with him.

How about "concept"? Concept also is something the physicist has or does; and just as operation involves planning, so concept involves empirical experiencing — fact — outer world — call it what you will. Simple evidence of this is the ease with which the words "the concept of" can be dropped out of many passages in Bridgman's texts with no noticeable alteration of meaning; as, for instance, where in place of "the concept of space" one may read simply "space." "Operation" and "concept," therefore, exhibit the characteristics of a common psychological world and of a common empirical world, so that some real possibility exists of development in a common system. They represent, nevertheless, different phases or aspects, of the types most commonly spoken of as "fact" and "knowledge of fact." For the term "concept," its extension, the range of its meaning, is plain enough in Bridgman's use; the sum total of concepts is the sum total of knowledge existing at any time.[9]

I have given a great deal of attention off and on for many years to Bridgman's words "concept" and "operation" with a view to their future possibilities when someone finds a way to produce a really intelligible psychology; and the best way I know to characterize them, in their signal-flag values indicated above, is that operation represents what goes on in the laboratory and concept represents what goes on in the library, the physicist himself in each case being present and at work.

In such a set-up as this it is plain enough that two great lines of inquiry open up. One is into the operations as they affect the concepts; the other into the concepts as they affect the operations. It is equally plain in Bridgman's work that he undertakes only the first of these two inquiries, that being in the field in which he himself controls expert accumulations of specialized knowledge. The other line of inquiry remains open, and is an enormously important line. But it is not sufficient to pick some kind of a concept off the ancient concept-tree to stick in. Much less is known about concepts today than about operations, and much difficult research will be needed before good constructions can be obtained. As to this, a word or two will be said later on. Instead of making a specialized inquiry in this direction, Bridgman just assumes that knowledge in the form of concepts is somewhere around in the neighborhood, and goes ahead. Adopting a common form of word-stress which he himself now and then uses, we may say that in his theory he employs a *concept* of an operation, but only a *notion* of a concept.

As to his own view of the "real nature" of his concepts there seems little question. At almost any stage of his career, if one asked him, his

---

[9] For example: *The Nature of Physical Theory*, p. 9: "At any moment our concepts are coextensive with the system of existing knowledge."

answer would doubtless be to the effect that they were a sort of little things kite-tailing along somewhere around a brain. The point about his work — the outstanding point — the great achievement — is that in his original construction he did not use in any way or attempt actually to use these little spooklets. Isaac Newton oozed theological speculations and worked long and hard at numerology, and indications remain that he may even have thought better of his output in these fields than of the *Principia*. But who cares today? The point is that the vermin were kept out of the mechanics and the cosmology. So with Bridgman. He did not let his " mentals " and his " consciousness," nor even his " self-consciousness " and his " solipsistic " soul, operate in his early work; and so long as such things do not operate they do no harm.[10]

In his inquiry Bridgman occupied himself with physical concepts without attempting to differentiate them sharply from non-physical concepts, if any; he did not even take the trouble to tell us definitely whether he was concerned with *all* physical concepts, or solely with the good ones, assuming some are bad; he left open various issues as to the presence of " mental " operations alongside the physical operations. These uncertainties are all to his credit, in the sense that an open chasm is less dangerous than one that is camouflaged.

His conclusions themselves he put in a great variety of phrasings, all impressionistic. These are so well known that all I need do is to recall such assertions as that the concept " means " a set of operations, or is " synonymous with," or is " equivalent to," or is " defined in terms of," or " names a group of " operations; or again that operational meaning is " the analysis of what we do," or is found in " making application," or in the statement that we can " maintain correspondences." Here again the very impressionism of his presentation is to his credit. It might be summed up in the statement " You can best keep your head by using your hands." This may not seem such a wonderful delivery; but the merit of it will shine when we come in a moment to examine what happens in the case of a physicist who insists that his head occupies a separate compartment from his hands, and must be appealed to all by itself in cases of deepest need.

Bridgman and Pavlov are akin in a very important characteristic. Pavlov pushed physiology out into psychological territory, and it was precisely because he refused to do any psychology directly that he became one of the world's greatest contributors to psychology. In a very similar

---

[10] Bridgman is critized both as " too subjective " and for " expelling the subjective." The one type applies to his incidental phrasings; the other expresses the temperament of his critic.

sense Bridgman pushed physics out into psychological territory, and just to the extent that he lets the psychologizing alone he gets sound psychological results. The "Pavlov" I have in mind is, of course, not the caricature offered us by the petty mechanists of the American psychological laboratories [11] any more than the one offered by their distortionist rivals, the "purpositivists." The real Pavlov is the grand old peasant who saw what he wanted and who went after it, and who was never satisfied until he got things under his own hands in a way that enabled him to talk definitely about them.[12] He first worked with stomach secretions and gained the Nobel prize. He next worked with salivary secretions in dogs, still always the physiologist. He then made the blunt observation that if a dog salivates in response to the presence of meat on his tongue, and if that is a physiological process, the process ought to be just as truly physiological when the dog salivates to the sight of meat two feet away. Why insert a spook in the latter case and not in the former? To answer this, he just eliminated a couple of feet of rigid Newtonian space from his investigational background; and incidentally he did that long before Einstein gave the rest of us the tip.

Pavlov quite early made a further observation which was that when his colleagues in the laboratory attempted to report results in terms of what the dog "felt" or "wanted" or "saw" or "thought" or "knew" they never got anywhere; their reports were always vague and imperfect so that no two workers could come to definite agreement they could stick to. So he issued a rule: Cut out all the bad language in this laboratory, and talk facts. His original collaborator quarreled and went off on his own account; his students were always violating the rule; he himself kept slipping; finally a penalty was imposed, kopeks and rubles, for every offense, and in time precision was obtained in a considerable degree. Outside this "mental" range for the dog, there was much of his work for which Pavlov could not get definite terminology; here he made no pretenses, but did the best he could and shifted as need arose. Bridgman's best work is like that of Pavlov in both these linguistic attitudes, and Bridgman's later reversion to mentalist terms only serves, it seems to me, to point a moral to the tale.

[11] For current carelessness in discussing Pavlov, see some comments by Liddell in his essay on the conditioned reflex in the volume *Comparative Psychology* edited by Moss.
[12] This does not mean that Pavlov was a scientific paragon. He was always sticking out his neck, getting into trouble, and jerking back. His laboratory made some serious mistakes, but he was never ashamed to admit it and start over.

IV

The Birth of the Concept

Before passing to our remaining exhibits we may spend a moment to consider how the concept got into the world. It was not always with us, as some faithful souls so strongly feel. The case was one of mountains in parturition, a mouse being born, but What-a-Mouse! The Middle Ages struggled with their pains for centuries before they recovered sufficiently to attend to the housework again. Men had words, and some of the words were nouns, and some of the nouns named "things," or at least they named what the men of those days were in the habit of calling "things."[13] What, then, did the other nouns name — those upstage nouns such as "animal" or "virtue"? The official view was that the upstage nouns also named things, and upstage things at that; the heretic view was that the upstage nouns were just words, and that this was all there was to it. Realism on the one side, Nominalism on the other. Along came Abelard, at least so the story goes (for he was the publicity man who got all the headlines) to produce and exploit the "concept." Here was one of the great verbal triumphs of history. This "concept," present in mind, was to be "*the* thing" that the upstage noun named. Thus thing and word were to be alike happy, and each was to have its due. This was plain shenanigan, but it got by.

The British line of descent was in a by-path around the practical-minded nominalist, Hobbes, through the spawn of "ideas" that the conceptualist, Locke, let loose in a Newtonian framework, and past the epic campaign which John Stuart Mill waged against the shade of Sir William Hamilton, in the course of which he emitted his despairing lament over the wreckage of the human intellect.[14] When George Henry Lewes wrote his history of these events he refused to tolerate even so much as an inkling that anybody could ever have been free from chronic concept-

---

[13] Such "things" we have still with us today in many places where they ought not to be. A pleasant confession of faith from the eighteenth century is that of Thomas Reid: "Every object of sense, of memory, or of consciousness, is an individual object. All the good things we enjoy or desire, and all the evils we feel or fear, must come from individuals; and I think we may venture to say, that every creature which God hath made, in the heavens above, or in the earth beneath, or in the waters under the earth is an individual." (*Essays on the Intellectual Powers of Man:* Essay V, Chap. 1).

[14] Hamilton had held at one stage of his work that concepts arise from judgments, and at a later stage that judgments are comparisons of concepts. Said Mill: "Coming from a thinker of such ability, it almost makes one despair of one's own intellect and that of mankind, and feel as if the attainment of truth on any of the more complicated subjects of thought were impossible." (*An Examination of Sir William Hamilton's Philosophy:* Vol. II, Chap. XVIII).

on-the-brain.[15] Today the common sense of the common man never dreams that a word may possibly be something other than a sign of such a concept, or thought, or idea, or whatever he may call it; while in the American laboratories not a tired rat can fall from his perch but some bright-eyed young researcher will discover in him " a concept just like a man's," with never a thought as to what that may be.

The physicist who fails to get the meat of this brief narrative may perhaps be willing to recall the verb " phlogisticate " from the earlier history of his science, and understand me to mean that " conceptualize " and " phlogisticate " are piggies from the same litter. If he thinks I am wrong, all he has to do is to show me a concept in just the same sense he might ask me to show him phlogiston, if I insisted on its presence; which means, of course, showing something definite, and not merely waving one's hand toward a general region of human behavior to which such a word as " concept " can roughly apply. The physicist is closer to an electron than he is to a concept; he is closer to a light-wave; he is closer to a probability-wave. He has more good sound practical reason for believing that he can some day grasp a " probability " in his strong right hand than that he will ever make contact with a concept in person. All he needs to do is to stop believing-out-loud, and try to observe instead — just for a moment.[16]

Such is the concept which Bridgman found and casually adopted, but from which he stripped most of the hokum. Without investigating its procedure directly, he allotted it some incidental work to do, but rejected all its claims to dominance.

V

Margenau

We turn now to two physicists who are deeply pained by such irreverence and who, in their blacker moments, see in it the overthrow of all knowledge and the destruction of all possibility of attaining knowledge.[17]

---

[15] " It seems almost inconceivable that an acute mind could believe . . . that names . . . are not . . . signs of ideas " (*The History of Philosophy*, Vol. II, p. 26).

[16] I acknowledge that several times in print I have indicated what it is I regard a concept to " be." I shall try to exhibit the situation in detail at some future time. The difficulties are increased by the fact that almost all programs of psychology in the last two generations have evaded the issues.

[17] Henry Margenau: four papers in *Philosophy of Science,* as follows: " Meaning and Scientific Status of Causality," vol. I, pp. 133–148; " Methodology of Modern Physics," vol. II, pp. 48–72, and pp. 164–187; " Critical Points in Modern Physical Theory," vol. IV, pp. 337–370. R. B. Lindsay: two papers in the same journal: " The Meaning of Simplicity in Physics," vol. IV, pp. 151–167; " A Critique of Operationalism in Physics,"

Margenau says little of Bridgman,[18] but has his eye steadily on him, and brings up the heavy artillery. Lindsay sniffs a beast in the underbrush, dubs it " operationalism," calls it the offspring of Bridgman, and starts to hunt it down with sidearms. Both men place all their faith and hope in the " concept," which they insist must be restored to its ancient throne, with " operation " reduced to the status of a humble, even if very necessary, slave. The word " concept " is used sparingly by Margenau (about once in two pages), but he has several alternate words, and his heavy specialization,[19] the " construct," dominates his entire treatment. As for Lindsay, he produces ninety-seven concepts in thirty pages of text, among them such specimens as " sophisticated abstract concepts," " intuitive and *a priori* concepts," " logically indefinable concepts," " instinctive and not analyzable concepts," "' economy of thought' concepts," " symbolic concepts," and " anthropomorphic concepts," apparently finding in them the proper ammunition for non-operational, though still soundly scientific, knowledge.

By distorting Bridgman grossly enough, either man can, of course, readily destroy what he has distorted. Both men distort alike; first by insisting " operations " must be all hands and no mind; second by alleging that no operation in this world can possibly have anything to do with

---

vol. IV, pp. 456–470. To show the source of citations from any of these papers, the page number in parentheses will be inserted directly in the text. Lindsay's fear is expressed thus: " A thorough-going adherence to the operational method . . . would necessarily imply the abandonment of the method of theoretical physics " (458). In their book *Foundations of Physics* (1936), p. 412, Lindsay and Margenau describe Bridgman's position as " a short-sighted curtailment of the realm of physics." Margenau has also three articles in *The Monist,* 1929, 1931, and 1932.

[18] In his *Monist* articles, Margenau describes Bridgman as " following Einstein and others," and objects to " the penumbra of uncertainty " and the " meaningless." He criticizes Bridgman's stress on differential equations in the analysis of causality as " mere description " and as " renouncing all attempts to explain it in terms which it does not itself offer without the intervention of reason " (1929, p. 328). He proposes to improve Bridgman's " principle of essential connectivity " by renaming it " the principle of consistency of nature," and gives three reasons why the operational theory " cannot be tolerated " (1931, p. 16): namely (a) that it would dissolve the world into an unmanageable variety of discrete concepts without logical coherence; (b) that it would impede science by emphasizing the changeable; and (c) that it would make physical concepts falsely appear to be different from other kinds of concepts. In his later articles in *Philosophy of Science* I have noted only one reference to Bridgman by name (62), but others will be found or suspected, as pages 139, 144, 170, 174, 343, 345. We may possibly include the remark (63) that " constitutive " definition enables us to reason, seeing that it is the " epistemic " definition alone that is allotted by Margenau to Bridgman.

[19] I doubt if I could find a definite statement to this effect anywhere in Margenau's papers. Lindsay, however, explains the situation thus: " In the interesting paper of Margenau, the term ' construct ' is introduced in place of ' concept,' presumably to emphasize the active constructive rôle of the mind in building physical theories. This is a worthwhile procedure. However the present paper will continue to use the more familiar term with the feeling that no essential ambiguity will result " (161).

any other operation, not even with its own repetitions of itself.[20] Bridgman may be destroyed either in person or in distortion, so far as we are concerned at the moment; what we are to observe is what the distorters do to themselves.

We shall begin with an examination of Margenau and we shall confine ourselves to the manner in which he undertakes his anti-operational interpretation of physical knowledge, to the coherence of his mechanisms, and to the uses he finds for his construction after he has obtained it. We shall be compelled to omit a showing of his physical objectives proper, and of his frequently interesting and valuable organization of the physical material; though to give a fair picture of his position all this should be included, especially by way of indicating how readily his normal physics [21] may be detached from the " mentalist " and " conceptualist " interpretations thrust at it, and how these latter exhibit themselves more as matters of " temperament " than of either " philosophy " or " science."

The first of Margenau's four papers analyzes causality with special reference to the quantum by the use of a construct, the " state," the development and application of which is his main contribution to the direct interpretation of the newer theories. The next two papers build a system of what he calls methodology, but which might better be called conceptual mythology, to underlie the construct " state." His last paper is oriented to issues of truth or fiction in physics; for these return to

[20] " On the basis of purely operational definitions, all concepts are strictly empirical and isolated " (*Foundations of Physics*, p. 412). Definition by operation " would dissolve the world into an unmanageable variety of discrete concepts without logical coherence " (*Monist*, 1931, p. 16). " Logically the operational method . . . implies that each concept is tied to a definite operation "; " the concept must be arbitrarily associated with a particular operation " (Lindsay, 458). Allegations such as the preceding merely apply the older association psychology or the newer psychology of mechanistic reflexes to the opponent without his permission.

[21] The basic differences between Margenau and Bridgman in actual physical criticism, so far as I am competent to judge, are very slight. Margenau's sketch of his methodological problem (48–52) is alone sufficient to indicate this. To make sure, however, we must first: (a) eliminate all conceptualizings and other psychologizings on the part of either man as totally irrelevant; (b) eliminate minor elements of technical difference insignificant for the main interpretation; (c) capture and banish to some remote desert island Margenau's overpowering, though partially veiled, interest in issues of " reality," which, when all is said and done, are nothing more than naïvely formulated distinctions of " common language " (346) " between physical objects and the observer's knowledge about physical objects "; and at the same time we must eliminate Bridgman's recent quibblings of comparable nature. We should then have our problem stripped down to what is truly significant: viz., the issues of causality, differential equations, simplicity, consistency, connectivity, and correspondence in the strictly physical sphere. Along with these we could inspect Margenau's " observations," his " operations " in the two forms, " preparations " and " measurements," (356–8) and his " states " as he actually uses them, in close comparison with Bridgman's constructions. My present essay began with this type of inquiry; but its continuation is wholly useless until the mythology, mysticism, and sentimentality is cleared away; and when that is done, almost any physicist can be depended on to reach better answers in immediate examination than I can with protracted discussion.

bother him in ways they never could have done, had the mythology been omitted.

What we should like to be able to do in a case like this is to examine the writer's *utterances,* which are not only the evidence but themselves the *very fact* of his construction so far as we can come into contact with it, with as much precision and care as a physicist would give to a study of tracks in a Wilson cloud chamber. Let the philosophers guess at what men mean and then squabble over their guesses; but we, in sharp contrast, ought to get down to the hard facts of the case, namely the specific assertions that are expressly offered us. We want to find out in which way, or in how many ways, Margenau's sentences curve, and how steadily they hold their curvatures. To accomplish this within any reasonable space we must select and sort, perhaps at times arbitrarily; and we undertake this task here with the disquieting sense that no matter what attitudes we may in this way most firmly assign to him, he will still be able to dig up out of his texts other and contradicting sentences to allege that we are wrong.

A. *A Breath of Preliminary Unity.* Deep down at the bottom of the pit of knowledge Margenau sees a frightful chasm opening to still lower deeps. Is Nature " merely a complex of awareness " or has it " the status of transcendental objectivity " ? (60).* To a similar question the early Bridgman had replied that the answer did not make much difference, and that the question was operationally meaningless anyway. Margenau adopts what he says is " the most cautious and possibly the wisest course " by decreeing Nature to be "*merely* the aggregate of our perceptible experiences." What light this throws into the pit the reader may decide for himself. Margenau makes the further suggestion that by " coining a new and strange term," *habita,* and substituting it in physics for *data,* much good would follow.[22]

B. *Essential Dichotomy.* Physical science, according to Margenau, begins with " perceptible matters of fact "; it then places these in " mental custody " where, " in the privacy of one's speculations," they undergo an " act of speculative creation " and become " endowed with abstract properties "; and it emerges again later in " the realm of perceptible facts " (57, 59, *et passim*). Such phrasings will answer anybody's purposes, anywhere, any time, especially under the qualifications Margenau

---

* See footnote 17 for method employed in citing Margenau and Lindsay.

[22] In his *Monist* paper, 1929, Margenau mentions his acquisition of this term from a " philosopher." Unfortunately he takes over only a small part of the significance of the word, and its extended investigation would be fatal to his " mental custody." In this same *Monist* paper he is quite frank in asserting his start from data that are " parts of our consciousness," in which we are " merely having cognitions."

slips into his sentences from the very start; all depends on how they are developed. Margenau's development is to declare a " dichotomy " (50–51); an " essential distinction between two kinds of entity " (170); a " formal bifurcation " necessary " in principle " (179); not " philosophical " and not " artificial " but instead merely such that one cannot " get along with less than two classes of things " (187), and that one errs if one ever ventures a tiny bit to doubt the reality of the " ultimate " abstract (187).

One " kind of entity " lies in the general region of " mind," where it includes such items as the " intrinsically non-empirical " (53), the " totally abstract " (169), the " imperceptible concepts " (55), and the " transcendental elements " or " transcendental notions " (52).

The other " kind of entity " lies in the region of " fact," or " sense," or " perceptibility "; and while it is asserted just as bravely, it is not pictured so well. Margenau defies the world to get along without the " transcendental notions," but he allows their consort, the " transcendental objectivity," as we have just seen, to become somewhat blurred; and indeed in another passage (345) he even tells us that the split between physical systems and our knowledge of them is not nearly so deep as the general split of epistemology — which to my mind is a very considerable concession to make to the enemy. We find, nevertheless, on this fork of the bifurcation, the " totality of all matters capable of sensory perception " (57, 59), and these must have " attributes of extension and duration " (60) and are sharply contrasted with items that involve even " simple processes of abstraction " (166).

C. *Organization by Concept.* Whatever fundamental criticism Margenau directs against Bridgman depends on this " dichotomy," which is unflinchingly vociferous despite the slight lameness in one of its legs. But Margenau's difficulty is that, with too much dichotomy in its materials, science can find no way to make any advance at all. Therefore, having forced a divorce, he now has to engineer a remarriage, or at least some kind of a conventionally tolerated, if not fully solemnized, marital status. (Mixed arguments make me sprout mixed metaphors, and I have no inclination to apologize, either here or for other passages in this chapter.)

He accomplishes this by a process of " conceptualization." Under a strong declaration of freedom of choice, he establishes the " physical universe " in high estate as number-one Concept. This concept embraces two " classes " or " domains " of concepts — one class " Nature," the other " Constructs of Explanation "; and these he labels " data " and " constructs " for short (59, 61, 166, 174, *et passim*).

These words, " data " and " construct," have most important functions in his system. When he so desires they indicate " concepts " as here. When he does not so desire, they are bifurcations (as in B, above). They are therefore notably disingenuous; and this is true of them, I believe, not only in his work, but in all those regions of philosophizing from which he acquires them.

D. *Chaos out of Cosmos.* For all this procedure one can find analogues in Hindu mythology, except that Margenau's course is rather from cosmos to chaos than from chaos to cosmos. The gods wanted to stir up the sea of milk to get hold of the philter of immortality. Vishnu, masquerading as the big sea-tortoise, sank to the bottom to give leverage for the stirring-stick; Margenau's " aggregate of experience " will do well enough for Vishnu. Out of the sea of milk finally popped up a White Elephant; Margenau's elephant unfortunately rises dichotomized, bifurcated — even, I fear, a bit schizophrenetic. On his back, Indra, Margenau's concept-maker, takes his seat, and proceeds to entrust himself with dominion over the firmament and the atmosphere, and to hold the earth in the hollow of his hand — quite some forerunner of the modern scientist. Our next step is to see what sort of immortal scientificity Margenau-Indra achieves out of it all. Again his sentences need much sorting.

a) *The Data.* Comparatively little attention is given to these; sometimes they are taken raw, sometimes conceptually; it is hard to disentangle. They include items like " pointer readings," " experimental decisions," and " countings of individual events " (61). In one illustration matter is a datum and mass a construct (61; and compare 69, footnote). Sometimes the " smallest part of nature " turns up " not a datum, but a collection of data," which seems hard on the bifurcator (66; though before the paragraph ends, a re-entry of the " single perceptible counterpart " is implied). Sometimes no experiment is practicable except by way of a theory (179) in which case datum is reduced to observation of the type which involves strict passivity in the observer, and this seems hard on the concept-maker.

b) *The Constructs.* The manipulation of constructs is Margenau's main activity. He offers three classifications of constructs proper, and a fourth classification, not of constructs but of " definitions of constructs," whatever such a distinction may mean. There are:

1. A classification of constructs into five manners of " existence " (164–6). This is not put to direct use, though it has sound value in eliminating various possible confusions and misunderstandings.

2. A classification, described as " more natural " (166) and again as " more qualitative " (174), into " sensible," " pseudo-sensible," and " abstract." Archetype for this is that magnifico among classifications

(though hardly a prize-winner in recent physics) into the "absolute," the "relatively absolute," and the "relative." What happens for Margenau is what always happens with classifications of this form. It will suffice to offer a sample or two from among scores:

"All constructs . . . possess necessarily some of the characteristics of nature" (171).
"The systems themselves" (abstract systems being here in view, and all systems being constructs) "no longer partake of the attributes of data" (175).

The Hamiltonian operator illustrates constructs that are "totally abstract" and "wholly insensible" (169–70); but it is "not entirely free from an admixture of sensible and pseudo-sensible constructs" (171); it involves space and time co-ordinates, and this is as it should be since "every abstract notion, if it is to be intelligible, implies some reference to sensory experience" (171). At a point like this, nine days' retirement to the desert for silent thought is indicated. The result of meditation will be that Margenau is obsessed by visualizability, that he merely suggests three degrees of it, and that the classificatory pretentiousness adds nothing to the import of his suggestion.

3. A classification of "definitions of constructs," ancillary to a third classification of constructs proper, into two typical forms of definition called "epistemic" and "constitutive" (61–62).[23] The epistemic is approximately "operational" and permits measurement, but the constitutive is much nobler since by it "we are enabled to reason" (63). The far echo of one of Kant's most famous phrases is in this wording. If the question is asked why Margenau offers a classification of definitions separate from that of constructs proper, the answer is probably that he has now reached the particular point at which he must command a dichotomy for his warfare against "operational" physics; and since he cannot exhibit such a dichotomy in the "constructs" directly, he pushes it back

[23] The word "constitutive" is derived from Kant, who uses it in an entirely different sense. The word "epistemic" is not found in Murray, nor in the technical dictionaries of Baldwin and Warren. The coupling of the two words was made by W. E. Johnson in his *Logic* (1921 to 1924, 3 vol.). It is interesting to note that whereas Johnson introduced the word "epistemic" to replace "subjective," which he disliked, and made it indicate "the relation . . . to the thinker" (vol. I, p. xxxiv), Margenau attaches his own heavily subjective stress to the opposed word "constitutive." I mention this merely as a curiosity, not in reproach, since all such terms are so slippery it is impossible to expect anyone to hold steadily to them, not even when criticizing them. Observe that Margenau first tells us that the two kinds of definition are "different," then that they are "interdependent," and then that epistemic alone will not suffice. His illustration for the electron is worthy of Schoolmen in their prime, namely that "it" cannot be measured, but that "we do not question the possibility of measuring its charge or its mass, etc." (63). Observe also his very first illustration in the case of "mass," where the "constitutive" is granted superiority, even though requiring auxiliary "epistemics" on which to rest (62).

into the region of "definitions of constructs" (even though he avoids so much as the implication of dichotomy for the definition-types) and on that basis proceeds to manipulate the definitions speciously with respect to the constructs to uphold his cause. The definitions thus act merely as a "front" in the old Wild West sense. This is at once plain from the uses to which they are put. He now obtains:

4. A classification employing the words "system," "quantity," and "state," which takes two forms:

4'; into systems and quantities, wherein the former permit constitutive definition only, while the latter may take both constitutive and epistemic definition; and wherein the state appears as "a combination of quantities with a system" (64).

4"; into systems, quantities, *and* states, with the last of these "a third class of constructs" and with the comment that "it is a matter of practical indifference" whether we look upon the states in this way or "as associations of systems and quantities" (70).

Since "state" is Margenau's greatest engine of war, his trusty catapult, one regrets that he should be so unclear about its status under his basic definitions. If (as in 4') a "state" is regarded as a combination or association in which one of its elements is already a combination, we certainly have a right to be told something about ratios, and whether the second stage of combination is merely additive, or involves, so to speak, a second power of the "constitutive."[24] If on the other hand (as under 4") the "state" is a third "class," then we should know its standing under "definition," if these definitions are to have the authority attributed to them. The sole schematic position Margenau has left open among his definition-types is "epistemic only"; and the use of this would involve a surrender to Bridgman which manifestly is impossible. If a third type

---

[24] Margenau's "simplest possible way" to form a state is by "a direct assignment" of certain quantities to a system (64), but he assures us that no one-to-one correspondence between constructs and data is involved in his procedure (66). Later, however, he attains the somewhat surprising presentation of a "one-to-one correspondence ... between states and probability distributions of observed properties" (341). Historically his definitions of "state" run back to "an agreement to consider those qualities as composing the state of a system which enter into a time-free differential equation describing its behavior" (145). Later he defined states for quantum mechanics "by means of *state functions*, functions of space and time coordinates which make no explicit reference to quantities" (175). And finally state or representative of state comes to mean in quantum mechanics "a certain function of a suitable number of variables" (340). Elaboration will be found in *Foundations of Physics* (401-413) where a "physical system" is "any object ... which in classical physics is thought of as an entity," its "properties" being called "observables," and its "state" being "simply a function in configuration space." In this connection he also tells us that, if classical mechanics is like a report on a man's actions and utterances, the "state" in quantum mechanics gives us "a story of the succession of all his thoughts, sentiments, and volitions" (401-2). Maximum illumination is here apparently cast upon the situation.

of definition is to be called on for the benefit of "state," no hint is given us of what this may be.

Difficulties like the above are academic and trivial, however, compared with what happens when "system," "quantity," and "state" are put to work. "System" is handicapped by an unfortunate Siamese-twin-like start in life, since it is not only "constitutive only" but also an "entity," the "notion" of which is "largely carried over from previous physical experience" (*Foundations of Physics,* p. 401). In neither of its personalities, however, can it very well be quantity or do measuring, since, also from the start, the "epistemic" is involved in that (63-4). And yet:

"All properties . . . with which physical systems are endowed must be measurable" (341).
"There is no consideration which compels that states be directly measurable" (341).

Of course Margenau has an "emergency exit," here as elsewhere. The first sentence above is in terms of "properties," not of "systems" direct, under the super-elegant distinction already noted in the case of electron-as-system. This "exit," however, opens upon a road which runs from a starting point in "reason," where system is "constitutive only," past a rough spot in which "properties" (341, *et passim*) crop out, to a terminus in which the systems have "behaviors" of their own (339). On such a road we need skis, waders, and dancing pumps, all at once. But for the "dichotomies," travel would have been smooth. No doubt Margenau can demonstrate my account here to be false. In doing it, however, he will not "refute" me, but rather illuminate still more brightly my exhibit of a linguistic mess, and of its uselessness.

We could perhaps overlook differences that seem to us incoherent at different stages of his development, or adjust ourselves to them without complaint since we are all errantly human, if only he would maintain separate coherences for the separate stages. But compare now these two sentences:

"A state function . . . is not at all linked with physical experience" (340).
"States which . . . fail to provide a *definite connection* with experience must be considered futile" (341).

Again there is a fire exit, but again one might as well stay behind and burn.

Margenau's idolized "mentality" is both origin and shield for these conflicts, giving him hope, or perhaps illusion, that behind the murky words the mind's still shining. It is this "mentality" which produces his concern over "reality" in his final paper, a concern which is intense and unchecked despite the devices he uses to disguise his very preoccupation from himself. After constitutive "system" has bobbed up as behaving "fact," we find him spending many long pages debating the relative merits of "system" and "knowledge of system" (344ff.); while even for "state" the comparable question comes up in the form: is it "state" or "representative of state" about which we are now talking? (340).

E. *And What Good Came of It at Last?* We have exhibited a chaos of inconsistencies and the presence of much wasteful rumination. It is further plain that Margenau violates every canon of simplicity. But he may retort that even though he exhibits inconsistency, wastefulness, and frightful complexity, this is the best one can do these days; and he may insist that despite all its defects the usefulness of his interpretative system still remains. The answer to this is the exhibit of its redundancy. After he has constructed his program, about all he does is occasionally to refer to it. Run through his illustrative matter (174–187) and see if this is not so. After an examination of "elementary diffuseness" which his section heading (174) suggests to be "a result of abstract physical constructs," he sums up: "By placing into prominence certain abstract features which have always been inherent in physical explanation it is possible to reconcile . . . etc." (177). This is a sound statement, matter-of-fact and true; it tells exactly what he is doing, and incidentally what everyone else does, but it certainly does not exhibit physical facts in any way as the "result" of constructs; it is unexceptional so long as he does not attempt to pursue the task, utterly hopeless under his "conceptual" methods, of making a basic development for the word, or procedure, "abstract." Continuing further with simple, direct statement, he feels apology necessary for his use of a "customary, technical lingo which obscures distinctions between constructs and data" (178), apparently not noticing that if this "lingo" is proper to the extent he has used it, then the whole distinction between data and construct might as well fall out. He next (179) reasserts his scheme "in principle," but with the admission that "in actual investigations it is often" (he should have said "always") "impossible to maintain a sharp boundary"; and he follows this with a practical statement as to how physicists make theories, but one which has nothing whatever to do with his own interpretative mechanism. Finally, entering upon a longer discussion of certain constructions of Dirac and Fermi, he frankly writes: "We shall exercise little care in distinguishing constructs from data . . . for the result would be . . . tedious . . ." (181). His actual appraisals of Dirac and Fermi are noticeably "operational" in tone.

Margenau's formal opinion has been that the only salvation of physics lies in a "dichotomy," but now after forty pages of dichotomic crutch-building he throws away his crutches and walks like anybody else — practically, instead of dichotomically. We may conclude that his theoretical interpretation has as little to do with physical science as a cutaway coat at a wedding has to do with the simpler facts of life. The world will always, one may suppose, include people who prefer the regalia to the reality. Margenau's essays will have served a useful purpose if they have demonstrated what regalia the physicist can most easily get along without.[25]

VI
Lindsay

Lindsay makes direct assault upon a certain "operationalism" he attributes to Bridgman (456, note). This may be treated much more briefly. It will interest us not only for the display of the weakness of the argument, but by showing how unscrupulous the anti-operational "conceptualist" can become when he goes on the loose with "ideas."

An "ism," in the general case, is just a lumping, and so to speak, personalizing, of misunderstandings, as opposed to efforts at their clarification. One thing that Bridgman certainly is *not*, is the creator of an "ism." If he has ever used the word "operationalism" a single time, I have failed to note it; and certainly it is alien to his entire attitude, since salvation from the "ismic" disease would be one of the surest by-products of any steady operational stress on meanings.

Notice Lindsay's procedure in his first two paragraphs under his heading "Operationalism" (456–7). Watch the words wriggle. Beginning with broad generalizations in terms of meanings and definings, he is ready by the middle of the paragraph to assert that the content of an "operationalist's" thinking is "glass and rubber tubing" and other "actual apparatus." He then admits that this is an extreme statement, and

---

[25] Alterations in Margenau's views may be in part responsible for his conflicts in expression. Thus as contrasted with his early demand that physics abolish the penumbra of uncertainty (see footnote 18), he now occasionally remarks that his method has no finality (51, 68, 179, 339, *et passim*). Another difficulty is that at times he regards his program as philosophical (337, and the preface to *Foundations of Physics*), at other times as not philosophical (187), and at still other times as a method for keeping other physicists from talking inconsistently (338, 345, 346). In the analysis in the text I have limited myself to inconsistencies of a special type. For slightly different illustrations, note how certain formulations such as that of causality can be at the same time both tautological and statements about nature (146); and how Heisenberg's principle can be viewed as a "consequence" of a certain vaguely worded axiom Margenau himself formulated a decade later (341).

grants the operationalist other methods of defining than this. He next changes the issue to one of consistency, but asserts emphatically that the operationalist has now bound himself to believe very definitely that " no contradictions can ever arise in actual physical situations," and must be willing to trust himself " always . . . to the test of such situations." " This thesis " (meaning thereby apparently the chaotic contents of the two paragraphs) is the " ism " which Lindsay proposes to examine and refute; and he proceeds in his attack without any effort whatever to explain to us what can be meant by a " contradiction " in an " actual physical situation " or why a physicist should find it so appalling to be asked to give his confidence to the " actual physical situation."

" Actually " Lindsay's arguments against Bridgman are as follows: He first assumes naïvely the existence of a certain " purely theoretical " element which involves " ideas in mind " and " purely mental planning." Putting this " Charlie McCarthy " on his physical lap, and holding his breath till he thinks he has made us believe that his Charlie is radically different from " actual apparatus," he profoundly proclaims that no " apparatus " can get along without " ideas " (457). This proclamation we are supposed to accept as knockout number one for " operationalism." He next asserts a rigorous isolation for all operations, each from every other, and thereby a second time puts " operationalism " on the floor for the count (458). Fearing, however, that he may have gone too far, he proceeds to assure us, like a true Charlie, that theories require verification, that experimental tests are still useful, and that the goal of physics is still ultimately " to describe physical phenomena "; adding that what he really means to insist on is a reservation of his right to use " concepts which are not defined *directly* in terms of operations " (459). He is apparently unaware that this matter of " directly," which I have taken the liberty to italicize in the citation, is the whole issue of inquiry. All he does is to assert a right of " indirection " as over against a crude falsification of " direct "; and there he stops, with no contribution at all to the solution. This, so far as I can find out, is his whole case against Bridgman's critical inquiry into physical knowledge.

He adds, however, a few minor considerations. He intimates that operationalists " flirt with the idea of emergence," leaving the implication that he is referring to Bridgman (465). Apparently he has not read Bridgman's own remarks on emergence (*Nature of Physical Theory*, p. 97). He dislikes the way Bridgman talks about " text," because " although it is of course true," yet " it seems to give a misleading impression " (459). He criticizes certain of Bridgman's attitudes toward models, probability, and statistics, but in ways only slightly relevant to the issues between "operationalism" and his primordial "conceptualism." He winds up with a summary of his overthrow of "operationalism" by declaring (a) that it is fascinating, (b) that it casts light, (c) that it has weaknesses, and (d) that "certainly it would demand the complete scrapping of the well-recognized methodology of physics" (469–70). In other words, he credits it with three trivialities and an absurdity. It is little above the level of devil-worship to believe that any such "ism" as Lindsay's imagination projects could ever have power to work such harm.

What this sort of "conceptualism" does to its advocates is to distract their attention from honesty of statement, and in large measure destroy all their sense of humor. What it does to Lindsay himself may be made evident in three brief examples. In his article on simplicity in physics he arrives at the fine pedagogical conclusion that the theory in physics which is the simplest, and thus presumably the best, is that one which the average student can learn most quickly (166). In his later article he speaks of space and time in mechanics as primitive, indefinable concepts (459), which would seem to indicate very slight effect upon his thought as yet from the Einstein relativity. After having built his main arguments on the "purely mental," he proceeds to set forth all physical theory as "but an attempt to *describe*" (459), while in the very next sentence he describes description itself as beginning "with certain intuitive and logically indefinable concepts" and advancing to the building of "more elaborate concepts by purely postulational methods." If this be "description," then Robin Goodfellow is a molecule.

VII

BRIDGMAN AGAIN

We return now to Bridgman in order to inspect the later stages of his development especially as we find it in *The Nature of Physical Theory* (1936).[26] His direct criticism of physics remains as fine as ever; the reviewers give it all the good words: matter-of-fact, common-sense, simple, direct, pertinent, hardheaded. Asserting the importance of the "physicist as critic" alongside the "physicist as theorist" he is in position to make sound progress on lines that recall Karl Pearson's use of Cousin's "*La critique est la vie de la science*" on the title page of the *Grammar of Science*.

But there is another side of his work. In place of the "naïve" view-

---

[26] Page references in the text will be to this book.

point he formerly took, he now seeks to insert " foundations " of a kind that require him " to map out the possibilities and limitations of the human mind in dealing with the problems presented it " (2). The world's long delay in getting to close quarters with this type of inquiry is probable evidence how much more difficult it is than the problems physics itself has solved. But Bridgman is not timorous. " Operationally " his indicated course would seem to be increasing caution and precision in the use of the words he draws from the surrounding psychological vocabulary in the general region he describes as that of " concept "; but this does not appeal to him at all. He simply adopts " mind " the way he has heard about it somewhere, and seeks results as mighty as Margenau's out of materials as frothy as Lindsay's.[27]

The moment he starts his examination he finds himself involved with " thought " and " language," and with their status with respect to a something known as " experience " (15). He is in the world's worst bog, but he goes merrily ahead. He gives us a chapter on thought and language, another on logic, and two on mathematics. Our complaint is not that he makes this inquiry, but that in it he employs all the bad devices he had ejected from physics, exploring, thus, " the properties of our mental processes " (13) by the aid of " essentially," " vitally," " absolutely," and " intuitively." The outcome for thought, language, and experience is as follows:

First Language must be differentiated from Experience. This is the way it is done (24):

" Activity is the basal property of all our experience."
" Language as language is divorced from activity."
" Language must be *language used*."
" *Language used* is obviously an activity."

The physicist, when he goes outside of physics, and whether he be concept-adorer or operation-priest, seems wholly without sense of linguistic shame.[28] The comment here must be the same as in the similar case for Margenau. If one must write contradictions such as these, why write at all? But this is not the worst. Bridgman next finds it necessary to differentiate Language from Thought, and this he does as follows:

---

[27] Reviewers of the book are almost unanimous in deprecating this development, even though each may have a different set of reasons for his objections. Malisoff's discussion in *Philosophy of Science*, Vol. III, pp. 360–364, covers the ground so fully that we may omit most of the details of criticism here.

[28] In fairness we must admit that psychologists and philosophers set him the example. In mathematics E. T. Bell is outstanding for inconsistencies arising from interpretative misuse of the " mental."

"The primary tool of self-conscious rational thought" appears to be "the tying up of experience into bundles which are capable of recognition" (26).

"Language separates out from the living matrix little bundles and freezes them" (24).

If Bridgman's exhibit of "the living matrix" is different from his exhibit of "experience," or if his "tying up" is different from his "freezing," then I am criticizing him unfairly. But I find no difference in his account. "Operationally" he shows us Language and Thought as "the same," as far as he goes. If they are in any sense "the same," then he ought to treat them so. But he does not. Quite the contrary. He thrusts them very far apart, even though he has nothing but conventionalized emotion to support him. Consider this:

"The two are not identical; thought is infinitely the richer, for it may contain awareness of the continually shifting background of connotation that is incapable of expression in language. . . . Thought is thus closer to experience than language" (26).

These words are all muddy; and the implication that a thing "'is infinitely' this because it 'may contain' that" is certainly queer for a realist to give us. But observe also how easily the assertion can be turned upside down with equally plausible results, as thus: "Language is infinitely richer and closer to experience than thought because it joins issues with precision, sweeps the cobwebs away, and pockets its gains," these motley nouns and verbs being just as safe and sane as any Bridgman uses.

All depends on what one thinks is "rich" or "close." Some like the gravy and some like the meat; but you can't build much muscle out of casual, personal preference.

Bridgman does, indeed, seek more definite statement than this, but never, so far as I have noted, without a hesitating qualification. Consider the words I have permitted myself to italicize in the following:

"Modes of thought . . . are possible from which the verbal element is *almost* entirely absent"; also some which go on "without *consciously* getting onto the verbal level" (25).

"The use of language is an activity" but "the fundamental device of *practically* all thought" is "analyzing experience into static bits with static meanings" (58).

Minor illustrations of the outcome of such procedures as the above abound. One will suffice. Bridgman repeatedly examines certain questions about *pi* (41, 43, 47),[29] especially as to whether men had a right to

---

[29] See also his essay, "A Physicist's Second Reaction to Mengenlehre," *Scripta Mathematica*, Vol. II, 1934.

say that it was either transcendental or not transcendental in 1881, the year before a proof was offered that it was. Somewhere in his discussion Bridgman applies his word "meaningless," but we can go a bit further than he does, and apply it even to his discussions of such issues, in which nothing can be found that is either appetizing or edifying. So vague is his wording that I would not even attempt to state precisely what the issue is. In front of me lie comments by four men, all no doubt impressionistic; one says Bridgman thought the question meaningless in 1881, another that it was meaningless to ask the question in that year, a third that Bridgman held the transcendental *pi* did not exist in that year, and a fourth that if he did not hold it non-existent, he should have, in order to be consistent. Bridgman is not that vague, of course; but his background of discussion is. He is far remote from operational procedure; and his recent shift in the type of his analysis bears most of the responsibility.

VIII

Faint Hint

A physicist cranking an ancient car with worn gears and leaky valves would never say: "What a wonderful machine. Its 'spirit' is right. I will use no other." Why, then, when he needs a behavioral carriage for his science, should he hold to a broken-down psychology of antiquated model?

What difference can it make to the physicist whether "ideas," "concepts," "minds" really "exist" or not, or whether anybody else thinks they exist or not? He has long since overcome his old imagined dependence on the "reality" of physical objects as a necessary presupposition for scientific work; he did not overcome this dependence because he wanted to, but because he had to; because the only way he could acquire sound physical descriptions was by abandoning some of his older rigidities.

The sole issue of scientific importance with regard to the "mental" is whether the mentalist vocabulary offers a sound technique for description or whether it does not. We know it does not. No one can put it to work properly. The more earnestly one tries, the better one understands its radical deficiencies. Modern logic offers a horrible example. We have examined what certain psysicists have tried to do with it. We may feel assured that their failures are not those of personal incompetence, but instead of the tools they have attempted to use, and of their almost hypnotic belief in the efficacy of such tools.

The "mental" cannot help other sciences because it cannot help its own. It is a breeding place of "schools," on the side of theory as well as on that of practice. Psychoanalysis is an illustration with its messes of Cs, Ucs, and Pcs, remote from possibility of scientific usage. Faculties and associations of ideas, reflexes, and brain cells [30] have had sounder scientific purpose, but no greater constructive success.

The strength of the "mental" in the past has rested in the certainty — as great a certainty as we can say we possess anywhere — that we confront actual phenomena, namely the behaviors of men, which do not attain adequate description in terms of spatial co-ordinates, and which thus, in a properly technical sense, do not exist "in space" at all.

The physicist may remind himself, however, that the "space" out of which "mental" phenomena have been ejected was the old absolute space-form of Newton, which was postulated as if something over and above all the events which happen within it. Despite the value this space-form retains, it can now no longer pretend to such great dominion. The new spaces that are succeeding it are much more tolerant to behavioral description. But they are more than this: they bring a new freedom to the enquirer into behavioral phenomena to construct and postulate whatever spaces he himself may need in which to examine his behavioral events; they come with the assurance that the sole criterion of their own validity and worth will be the success of the descriptions made by their aid.

Since the "mental" as we have known it in the past was a squeeze-out from Newtonian space, the physicist may be asked to ponder how it can still remain a squeeze-out when the space out of which it was squeezed is no longer there to squeeze it out.

If this faint hint aids the physicist, it will only be as he learns to distrust the reports of the pre-scientific psychology and do some of his spadework himself.

---

[30] Brain and nerve research lies in one of the soundest regions of experimental psychology, and K. S. Lashley is outstanding in this field. Here is what Lashley says of his own branch of inquiry: "It is doubtful if we know anything more about the mechanism of learning than did Descartes when he described the opening of the pores in the nerves by the passage of animal spirits. His statement sounds remarkably like the reduction of synaptic resistance by the passage of the nerve-impulse." (In *Handbook of Experimental Psychology,* edited by Murchison, p. 493.) Lashley's view in this respect is not isolated; rather it is typical of what outstanding investigators in any special branch of psychological inquiry will say of the status of knowledge in their particular branch. An examination of a dozen American psychological systems, under standards such as those that have been used in this essay, will be found in my book *Behavior, Knowledge, Fact,* 1935.

CHAPTER EIGHT

Situational *vs.* Psychological Theories of Behavior*

I

SIGHTS-SEEN AS MATERIALS OF KNOWLEDGE [1]

Most modern psychological inquiry is conducted under postulation expressible thus: Confronting various material objects are to be found certain experiencing beings, whose experiences (including their knowings) may, and for scientific purposes must, be isolated as subjectmatters in behavioral inquiry.[2] Upon psychologies so constructed (as a rule in their crudest forms) practically all our sociologies are based. To such psychologies likewise the current philosophizings about science as knowledge are steadily oriented.

This manner of postulation is not always — indeed, not even commonly — explicit. For the most part it takes itself for granted as plain common sense. Where affirmed, it exhibits shadings of stress ranging upward to a supreme self-confidence in the eternal verities. It will concern us solely as it enters scientific inquiry as guide to operation. In this form it declares with reasonable modesty, and with presumptive clarity, that investigation into behaviors is to be undertaken, and construction made, *as if in fact* the materials used consist definitely and precisely of non-organic objects, human beings (or other organisms), and experiences, with specialized isolation of the third of these for technical examination.[3]

Considered in this way with respect to their operative usefulness, such

---

* From *Journal of Philosophy*, Vol. XXXVI, No. 7 (March 30, 1939), pp. 169–81; No. 12 (June 8, 1939), pp. 309–23; No. 15 (July 20, 1939), pp. 405–13.

[1] This discussion in three sections is an expansion of remarks made at the Third Conference on Methods in Philosophy and the Sciences, New York City, May 8, 1938.

[2] For exceptions, see Section II.

[3] Let it be flatly stated now, and given maximum emphasis, that " reality " and " truth," and dogmatic concern over either, are wholly irrelevant to our present purposes. We shall consider only the status of scientific, pseudo-scientific, and expectantly scientific inquiry, with respect to what is taken to be fact, used as fact, or assumed to be on its way toward improved specification as fact in the advance of inquiry.

postulates have one test to face and only one: do systems constructed in their terms attain coherence of formulation and solidity of factual interpretations? Under this test the postulation is bad, because its works are bad; it has far outlived its usefulness. Some small parts of our current psychologies and sociologies are satisfactory to some workers in some small corners of the field, but the general condition of both branches of inquiry is notoriously unsatisfactory with respect to consistency and to factuality alike.

Any philosopher can tell us of dozens of accusations that have been cast against the materials thus postulated, and of dozens of philosophical efforts at their reformation; but the philosopher will also admit when pressed that no philosophy has ever accomplished anything toward reform that has stayed accomplished. Something of importance has been occurring in the last generation, nevertheless, that affects the entire method of initial observation which both the philosophies and the sciences have been employing. As a first approach I shall describe and develop to some extent a transformed method of inspecting the simplest factual situations that enter behavioral inquiry. In a following section I shall examine a number of recent psychological attitudes and constructions which tend to break away from the old forms and move toward the new ones. In the third section I shall consider the probable frame of postulation which the newer method of construction will require.

A Key to Progress. Professor Woodbridge, in a renewed examination of the problem of consciousness, declared in the *Journal of Philosophy* that "consciousness is seeing, hearing, and the rest," and that "seeing and hearing — and the rest appropriately — are sights seen and sounds heard"; that they "are materials of knowledge," not readily to be appraised as "functions" of anything.[4] His procedure in reaching this conclusion was to focus consideration upon "consciousness" as field of inquiry and as subject of discourse. After long-continued examination of the common-sense applications of the word and of its philosophical and scientific uses, and after a searching genetic appraisal, he achieved an immensely improved description and naming for the involved phenomena. I shall take the "is" and the first "are" in his cited words as asserting full equivalence in the naming of fact, so that when "sights seen" and "the rest appropriately" are specified, a comprehensive naming of the phenomena of consciousness has been given,[5] and no double-naming,

---

[4] *Journal of Philosophy*, Vol. XXXIII (1936), p. 567.
[5] These phenomena include also "thinking about . . ." and "expressing the result . . ."; *op. cit.*, p. 563. Discussion of the status of this inclusion will not be reached directly in the present essay.

collateral or summative, is permissible. We have here, then, a formal substitution of naming, and our procedure will be to start directly upon the basis of the substitution thus achieved. When we specify sights seen, and the rest, we shall regard ourselves as having exhaustively specified all that the word " consciousness " covers, so that nothing further will be implied or supplied by further use of the vocabulary of the " conscious," which may then drop out of the discussion altogether, except as it appears in occasional cases of critical offsetting.

Let us now take the words " sights " and " seen " and hyphenate them to sharpen their status as a single term which offers scientifically definite phenomena for our consideration. Let us then add an " etc." to permit ourselves to escape repetitional detail of naming when we include the correlated phenomena Professor Woodbridge has set forth, which are assimilable for *all* the purposes of the coming inquiry to the sights-seen proper. Taking these " sights-seen, etc." directly as " materials of knowledge," and proceeding to examine the forms of observation that may now be employed and the actual observations that can be made, we shall find that we have acquired an extremely efficient tool for further work.[6]

Absent entirely from our development will be any preferential imputation either to the " seeing " or to the " sights " in the term " sights-seen." In its freedom from such imputations lies one of the term's highest merits. Precisely here, however, appears a problem as to the localization of the phenomena " sights-seen, etc." which we may not at all evade. If the locus of these phenomena is not assigned exclusively to the organism in severance from the object (the changed status following at once if neither seen-object nor seeing-process has preferential stress), *where* are we to say that they are to be looked for and found? The answer to this question is not to be given out of hand. It is evident, however, that man's anatomical skin no longer is master in the old sense over the full scheme of observation and description. For the moment it will suffice to say that the locus may be assigned to a " situation " that includes organism and object, not as isolated beings forcing themselves or being forced into contact with one another, but as phases of one common, naturalistic process or event.

[6] The following additional expressions by Professor Woodbridge are well worth consideration as illustrative of his development in this field. The citations are from essays of the dates noted, as reprinted in his volume *Nature and Mind: Selected Essays* (1937). Consciousness . . . a type of connection (1905). Life . . . an interaction between organism and environment . . . not between consciousness and objects (1912). To expect a brain to think seems to be about as unreasonable an expectation as one can entertain (1925). Cognition is experience; only analysis of our subject-matter . . . increases our knowledge (1932). Vision . . . living and dynamic intimacy with nature; . . . Language . . . a living and natural communication with nature (1935). Seeing and hearing . . . the natural existence of sights and sounds; Knowledge . . . the elaboration of perception (1936).

Any such localization will, of course, be a provisional device for purposes of study, a possible first approximation to spatial form, and not at all a purported determination of reality.

Sights-Seen, Etc., in Evolution. Sights-seen, etc., enter the long array of evolutionary forms — sidereal, terrestrial, vital, and social — at the same stage at which an individualized "consciousness" is commonly averred to enter. They enter under slow gradation and differentiation just as an evolutionist might hope to make such a "consciousness" enter. They enter, however — and here lies an important difference in the outcome — as newly elaborated *process,* not as newly created (or creatively evolved) *things.* This contrast of process versus thing is not one that primarily involves the older specifications of "substance," whether material or immaterial. Rather it is a question of *force,* whether as a settled resident of a locality, or as distributed across a field with only such stress on localization as the conditions surrounding inquiry provisionally require.

An individualized "consciousness" entering the evolutionary train presents itself as a new "thing," or "quality," or "possession," or "capacity," or "power," or "force." "Emergent evolution" is friendly to it, and indeed the term "emergent" seems employed peculiarly to signalize this attitude, emphasis being placed upon the "new," not merely as produced through the processes of evolution, but more emphatically still upon this "new" as "present at" and "active at" the spot where it is thus "produced." Such an emergent "consciousness" acquires residence in or upon an organism or perhaps a brain, with all the possible consequences therefrom up to and including full theological dignity.

In sharp contrast with this, the evolving *sights-seen,* etc., acquire no such residence. They remain process under way across a field, with their localizations having the rank only of descriptions within inquiry, to be maintained to such an extent, and only to such an extent, as proves continuingly useful.[7] They are not "things" in the defective sense of that term; they are not closely localized residents of cerebral or other narrow areas; they make no claim to the possession of independent powers of their own.

Circularity. While sights-seen, etc., are thus established in an evolutionary setting, this setting itself is an outgrowth of knowledge, and this very "knowledge" arises directly out of the sights-seen, etc., which provide its materials. We face the great circle of all circles. So far as we

---

[7] The history of physics as knowledge exhibits just such transformations. Although in their book *The Evolution of Physics* (1938) Einstein and Infeld still speak with the tongues of the "psyche," nevertheless they clearly set forth the steady advance of their own science away from the old psyche's correlate — matter — and their own very strong hope for the ultimate complete displacement of "matter" in favor of "field."

know, such a circle of knowledge is inevitable under our present conditions of living, being, and knowing. Our age has overcome the heaviest of the ancient fixations and dogmatisms, but it has not yet reached the possible future stage of calm assurance; it shows itself at its best where it attains maximum freedom for search and discovery in the manner called scientific. What here concerns us, then, is not the fact of circularity, but only the type.

Where "consciousness" enters as a quasi-thing with a definite organic location, alleged to possess and exercise a power-specialization of its own, it carries with it all the old embroilments of solipsism and realism. A "mental" which eschews its old linguistic companions and parades itself in a fresh disguise as "emergental," remains after all the same old "mental":[8] a device for practical communication, a grammarizing of fact, a crude and imperfect manner of talking, a bit of mysticism. In it the "knower" is still opposed to the "known," with little change except in the stuff out of which he is assumed to be made. The same old duplicities appear, as well in the knower when he is appraised in terms of the known, as in the known when it is appraised in terms of the knower. The old difficulties with "raw" sensation are not very far away.[9]

In contrast with all this is the situation when sights-seen, etc., are taken in direct view. The distinction of subjective and objective no longer dominates. Concreted oppositions of the type of knower and known lose their microcosmic pretenses. The processes under way cease to appear as personality-masses in particle-point construction, but instead are broken down and spread over the long course of the evolutionary series, under conditions which give inquiry greatly heightened prospects of success. Sets of descriptions may now connect with one another the full length of the evolutionary chain. Well-knit descriptions will pass from stages prior to the entry of the sights-seen, etc. (as displayed in terrestrial time), not only up *to* the sights-seen, but straight on through them (now in a time in which the terrestrial clock seems shrunk in significance) into descriptions of the processes called concept, word, thought, and symbol, and into those further processes called "constructions," which in the end set forth that very evolutionary background within which the sights-seen, etc.,

---

[8] The evidence lies in the way its proponents *make use* of it in their further procedures.

[9] E. A. Singer, Jr., twenty-five years ago or more, laid the foundations admirably for the transition from the older views, although he himself did not push the conclusion its full distance. "The beginning of our epistemological building is not a datum which might be known by itself . . . but just any point at which it occurs to us to ask ourselves, What is it you know? and, How do you know it?" . . . "Two wearily endless ways. The one leads toward, but never arrives at, the real object; the other leads toward, but never culminates in, the bare datum" (From an essay of 1910 included in *Mind as Behavior* 1924, pp. 13–14).

themselves are described. The "circle" is not lost, but its radius now becomes so great that along a segment of our working lives we may attain what seems to us to be direct vision forward or backward alike; this, however, solely when our "feel" is that of inquiry, and when we disregard the assertion of realities, and concern ourselves neither with *terminus a quo* nor *ad quem*. We have thus indications of an empirically established empiricism, in significant contrast with the older patterns of empiricism, rationalistically proclaimed.

Seeing Sights-Seen, Etc. If a sight-seen is material of knowledge — if, indeed, there is any system in knowledge and observation — then we may expect the sight-seen itself to be observable. To what observation can we attain?

We start with a handicap. In current ways of talking, an observation is an organism's "act." For us, in contrast, it is the existence — the very phenomenal presence — of a sight-seen, which is not a "function" of anything. In current speech the conventions of our pre-scientific language, particularly its grammar, dominate report, belief, and in a well-known sense the observing itself; an illusion being no less an illusion where ancient respectability is its boast.[10] The current form of speech is a recognized obstacle to progress in the psychological and social sciences, the existing status of these sciences being evidence enough of the fact. In replacing the current form — if replacement is to come at all — we need the simplest and most efficient direct description we can obtain. The description must be verifiable, and it must be uncompelled; otherwise we do not want it at all.

Observing the situation set before us by the report "I see a tree," we have a right to take it as event, as *an* event, and to approach thus its examination. We lay aside the usual inattentive procedure of resting casually on the items "I" and "tree" under the impression that we are safe in allowing these items to explain, or serve as bases for, a possible third item, "see." The barest hint of the dubious status of the first two items should be enough to require us to seek as closely as possible the observation of the event, regardless of what possible reorientation of the items "I," "see," and "tree" may follow.

The position now briefly to be sketched occupies ground common to many men of many views. The outcome depends on how far one proceeds, on where he stops, and on what he does at his chosen stopping point.[11]

[10] Whether grammar precedes factual scheme historically or factual scheme grammar, in such a case as the one involving "I," "see," and "tree," is a question not here at issue. We examine conditions as we find them coming before us *now*.

[11] A most interesting recent review is by E. B. Holt, "Materialism and the Criterion of the Psychic," *Psychological Review,* Vol. 44 (1937), p. 33. Professor Holt summons

Our first step is to note the extreme over-generalization of the expression " I see a tree." In its place we may substitute and use for introductory purposes an expression that is much closer to the event, thus: " Standing at my window, I look out and see a tree on the hill." Even this must be made more definite in terms of " my present organism now," " this window to my left," and " that white oak beyond," and by recognizing that the " see " in question is no longer some generality of " power " or " act," but instead the indicated process of a much more definite verb than " see " — namely, " to see a," expressing precisely a present event of seeing.

In my own case the more clearly I narrow observation down to the immediate instance, the more certainly I identify the form " sight-seen " directly, without further differentiation into components such as " I," " see," or " it." I identify no component such as tree-object (apart from observable presence), no separate " idea " or mental element, or capacity, or personality factor, and no separated " act " of observing, separately performed. I observe no array of performers or performances under the conventional linguistic specifications, but instead precisely the immediately present event. Lurking in the underbrush around the edges of observation may be myriad candidates for attention, but the behavioral techniques of their entries and exits is not our problem at this moment; once entered, they exhibit themselves in the form of sights-seen, etc.[12]

The illustration, " sight-seen," will suffice for the full range of " sights-seen, etc.," although if the presumptive procedure under examination were that of an independent mind-thing, with a private array of powers of its own, a single specimen — such as a " seeing " — would fall far short of being adequate. In our case, consider in differentiation: (a) the sight-seen as an instance of observation, and (b) the sight-seen as an object-phase of observation, where the form in place of (tree-sight)-seen is (sight-seen)-seen. The two cases reduce to one, and although they exhibit an immense range of complexities greatly in need of exploration and organization, everywhere in them is also exhibited the characteristic process or event. Case (b) is an instance within the phenomena of sights-seen, etc., just as fully as was the special instance of a single sight-seen we considered above. The outlines of coherent scientific construction are clear. This is in sharp contrast with the painful problems that arise where " observation " is the

---

as witnesses James, Russell, Palágyi, Mauthner, Müller-Freienfels, and others, but stops at a point that enables him, according to his own desire, to reduce all process to physiological " body," and to declare positively (p. 53) that " awareness is *created* by motor response " (italics mine).

[12] No atomism or particularism is implied by the statements of the text, nor is incidentally any " infinitism." No position is taken as to how " big " or how " little " a sight-seen, or any of its company, may be, to accord with any current specification of bigness or littleness.

"act" of an "I." The words "solipsism" and "introspection" tell enough of the story. The latter word reports certain sporadically plausible attempts to make direct contact with a linguistically engineered fiction. The former recognizes that a comparable fiction inserted into any "other" organism is beyond plausible reach of such contact. Where observation proceeds under the form of sights-seen, etc., the fiction is eliminated, and along with it the full nest of fictive problems.

Obstacles to Observation. My observation and report, as I have above set it down, may, of course, be erroneous. I cannot claim validity for it unless it is also valid for other organisms like mine. The decision, however, is not a matter of statistics of attitudes at a given moment, nor of personal likings. Verifications or rejections that count come only when issues are analyzed, goals identified, obstacles overcome, and sufficient training obtained; the use of a great telescope requires all of these, and much more does our problem require them. We may mention the main obstacles that interfere, and then indicate the influence of prominently recognized objectives.

If, despite all the characterization that has been given them, a reader still regards the sights-seen, etc., as "subjective" in contrast with things-objective, he illustrates a manner of obstacle, perhaps to be styled propaedeutical inelasticity, of which nothing further need here be said. In specific experience such as memory-image, however, a quasi-subjective influence may assert itself, despite high discipline of attention. One may grant, tentatively at least, a basic observation of sights-seen where tree and man confront, but feel forced to deny it when man has moved five minutes and a thousand feet down the road and memory-image comes. Hobbes in his time and in his matter-of-fact way found no difficulty here.[13] Have we such clarity of knowledge about light-waves-at-an-instant that an event of light-waves-with-neural-continuations is in contrast a mystery?

The above difficulty under analysis shows itself to involve the particular space and time backgrounds of our ordinary reference and our connected attitude which sees events as the results of impact-causation. Our three-dimensional surveyor's space rose to unique magnificence in Newton's mechanics, but has been shorn of its older claims through the extensions of physical observation which modern physics has achieved; yet it still dominates the description of most things "psychological"; which is to say that it dominates the very region in which its standing was *never* sound, and its descriptive powers *never* adequate. Confirmed addicts of

[13] *Leviathan,* Chapters I and II.

such space and time and causation bar themselves automatically from improvement of their observational processes beyond what these forms will permit.

But again these space and time backgrounds are complexly involved with our language systems.[14] Perceptional phases are entangled with " categories " and other expressive phases. Obstacle of obstacles to progress is the too highly specialized verbal device, good enough, perhaps, in its special uses, but allowed to dominate problems far beyond its proper competence. So many enterprises are under way at present toward setting the world right linguistically [15] that it is enough here to mention the situation.

Not as direct obstacle, but more widely as conditioning of opinion, we come finally to the nature of the problems men set themselves, in their respective times and places. We possess as yet no usable sociological theory of the conditions of progress, that is, of the nexus of change with change in social life. We may nevertheless very simply note that devices good for older uses, in time prove defective and must undergo replacement; and that the present age is one in which a basic " I " which " sees," and a basic " it " which " is seen," are both devices which have fallen into disrepute because of their failures to do sound work where sound work is scientifically most needed. The sights-seen, etc., appear in replacement, precisely to attempt to perform the task.

Favoring Signs. Is there a serious student of behaviors today who asserts the existence (i.e., presence for study) of " mental states " (ideas, concepts, or whatsoever) devoid of all " content "? Probably, no. Suppose, now, an inquirer *includes* this admitted " content " fully and honestly in his behavorial materials, and then, in disregard of minor aims and games, seeks the most comprehensive construction for behavior he can get. Can he stop short of full recognition of sights-seen, etc., as basic phenomena of observation? The answer is, I think, that he cannot. An accompanying incidental comment is necessary, however, to the effect that few inquirers have either occasion or desire to seek so far.

William James was our greatest observer. His " stream of thought " (with " thought " the equivalent of " consciousness ") was perhaps his

---

[14] Compare E. Durkheim, *The Elementary Forms of the Religious Life,* pp. 1–20, for pertinent facts, presented, however, under a widely different plan of statement.

[15] Thus Korzybski; Ogden and the shades of Bentham; Chase's troubled effort to spread the sad tale; the companions of the *Encyclopedia [of Unified Science]*; and many others. I have yet to find, however, that any of these have applied their proposed linguistic procedures to their own accepted operator-egos; till that is done I suspect all our wings will continue to flutter feebly.

greatest observation. He saw, of course, with the eye of the physiologist, and located this " stream " within the skin; but even that localized setting did not suppress his feeling that by rights he should be using the impersonal verb to report " simply and with the minimum of assumption " his observation that " it thinks." " Every thought," he continued, "*tends* to be part of a personal consciousness " (italics mine).[16] In our present generation with its greatly widened knowledge of environing and social processes, James's impersonal observation " it thinks " moves readily from intra-organic localizations into the full situations of organism-object, where the form " sights-seen, etc.," becomes characteristic of it.

The strongest evidence for the phenomena, sights-seen, etc., so far as my own feeling goes, lies in the duplicity of perhaps all of those words in our language by which specific instances of " mental process " are displayed. This evidence is strong because it exhibits the utmost that speaking beings, all together across the millennia, have been able to accomplish toward isolating factually the " psyche " of their belief; and this utmost is just nothing. Long-range word-couples like " mind " and " matter," or like " subjective " and " objective," are easy enough to emit and to hold in plausible imaginative severance; but when we come down to particular instances of behavior, this is no longer possible. The philosophical ins and outs of the word " idea " in its specific applications are notorious. The word " observation," considered above, exhibits much of the same condition; it fades in and out between the observing and the observed, and is never safe until these are brought frankly into fusion, and the start is made thus. Such words as " thought," " knowledge," " meaning," " percept," " concept," all have the common affliction.[17] Even the word " operation," since the enormous increase in its use following Bridgman's brilliant application, swells with confusion; a certain recent inquiry into operational constructions employed this word in closely succeeding passages, first with the implications we call " subjective," next with those we call " objective," and finally in a way hardly otherwise to be labeled

---

[16] *The Principles of Psychology*, Vol. I, pp. 224–227. James proceeds somewhat apologetically to say that phenomena like the split personality were what led him to use the word " tends," and that " no psychology, at any rate, can question the *existence* of personal selves " (italics his), a cryptic remark one may read as one will. For a check on James's later views, see his presidential address, " The Experience of Activity," *Psychological Review*, Vol. 12 (1905), pp. 1–17, and particularly p. 9.

[17] In a similar sense John Dewey calls " belief " a " double-barreled " word, and refuses to waste time with it in discussing the outcomes of logical procedure (*Logic, The Theory of Inquiry*, 1938, p. 7). Professor Dewey's new work is of the very highest importance in the development of interactional interpretation of behavior, but it was not available to me when these essays were prepared. To take full account of his presentation would require such extensive recasting that I have been compelled to limit myself for the present to a note appended to the final essay.

than " mixed." The more remote we place ourselves from specific facts, the more easily we proclaim the separateness of the poles of knowledge. The closer we come to specific facts, the more certainly these poles fuse into the processes of one common field.

Comment. To adopt sights-seen, etc., as materials of knowledge brings no interference whatever with the procedures of the established sciences. Physics can select its objects for inquiry, and bring them toward precision just as it does now — indeed it will be released from some of its present incentives to paradox-hunting. Physiological psychology can carry on its researches without either present interference or any suggestion of limits to be placed upon its expansion. Only the physicist who craves to orate over God and Nature, and the physiologist or psychologist who, with similar futility, burns to instruct us of Man and Society, will fall victim; and they only as respects these particular splutterings of their linguistic energies.

No summation of physics and physiology has ever yet shown signs of yielding behavioral knowledge. In the "psychological" range of behavioral inquiries, the enterprise of most pressing importance (noted incidentally under the heading " Circularity " above) is the development of an interpretation of the processes called " concept " and " word " directly out of perceptive and sub-perceptive processes. The steps here to be taken are fairly plain (though if I had not already explored them to a considerable degree, I should probably not feel justified in so positive a stand as I am here taking). A very real progress had been made in this direction a generation or two ago, only to fall forfeit when an upsurging physiology took into its bosom most of the evil of the old " psychic," while tossing away much of the good.

From the " social " range of behavioral inquiries, an illustration — a vivid one to all students of the subject who are sufficiently interested — will suffice. This is the case of the " institution," most plainly inspected as economics has struggled to develop it. Veblen's magnificent insights and analyses were in terms of " institution," yet the best description he could give was in such phrasing as: " the institutions — that is to say the habits of thought — under the guidance of which men live "; [18] and such phrasings are wholly non-informative where the " habits of thought " themselves are not technically examined and established in their operations. Commons has created an institutional economics around a definition of the institution as " Collective Action in Control of Individual Ac-

---

[18] Thorstein Veblen, *The Theory of the Leisure Class,* p. 191. I do not recall his stressing such descriptions in his later work, but neither do I recall his making improvements upon them.

tion,"[19] although such a "collective" is the purest fiction, since no behavioral processes are anywhere known except as those of individual organisms. Mitchell calls the word "institution" "merely a convenient term for the more important among the widely prevalent, highly standardized social habits";[20] in other words, he avoids characterization altogether, and this is wisdom on his part so long as the older "psychic" terms and implications are all he can muster for his uses, even though his own admirable manner of placing the "psychological" in the framework of the "institutional" runs far beyond the import of that older terminology.[21] The social sciences require specifications for their important terms such as "institution" — not in any miracle of precision, but at least to the extent of distinguishing fish, flesh, and fowl — as much as do the physical and physiological sciences. The construction "sights-seen, etc.," puts an entirely new face on the issue, since the materials we call physical and mental, and individual and social, now enter from the start in system — a system which needs only phenomenal development, not miraculous intervention, to become workable.

By Way of Contrast. Typical working programs with which the above suggestions are radically out of harmony may be exhibited in two well-known older formulations, and in one newer one:

Bertrand Russell: "I wish to preserve the dualism of subject and object in my terminology, because this dualism seems to me a fundamental fact concerning cognition."[22]

Sigmund Freud: "What is meant by 'conscious' we need not discuss; it is beyond all doubt."[23]

Edwin B. Holt: "When entities are combined into wholes, novel properties emerge." "A genuine analysis of the mind and the cognitive process will inevitably analyze these into things and processes which are neither mental nor cognitive."[24]

---

[19] John R. Commons, *Institutional Economics: Its Place in Political Economy* (1934), p. 69. Compare also the opening sentence of Chapter I. The difficulty, of course, lies only in the psychological setting of the "definition." Commons' high rank as observer of the economic scene and as interpreter of economic history is everywhere recognized.

[20] Wesley C. Mitchell, *The Backward Art of Spending Money, and Other Essays* (1937), p. 373.

[21] Walton H. Hamilton was one of the early "institutional" economists, but even in a late book of which he is co-author, *The Power to Govern* (1937), the heading for the section of the book dealing with institutional transformation is the wholly decorative one "The Paths for the Mind."

[22] *Proc. Arist. Soc.*, 1910–1911, p. 109. In a later stage Russell developed a strong interest in unification by way of "neutral stuff" (*The Analysis of Mind*, 1921); and still later he made an effort at situational treatment, declaring knowledge to need study not as "inner," but as "a manner of reacting to the environment," as "a characteristic which may be displayed in our reactions to our environment," though still referable to events occurring in heads with brains (*Philosophy*, 1927, p. 17, p. 88, p. 89, p. 285).

[23] *New Introductory Lectures on Psycho-Analysis* (1933), p. 99.

[24] *Psychological Review*, 1937, p. 36, p. 43.

II
SITUATIONAL TREATMENTS OF BEHAVIOR

The preceding pages [25] gave attention to the observability of sights-seen and of certain comparable perceivings, thinkings, and expressings belonging to the field commonly called " conscious." It permitted the tentative localization of such phenomena in regions broader than the anatomies of the organisms most manifestly active in them. It asserted that observation in this form, if once in common use, might lead to a reconstruction of the psychological and sociological sciences. Let us now consider certain recent advances toward this attitude as we find them in the works of Pavlov, Klüver, A. Meyer, Kantor, and Lewin. If comparably important developments go unmentioned through my lack of acquaintance, I can only express my regret.

The commonest and most broadly used name for the phenomena these men investigate is " behavior." Since " psyche " lost its last shreds of respectable status, " behavior " has become the word that stands as fact-indicator for psychology much as " social " stands for sociology. This " social," however, is itself a form of behavior, so that psychology and sociology alike now appear to be dealing with common fact under common basic name, and the outcome should be a final fusion of the two sciences much as physics and chemistry are now fused — unless, indeed, some wider and richer knowledge comes to yield new grounds of distinction.

The word " behavior " has, of course, applications running beyond those of psychology and sociology, as when physicists use it for electrons, or physiologists for genes and cells, but this is no disadvantage to its use. Rather we are stimulated to search for more precise differentiation. We find that if we talk of "*psychological* behaviors," we are merely using a form of double-talk which tells nothing. We may wisely look to the physicists and physiologists for aid or suggestion. If we do, we shall note that these scientists strive ceaselessly for precision in their localization of the special physical and physiological behaviors they study. They demand of themselves ever more definitely that they be able to put their fingers on the spot and on the instant of the event, even though thereby they are led to field and wave.

In appraising the five behavioral constructions above listed, we shall follow this hint from physics and physiology, and use as our test the type of localization which the work of each psychologist (though not nec-

---

[25] " Sights-Seen as Materials of Knowledge," *Journal of Philosophy*, Vol. XXXVI (1939), pp. 169–181 [Section I of this chapter].

essarily his accompanying comment) gives to the behavioral facts he studies. However, we shall not push this test beyond the elementary range of a surveyor's space and an ordinary clock's time. Evidences of spatial and temporal definiteness are all that we seek: if any, then what? Our assumptions will be: (1) that behaviors are facts; (2) that facts must be isolable in instances if scientific techniques are to be employed in their study; (3) that in consequence it makes sense in the psychological case if we venture to speak of *a* behavior — of a *single* behavior — as recognizable, describable, and in some form manipulatable; (4) that in this event we have the right, and are indeed obligated, to ask the simple questions, " Where is this behavior to be found? " and " When is it to be found? "; finally (5) that we have the right to expect a rationally worded reply in a usable form. This is no more than to employ the simplest common sense in a simple situation, so that if " we keep the pig in the parlor," we at least know parlor from pig-pen. We may, if we wish, fortify ourselves by recalling William James's opinion that " the word ' I ' is primarily a noun of position, just like ' this ' and ' here.' " [26]

One great step toward localization has been taken in the last generation, but it is only a preliminary. This is the bringing of behaviors down from Cloudcuckooville, and their establishment upon the common earth. " Soul " had enjoyed as its spectacular environments, God, Flesh, and Devil. " Mind " — attritus of Soul — stood closer, but not too close, to earth, performing neatly on a " parallel " trapeze. Both of these were viewed as " at," or " attached to " the body, though not " of " it, so that, when they finally came to earth, this body — the organism — provided a ready home for them. Overt movements, neural linkages, glands, and cerebrums — even cerebral arteries — soon were claimed as the very liver and lights of behavior itself. But something went wrong. No matter how busily one talks about these organic items, not a single one of them in its own direct description has ever successfully set forth behaviors in recognizable forms of their own. The result is that we find, now behaviors in the guise of " personalities," and again behaviors in the guise of " whole-organisms," where " person " and " wholeness " are treated as something over and beyond the organism proper — simulant auras floating off from, or above, or around organic events. The preliminary step — the transfer from " psyche " to earth — has thus yielded no proper localization in the sense of our assumptions, but has resulted instead in psyche-substitutes, referable to the organism, but not describable in its terms.

All such theories of behavior as the above we may call " psychological." In contrast with them we may consider a group, or the beginnings of a

[26] *Psychological Review,* Vol. 12 (1905), p. 9.

group, of theories employing a different type of localization, and these we may call "situational." The differentiation lies in the fact that in this second group the locus of the behaviors no longer is placed in the organism alone. While the differentiation between the two groups is vital, the particular manner just suggested for their naming is merely a convenience of the present essay, and is not indicated or recommended for use beyond.[27]

Situational Behaviors in the Laboratory. Let us begin by considering experimentation rather than attempts at formulation and construction. First to inspect is Pavlov. He is commonly spoken of as a psychologist, and as such is classified as mechanist and atomist. This was not his own view of the case at all. He regarded himself as physiologist — first, last, and all the time. He thought of his experiments as extending physiology directly into fresh fields *of its own;* these last three words set forth the essence of the matter.[28] As a physiologist the work of his hands counted much more for him than his voice.

His great inquiry began with a study of stomach secretions which early won him the Nobel prize. He passed to buccal secretions, and from there — still steadily the physiologist — to the examination of cases in which a dog's stimulation to secretion comes by eye instead of by palate or tongue. Of this step, it is literal and precise to say that Pavlov, the physiologist, not for an instant departing from his physiological footing, crosses the borders of a dog's anatomically specified skin, and experiments with a physiological event which *includes* phases lying several feet "outside" of the thus specified skin. Our matter-of-fact program of localization requires us to make this direct report, no matter how erratic the statement may seem to those who ascribe behavioral events to the operations of

---

[27] In the text I consider only certain theoretical constructions or experimental approaches thereto. For a fuller review much surrounding territory would have to be covered. Philosophically, Aristotle, Aquinas, and Fichte come to mind. In physiology there is a strong "situational" trend, though limited to cellular and similar interior events, and with manifest lack of sympathy for any extended psychological application. Cultural studies, institutional economics, modern criminologies, and rehabilitation programs all show a practical departure from the old stresses on individual power and responsibility in favor of the new "social" and "ecological" stresses on situations. Even our everyday forms of conversational comment are charged with this attitude. The philosophies, however, are remote from our present specialization of interest, and the practical inquiries and appraisals, no matter how they stress a form of *conditioning,* distinctly imply that there is a separable person-thing that is thus *conditioned,* and are usually vehement in their hostility to any full theoretical generalization. The absurd terminology of the "social environment" is in point: the only thing this form of "social" can environ is a something that itself is a "not-social"; the explicit recognition of "facts," toward which the terminology strives, is thus accompanied by their implicit denial.

[28] *Lectures on Conditioned Reflexes,* translated by W. Horsley Gantt (1928), p. 213; p. 241. See also "Reply of a Physiologist to Psychologists," *Psychological Review,* Vol. 39 (1932), p. 91.

psyche-powered — or psyche-simulant — brains. The anatomical skin now ceases to be the behavioral " skin " in that region of physiological inquiry commonly covered by the word " behavior." If there is a sense in which a physiological event can be given a locus running from " taste-organ " to " muscle-movement," just so surely a Pavlov conditioned reflex may be seen as having its continuously physiological localization in a region running all the way from " meat-powder " or " bell-peal " to " saliva-flow," rather than as being physiological part of the way and something else the rest.

The individual student is of course free to describe Pavlov's procedure as he wishes and to interpret it in his own way; among us all we may have a hundred forms of report. Two of these stand out most prominently: one in which a mentalist's view of a mechanist's space and causation is used as a framework, with Pavlov conventionalized to fit; the other, in which Pavlov's experimentation is permitted to run its own free course, while the " space " distinctions are allowed to adapt themselves to the experimentally recorded facts. (I repeat: it is Pavlov's *procedure,* and not his *views,* or the views of others about him, which I here appraise.) Despite his *obiter dicta* — and these appeared in motley collection during his long busy career — he was not dogmatically a disbeliever in the " psychical," his language about it being often that of a true believer. The roots of his criticism run deeper than either dogma or dogmatic rejection of dogma. As a scientific seeker, his observation and his repeated report was that whenever he or his associates used psychical expressions for the description of their experiments — speaking, perhaps, of a dog's feelings, wishes, or intentions — they lost precision, and weakened the further course of observation.[29] Hence the fines imposed in his laboratory through a large part of his career where lapses into slovenly expression occurred.

Pavlov's familiar key-words, " conditioned " and " unconditioned," have acquired in translation, it is said, a measure of false coloration; certainly many of their current applications yield a distortion of the phenomena of inquiry. He tried various other phrasings, such as permanent and temporary, constant and inconstant, inborn and acquired, species and individuals, but none of these seemed satisfactory. More and more as the years went on he came to talk in terms of signaling, until finally in his lectures on cerebral activity he set down " signal-reflexes as the most fundamental physiological characteristic of the hemispheres." [30] What is more, this signalization, however crude Pavlov was

[29] *Lectures* (Gantt tr.), p. 38.
[30] *Conditioned Reflexes: An Investigation of the Physiological Activity of the Cerebral Cortex,* translated by G. V. Anrep (1927), p. xiii, p. 15; also pp. 14-24. *Lectures* (Gantt

in his later attempts at its linguistic extension, is much closer as a technique to the outcome of the long line of factual inquiries in Great Britain from Reid to Romanes than it is to the gymnastics of our atomist mentalists on mechanist stilts.

By the side of this development in terms of signaling, two other characteristics of Pavlov's procedure stand forth when we look at it realistically. One is the emergence and steady increase in significance of what he at first called the "investigatory reflex,"[31] a name which in mechanistic application lends itself to base ends, but which in Pavlov's hands marked a phenomenon of inquiry which came to annoy his assistants so badly that they labeled it "the enemy," and finally recognized it as neither a "conditioned" nor an "unconditioned" reflex, but as in a classification to itself,[32] where its revolutionary possibilities now begin to appear. The other characteristic is the steady difficulty Pavlov and his followers have had in the use of the words "internal" and "external." The slippery use of such terms by systematizers always leads one to fear the worst; but in Pavlov's case the difficulty is the honest laboratory record of phenomena to which the slide-rule of our ordinary language will not accurately apply, with important consequences for the old anatomical "skin" wherever behaviors are in question.[33]

Pavlov's scheme of signalizations may be readily brought into close correspondence with Woodbridge's sights-seen. Both procedures are the type that insist on examining phenomena as they come. Each refuses to accept a shift in wording as an explanation. Pavlov's phenomena are no ganglionic reflexes in physical-chemical report, but processes involving

tr.), pp. 52, 123, 127, 214, 297, 372, 381, 382, *et al.* *Psychologies of 1930*, pp. 208–211. Y. P. Frolov does not index the word "signal" in his recent book *Pavlov and His School* (1937), but he describes late extensions of its use, pp. 78, 81, 90, 91, 228, 234. Frolov's interpretations (i.e., his manners of verbalization) are throughout alien to the attitude I am here taking, but that does not affect the point under consideration.

[31] *Conditioned Reflexes* (Anrep tr.), p. 12, *et al.* See *ibid.*, p. 115, and *Psychologies of 1930*, p. 211, for the general environmental influence. G. E. Coghill, in his paper "Individuation versus Integration in the Development of Behavior," *Journal of General Psychology*, Vol. III (1930), pp. 431–435, interprets the general trend of Pavlov's actual experimentation as in line with his own important results with Amblystoma, and lets his criticism run against "units" of the type "generally accepted." Needless to say, Coghill's own work is heavily relied upon by me in my present development, his "total pattern" not being subject to the objections to the "whole-organism" in this latter's "generally accepted" form.

[32] Frolov names it the "boundary reflex," *op. cit.*, pp. 62, 64.

[33] The fact that Pavlov has a coherent theory of sleep (*Conditioned Reflexes*, Anrep tr., Chap. XV) may also be stressed. Many outside observers find it astounding when psychologists describe consciousness as awareness in the sense of awakeness, and then relegate sleep to an inferior region as a "special" topic. Kantor is one of the very few psychologists along with Pavlov who seem to have made progress toward bringing sleeping and waking states into system, behaviorally.

percipient characteristics, cerebrally mediated. If we take sights-seen, etc., as basis for our generic term, then the Pavlov reflex enters association with it as specific process. If we take sights-seen as one process and Pavlov reflex as another (recognizing the terminology as inchoate), the term "signalization" will supply a clue to their further organization, and also to the introduction of still more complex processes arising from them. Interfering with recognition of this intimate correlation is merely the intrusion of the verbal opposition, "subjective-objective," which forces itself upward from our lower language deeps, often against our best resistance. If sights-seen have suppressed this opposition in one way, and if the Pavlov signalization has suppressed it in another, a critic would seem to fall far short of the reasonable proprieties if he permits its resurgence to lead him to deny the right of broader alliance to the joint victors.

For an additional exhibit of behaviors as situational we may examine the laboratory work of Heinrich Klüver. He approaches from the viewpoint of Gestalt psychology, and finds frequent occasion to differ from Pavlov. So much the more striking, therefore, are the indications provided in his book *Behavior Mechanisms in Monkeys* (1933).[34] His word "mechanisms" stands for "general modes of functioning" (p. 1) which as processes or events can get adequate statement only in terms of a monkey and its situation jointly. Not in his formal pronouncement, but in the detail of experiment and description, he abandons monkey-itself as locus of behaviors. He shows us neither monkey-faculties nor outer-world controls upon specialized monkey-entities, but instead "conditions under which" (p. 328) events occur; "organisms which under certain conditions happen to function in such a way that" (p. 333); responses which "occur along certain lines and in certain directions" (p. 345); the "this and not that" of the event (p. 347); and "properties that become effective" in given situations (p. 355). In grammatical structure and in direct assertion his sentences leave the behavioral organism with a status apart from environment, and make no further generalization. Factually, nevertheless, they report phenomena which in simple direct description cross the animal's skin, and are of the nature of sights-seen rather than of seeings, or things, or mechanical or other combinations of the two.

In reports made by specialists in animal behavior, even by some of those who employ the simplest of mentalist backgrounds in which to display their work, it is more and more common today to find phrases of

---

[34] Page citations in parentheses in the text are from this book; see also pp. 355-359 on "capacities," and items 3-6, pp. 365-366.

Situational vs. Psychological Theories of Behavior

"situational" intimation. Consider "behavior *in situ*,"[35] and "expressions as they occur in a given type of situation."[36] Professor K. S. Lashley in his introduction to Klüver's book just cited (p. vii) speaks of "the properties in complex sensory situations," and of "the relational properties of the situations," using phrasings of an older model, but approximating recognition of a situational status.

The Growth of an Attitude. In his special field, psychiatry, Adolf Meyer holds foremost place in the United States. He is noted for his steady calmness in viewing facts and — what is much the same thing — for his freedom from the psychological clichés which become the reliance of many practitioners.[37] To re-enforce his psychiatry he required a psychology. Finding none to meet his factual demands, he proceeded slowly and cautiously, but steadily, over a period of twenty-five years, to develop not a system but rather a working attitude for the guidance of himself and his students. His original stress was upon the organism — whence the name he adopted, psychobiology; it was designed to gain freedom from the fictions of the subjective psychologies.[38] This stress he still retains, but gradually he has overlaid it with an even heavier stress on the need for freedom from prevalent physiological dicta, as against which his psychobiology has come to yield the "biologic" antidote. Today he observes and investigates the "whole organism" as itself comprised within a wider whole, the very "situations" of its living. His "person" becomes a "functional inclusion of a varying scope of relations reaching far beyond the structural organism";[39] it is "body in action" in circumstances such that it is a "responding to varying situations" in

---

[35] R. C. Tryon in *Comparative Psychology* (edited by F. A. Moss, 1934), p. 442.
[36] Otto L. Tinklepaugh, *ibid.*, p. 477.
[37] "We use terminology where it serves a purpose; we do not serve traditional terminology." (*Address before the Massachusetts Psychiatric Society*, Dec. 9, 1927, p. 14.)
[38] "Objective Psychology or Psychobiology with Subordination of the Medically Useless Contrast of Mental and Physical," *Journal of the American Medical Association* (Sept. 4, 1915); "The Contributions of Psychiatry to the Understanding of Life Problems," from *A Psychiatric Milestone*, privately printed by the Society of the New York Hospital, 1921.
[39] This phrasing is from his abstract of one of his lecture courses. The citations that follow in the text, with page numbers in parentheses, are from his contribution "The Psychobiological Point of View" to the National Research Council's report, *The Problem of Mental Disorder* (1934). See also his paper "Spontaneity" in *A Contribution of Mental Hygiene to Education*, published by Illinois Conference on Public Welfare (1933), and his contributions to a symposium appearing in *American Journal of Psychiatry*, Vol. 92 (1935), p. 271, p. 353. C. Macfie Campbell, describing Meyer's position in *Archives of Neurology and Psychiatry*, Vol. 37 (1937), p. 724, writes that in psychiatry the student is always dealing "with a human personality at grips with its environment." The import of such a sentence varies, however, in accordance with the manner in which the key-words are stressed. Neither Campbell nor, so far as I have observed, any of Meyer's students is accustomed to give the full "situational" value to such words that Meyer himself seems to me to give.

ways that are "open to observation" as "states of function" which do not exist "without specific 'content'" (p. 56). These assertions by Meyer are not the mere protective verbal discolorations which we so often find in works built loosely on scattering foundations. They are careful and positive expressions of his factual approach. "I should emphasize," he writes, "the definitely biological rather than physiological character of the problem. . . . What interests us is the functioning in a situation with content of varying bearing upon the *life-curve*" (p. 68). His term "ergasia," covering "actions, and reactions, and attitudes" (p. 55) is a phenomenal naming of processes on the behavioral level under way in a situation, and as a working attitude goes far toward the suppression of the old pretense that the human epidermis is the most vital line of demarcation in the universe.

Expressions of Meyer's earlier "organismal" view, as he at times calls it, still occur in his writings along with "situational" stresses. Thus: "the reduction of man to singularity and unity" (p. 51), and "the individual organism as the entity" (p. 56); but these latter in their turn are offset by the emphatic assurance that "the person and the group" furnish the problem, that "units" are matters of choice, and that when "person" appears as a "unit," it is "personality function" that is meant (p. 70).

Precisely this emergence of the "situational" in the arms of the "organismal" is our great interest and concern. The issues which this emergence involves are now to appear more clearly in the specimens of formally "interactional" and "field" construction which we are next to survey.

Direct Situational Construction: Kantor's "Interactions." Professor J. R. Kantor has produced what I take to be the earliest of such constructions. His *Principles of Psychology,* Vol. I, appeared in 1924.[40] A characteristic assertion is: "You do not see or hear unless you see an object or hear some kind of sound" (*S*, p. 1). This is a type of statement in which, by a slight shift of emphasis from one key-word (such as "you," "see," "object," "kind," or "sound") to another, a startling

---

[40] A later statement is in *A Survey of the Science of Psychology* (1933). Citations in the text will use "*P*" for Vol. I of the Principles, and "*S*" for the Survey. Three recent presentations may be found in "The Operational Principle in the Physical and Psychological Sciences," *The Psychological Record*, Vol. II (1938); in "Interbehavioral Psychology and the Social Sciences," *Journal of Social Philosophy*, Vol. III (1937); and in "The Rôle of Language in Logic and Science," *Journal of Philosophy*, Vol. XXXV (1938). It is possible that Kantor's priority in construction in this form is such that all discussion should be organized around his work. Being without competence as an appraiser of such values, I can only present the issues in the way I am able to see them at the present time, and I shall gladly concede to Professor Kantor whatever independence or special rights may be claimed by him or by any of his friends for him.

Situational vs. Psychological Theories of Behavior 161

difference in understanding may result; it gives a good illustration of the difficulties which beset any effort for thorough theoretical construction and expression in this field.

Kantor has variously named his psychology " organismic," " objective," " interactional," " operational," and " interbehavioral," his claim to the first of these names antedating that of most others who use it. The first name and the third have been his main reliance, the second and fourth having many rival claimants, and the fifth having but recently been put into use. " Organismic " primarily exhibits psychological phenomena as the ways an organism " acts as a whole " (P, p. 57), while " interactional " primarily specifies that the data are " concrete interactions of organisms and things " (P, p. xvi). Kantor's construction consolidates these two positions, and he makes frequent use of phrasings of the one form in specification of namings of the other form (thus: S, p. vii). Even though we may be doing a certain violence to his work, we may *for our immediate analysis* venture to hold the two apart, since the issue involved is plainly an explicit form of one which we have already seen rising indirectly into prominence in the course of Adolf Meyer's thought.

" Interactionally," Kantor starts with organism and thing (object), setting these over against each other naturalistically, and making the psychological event a correlation, or reciprocal activity, or " function " of the two (P, p. 47, p. 57; S, p. 21, p. 23, pp. 27-32). The participation of the object (in the form of stimulus) is held to be just as essential to the " psychological " as is the participation of the organism (in the form of response). Psychology then is " the study of the interactions of organisms and things, or more exactly the interactions of responses and stimuli " (S, p. 1). We cannot undertake here to examine the complexities of interpretation which are possible as to " organisms," " things," " functions," and " interactions," but may only note the form that basic description takes in this presentation.

Suppose a student needs, or imagines that he needs, a sharp specification for the word " behavior," and suppose that as a step toward it he undertakes to establish a " location " for " a behavior " in the simple matter-of-fact manner we have adopted as guide to appraisal. Putting ourselves in the place of this student we shall find that Kantor sets up " interactionally " a " unit " of inquiry which he names the " segment of behavior," that he describes it as " an interactional event," and specifies that it " consists of a single stimulus and its correlated response " (S, p. 21). In Kantor's accompanying text, however, we shall find " organismic " assertions to the effect that this " segment " is " cut " from the "continuous activity of an organism," and also other statements to the effect that the activity, the "something that the organism does," is a *response*, although such a response is, as we have just seen, one of the two parts, or factors, or termini, of a "segment" (S, pp. 21-22). With a fusion of the "organismic" and the "interactional," and with a specialization of attention on the "reactional biography," which was Kantor's primary field of exploration, we may well believe that no friction is felt as between these two manners of statement. But we have been assuming for our suggested student a further specialization of interest, one which not unreasonably requires him to decide whether "a behavior" (so far as his own work goes) is a "response" or an "interaction," and which requires him further to hold precisely to the one or the other localization after he has once adopted it. Here internal friction may show heat.[41]

We find evidence of this in Kantor's own latest development as he makes it in terms of the "interbehavioral"; he tells us that "the interbehavioral hypothesis signifies that all human phenomena . . . consists of the concrete interbehavior of specific individuals with things"; but also that "interbehavior must be distinguished from the objects interbehaved with."[42] Here the status of "a behavior" with respect to "an interbehavior," and that of the process "inter" with respect either to a "behavior" or to "an interbehavior," present difficulties.[43]

The presence of issues such as this does not at all invalidate Kantor's

---

[41] It is, of course, not impossible that the "organismic" and the "interactional" may be established as the same. This will, however, require a factual determination, accompanied by the adoption of a single name, such as "organismic-interactional" with rigid care in the use of that name. The indications are that this would place great restriction on the current uses of the terms. In Kantor's *Principles* the same issue appeared, though under a slightly different phrasing. His primary statement there was that the "data" of psychology are "bipolar acts," with the "segment of behavior" defined as "an arbitrarily selected portion of the activities of a person or animal" but also as a "psychological act," in a context in which such an "act" is stated to consist of *both* stimulus and response (P, p. 36).

[42] *Journal of Philosophy*, Vol. XXXV (1938), p. 449; p. 462. Similar phrasings are frequent: thus, "the interaction of the individual with occurring events," *Journal of Social Philosophy*, Vol. III (1937), p. 43; and "interactions" or "interbehaviors" with "operations," "relations," "colors," or "own constructions," *Psychological Record*, Vol. II (1938), pp. 9, 10, 24, 28.

[43] Other difficulties of development similarly connected with the issues of "organismic" and "interactional" may be found in the status of "personality," whether as "a complement of . . . events" ("totality of . . . reactions"), or alternatively, as "a *product* of reactional biography" (S, pp. 118-119, italics mine; S, pp. 5-6); in the status of stimulus objects which are "created" by organisms (thus, "objects . . . derived as products of interbehavior," *Journal of Philosophy*, Vol. XXXV (1938), p. 462; see also P, p. 48; S, p. 28, p. 136); in the status of *semi*-implicit behaviors with respect to "implicit" behaviors, after the latter have been defined as cases in which stimulus objects are *not* present (P, p. 51, p. 68, pp. 242-243, pp. 295 ff.; S, p. 153, p. 173); and in the status of "knowledge" and "meaning" with respect to orientation and adjustment (P, p. 47; S, p. 4, p. 152, p. 190).

initiative or procedure. It merely raises further questions as to the safest course to follow in future work. The problems are most annoying in certain regions of conceptual and logical construction where the tendency in inexpert hands may easily be for the " interactional " to lose its prominence and for the " organismic " to acquire some of the characteristics of earlier " psychological " construction. The form of phenomenal unification presented by the observation, " sights-seen," in this region of inquiry is worthy of the strongest consideration.

Direct Situational Construction: Lewin's " Field." The problem which Kantor attacks naturalistically in terrestrial-geological space and time, Lewin proposes to deal with in a manner he calls " mathematical." He sets up a " field " as the formal frame of his psychological presentation, and for it he seeks " topological " and " dynamical " determinations. A characteristic form of his assertion is: " Any behavior is to be considered as resulting from *one* total field which includes as dependent parts the person and his psychological environment," to which he adds that science *must* use " ' constructs,' the conceptual properties of which are well defined."[44] Unfortunately, despite his repeated assurances that his method not only permits, but attains, mathematically rigorous treatment of psychological facts,[45] it is clear here, as it was with Kantor, that the keywords employed are subject to many shifting interpretations, and that precision is among the less conspicuous of their qualities.

With apologies to both of these psychologists for a comment to which, no doubt, each will strongly object, we may suggest that, just as in Kantor's case his mechanistic envisionment of the universe interferes with his attempt at " functional " description, so in Lewin's case an underlying *Seele* is present that *stets verneint* all that his " mathematics " attempts. We may here mention merely a few of the more prominent inconsistencies in his development.[46]

[44] Both citations are from the mimeographed abstract furnished by him for a paper read at the Third Conference on Methods in Philosophy and the Sciences, New York City, May 8, 1938.

[45] " Der Richtungsbegriff in der Psychologie," *Psychologische Forschung*, Vol. 19 (1934), p. 249; *Principles of Topological Psychology* (1936), p. 42, p. 78.

[46] These are selected from an unpublished analysis which in thirty-five pages of manuscript, using some twenty-five headings, goes little beyond a bare listing and classification of confusions. The items to be presented should be tested primarily by accurate comparisons of the formal definitions Lewin offers in his " glossary," pp. 213–218 of his *Topological Psychology;* the page references in parentheses are merely to pertinent incidental discussions in his text. For his postulatory background, see essays reprinted in his book, *A Dynamic Theory of Personality* (1935). For his latest tribute to a Freudian " soul," see " Psychoanalysis and Topological Psychology," *Bulletin of the Menninger Clinic*, Vol. I (1937), pp. 202–211. Incidentally it may be of interest to recall that the phrase " topographical-dynamic " (" *ein topisch-dynamischer Begriff* ") was used by Freud himself as early as 1917; see *Introductory Lectures on Psycho-Analysis*, Riviere translation (London, 1922), pp. 287, 288.

If we appraise "behavior" as he describes it, we shall find the same uncertainty we have met in other cases as to whether it is an event of interaction, situation, or field, or whether alternatively it is the organism's share as "factor" or "actor" in such an event. Behavior (B) is specified as a function (f) of a life space (L) which itself is a function of person (P) and psychological environment (E). The formula is: $B = f(L) = f(P, E)$. In one formal definition we find B to be any change in the L which is subject to psychological laws. In another we hear of the "B of an individual." In still another the L is influenced by facts "from outside," which are specified as themselves not under "psychobiological" laws. Whether the B has a locus in an L, or in a P which is "part" of an L, is indeterminable; even the sense in which the L is psychological (or perhaps "psychobiological") is uncertain.

The L is firmly asserted to be that "of an individual" (cf. p. 68, p. 75); nevertheless it is made to cover "group" phenomena (cf. p. 95, p. 100, p. 126). Although it exists "at a certain moment," and its B "at a given time," it regularly covers "locomotions" and other "changes," and it may even represent "the totality of possible events." It is discussed in terms of "dimensions," though not always in terms of the same set of dimensions; and these dimensions sometimes appear to belong to the P, or to the E, rather than to the L (cf. the headlines, p. 193, p. 195, p. 200), and are curiously involved with the "outside" hull (cf. p. 203); different types of phenomena appear as dimensions (p. 73, p. 199), including "properties," despite strong and repeatedly urged objections against the confusion of "properties" and "dimensions" by other writers (cf. p. 76, p. 194).

The structural terms "dynamical," "vector," and "topological" are shiftingly used, appearing at times with meanings that flatly contradict earlier meanings assigned to them.[47] Even the boasted term "field" presents itself in specialized (and contradictory) deviations, such as a collection of objects (which is what most writers assume Lewin to mean) (p. 115, p. 166),[48] or as the power-range of the P (p. 129).

[47] To appreciate the full complexity of such confusions, examine some of the following passages as grouped: For the organization of the three words, cf. pp. 85–86 with 159; and also pp. 129, 173, and 205 with p. vi of *A Dynamic Theory of Personality*. For the status of space with respect to them, cf. p. 62 with pp. 64 and 205. For the status of change, cf. p. 159 with p. 205; For possibles, cf. p. 15 with pp. 85 and 205. As to the status of force and vectors, cf. p. 58 with p. 93, and again with pp. 159, 205, and 218, and for the incidental status of causation, cf. pp. 32 and 63. The prominent term "communication" as connected with "dynamic" and contrasted with "locomotion," is in even worse difficulties, because of its more intimate contacts with presumptive "facts."

[48] Compare "objects from which force goes out," *A Dynamic Theory of Personality*, p. 50; also the "outer" and "inner" fields, and the "valences" of Lewin's earlier writings.

A growing concentration of force in the P is seen developing in a way which splits the P and the E widely apart, although both had been defined as alike " regions " of a " topological " L. In the end, it is found that three incarnations of the P have appeared in the work: an epistemological P, underlying the primary representation of an L; a regional P, having presumable status within an L; and a power-P, which dominates the stage after the prestidigitations of the two other P's are completed, although this power-P itself is neither prime positer nor posited region.

Spatial precision is Lewin's claim. But he makes his bid for it prematurely and pretentiously, before he achieves that simple, practical matter-of-fact localization of observation which must be the beginning of constructive knowledge. Mathematics, whether topological or other, is not a form of magic; one may profitably bear in mind that it is the veritable practice of precision.[49]

Summary. We have now sufficient indications of a strong recent trend toward the localization of behaviors in organic-environmental situations rather than in organisms separately viewed. This trend has shown itself to be an extension of that earlier trend which brought behavorial phenomena down from the clouds to earth. When vitalism (and with it also the vitalistic treatment of the gene) is fully overcome — when physiology not only recognizes, but fully uses, its environmental frame — then a situational inquiry into behaviors, we conclude, may be differentiated

---

[49] Among other investigators who have advanced along this line, Albert P. Weiss (*A Theoretical Basis of Human Behavior*, sec. ed., 1929) should have foremost mention, his early death having been a great loss to psychology and sociology. In the last few years important work has been accomplished by J. F. Brown (*Psychology and the Social Order*, 1936). A direct follower of Lewin, Professor Brown shows great superiority by developing " field " much more as a " social " frame of expression than as an " individual " emanation; however, his earnest hope that the Freudian makeshifts will incorporate themselves into a future theoretical sociology results in serious but, we may hope, temporary flaws in his postulation and procedure. Clark L. Hull (especially in " Mind, Mechanism, and Adaptive Behavior," *Psychological Review*, Vol. 44, 1937, pp. 1 to 32) makes, so far as I am aware, no direct " situational " assertions, but his powerful demand for linguistic integrity (less impressive, unfortunately, under the " logical " pretense with which he garbs it than it would be in its own authority) seems bound to lead in this direction. Several other enterprises might be mentioned which make situational or quasi-situational assertion, but which had their definite work at so early a stage that their presentations become little more than camouflage for earlier forms. An essay undertaking to construct a psychology by " selecting the processes in an organism from the point of view of their relevance to achievements in the environment " is being prepared by Egon Brunswik and Arne Ness for interpolation into " logical positivism," and is announced to appear in a proposed Volume II of the *International Encyclopedia of Unified Science*. [See Egon Brunswik, *The Conceptual Framework of Psychology*, Volume I, Number 10, of the *Encyclopedia* (Chicago, 1952).] The characterization as cited is by R. Carnap on page 48 of Volume I, Number 1, of the *Encyclopedia*. Brunswik's preliminary statements may be found in his papers in *Philosophy of Science* (1937), in an anniversary volume published by the University of Southern California (1936), and (with E. C. Tolman) in *Psychological Review* (1935).

from other situational physiological inquiries by the greater complexity of the processes of organism-environment it studies: processes that show themselves in their most characteristic forms above the level at which "externalizations" appear.

We likewise have sufficient indications of the undesirability of halfway steps in construction. Attempts which retain a leaning for "mind," along with those which place strong emphasis on "matter" in contrast with "mind," alike exhibit deficiencies in inner coherence. As our test of coherence we have used the type of localization which the word "behavior" is made to deliver. We know that coherence has never been attained by dualisms. We know that retention of a "mental" after abolishing the "material" gets nowhere; and we certainly ought to know that retention of a "material" after abolishing the "mental" is equally futile. If the needed coherence of expression is to be attained, we may anticipate as a necessary condition to it that the behavioral isolation of the organism must be overcome, and this without any remaining adhesion to either "mental" or "material" wordings.

III

Postulation for Behavioral Inquiry

Having discussed, first the possibility of observing behavior in a locus wider than that of a single organism, and next the recent trend among psychologists toward "situational" construction,[50] we may now sketch the main features of postulation which are necessary if such observation and construction is to be successfully maintained as knowledge.

Older theories treat knowledge as a process that takes place, or as a status that has place, in or at an animal organism — human, primarily. The newer theories tend to examine it, not as the capacity of an organism, but *directly* as itself a process that arises in the situation: "organism-environment." The organism remains central — "nuclear," if one will — but abdicates as Lord Proprietor.

I shall assert five propositions and call them postulates for "situational" inquiry into behaviors. Each of them, separately taken, is in definite accord with important phases of modern scientific inquiry. No one of them is repugnant to scientific procedures in general, however repugnant some of them may be to non-scientific talk. The postulates are *not* items of belief. They are tools to work with. They concern us *only*

[50] *Journal of Philosophy,* "Sights-Seen as Materials of Knowledge," Vol. XXXVI (1939), pp. 169–181; "Situational Treatments of Behavior," Vol. XXXVI (1939), pp. 309–323 [Sections I and II of this chapter].

as we work with them. Their value depends *solely* on how well they do their work — apart, and together. If they do their work so well that we retain them for any great length of time, they themselves may expect to undergo modification in and through that work.

Prior to their assertion and as introductory to them, let us assume recognition of an attitude which we may speak of as the uniformity of *knowledge* as process and field of inquiry. This attitude is prevalently atmospheric, but not to be taken as a matter for proof or for belief or disbelief in our day. Being an affair of knowledge, it is in contrast with realistic assertions of a uniformity of *nature,* and persons unsympathetic to it may know in advance that they will also be unsympathetic to the postulates that follow, and this to such an extent that they may well spare themselves the labor of a reading. This attitude is: that *all* physiological and behavioral knowledge is legitimately open to scientists for physical inquiry and interpretation; that *all* behavioral knowledge is legitimately open to physiological inquiry and interpretation as this develops in a physical setting; that in such inquiries claims and boasts have no significance, but only work accomplished; that, when all is said and done, physical and physiological knowledge, along with all the rest, is behavioral process, subject itself to behavioral inquiry and interpretation.

The five postulates now to be laid down for working purposes are:

(a) Organism and Object. In behavioral inquiry, organic and non-organic participations cover the field, without third participant.

(b) Activity and Passivity. What is active in behavior, and what is passive, must be appraised as such through the study of behavior itself, and not under conventional or other external prescription.

(c) Factual Observation. Direct observation shall be permitted for all organism-object situations, with freedom for direct factual report thereon.

(d) Space and Time. Behavioral space and time shall be established in whatever ways are germane to behavioral construction. No space and time forms, elsewhere in use or approved, shall usurp control of behavioral observation and report.

(e) Existence. All existence asserted shall be stated-existence, not named-existence. Naming shall be subsidiary to statement, and no named-existence shall be permitted to claim authority beyond its range of coherent statement.

These five propositions have been set down in an order advancing from the more specifically behavioral to the more general. They will be discussed briefly in the opposite order.

Stated Existence. Name a thing — assert with vehemence the existence of what you name — and you at once leave the route of knowing. State — develop and expand your statement — then, in the favorable case, you are on your way forward. A large literature of this import, running from erudite to popular, marks recent years; the varieties of expression are very great, none of them as yet satisfactory. The roots go back of Socrates. The overthrow of logical, as well as of verbal, pretense is everywhere involved. Expansion of statement is made our safeguard against our fallibility of first report. I need do no more here than to call attention to this postulate and give it emphasis.

Behavioral Space-Time. Newtonian space and time were established in rigid severance from the phenomena investigated and, thus viewed, were called " absolute." More recent physics absorbs its spaces and times into its observed facts; it passes beyond namings to statements; its facts and its space-time become in their way obverse and converse expressions of event. Into the Newtonian space " mind " could not fit itself, but as Protuberant Psyche there stood forth. In the new spaces and times " psyche " ceases to protrude and becomes at last itself event in the world. Physics, out of its own experience of growth, now gives students of behavior justification for choosing their own frames of space and time to fit their facts. It frees them from the old rigidity. An opening for work appears, for which all determined students of behavior give thanks.

The Right to Observe. Consider hound-running-hare. Named-hound and named-hare come before our attention as differentiated under the stresses of our practical living. Inspected in rigid Newtonian space, the " names " dominate and the " running " gets into difficulties. The resulting paradoxes are known from antiquity. Nevertheless both hound and hare, thoroughly enough explored, are seen to be made up of runnings, " and the rest appropriately."

I postulate the right, if my purposes require it, to observe hound-running-hare, and all similar events, *directly,* and not as inferential to named-hound and named-hare. The " right " is all I postulate. The utility of procedure under the postulation remains for results to show: and this in the long run.

If I have the right to observe directly hound-running-hare, I have the right to similar direct observation of hound-perceiving-hare, and of man-knowing-hound-running-hare — or of whatever it may be that such phrasings turn out factually to indicate. Recall Singer's words.[51] Start where you are (when you find out as best you can where this is), and take what

---

[51] See footnote 9 above.

comes (as best you can). Give the other man likewise his full right to start, to take, and to see. Suppress the waste forced on you by old authority.[52]

Active and Passive. Newton's third law of motion made action and reaction equal; both termini became parties to the event. Physicists for many generations, even while they *worked* true to the law, could not *see* facts in that form, and could not expound in that form what they saw and did; their " force " still claimed for them its punch. This lag is past for physics, where more and more the differential equation becomes the great central expression — the very description itself — of causation.

" Psychology," in its standard procedures, still concentrates activity, as cause, at a spot. However elaborately it may discuss environments, however strongly it may stress them, it still treats them as alien " things "; its basic construction makes of them in the end passivities as over against its own stressed " psychic " powers.

Body-and-mind conflicts bother few inquirers today. Subject-and-object severances are of little prominence under that naming. But concentrations of activity, heavy stresses upon " force " at certain spots, leading to degradation of " force " at other spots, enter everywhere.

Reliance on stated-existence as opposed to named-existence, permitting freely spaced and freely timed factual observation, cannot, of course, guarantee balanced treatment of activities and passivities in joint system, but it at least opens the way toward that end.

Organism and Object. " Psychological " construction, in contrast with " situational," introduces and employs — indeed, capitalizes — a " third " component in addition to organism and object. This is manifestly the case with " mentalist psychology," and it is equally the case with the " mentaloid psychology " of the physiologist. In this latter the physiology is (or " is usually," or " may be ") soundly scientific, but its affiliated " psychology " merely succeeds in substituting a new " third " component for the old " third "; " souls " and " minds " may be gone, but " brains " or other imitative devices have taken their place.

Such " third " components are named-existences of the kind that do not bear careful statement; they are assigned to a defective and inappropriate time and space; they are incapable of being factually observed;

[52] Argument is not here in place; but (1) we may recall how far physics has traveled from rolling stones, by way of electricity and optics, to the electron and its company — so that now, whether we approve of it theoretically or not, the photo-electric cell opens the door at our approach; (2) we may recall " psychological " report on perceptional build-up, and semantic report on verbal precipitates and defaults; finally (3) we may keep in mind the ceaseless backward and forward swing in the growth of knowledge — old " things " breaking down, new " things " building up — with no one man, and no one generation, having power to settle matters soundly for all time.

they unduly assert the presence of active powers-at-a-spot. They are out of accord with all five " situational " postulates.

Organism and object together furnish a sufficient, as well as a necessary, base for behavioral inquiry. Thus taken, and literally maintained without evasively intervening " thirds," organism and environment may be coherently investigated in accordance with the proposed postulates. Behaviors are then seen as " situational " rather than as technically " psychological," and run their course as durational events without spectacular concentration at the organism in degrees beyond what phenomenal description will justify. Organism and object become statable as organic and non-organic participations in behavioral events. Their spaces and times are " situational." Direct observation is always practicable. Activity is not arbitrarily concentrated as " force," but becomes that which can be observed and described — wherever it can be observed and described — and nothing else.

The " thirds " are hard to eject. Many have proclaimed success in ejection, but no one, perhaps, has achieved it. Good-will alone is not enough. To assert strongly the present postulate is not to claim as yet full success in its use. Concealed " thirds " may still be found by others in some of the work we do, and this may long remain a possibility. If they are found we face anew the requirement of either pursuing them till they are ejected, or else of amending our postulation to fit whatever in them shows itself most definitely to be " fact."

Deeds, Not Words. All of the above postulates are meant to be taken literally, but for taking them literally lip-service is not enough. Their program is action. Observation — widened and sharpened observation — is the heart of them. The assertion is that even a small measure of such observation is enormously helpful, and that a full measure can be achieved, if labor is not spared. Liking or disliking the wordings of the postulates in detachment from action has no significance.

In the two preceding sections I have once or twice asserted, and several times hinted, the probability of a future radical theoretical reconstruction of sociological inquiry. While present intentions do not run in this direction, perhaps a pertinent remark or two should be made.

1. If the two promising types of situational inspection — those of Woodbridge and of Pavlov — can be so organized and put to work by others as to eliminate the last remnants of matter-mind conflicts in their procedures, then *all* constructions in which *mental* (or substitute-mental) elements are made to operate *upon* non-mental would quickly disappear. The reader will probably at once remark that in this event practically

nothing of the structure of what now calls itself a "science" of society will remain.

2. What will then force itself upon attention will be a certain specialization of behavior-being as apart from that of living-being. A behavior organism will appear which will require portrayal within boundaries not identical with those of an established organism of biological inquiry. The distinction will lie in the particular manner in which the requirements of research lessen or heighten stress upon anatomical skin in delimiting subjectmatters. The stress upon skin that is already weakened in many physiological inquiries declines further and more radically for these new behavioral purposes.

3. From this we are quickly led to ask whether we may not perhaps be able to identify something of the nature of cellular structure in the situationally inspected behaviors. Such cellular structures, of course, will have to be themselves situational: i.e., not now capable of adequate description in any mentally, organically, or environmentally isolated phenomenal forms. The Pavlov signal-reflex (when not given crude, mechanistic distortion) and the Kantor segment-of-behavior (in its more straightforward uses) come at once to mind as two such structures, probably capable of development and maintenance.

4. A different, and additional, cell-form seems, however, indicated for situations which involve the more elaborated activities of speech-using human beings. In earlier work I have made some preliminary development along these lines.[53]

5. Reverting to Woodbridge's envisionment, his inclusion of "thinkings" and "expressings" along with "seeings" and with "the rest appropriately" remains unexamined in the preceding pages. In this region we find the first great problem for expansion on the changed basis. Pavlov's speculations in his final years about a third cerebral or second cortical system (also called a "second signalling system") are very weak so far we can make them out from the available reports;[54] but this is manifestly because Pavlov's "cell," if we may call it that, is inadequately framed for this particular extension of inquiry. Kantor's attack in this region is elaborate,[55] but his results — to my eye, at least,

---

[53] My *Process of Government* (1908) was put forth as "an attempt to fashion a tool," and a recent commentator has cited a passage in it (p. 175 ff.) which he thinks carries something of the present line of argument. In *Behavior, Knowledge, Fact* (1935), I have discussed "isolationality" in Chapter XIV of Part I, and "observation," "communication," and "behavioral space-time" throughout Part III.

[54] Y. P. Frolov, *Pavlov and His School* (1937), pp. 78-82, p. 228, *et al.* For Pavlov's earlier attitude toward language, see *Conditioned Reflexes* (Anrep, tr.), p. 407.

[55] *An Objective Psychology of Grammar* (1936); also three late essays cited in footnote 40 of the preceding section.

and for my personal uses — are far from satisfactory. Adolf Meyer's position, though not running beyond suggestion,[56] has great promise.[57]

6. If "sociology" is to be technically "scientific," it should exhibit basic systematic organization with physics and biology, which two sciences are the veritable *science* of our era. If it is to use physical and biological materials at all, it should use them in the forms in which the physical and biological sciences present them, and not in some ancient crudity or naïveté which those sciences have long ago overcome and discarded. If "gold" is to enter, it should be in the sense of the gold of physics, and not the gold of a hog that scratches its back on a piece of ore or the gold of some behaviorally degraded speculator on a stock exchange.

7. We find today that most physical, physiological, and behavioral materials enter their various sciences in forms called "conceptual." To deal decently with behaviors in conceptual forms (however the issue may be temporarily evaded in other sciences), we are obligated to gain some understanding as to what the word "concept" stands for *factually* in its current uses. The scholastic and mentalist "definitions" found in dictionaries and elsewhere have no pertinence to present needs. Factual determination is lacking and must be gained. One may today go back and forth across the land indefinitely seeking information: he will garner sneers, scorn, and anger, but never a hint as to "facts."[58]

8. From various points of approach we thus come to the conclusion that the development of the *situationally* conceptual, including the linguistic, out of the *situationally* perceptional, as this latter is developed out of the *situationally* physiological, is our most pressing requirement. Once this task has been reasonably accomplished, then, and I believe then only, will a sound behavioral base be available upon which an acceptable construction of social science can begin to arise.

9. It is improbable that a single technical pattern of speech will be

[56] "The Psychobiological Point of View" in *The Problem of Mental Disorder* (National Research Council, 1934), pp. 57–60.

[57] A recent discussion from a non-situational point of view is that of Charles W. Morris, "Foundations of the Theory of Signs," *International Encyclopedia of Unified Science*, Vol. I, No. 2, pp. 1–59 (1938). Typical of the "psychological" approach is his inability to attain a coherent statement even for his two or three basic presentations. Thus (p. 3) we are told that the "three components in semiosis" are Sign Vehicle (S), Designatum (D), and Interpretant (I), with "interpreter" as a possible fourth; while only three pages later (p. 6) the "triadic relation of semiosis" involves three correlates, S, D, and the "interpreter" — the "I" now being omitted. On the side of "object" corresponding confusions are continuous, the remarks on the status of S, p. 4 and p. 49, offering fair illustration.

[58] Recent abuses of the word "concept" are described in my papers "The Positive and the Logical" and "Physicists and Fairies," *Philosophy of Science*, Vol. III (1936), p. 472, and Vol. V (1938), p. 132 [Chapters 6 and 7 of this book].

competent to handle all behavioral constructions. Several patterns will be necessary, and these *must* be accompanied, if they are to perform well their work, by definite methods of making transformation from one pattern to another. Physics, physiology, and behavioral sciences are alike in this respect. Even mathematics — in the very simple case — needs a rule to transform the pattern of ⅓ into that of .33333 . . . , and *vice versa*. The Pavlov signal-reflex provides one such speech-form, the Kantor interaction provides another, and a third non-isolational type of expression seems likewise indicated as necessary. If cell-types are set up factually within behavior, then expressive speech patterns must be established to conform to them.

10. Finally we may say: Not some picayune man's ultimatum as to which is "true": Pavlov's, Woodbridge's, or Kantor's construction, is what we need. Rather it is the power to use many such constructions, and to read each report in the light of the others, so as to get from each most soundly its working values.

John Dewey's book *Logic, the Theory of Inquiry* (1938) was not yet available when the preceding pages were prepared. Professor Dewey uses the interactional approach for his biological foundations, and proceeds to a naturalistically interactional development of the theory of inquiry (warranted assertion, knowledge) as human behavior, this development including, of course, a thorough rejection of all forms of mentalistic "interactionism." He expressly asserts the first two of the five propositions which the present essay suggests for postulatory status, and under somewhat different formulation employs procedures closely related to the three others.[59] Certain criticisms which at an earlier date I had felt might lie against his attitude [60] are thus not justified as against his fully developed presentation. However, he emphasizes our present lack of "a general theory of language," and I take it that this very incompleteness finds illustration in his own work by his retention of certain words from the older vocabulary of philosophy and psychology. The word "conceptual," for example, is employed by him in a great variety of im-

[59] "Behavior is in fact a function of the total state of the organism in relation to environment" (p. 31). "What is designated by such terms as . . . idea, conception . . . must be located and described as behavior in which organism and environment act together, or *inter*-act" (p. 33). "Observation . . . the restrictive-selective determination . . . within a total environing field" (p. 150). "Inquiry effects *existential* transformation" (p. 159). "Observed facts . . . are operational" (p. 112). "I doubt whether there exists anything that may be called *thought* as a strictly psychical existence" (p. 21). Compare for "interaction," the full discussion, pp. 23–36; for the "mental," pp. 57, 106, 159, 287, 525, 530; for the temporal quality of inquiry, p. 118; and for space and time as outcomes of measurement, p. 217.

[60] *Behavior, Knowledge, Fact* (1935), Chap. XI.

portant logical situations, and while he undoubtedly makes it stand for phenomena that are linguistically operational in non-mentalistic ways, it has not yet attained for itself a sharp existential reference. While I am prepared to accept and employ probably every positive determination Professor Dewey has made, I find myself at the same time strengthened by his inquiry in the opinion that much further research will be necessary on the lines above discussed, and that for such work the organic-interactional and social stresses will require supplement by stresses of the full situational type.

CHAPTER NINE

Observable Behaviors*

In a recent paper in the *Psychological Review* (23)† in which he discussed types of constructional background for psychology, Professor Reiser cited with significant emphasis Eddington's remark that the electron by itself has no physical properties and that there would be nothing whatever to say about it if it were absolutely alone, not even that it was an electron. The electron does not renew on its smaller scale the status of the old atom-thing, but enters, we may say, as an ingredient of a new type, modifying the atom even to the extent of extirpating its ancient boundaries and manners of localization in Newtonian space. An electron not only requires a universe for its adequate description, but it proceeds to dissolve the very walls of its former homestead.

Now we know very well that psychology has had to struggle all through its scientific history with certain boundary-transcending characteristics of the phenomena it has under investigation; also that the spatial localizations it has assumed for these phenomena in the Newtonian scheme of things have remained dubious wherever anything more than vague generality of reference has been required. Man's seeings, desirings, knowings, purposes, and plannings leap toward objectives in defiance of Newtonian boundaries in space and time, and man acts thus " at a distance " in the sense that " connective "[1] processes of Newtonian types cannot be precisely traced in research, however they may be indicated or believed to be collateral. This region of psychology's difficulty is labeled that of subject-object (*S-O*)[2]; it once aroused endless discussion

---

* From *Psychological Review*, Vol. XLVII, No. 3 (May, 1940), pp. 230–53.
† Parenthetical boldface figures refer to References at end of chapter.
[1] The word " connection " will be employed throughout this paper in the technical sense proposed by Dewey in his *Logic* (**12**, p. 55). It is there brought into system with the words " reference " and " relation." We may understand as follows:

Connection: any thing-to-thing event, whether its report is the outcome of physical, physiological, or behavioral research.
Reference: any word-to-thing event, such as naming.
Relation: any word-to-word event, such as symbolizing.

[2] Understand the use of the abbreviation "*S-O*" in system with two companion abbreviations as follows:

in terms of mind *vs.* matter, though the issue in this form retains little interest and no value at all for us today.

Take perception as an example, and take as a test our ability to make a firm report upon significant fact. We possess large accumulations of approximately envisaged fact, and it is easy enough for our blunt approaches, whether by way of psychical or physical terminologies, to erupt in doctrinaire assertion. But cautious and discriminating inquiry running direct to the point has never yet been able to maintain clear distinction between perceived object, mental percept, and perceiving process, although all three of these possibilities of factuality force themselves upon attention, along with their conflicting implications of " outer," " inner," and " connector." This vagueness is *fully as great today* as at any time in the past. The confusion is still more troublesome for other psychological phenomena such as those labeled concepts, thoughts, ideas, meanings, and knowledges.[3] It is present no matter what form of " mental " or " sub-mental " is used, and equally when the whole flock of " mentals " is expelled and some form of " mental substitute " inserted. The phrasings of the dictionaries, textbooks, and laboratory reports all offer overwhelming evidence.

The great task of psychologists, as of all other scientists, is to observe. Precision of observation is their goal. Without it their science stumbles. If physicists in the development of their observation have found themselves transcending the atomic pattern, and if psychologists in their attempts to copy atomic patterns have never attained to an adequate, specific observation of a definite behavior, located in a definitely determinable time and place, nor to one which (except in make-believe) can be precisely attached to a definite name valid throughout research, then it may well be that the physicists' most recent experiences with atom and electron have, methodologically, an import for us today.

I wish briefly to examine some of the problems and difficulties that are involved, and some of the possible outcomes. We have to do with the types of observation psychologists have made, or have endeavored to make, or have believed they were making, in the past, with the deficiencies they have revealed in these types of observation, and with certain newer

---

S-O: the subject-object differentiation in its more general expressions: popular, tentatively psychological, or philosophical.

P-E: any current form of differentiation between person and environment, useful as broad description, but still lacking close specification for inquiry.

Org-obj: the recent naturalistic confrontations of organism and object in behavioral research.

[3] For the status of " belief " and of " desire," note what steps Dewey has been forced to take in the development of logic and of the theory of value (12, p. 7; 13, p. 16).

types they are now attempting to make or believe they find indicated for the near future.

Observable behaviors will be our subject of inquiry. Preliminary to such inquiry we must have a tentative, introductory accord as to what we are to understand by " observation ": an inspection of what Bridgman calls " text " — the context of our assertions — the texture of our inquiry. The word " observation " is itself a psychological term, naming psychological fact; as such it is subject to the characteristic psychological indefiniteness above indicated with respect to its own proper factual-observational status. We have many imperfect theories of observation which, when we take them too seriously, interfere with us more than they aid. If we refrain from emphasizing such theories too strongly, and if we postpone quibbles over the imperfections of our immediate statement and consider for the moment solely our need of *preliminary* orientation, then perhaps those of us who occupy central ground as to scientific method may agree on certain provisional attitudes. Let it be understood that our resulting conclusions will be qualified as subject to the validity of the method of observation here adopted, though this latter in turn is to be checked back from the conclusions under the ordinary tests of coherence.

Our provisional attitudes toward observation will be as follows:

I. *Data upon Observation*

Scientific observation is concerned, not with generalities, but in each case with *an* item, *a* thing, a *specific* fact or candidate for factual status.

It has direction.

Its direction is engineered or maintained — to use a roughly descriptive expression — through signs, where by " signs " we understand behavioral connections with a range all the way from sense-stimulation to symbol.

These signs have cultural-historical connection with previous observations — our own, and those of others.

In highly developed knowledge the linguistic signs, and among these peculiarly the mathematical, have outstanding importance.

All these signs, sensational, perceptional, verbal, symbolic, show ordering or pattern (again to employ roughly approximate expression); our observations are thus patterned; the closer knit they are, the more dependable the science.

Since they arise in naturalistic evolution which we take to be an unfinished process, observations cannot safely or sanely claim perfection and finality among their characteristics. Observation grows.

We may further say that under the above approach no *fundamental* cleavage of one realm of observation from another rises, nor of observation from interpretation, nor of description from theory. Child under mother's guidance looking with bare eyes at monkey in zoo observes within the scheme of an ancient naturalistic system of physiological organization and cultural growth. Microbiologist in laboratory and astronomer reading photographic plate observe in a naturalistic system, naturalistically expanded from what came before. The many differences of detail remain greatly in need of investigation, but distinctions stressed as "fundamental" are sentimentalities to be dropped — or at least they will be so regarded here — since in neither early nor late observation, whether simple or profound, may we assume (scientifically speaking) that we possess exclusive or even predominant hold on what folks in folkish confidence call "reality."

If the above characterization may seem to lack certain of the everyday stresses on observation, it emphasizes in their place the important and necessary features both of everyday and of scientific procedure. Scientific observation strains above all at definiteness: *the* fact which it observes must be observable at *a* place and at *a* time. This approach is basically quantitative, even though employing, as it sometimes may, no other number than "one." [4]

An electron is definitely observable under this attitude and approach. The fact that nothing can be said about it *solus* — I shall occasionally use this word in reminiscence of Eddington's "by itself" and "absolutely alone" — does not obliterate the vastly more important fact that within its own proper system of observation so much of the utmost scientific interest and importance actually *is* being said. *An* electron cannot be discarded as a mere "construct," for to do so is to attempt to judge and sentence it in terms of a defective "mentalistic" theory of observation. An electron, to be observable, requires its own proper factual background which happens to be one, not of Newtonian space but of relativity, and not of Newtonian mechanics but of undulations. Thus observed, an electron is given its measurement and localization. Thus established, experiment and observation re-enforce each other to greater exactness for its further examination. Herein lies its factual and observational definiteness.

How will *a* behavior stand as *an* item of knowledge when comparably considered? This is not a question of analogy, but of method, and especially of the method of free research. If psychology is to advance as a science, and if scientific advance rests in observation (which in the older way of talking is merely to say: if *sensus* and *intellectus* go ahead together), then certainly psychological observation will in time come to concentrate upon definite behavioral facts and things which it can definitely show as belonging to its own subjectmatters. The old generalities of expression will no longer suffice. For this purpose psychologists will

[4] Unfortunately much laboratory research and statistical technique is at times wasted on material that contains no observable datum capable of specification in terms of "a" or "one." A recently fashionable series of investigations into "*the* concept" is very much in point. What precisely is meant by "*a* concept" one can nowhere discover (14, 15, 16, 17, 18, 19, 20, 24, 25, 26).

require and must be allowed their own observational base, and this base from time immemorial, psychologically speaking, has sought to take into account the boundary-transcending characteristics of psychological subjectmatters. Presumption, then, should strongly favor the search for special instances of *a* behavior, as *observable,* having *localization* in psychology's own proper background of knowledge. However suspicious this may look from certain earlier viewpoints, it amounts simply to saying that if the word " mental " has any factual reference at all, our business, scientifically, is to observe and study this factuality.

I shall employ henceforth the expression Observation Base [5] to name the texture of thing-observed in its observational setting, without either distorting the background of observation into " construct " or the observation itself into " inference."

We may begin by tabulating certain of the more striking stages in the advance of the older sciences as usable knowledge, pretending neither to expertness, completeness, or precision, nor even to accuracy in dating the stages, but holding steadily in view the Observation Bases employed and their transformations.

In the case of physics we find:

II. *Data upon Physical Observables*

A pre-scientific view of thing-acting — as spirit, form, or force — benevolently, malevolently, or even neutrally; with Molière's *vis dormativa* a fair example in a late charlatan survival.

A powerful, sustained observation of gross motions — Galileo's is the name we stress.

Newton's third law: equation of action and reaction in an organization [6] of contraposed mass-things taken as present in a rigid, independently " existent " space and time; the old " force " now becoming reduced to the status of factual description.

Energy entering, becoming seemingly the dominant " real," then being transformed into a characteristic of physical system.[7]

Light, once seen as instantaneous and then as simple velocity, coming to establish itself, along with other undulations, as fixed maximum velocity, and as such no longer a proper member of the family of speeds bred out of space by time.

Newtonian space and time ceasing thereupon to be rigid separables and (as approximations) becoming constituents of system.

---

[5] Since Observation Bases rise and decline as stages of science, not as realities or unrealities, truths or falsities, we may use the qualification *Nascent* for any old Observation Base as it may be viewed from our present standpoint, or for any present Base as we may appraise it with an eye to the future possibilities of knowledge. Thus, as we shall later note, an Observation Base as " force " has been historically nascent to a Base as " thing-*solus*," and this latter to one as " system."

[6] Understand this word to indicate any scientific development in terms of things-*solus*.

[7] *System:* Understand this word to indicate any scientific development methodologically comparable to the treatment of the electron by physics.

Wave formulations joining, and for the present at least showing signs of dominating, particle formulations.

Radiation, once an alien among the "things" of physics, becoming thus its now dominantly factual "thing."

In the sciences of life comparable changes show themselves, though here rather as overlapping attitudes of approach, the trend of which, however, is plainly visible:

III. *Data upon Organic Observables*

The animal organism, together with the human, is included in natural evolution.

Vitalisms, once strongly favored, pass under steady replacement.

Physiological organization presents itself as competent to do the needed work.

Ecologies prepare the way for widened organization running beyond the more narrowly physiological.

Primary data begin to be observed in durational forms, complementing and threatening possible replacement of the static-structural.

Atom-patterned lines of causation begin to yield to system-patterned, as in Coghill's work with Amblystoma (11).

The gene ceases to breathe fire through its nostrils in pretentious independence, and begins to become reconciled to a place within the system of life.

Pavlov makes specific extension of physiology beyond the human skin so as to include "outer" facts directly within the organism's working process, forecasting thus a wide extension of inquiry (3, 311ff).

Still without stress upon historical order, but concentrating upon types of Observation Base employed, and avoiding control by ordinary language-conventions as well as by any insistent dogma, we may note among the phrases of the advance of psychology as science the following:

III. *Data upon Organic Observables*

An initial period of Souls and Spirits, enjoying power, initiative, and responsibility.

The failure of behavioral phenomena (the lookings before and after, the purposings, communicatings, influencings, and idealizings) to exhibit causal connections of types determinable for physical phenomena in Newtonian space and time; their distinctive display of "boundary-transcending" and "distant-acting" characteristics, and their consequent status (in the scientist's preliminary inspection, at least) as a group of remainders left over from the world of Galilean and Newtonian motions.

Assignment of these remainders to an Observation Base taken in divorce from the physical, and lumping together the contrast of spirit to body, of subjective to objective, and of psychical to physical.

A long period in which "mind-body" was the dominant formulation for the boundary-transcending behavioral problems.

A comparatively early determination by psychologists that when they used

"Mind" as their Observation Base, no item such as *a* mind could be observed or cleanly examined by them as *a* fact; this being followed by the abandonment as non-observable (though with the common retention of many accompanying language-forms for purposes of rough description) of all hypothetized "faculties" of mind, down even to the late revival of a facultative "I" in an I.Q.

"Mental" or "psychical" *particles* viewed on the atomic model in their turn fail to attain definite experimental observation as specific items. Note: the chaotic flutterings of "*an* idea," notorious ever since Locke; the recent rise and fall of "*an* instinct*"* (regarded as a "mental" item, rather than as a rough verbal description); the "emotion," since James' and Lange's insisting upon physiological observation; the technical Titchener "sensation," not able to maintain a usable status in inquiry; "feeling" alone retaining fairly sound determinability, but this rather as physiological than as behavioral description, even where the "psychical" label remains attached to it.

The "mind-body" formulation now loses interest, and the direct use of a "mental" or "psychical" Observation Base comes to be abandoned; this occurring precisely because the "mental" has failed to yield dependable observations of definite facts.

The boundary-transcending subject-object (S-O) phenomena remain as much as ever in need of an adequate Observation Base. Their "connections" are not physical in the technical scientific sense of that term, and since they are no longer referable to "powers" of the "mind" or to the magic of mind-bits, they cry even more loudly than before for a direct inquiry.

As a tentative approach, however, prior to the direct inquiry, a substitute for the old "mental" is sought in the overt mechanistic movements which the original Behaviorists took as their Observation Base. Good as far as it went, this substitute did not reach far enough to have lasting importance.

Another substitute for the "mental" as Observation Base is then tried, namely, physiology. The physiology itself is fine, but it can only report on S-O behaviors by assuming them as collateral, helplessly and harmlessly, to nerves and brains. Its reports never reach behavioral phenomena proper, and the Observation Base it establishes remains physiological instead of becoming psychological.

Various "whole-organisms," "sub-mental" Freudian items, emergent shadow-mentals, and ideologies capitalized as "causes" are found, all of them makeshifts for observation in clean-cut naming.

Enormous laboratory accumulations of nascent observations, mostly proclaimed with thing-*solus* assertiveness, are at hand awaiting directly coherent behavioral formulation and perfected organization upon an adequate Observation Base of their own.

To sum up for all three realms of scientific inquiry:

V. *Summary for Changing Observation Bases*

Physics has transformed its Observation Base from one of initiating powers or forces, through one of things-*solus* in organization, to one of full systemic description.[8]

---

[8] Or, one may say: from the arbitrary through the compulsory to system; or again: from ignorant imputation, through objectification, to factual knowledge.

Biological sciences show comparable trends of transformation, though not in such sharply marked succession of stages.

Psychology, much more complexly, travels the same route. It has used " psychical," " physical," and " physiological " Observation Bases, and in each of these (though in varying degrees of prominence) it has employed " power " patterns and " thing-*solus* " patterns, but has not as yet firmly established itself in any stage beyond.

Fluidly phrased, our report thus far is that psychologists do not as yet make direct, literal observation of their own primary phenomena of inquiry in the sense in which other sciences observe: not as psychical, whether as selves or as self-dust; not as physical, whether as mechanistic or as post-mechanistic; nor yet as physiological, despite all the riches physiology has brought. Their raw material of inquiry — the behavioral itself — still fails to obtain distinctive observation of its own. The many interesting and valuable observations they make, whether in psychical, physical, or physiological form, prove on test not to be distinctively and observationally behavioral. Their science is thus ripe for an important step forward.

We shall next proceed to consider some of the newer psychological procedures that are endeavoring to overcome the defect; but since the nascent physiological base for psychology is now at the height of its popularity as confident claimant to the psychological throne, and since it is this base that provides the starting point for the next advance, we shall do well first to secure a sharper and more complete statement of the actual situation of knowledge in this region at this time:

VI. *Detail for Physiological-Psychological Observation*

1. Behavioral clues have opened wide physiological vistas.

2. The resulting physiology is fine *physiology*.

3. This physiology undoubtedly gives the death-blow (if one is still needed) to the old " mental."

4. This physiology has nevertheless not itself yielded (Pavlov alone excepted — and he only through experimental disregard of the normal physiological boundary-line) one single direct report or description of any characteristically behavioral S-O phenomenon.

5. The most competently explored neural train in the science has not yet shown a capacity in its own right to report upon any such phenomenon as " horse-seen," much less " word-understood."

6. The only way this physiology succeeds in labeling itself " psychological " is by treating behavior as collateral to neural process.

7. How behavior is thus " collateral " is a pressing *scientific* issue — assuming that " science " is really a passage from guessings to knowings — and here physiology has nothing to tell us.

8. The common procedure is to employ a collateral quiddity or dummy of the old " psychic " type, thus admitting at the back door in an inferior capacity the very nuisance that had been lustily kicked out the front.

9. Characteristic of such a quiddity is that " behavior " is treated as some sort of an act which the dummy " performs " at a spot — anciently a psychical spot, now a physiological spot.

10. This rates more as a change of name than as progress in primary behavioral observation and report.

11. The one requirement, namely, matching the physiology against the fully characteristic systemic behavioral process, is just what the physiology in its own terminology does not accomplish. The " quiddity " it offers remains as mystic as was ever the old straight-psychic, and the Observation Base it offers remains physiological.

12. The psychologist is unquestionably to be controlled by physiology in everything it establishes within its own Observation Base and by its own exact methods. Such control, we may fully believe, will endure and increase. But beyond this, for the present at least, the psychologist must seek for himself.

13. To sum up: Physiology as it now stands offers *no guarantee whatever* that the locus of *a* behavior is within a skin, nor even a first hint that that is where *a* behavior should actually and factually be sought. If or when a physiologist or anyone else talks of phenomena without locus, we have no need to listen.

The newer forms of observation which we are now to examine have a right to regard themselves as attempting to deal with the psychological proper as distinct from guesses, substitutes, and approximations of language. Recently in another place (3) I have appraised some of these procedures. Without repeating the discussion, we may here recapitulate by displaying three typical forms of attack. It will be manifest that our cues come from Lewin, Pavlov, and Kantor, but our sketches of three cases to be known as *A, B,* and *C* do not hold minutely to these men, since it is types of approach to the problem rather than professional biographies that concern us. It is essential to recognize, however, that Kantor's initiative and leadership in this field is unquestioned (21). In comparison with him Lewin offers us a belated " mentalist " shadow, while the peculiar significance of Pavlov's procedure could not readily have been appraised free from its ordinary mechanistic discolorations until after Kantor had established the background of observation.

Case *A*. Suppose that, under various current influences, a psychologist excellent in special research, but still wearing the linguistic harness of the old " psychic," should say: " Come, let us make a ' system ' in which we can hold S-O phenomena in union for study "; and suppose he should look around and discover a mathematical technique flexible enough for his use. Suppose he should select as components of his system, and as representatives of S and O, the two presentations " person " and " environment," symbolizing them as "P" and "E," and should call their system a " field." Surely we will have sympathetic interest in his undertaking. But suppose our examination of his accomplishment with a view to its adoption shows it making use of three or more warring items under the symbol "P," and does not enable us to become clear just what is the status of E with respect to P within the " field " in terms of the typically physical, physiological, and behavioral issues that arise. Then we will doubtless conclude that the time has come for us, if our understanding is to progress, to concentrate upon direct inquiry into the status of the phenomena P and E themselves within the field. In a case like this, if we find that the P and E enter *solus,* then we have " organization " rather than " system " to investigate, and our business will be to build up the " connections " [9] on that basis. If, however, the field is properly " system," as in the mathematical-physical procedures from which its name is taken, then our business is its free observation and delicate analysis into its constituent P and E or whatsoever. Here again " connections " will be the exhibit in the outcome. Despite difficulties such as these, the mere appearance upon the scene of procedures such as Case A must be taken as having high symptomatic import at the present stage of psychological advance.

Case B. We suppose a physiologist of outstanding ability who arrives in due course at experimentation with the buccal cavity on a basis comparable with his earlier work with stomach and brain. He finds himself observing animal activities involving eye, tongue, touch, smell, hearing, and other stimulus-reaction situations as direct contacts of organism and object, on a basis which we may style org-obj,[10] without drawing any *radical* distinction *in his experimental procedure* between inside-skin and outside-skin phenomena. The resulting opportunities for research prove magnificent; they justify lifelong activity for himself and for scores of keen associates; even after forty years their attractions are increasing rather than declining. Our physiologist discovers and insists that whenever he makes his reports in the old " psychic " terminology he blurs the facts, but when he adheres to straight behavioral description as he understands it, he makes a gain in precision of inquiry. He asserts vigorously that he is a physiologist, not any kind of a psychologist he knows of; also that as a physiologist he is expanding physiology across new territories. What concerns us here is not whether the investigator of Case B " believes " or " disbelieves " in a psychic, nor what *obiter dicta* may come from him about world and man. Rather it is the fact that

[9] For " connections " refer to footnote No. 1.
[10] See footnote No. 2 for status of org-obj with respect to P-E and S-O.

Observable Behaviors

when he discards the older terminology he is in effect replacing his old Observation Base with a new one; further that his new base is just what he calls it, namely, an expanded physiology (*i.e.*, expanded beyond skin-limitations), and not a physiological sentimentalization purporting to *be* in its own right a certain " something " which it had previously discarded as *not*-being. Clearly such an exhibit is neither itself old-psychical, nor old-physical, nor old-physiological. Its range of experiment is limited, indeed, to animal perception-behaviors, and we cannnot be too certain as to whether its trend in the long run will be toward " organization " or toward " system," but we certainly can see in it at least a possibility of full system-development in the present sense.

Case *C*. We assume a psychologist concentrating naturalistically on the materials of his inquiry who comes to the conclusion that the " psychological fact " is to be found only where organism and environmental object confront. He finds such confrontation almost everywhere recognized as a necessary " condition," but this in the main grudgingly and as a handout to philosophy in the *S-O* form, and nowhere used as a building block for scientific psychological research. He determines so to use it, and he puts it definitely in the form org-obj. He proceeds thereupon to assert that for behavioral inquiry organism and object are both necessary, that they are all that is necessary, and that behavior is their " interaction," with the " function " of the object — the part it plays — just as essential to any behavior as is the part played by the organism. Our psychologist we may regard as having been fortified in his purpose by his clear view of the manifest defects of current constructions: the " psychical " cannot be seen; what one sees as " physical " is not itself in that form behavioral; the physiological may ape the behavioral, but does not itself arrive at it. In his development he employs as locus of all his phenomena a specifically successional geologic time, and a specifically terrestrial extension of space. In this background he sees the course of natural evolution as yielding successively objects, then organisms, and still later phenomena we call behaviors — those in which objects and organisms enter into organization with one another in super-physiological style. A procedure such as that of Case *C*, appraised in the perspective afforded by our general survey of scientific Observation Bases, offers a striking parallel to the case of physics when Newton introduced his third law of motion. Things-*solus* are set up in fixed temporal and spatial frameworks, and events are presented as equated in interaction. This treatment expels violently the older " force " regarded as that which " puts things over," and it replaces all such forces by descriptions, but it offers these descriptions in terms of " things " which are assumed to be capable of independent preliminary characterization on their own accounts (in Newton's case the mass-particles, in Case *C* the existent organisms and objects) *before* the description of their interaction is undertaken.

Given Cases *A, B,* and *C,* we may make the following comments: In the Newtonian organization of physics there was a defect so subtle that it required two hundred years of accumulating observations before the physicists got their first hints that it was becoming necessary to transport " masses " (and " space " and " time " as well) from the status of independent exterior facts or conditions into the physical " system " proper. For psychology, in contrast, such system (S-O) has been all too disturbingly in evidence from the start, and psychologists have evaded it by turning it over to magic (psyche) or to the pundits (philosophy) to be dealt with, while they themselves have endeavored as best they could to imitate the still imperfect physics of their period. Only now at last is the characteristically systemic behavioral fact beginning to obtain direct investigation in the scientific form by its own right. We have Cases *A, B,* and *C* as types of change. But procedures of type *A* must certainly free themselves from empyrean pretensions, and must operate on earth where immediate observation can be made; those of type *B,* however epoch-making, offer us as yet only a firm start; while those of type *C,* assuming any such to be found in the form we have given them, must show that their " organization " is technically adequate to deal with S-O system in its more difficult ranges, if they are to become the dominant pattern of inquiry.

In our earlier discussion of developments such as the above, the word " situational " was employed (3, p. 311) to name all treatments of behavior in which " the locus of the behaviors no longer is placed in the organism alone." The word was there brought into contrast with " psychological " because of the latter word's etymological involvement with a " psyche " now become decrepit and confined by feeble wing-power to an intra-dermal home. This contrast was solely for the convenience of the moment. " Psychological " is, of course, the permanent name to give to all behavioral research and knowledge, of whatever type. Let us here, therefore, while still retaining the specification of " situational " cited above, regard its application as limited to those varieties of psychological inquiry which employ a widened Observation Base in contrast with the older varieties which retain psychical, physical, or physiological localizations in or directly at a skin-bounded organism. " Situational," thus used, will cover cases both of organization and of system within psychology, since both employ loci wider than the organic body — the former compounding behaviors from independently specified components, the latter proposing to establish the scientifically valid differentiation of organic and objective constituents within and by means of the behavioral research-in-progress.[11]

Let us now establish as vividly as possible what it means for a behavior, *literally,* to be localized not in a mind or in an organism, but in a place (situation, field, " cell," or whatever it may be called) within which an organism holds status as at most a nucleus. Such localization may look queer at first, but this need not trouble us, since queerness is common enough in the appearance of knowledge rising wet from the pit. Actually the procedure is matter-of-fact, and can quickly be identified as such. Start with a behavior, fully, richly, concretely before you: say, John-loving-Jane, or Bolshevik-hating-Banker. Then *in your capacity as scientist, and for scientific purposes,* instead of taking it for granted in simple, naïve, unquestioning innocence that you have primarily before you the separate items John, Jane, Bolshevik, Banker, and consequently also " the " or " a " hate, and " the " or " a " love, which it becomes now your duty to patch together with sealing-wax, interpret, explain, or otherwise control by your own mental power as prime mover (or is it as fifth wheel? — you may not be at all sure), you determine to examine the situation as it comes just-so. You do some violence, indeed, to conventional attitudes and speech-forms, but it happens that under the conditions given above and for your specified purpose, namely, the increase of knowledge of the type we call science, your primary goal is *not* conventionality. You quickly find as you proceed that you are gaining immensely in directness of observation, and this is what you *do* want. You will also find upon due consideration that your procedure now agrees quite remarkably with your ordinary everyday " knowledge-of-acquaintance " of the behaviors taking place around you, and that nothing has been done away with except a conventional magic or semi-magic pretense of " knowledge about." Having this much start, your job is to " stay put " in observation, and

[11] No apology is needed for altering the earlier application of " situational." Verbal rigidity is always our danger, and free experimentation with words our need, so long as factual report remains imperfect. " Interaction " would be a preferable word especially because of its priority of use; but if I am right in my appraisal it is barred in the present discussion because it offers itself so emphatically in the form of " organization " and with subordination of " system." " Field " has great advantages if we could take it pure from its mathematical-physical uses, rather than as a corrupt emanation from an S or a P, devoid of all observational standing of its own either with respect to its factual or its systemic characteristics, but it is doubtful whether its originators would permit us any such liberty. J. F. Brown has adopted the name " vector-field," and has made important forward steps in its use, especially through stimulating investigations of vision (8, 9; see also Orbison, 22). My attention also is called to the early stress by M. Bentley on the function of the environment in psychology, and to researches made under his supervision in this intent (6, 7, 10).

not backslide into slovenly makeshifts as you proceed. Here now will be your difficulty. No longer may one fall back when puzzled upon a non-observable psyche or psyche-substitute, nor may he let the Eternal-Bodily serve as his sentimental reliance, nor require God the Great Geometer to be a purely Euclidean God. One must face the issue squarely: Are " hate," " capacity to hate," and " hater," " love," " capacity to love," and " lover," the phenomenally vivid, concrete, and " real " scientific facts? Or should this status be given instead to the full observable hate-situations and love-situations as we can actually anywhere and any time run across them? If this last is the case — and if we face it squarely — then " situational " psychology presents itself at once as proper hypothesis and procedure of research.

What now as to the respective status of organization and of system within situational psychology?[12] For science generally our exhibits indicate the former as a stage in the advance toward the latter, but this is not decisive. *Solvitur operando,* one is perhaps permitted to say. The issue will not here be discussed. The difficulties psychology has always had in applying the organization method to its materials will be taken for granted as well enough known. We shall confine ourselves to a brief sketch of the possibilities of the contrasted " situational-system " development in three regions, perception, culture, and language-thought, corresponding roughly to regions which in older days were known as senses, will, and intellect.

Take perception first. In Case B we considered perceptions as if directly localized in areas of a rod-or-so radius around a cortex, without introduction of an anatomical skin as a dominant boundary; in Case C we considered them, where treated, as themselves directly interactions. As background for such presentations we have much pertinent experience to draw upon. In all ages " philosophers " have found themselves — and with few exceptions — compelled to have dealings with S and O in fusion; the bare fact of their being thus forced is informative. In science, if physics is a sound guide, the day of the old atomisms is past except for use as approximate expression in special regions. Probably every psychologist has sometime found himself recording immediacy of perceptional event, no matter how surprised at himself he feels. The word " percept " forever winks back and forth, refusing to stay fixed, whether as S, or O, or connecting process. We forever hypothetize " things," which forever we must struggle to dismember again; and in behavioral regions our Occidental sentence-structure offers so many rigidities that

---

[12] For " organization " and " system " refer to footnotes No. 6 and 7.

often our hardest struggle is to set ourselves free. This last item — it is the well-known rhythm in the advance of knowledge — gives us our general justification for our course, added to the many direct clues we have secured, when we undertake an experimental technique of scientific envisionment which grasps the S and O aspects of perception together as they come, and when we propose this as a basis for still further inquiry. Elsewhere I have used Woodbridge's phrase " sight-seen " as a verbal aid (not, however, as a valuation) in dealing with this manner of observation, affirming that it conforms to my own long-maintained personal habit whenever I take sufficient pains to strip away certain well-known linguistic distortions (2). Such observation, always taking it in the specific case such as tree-sight-seen, is directly " system " in behavior. Many approximations to illustration can be found. We do not look upon tropism as involving differentiation of S and O, but still we treat it as lying in a region of transition toward such a differentiation. We do not suppose a toad to remark " Lo, me; Lo, it " before it swallows a gnat, but no more do we reduce its behavior to a presumed mechanistic pattern brought over from an older physics. Similarly (except for verbal bondage) we are under no compulsion (above all not in science) to regard tree-solus and man-solus as basic specimens of the way " God made the world," nor to place them eternally in pseudo-mechanistic contraposition to one another before we venture to ask ourselves how in fact perceptional-behavior-in-action is to be viewed. We may readily claim that we make a sound improvement in our practice when we treat the differentiation of tree and man as itself an evolutionary outcome, and our present formulation of any such differentiation as itself conditioned by the present stage and status of evolution, including our own place in it, perceptional, cultural, linguistic, and all.[13] Even though the ordinary chores of psychology may not need any reference to this direct systematic envisagement, we are justified in employing it whenever it helps us organ-

---

[13] It is common to sentimentalize over our speck-like status in space and time, often, indeed, with a bit of flattery to our intellects for their modesty in thus admitting our corporeal limitations. It may be useful to consider for an instant the deeper-lying *thermal* limitations of our knowledge itself within the frame of its own report on nature. We allow our universe, physically speaking, a temperature range of many millions of degrees. However, quite unbroken accumulations of experience seem to assure us that our process of observation and report is confined to occupants of a region which has an intra-dermal thermal tolerance with a range of possibly 20 degrees Fahrenheit, an extra-dermal range of less than 100 degress, and an extra-domiciliary range of possibly 200 degrees. How the universe might appear to beings otherwise localized with respect to temperatures is a question of no more scientific importance than whether any such otherwise localized beings " exist." What is important is that with respect to thermal tolerance we may appraise the validity of our ordinary dogmatic " realisms " as something of the order of 10^{-5}; and if we are wise we may perhaps behave accordingly.

ize those ordinary chores with one another or with other ranges of inquiry.

Turning to cultures, we find that our various social sciences from anthropology to economics have already made long advances on the route toward systematic statement. We no longer ask: "How *can* a man be a Persian?" nor even: "What *causes* are needed to produce a Persian?" We are, scientifically speaking, as well satisfied with Persians as with — let us say — Americans: sometimes, perhaps, even better as more remote, and so in better perspective. One no longer demands a principle of self-interest or a greed to give a foundation to economic institutions, nor of piety for the founding of religion. One can see a savage as so-acting, and himself likewise as so-acting. A totem-pole is no longer required to be a mechanistic (or perhaps a mystic) application of a man to a tree, but can be taken directly as behavioral fact. The fuller and richer one makes his descriptions, the more he finds description itself superior to imputed exterior factors of causation. Just as has happened with physical description in respect to objects-*solus,* so in the case of behaviors: the less one knows to say about the facts, the more is he inclined to introduce an independent mental-*solus* to "explain" them; the more one knows about the facts — in other words, the more strongly cultural research advances — the less need and the less plausibility is there for such professedly "independent" items. Ignorance requires sops, but advancing knowledge gets along without; and in cultural research the old "psychic" powers (and in prospect all their specious substitutes) prove to be such sops. Stylish revivals like the Freudian remain recidivist, no matter what fragments of information they assemble. The old creaky combinations of psychic with other-psychic or non-psychic items come ever more clearly to appear as cases of double talk, in which one says over again the same thing in changed words, without increment of meaning, under the pretense that word-reduplication is itself by some magic an explanation. All that this really represents is, however, the slovenly dodging of the painful effort of research. It thus comes about that the *S-O* separation appears rather as a subordinate tool of inquiry for cultural research than as a dependable framework of explanation. This is not to say that the majority of investigators already assert this attitude, but that the practice of the advance guard clearly shows the trend. The disappearance of the older "forces," which is the first step in the disappearance of all facts-*solus,* is here already far on its way, even among workers to whom the recognition of the trend, and much more its friendly acceptance, remains still abhorrent.

Finally, consider the region of language-thought-knowledge. The closeness of language and thought to each other and their possible identity has been stressed since the earliest days of Greek philosophy. In era after era groups of inquirers have asserted a oneness, *almost* convincing themselves of success in demonstrating it. But opposed to these stand always other groups who strive to herd thoughts off into pure realms of wordlessness, and who in their turn *almost* believe they succeed. A dilemma like this manifestly means failure as yet to secure sufficient analysis for the situation that includes both language and thought, so that neither language nor thought can as yet attain a formulation for itself which makes sufficient allowance for the other. It is common report both for language and for thought that each hypothesizes and that each recombines. When, however, the full complex is broken down into elements which openly or secretly are taken as basic, such as an " I " that thinks, a " body " that speaks, and some rigorously independent " other-thing " that is thought of or spoken about — when we find physical-thing and concept-thing shading into one another in such way that no one can tell just where or how — when words apart from thoughts prove meaningless and thus not behavioral at all, while thoughts apart from words vanish mistily except as other words are brought in to proclaim their " real " apartness — then the language-thought problem surely lies unsolved. Development on the basis of behavioral system offers hope, for here we shall look at the full situation directly; word, meaning, and object will begin to have their specifications developed within the inquiry. Certainly until such development is secured we can expect no success in our search for coherence, psychological, sociological, linguistic, or logical; in the last of these least of all.[14]

We have thus sight-seen, culture-fact, and language-thought-knowledge all exhibited as possibilities for study as localized in situations wider than the separate organism. As such we have them susceptible of systemic treatment in which S-O phenomena are approached head-on as problems, and no longer under the dominance of an isolated " S " which is assumed to be necessary, no matter how dubiously known. In the first of these three regions direct systemic observation is already practicable, if our inquiry needs it, and if we are willing to submit to its discipline. In the second, systemic presentation is already far along toward establishment. In the third, we have at last real hope for solving the most crucial of all our problems — that of the connection of our per-

---

[14] John Dewey's *Logic* (12) may safely be appraised as a full generation in advance of the technical logic now currently displaying itself as half-chess and half-faith. Even his work, however, remains in large part an exploration of difficulties, with language-knowledge chaos presented as the greatest immediate obstacle to progress.

ceptional and cultural behaviors by way of our language-thought-knowledge processes, themselves taken as behaviors in full system with the others.[15]

When psychology made its advance from its older psychical to its present intra-dermal physiological Observation Base, the strongest pressure in that direction came from organic evolution fresh arrived in knowledge with a sound demonstration of man's place among primate mammals. The initial inclusion of the organic body of man within nature has had this great result for improving our envisionment of behaviors.

The further advance from intra-dermal to full situational observation proceeds today under the same naturalistic pressure. The present step requires, however, much more than a curious, or grudging, or partial acceptance; it requires a full and frank adoption free from all qualifications or concealed evasions. Demanded of us now is that we recognize the absorption of all of the behaviors of men (and most emphatically for each one of us, of our very own) including all our talkings and thinkings and knowings into " nature " in the sense of a scientifically naturalistic system of events.[16] Charles Sanders Peirce, America's greatest leader in knowledge, comprehended this the instant that he felt the impact of Darwin upon his own solid scientific equipment and Kantian protective structures, and he quickly reported it to the world in his " pragmaticism " and " fallibilism," two techniques for gaining competence and stability in research which have power for the future, however they have been neglected by the past generation except in watery dilution. The verbal and other technical facilities available to Peirce in his own day for the examination of such phenomena as " ideas " were too limited to permit him to attain his objectives, but he gave us guiding principles and took powerful steps forward which only now the world begins to follow.

A full naturalism (the " ism " here implying merely a program for observing men at work in nature) will be determinedly observational, ever modifying its reports with improving vision. The observation, however, must itself be naturalistic, and this it cannot be if it distorts its reports as if they arrived by way of " powers," mental, organic, or other, not themselves naturalistically under observation. Naturalistic observation in a " nature " itself observationally established is " system " as we have used the word. The observer professes no creed based on the as-

[15] I may perhaps add that my examination of recent psychological progress has been forced on me by my great personal need for a better understanding of language-process than I have been able to obtain by way of the older psychologies.

[16] Certain recent specimens of surviving disregard or miscomprehension are elsewhere exhibited (4, 5).

sumed dominance of one single item of observation. He proceeds without any tortoise to hold up his world of research — even without dependence upon whatever testudinal mentality he has been wont to claim.

Concerning such situational system our most insistent assertion will be that it brings behavioral connection directly under inquiry.[17] Fast disappearing now will be the endeavors to compress S-O phenomena into an S-terminus, there to be studied as S, P, org, or as some alternative form, such as a mystic " id," a foggy " whole-organism," a " cortically-potent " artery, or whatever else happens most to please the performer. Instead the S-O phenomena will be held steadily in view as they primarily come. Studied thus, their connection enters attention in its own right with demand for direct observational report. No longer is there need for painful struggle to explain how a " power " of the S form, after it has once been set up *solus* (usually with its handful of assertively " realistic " credentials) can possibly perform such work as it has been set up to perform. No longer will problem-solution in this field have to be turned over to experts like " philosophers " to deal with. The work itself's the thing, the behavioral event itself, just as the event's the thing in all highly developed modern science; the S, P, or org, the O, E, or obj, must exhibit itself within it, not as above, or beneath, or otherwise presumptively fundamental to it.

In conclusion — as possible safeguard against word-distortion — the following statements are emphasized:

Observation, presented as situationally operating, has been frankly and openly used as implement for gaining knowledge of situational psychology. This is a " circle," but one without a trace of concealment. Outcomes are explicitly recognized as qualified by methods.

Observation Bases are regarded as appearing in science in successive stages, with early bases regarded as approximations on the way toward later; and likewise with future and better bases anticipated.

Whoever succeeds in establishing any piece of knowledge as resting securely in his own (or in anyone else's) point-blank contact with an object will send situational psychology crashing. No general theory or creed can accomplish this, but only the proffer of specific fact so established. The world as yet possesses no such fact, vehemence being still in inverse ratio to demonstration.

Situational psychology, in all of its tentative forms, asserts that its dealings with behaviors are concrete and direct, in comparison with the

---

[17] For " connection " refer to footnote No. 1.

sundry fictions and abstractions of the older organically localized Observation Bases. It places no obstacle, and has no thought of placing obstacle, in the way of intensive research into personality and person. If one sees the organism entering as nuclear in behavior rather than as an isolated locus, one is still as free as ever to specialize to the scientific limit on nuclear studies. Such free specialization is the life of science. Sole condition is that the report of outcomes be made under qualification as to objectives and methods, and not *sub specie aeternitatis*.

REFERENCES

1. BENTLEY, A. F. Postulation for behavioral inquiry. *J. Phil.*, 1939, **36**, 405-413.
2. ———. Sights-seen as materials of knowledge. *J. Phil.*, 1939, **36**, 169-181.
3. ———. Situational treatments of behavior. *J. Phil.*, 1939, **36**, 309-323.
4. ———. The positive and the logical. *Phil. Sci.*, 1936, **3**, 472-485.
5. ———. Physicists and fairies. *Phil. Sci.*, 1938, **5**, 132-165.
6. BENTLEY, M. Environment and context. *Amer. J. Psychol.*, 1927, **39**, 54-61.
7. ———. Individual psychology and psychological varieties. *Amer. J. Psychol.*, 1939, **52**, 300-301.
8. BROWN, J. F. The dynamics of visual speed, time, and space. *J. Psychol.*, 1938, **8**, 237-245.
9. ———, & VOTH, A. C. The path of seen movement as a function of the vector-field. *Amer. J. Psychol.*, 1937, **49**, 543-563.
10. CHRISOF, CLEO. The formulation and elaboration of thought-problems. *Amer. J. Psychol.*, 1939, **52**, 161-185.
11. COGHILL, G. E. *Anatomy and the problem of behavior.* Cambridge, England: University Press, 1929.
12. DEWEY, J. *Logic, the theory of inquiry.* New York: Henry Holt, 1938.
13. ———. *Theory of valuation.* Chicago: University of Chicago Press, 1939.
14. EWERT, P. H., & LAMBERT, J. F. Part II. The effect of verbal instructions upon the formation of a concept. *J. gen. Psychol.*, 1932, **6**, 400-411.
15. FIELDS, P. E. Studies in concept formation. *Comp. Psychol. Monogr.*, 1932, **9**, No. 42.
16. ———. Studies in concept formation. II. A new multiple stimulus jumping apparatus for visual figure discrimination. *J. comp. Psychol.*, 1935, **20**, 183-203.
17. ———. Studies in concept formation. III. A note on the retention of visual figure discriminations. *J. comp. Psychol.*, 1936, **21**, 131-136.
18. ———. Studies in concept formation. IV. A comparison of white rats and raccoons with respect to their discrimination of certain geometrical figures. *J. comp. Psychol.*, 1936, **21**, 341-355.
19. GENGERELLI, J. A. Mutual interference in the evolution of concepts. *Amer. J. Psychol.*, 1927, **38**, 639-646.
20. ———. Studies in abstraction with the white rat. *J. genet. Psychol.*, 1930, **38**, 171-202.
21. KANTOR, J. R. *Principles of psychology.* New York: Knopf, Vol. I, 1924; Vol. II, 1926.
22. ORBISON, W. D. Shape as a function of the vector-field. *Amer. J. Psychol.*, 1939, **52**, 31-45.
23. REISER, O. L. Aristotelian, Galilean and non-Aristotelian modes of thinking. *Psychol. Rev.*, 1939, **46**, 151-162.
24. SMOKE, K. L. An objective study of concept formation. *Psychol. Monogr.*, 1932, **42**, No. 191.
25. ———. Negative instances in concept learning. *J. exper. Psychol.*, 1933, **16**, 583-588.
26. ———. The experimental approach to concept learning. *Psychol. Rev.*, 1935, **42**, 274-279.

CHAPTER TEN

The Human Skin: Philosophy's Last Line of Defense*

Human skin is the one authentic criterion of the universe which philosophers recognize when they appraise knowledge under their professional rubric, epistemology. By and large — except for a few of the great Critics and Skeptics — they view knowledge as a capacity, attribute, possession, or other mysterious inner quality of a " knower "; they view this knower as residing in or at a " body "; they view the body as cut off from the rest of the universe by a " skin "; all of which holds for philosophizing physicists and physiologists even as for the professionals of the arcanum itself. If this assertion seems crude, one may recall that there *are* times when a bit of crudity is a fair physic for an inflamed subtlety. In the case before us the factual crudity lies in the use of " skin " for a criterion, not in our calling attention to the fact. The " skin " that is so used is, indeed, that of ancient anatomical schematism, unaffected by the transformation of understanding which modern physiological research has brought about. Yet if philosophers cease thus crudely to employ it, all their issues of epistemology will vanish, and the very type of attack they make on cognition will be discredited; whereupon the task of determining the status of knowledge itself will pass from their hands to those of the scientists who have taken over so many regions of philosophical arrogation in the past. This is what I propose here to show.

Assuredly skin is a proper subject for examination in connection with the processes of knowledge, and assuredly matter-of-fact observation and report is appropriate to it. If there is a " knower " and if there is a " known," if one of these lies apart from the other and if there is a process of " knowing " which involves both, then skin lies somewhere along the line of march, and must be taken into account.

The philosopher will enter demurrer. He will deny on principle that knowing can ever come to be dealt with by matter-of-fact techniques that concern themselves with the status of skins inside the course of the

---

* From *Philosophy of Science*, Vol. VIII, No. 1 (January, 1941), pp. 1-19.

knowledges themselves. He will assert that it is necessary to get behind the process in some highly specialized way to gain a vantage point for its appraisal, and that such an undertaking is his professional prerogative, its sacred maintenance his obligation. Symbolic logic, that curious mixture of skill and superstition, is today claiming to occupy such a vantage point. One of its flanks (the right flank it should doubtless be called, since it is the flank in which the superstition far outweighs the skill) even boasts its putative capacity to *unify* — God save the mark — all science. "Getting behind" is, of course, a necessity in all research; it is also a characteristic of all behavior, including as Jennings found that of the infusoria.[1] It is not an exclusive privilege of the philosophers, and our concern is solely with the technical efficiency of their method.

The philosopher, having no open truck with skin, leaps from essence to essence — from the essential knower to the essentially known. He leaps with never so much as the twitch of an eyelash to mark that he glimpses anything of significance lying in between. Yet it is simple to show that skin — and indeed skin in its primitive anatomical character — dominates every position the philosopher occupies and every decision he makes. Stripping off the subtle philosophical veilings, let us get down to the naked evidence.

"Inner" and "outer" are ever-present distinctions, however camouflaged, in philosophical procedure as well as in conventional speech-forms and in the traditional terminology of psychology. What holds "inner" and "outer" apart? The answer must come not by way of transcendental build-up but by indications of pertinent fact. Bluntly, the separator is skin; no other appears. Trace the varieties of description historically, beginning with the early days of "soul." Apart from minor flights of fancy, "soul" reports itself as inhabitant of body, so long as mortal coil endures. Body has skin for boundary, and skin thus fences off the mortal residence. Skin in its way even operates as that which demarcates those bits of the universe destined to sing in the hereafter, and those destined to singe. Soul is tempted by world, flesh, and devil, and skin is what keeps world and flesh apart, yielding also, it is said, many satisfactions to devil. The later "actors" of psychology are all modeled on soul, down even to the last of the Freudian sub-mentalities and of the physiological substitutes, the difference being mainly in the degree of attenuation. Psyches, minds, personalities, all belong in this class; skin is what holds them "in." Singly or in groups they are made to fill the intra-dermal region, whenever behaviors rather than physiological processes form the subject of discussion. The greater their attentuation the

[1] H. S. Jennings, *Behavior of the Lower Organisms* (1906), p. 296 ff.

more stridently they are apt to assert themselves as "real," but also the more absured becomes the account that is given of them. Take the "internal environment" of current professional gossip. An organism has an "external" environment. This lies outside its skin. Inside the skin we find, if we look closely and talk bluntly, the organism itself. If there is an "internal" environment, then, where is it? And what is it environment to? Its professional exploiters seem never to ask. Claude Bernard meant by internal environment the blood as environing the bodily organs. This is sound physiology. Later physiologists have followed with valuable studies of the environing status of certain parts of the body to other parts. This also is sound physiology. But the psychologist's case is sharply different. In his use "internal environment" seems to require something akin to the aura of an Annie Besant for its focal reference (P, v. 48).[2] Leibnitz made what was probably the most powerful effort in all philosophy to face the issues of "inner" and "outer" and get rid of the domination of skin. His monads were to "mirror" the world without actual contact. They are thus "windowless" in the sense that no path is traceable across their boundaries. They are skin-impounded but not skin-traversable. The private difficulties a monad would have with its privacy have been amusingly traced by Malisoff.[3] Modern science stresses paths. Leibnitz destroyed paths to preserve innerness. Nevertheless Leibnitz rates high today; the integrity of his attack brings illumination to every inquirer above the level of the "internal environment." Those who hold the "inner" apart from nature may take him as they find him, while others gain ample incentive to trace the paths of nature across all knowledge.[4]

The above presentation of the basis of the "philosophical" technique must be left for the moment with this sketch. It is a technique of the

[2] Citations from some of my recent papers will be made in the text by the use of the letter "J" for the *Journal of Philosophy,* and "P" for the *Psychological Review.* These papers are:
Sights-Seen as Materials of Knowledge, *J. Phil.,* 36, 1939, pp. 169–181.
Situational Treatments of Behavior, *Ibid.,* pp. 309–323.
Postulation for Behavioral Inquiry, *Ibid.,* pp. 405–413.
Observable Behaviors, *Psychol. Rev.,* 47, 1940, pp. 230–253.
The Behavioral Superfice, *Ibid.,* 48, No. 1, 1941.
[3] "What Is a Monad?" *Phil. Sci.,* 7, 1940, pp. 1–6.
[4] The generalization of the "inner" into a comprehensive or "absolute" form is a more recent program of philosophical escape. Trailing its initial "innerness" with it to the end, it remains a program rather than an achievement, critically of high importance, constructively of none. Its justification has rested in its importance as complement to the Newtonian absolutes, space and time. When these last disintegrated in modern physics this justification disappeared. When science ceases to have a base that is all "outer," then a complementary "pure inner" is no longer needed; scientific techniques become available for direct application to cognitions, once we discover how to develop and use them.

past surviving into the present. We shall later summarize its ruinous defects. Turn now to the techniques of the present — those we call "scientific" — and to the forecast they give of the future. They are in sharp contrast. They gather their facts where they may, and make a bouquet of actuals instead of one of stylized artificials. They look closely at skin as interior connective tissue of the events in progress. The old pretense of skin to dominate everything vanishes instanter. It is like having been scared of a ghost, and getting over being scared when you catch the cat. Skin now enters for what it is worth in the process and for nothing more.

Knowings are forms of human behavior (P, v. 48). By "behaviors" let us understand that special class of biological adjustments and adaptations which remains for inquiry after both the slow evolutions and the technically physiological processes have secured their separate study. The word "behavioral" will thus cover the same field as "psychological," *provided*, that we take our data as they are *biologically* presented without presumptuous recasting into either psychic or mechanistic forms. Only because of the many hidden implications of "psyche" in current uses of "psychological" is the term "behavior" here preferred.

The reader may already be commenting that physiology has long since reduced skin to its proper place in behavioral process. This comment he might support on the results of research into stimulations and reactions. He is wrong. Almost all of our present physiology, so far as its results are applied to knowledge behaviors, is in the same position with respect to skin as are the defective philosophies; its reports about behaviors are skin-dominated. A display of this situation is a needed preliminary to further examination.

Physiological psychologists sometimes talk of physiological facts and psychological facts as the same; sometimes they talk of them as fellow travelers; always they insist that when physiology has advanced far enough it will produce both physiological and psychological descriptions in one breath. The discouraging truth is, however, that up to date physiology has not itself made one single psychological report directly in its own terms (P, v. 47, p. 238). Even in the simplest physical-physiological stimulation train, the meanings of the words "stimulus" and "reaction" change sharply when shifted from physiological to psychological application. We certainly agree that physiological knowledge is the background of psychological just as physical is the background of physiological; [5]

---

[5] The view of science here taken is substantially that of the "levels of description" used by Malisoff in his presentation of "Emergence Without Mystery" (*Phil. Sci.*, 6,

likewise that tropisms and sensitivities are transitional at their proper stage of inquiry just as viruses are at theirs. But this in no way justifies current theorizing which proclaims physiological-psychological identity on the basis of a pun backed by faith, without positive advance toward organization in simple, direct, steady, scientific report.

This may best be displayed if we join some of Pavlov's results with some of Dewey's and bring them together into contrast with the current physiological-psychological attitude. The labors of these two investigators admirably complement each other. Back of them stand Darwin and Peirce, who put the problem of knowledge " on location " for inquiry. The Pavlov to consider is not the presumed mechanist of academic degradation, any more than the Dewey is the figure in whose name so many educational tradesmen have perpetrated misdemeanors and crimes. The Dewey is he of the *Logic* [6] and of the fifty years of co-ordinated inquiry that have gone into it, just as the Pavlov is the technician of his own laboratory and none other.

Some forty-five years ago when the correlation of psychological with physiological states first became general Dewey noted [7] that the " reflex arc concept " of then current discussion had been adopted by psychologists as a convenient figure of speech to enable them to organize their rapidly growing masses of factual detail, and that its service to them was pictorial. This was unquestionably correct report on what was then taking place. He regarded it as progress but as not enough progress. His objection was that too much of the old was still retained in the figure of speech — that the old was still " not sufficiently displaced." This very objection remains valid today. Dewey proceeded to show that what the psychologists called " stimulus " and what they called " reaction " were, when isolated, not immediate data but truncated part-statements, while conversely the definite immediate data were functional in the sense that both stimulations and reactions had to be combined in description as phases of common event, if the description was to make sense and be

---

1939, pp. 17-18). Such a view introduces a new dimension of freedom for scientific advance. The older science accepted as " reals " what were little more than remnants of primitive guesswork. The newer science becomes able to express itself frankly on the level of its own skills. In slight illustration, a generation ago physics and chemistry were differentiated in terms of " fact "; today in terms of objective and technique. In the case of physiology and psychology the current differentiation is still in terms of " reals," mitigated only by a credal consolidation. The view advocated in the text makes technical achievement the test. The sciences then appear not as reflections of " realms of reality," but as " realms of inquiry " in their own right. See also my *Behavior, Knowledge, Fact* (1935), p. 275 ff.

[6] *Logic, The Theory of Inquiry*, New York, Holt, 1938.
[7] " The Reflex-Arc Concept in Psychology," *Psychol. Rev.*, 5 (1896), pp. 357-370.

safely usable. Manifestly there is no attribution here of intra-dermal localization to psychological fact.[8]

Only in very recent years [9] has psychology begun to produce a series of constructions following out the lines of Dewey's observation (J, pp. 311-321; P, v. 47, pp. 239-243). However, from a very different quarter has come a development in thorough accord with it, if we are to judge not by casual verbalisms of the moment, but by long-range trends of research. This is Pavlov's work with perceptive activity, primarily in the case of the salivating dog.[10] In the pursuit of his conditioned reflexes Pavlov arrived at a manner of description in terms of signs and signals which was radically opposed to the old "psychic" description and just as radically to all physiological camouflages of the psychic. Psychic terms were barred in the laboratory as clumsy disturbers of the communicational peace. He regarded himself neither as a psychologist nor as a "physiological psychologist," but strictly and exclusively as a physiologist. The difference is sharp.[11] As a *physiologist* he declared that he was expanding physiology into new territory. He divided physiology into two branches, a narrower or lower dealing with the integration of the work of all parts of the organism, and a broader or higher exploring the connection and equilibration of the organism and external conditions.[12] This latter branch he stressed in terms of the activity of the

[8] If anyone is surprised at seeing Dewey, "the philosopher," listed on the side of science in the matter of cognition, his late address "Nature in Experience" (*Phil. Rev.*, 49, 1940, pp. 244-258), may be consulted. He has asserted again and again his naturalistic approach. Thus in 1908 (*J. Phil., Psychol., & Sci. Meth.*, V, 375) he wrote that the uncritical psychology which regards "intellectual operations ... as having an existence *per se* ... [and] as ... distinct from the *things* which figure in inference-drawing" makes "the theory of knowledge, not logic ... but epistemology." He has, of course, used the "personal" phrasing in much of his writing. This is convenient, and often necessary when addressing certain large groups of hearers. Not his mere use of a word, however, but his own statement of his intent in using it, must be taken as governing his theoretical approach.

[9] Thus J. R. Kantor, *Principles of Psychology*, 2 vol., 1924, 1926; *A Survey of the Science of Psychology*, 1933. K. Lewin, *Principles of Topological Psychology*, 1936. J. F. Brown, *Psychology and the Social Order*, 1937. Frequent phrasings in the earlier writings of Wertheimer and Koffka remind one of Dewey; and the most successful work of the Gestalt psychologists — that with colors — permits a very complete statement in this manner, even though the habitual Gestalt dualisms of sense and form, of outer and inner, and of physiological and psychological, cause serious deterioration in most other branches of their inquiries.

[10] *Conditioned Reflexes: An Investigation of the Physiological Activity of the Cerebral Cortex*, 1927. *Lectures on Conditioned Reflexes*, 1928.

[11] One may perhaps say that the psychologist follows psyche, the physiological psychologist follows flesh-bound psyche, and the physiologist in Pavlov's sense expands inquiry to full organic activity. The difference between the last two, so far as behaviors are concerned, is like that between duplication of phrase and straight research, or between rubber stamp and test tube.

[12] "A Brief Outline of the Higher Nervous Activity," *Psychologies of 1930*, Chap. II, p. 207.

cerebral cortex. The stress covers one phase of the full activity: the intra-dermal phase. The full physiology cannot be developed exclusively there nor kept permanently in close confinement. Pavlov's own laboratory procedure does not hold it there. The cerebral activity, as he saw it, was not assigned to the cortex as a power or capacity; his frequent researches into localization were of the legitimately factual type, and were not efforts at physiological-psychic identification. What he studied was a process directly involving phenomena outside the skin along with phenomena inside, so that the region in which the physiological event took place — its locus — was literally wider than any region enclosed by a skin. This characterization is not developed out of statements Pavlov himself made in commenting on his own work; indeed various expressions he used at one time or another in the course of his long career conflict with it. It is a proper statement, nevertheless, of his actual procedure, of its lines of expansion, and of safe forecast for its future (J, pp. 311–314; P, v. 47, pp. 240–241; P, v. 48). The very difficulties Pavlov had with the words " external " and " internal " [13] support this view if we remind ourselves that he was not a word-spinner but a fact-finder, for whom even a fumbling approximation to well-stated fact rated higher than the last word in verbal sanctification.

In exhibiting the manner in which Dewey on the one side and Pavlov on the other disregard skin as critical boundary and join thus in marked contrast to the conventional physiological-psychological attitude, we are already well on our way toward a consideration of the modern approach to inquiry which succeeds the traditional. The modern setting is this: For special purposes biology may study an organism " as if alone." Nevertheless biology knows no " organism alone " as fact. The words " organism alone " when used positively make no sense at all. The facts for biology are " organisms-in-environment " — " organisms-on-earth," if one wants it pictorially phrased.[14] Inquiries into behavior are primarily biological, but they differ from other branches of biological

---

[13] At times he treated the sub-cortical centers as the animal proper, with cerebrum environmental to it; again the cerebrum was connection between inner-sub-cortical and outer-environmental; other expressions seem to make " the rest " of the body environment to the cerebrum. His hemispheres " analyze " for internal as well as for external: " Some of the most delicate elements and moments of skeleto-muscular activity become stimuli." Excitation may " originate " in cortex and be " initial stimulus." Pavlov's manner of handling difficulties of this kind scientifically may profitably be compared with works in which similar difficulties appear, but in which essential existential statement is sought. Burrow's *The Biology of Human Conflict*, 1937, developed out of Freudian antecedents, will well serve for this purpose.

[14] From the biological point of view, and in terms of the organism as a whole, this functional status of stimulus with respect to organism is well brought out by Kurt Goldstein, *The Organism* (1934; Eng. trans. 1939). He does not, however, expand his statement in terms of the full situation of organism-environment.

inquiry in that they find greatly increased intricacy in the ways in which the organisms are involved in the environments, and the environments in the organisms. Moreover, in comparison with the slow adaptations that are the rule in biological evolution, behavioral adaptations are lightning flashes. But even lightning flashes are no longer seen as coming from the hand of Jove; they are instead readjustments of distribution. The more this comes to be understood in its full evolutionary setting, the more intimately will the fusion of organic and environmental participations in behaviors be manifest, even though this is in the sharpest contrast with the primitive view which continues to insist on " spirit " severance.

Let us return now to a consideration of the basic technique of the philosopher with his " inner knowers " and his " outer knowns " kept apart by an etherialization of an anatomical skin. We have already said that it is a technique of the past surviving into the present, and that it has ruinous defects. Examination of it shows:

(a) that despite its luxurious flowering in the form of philosophical systems and creeds, it has never produced any generally acceptable organized knowledge of knowings;

(b) that the inner " knower " it employs is a force, capacity, faculty, actor, or power belonging to that type of " forces " which competent sciences expel (P, v. 47, pp. 235-237) — physics today wholly, biology to sufficient extent so that the outcome is already clear.

(c) that no such force or actor has ever been observed directly, it being a phenomenon of ascription rather than of description;

(d) that terminological clarification fails whenever inners and outers must be closely examined as cases of fact (P, v. 48);

(e) that even ecology has difficulty at the line of skin in seeking precise formulations for organism and environment (P, v. 48);

(f) that closer descriptions are very greatly needed here as in all cases in which vehemence of belief is found in direct proportion to extent of ignorance;

(g) that once we have abandoned attributions to isolated inners of the sub-scientific type, we can attain no description that makes sense at all for actual human behaviors — lovings, hatings, buyings, votings, fightings, helpings, talkings, schemings — without observing and describing the behavioral activity as itself positively and directly trans-dermal (P, v. 48).

The assertions in the preceding paragraphs are " factual " in the sense that, giving sufficient detachment of purpose, any inquirer can make independent verifications. The appraisal of their bearing upon inquiry into knowledge is not so easy, running as it does far beyond the usual ranges of detachment. To proceed to it we must not only assume the natural evolution of organisms in terrestrial environments, but we must do this completely, making it cover not only the *structure* but *all of the behaviors* of organisms, and we must do it honestly and sincerely, weeding out every reservation and every exemption that we may secretly make (P, v. 47, pp. 250–251; v. 48).

Under a thoroughgoing assumption of evolution we may expect:

(1) that " forces " of types that disappear from the advanced sciences will in the course of time disappear from the less advanced;

(2) that radical reconstructions such as occur in the advanced sciences when incoherences of expression have been found insoluble will under similar conditions occur also in the less advanced;

(3) that behaviors should be investigated where they *are* — that is, where observation of them can be made — without limitation to spots where grammatical convenience guesses them to be;

(4) that knowledge processes are included with other behaviors, and can no longer claim special privilege as a unique type of " thing " or " event " in the world.

On this basis the procedures called "philosophical" are no longer sacredly untouchable but permit direct factual examination, so that their deficiencies can be appraised in their full gravity, and inferences as to needed reconstructions can be drawn. In simple illustration of the type of change that may be involved, consider our grandfathers, who in their innocence quite commonly believed in innate depravity and in the personal devil. The grandsons, leastwise those of a scientific bent, have quit that simple view. But these same grandsons for the most part still believe in a solipsistic intellect and in a regnant truth which, if they are good, they may some day look upon face to face. The data we have marshaled serve, however, to indicate that the sweet odors of mentality are at one with the sulphurous fumes of the devil, and the isolated " I " of the single organism is no more to be assumed to have personal dealings with eternal truth than with eternal evil or with any other of the personally guaranteed eternities the world has now discarded.

The philosopher faces a dilemma resting in the fact that the Newtonian space and time go hand in hand with the skin-encompassed knower, this latter being just a receptacle for the overflow of phenomena the former cannot contain (P, v. 47, p. 236). If the philosopher sticks to the knower in its old space and time, the only way he can get his knower to achieve its knowing in regions beyond the skin is through some form of magic, and the only path of escape he has ever found from the primitive magics is by way of verbal subtleties which are themselves just magics of an upper caste. If on the other hand the philosopher discards the Newtonian scheme under the influence of modern physics, and if he discards the magic knower under the influence of modern cultural studies, then he will find his phenomena of inquiry developing a phase space — a *system* of their own — for their formulation, and his whole inquiry will pass beyond the range of official philosophical technique and fall fully within that of freely advancing science.

What, now, under the newer approach, will be the status of knower and known, of knowing and of knowledges, in terms of direct observation and description? Where, in short, will one find the *facts,* if one looks for them? The answer cannot take the Newtonian form of " in the third pint-pot on the second shelf of the cupboard," or " in the upper right-hand corner of such-and-such a section of a cortex." The kindergarten class must wait a little longer before it can be told.

The first step toward considering a " where " under the new approach will be by comparison with the kind of " where " that was offered under the old. Under the old approach Cartesian co-ordinates could indeed be applied to the skin of the organism. The result was not localization, but a pseudo- or quasi-localization. The " knower " and the " known " entered as " existences," whether frankly or in subtle shadings. With soul weakened into psyche, and with psyche yielding to body as its " stand-in," " knowing " could in a way be viewed as physiological process within the skin. This supplied a confused pretense of definiteness to three of the four terms, viz., to knower, known, and knowing. But what kind of definiteness could then be given to the fourth term, " knowledge "! Knowledge, substantively viewed, was left to bear the brunt of the inquiry: Was it inside the skin, or out? Was it flesh, or spirit? Was it fact, or thought, or word?

To the direct question as to *where* knowledge is located, nobody under the old procedure has ever given a coherent answer. Even to put such a question and press it steadily is regarded as ill-mannered. Such possibilities as " in the head," " in the mind," " in the brain," " on the library shelf," " in the absolute," or just " out there " in the facts are all sad answers; you cannot stick to any one of them for three sentences without being in trouble. A knower with nothing it knows, or a known without a knower to know it, is absurd, not in subtlety alone, but as an affair of the simplest verbal integrity; yet the discussions result in demanding one, or the other, or both, or neither — you can take your choice.

The issue does not appear in its full absurdity so long as one potters around with generalities. When one gets down to the specific instance and demands the location of *an* item of knowledge — and this question the newer approach is compelled to ask, if it is to consider the matter at all — then the absurdity becomes violent. The word " concept " is everywhere found in recent discussions about science to designate such an " item " of knowledge. Its old scholastic implications have long since disappeared, and we may properly demand of the modern user of the word: *Where* can you show us a sample of these concepts you talk so much about? We get no answer whatever in any modern sense. Plenty of material is available for examination if we wish it: thus, Bridgman's *Logic of Modern Physics,* Dewey's *Logic,* almost any paper in *Philosophy of Science,* and many of the reports in technical journals such as the *Psychological Review.* My own inquiry indicates that in perhaps half the cases of its use the word " concept " may be omitted and no reader ever be aware of the difference, while in nine-tenths of the remaining cases simple rephrasing will just as completely get rid of it. An occasional instance remains in which the word suggests a slight hesitancy in assertion, perhaps about the equivalent of the quotation marks often used to hold a doubtful word up for inspection, and sometimes this takes the firmer form of a " planning." But at its best it is a mere schematic term. So far as any " existence " of its own in the way current uses imply is concerned it is abracadabra. If anyone who is not a psychist, and not merely wearing a verbal parade uniform, but who is seriously intent on precise statement in terms of the opposition of knower and known will indicate to me *where* a concept can be found as *a* fact, I shall be very grateful.[15]

The modern approach does not involve this confusion at all. It gets rid of it at a single stroke. Instead of starting with knowers and knowns which it proclaims as basic without pretending to " know " what they are, it starts with knower-known-knowing-knowledge complex to investigate. It does not talk generalities about system; it investigates system as fact. To be investigated as fact, system must be present somewhere. It must be terrestrial. Location must be assignable, for knower, for known, for knowing, and for knowledge, in definite terrestrial spaces and times. These spaces and times are biological. To call behaviors biological without giving them literal terrestrial location is delusion. Biological regions are regions of organic-environmental differentiation on earth,

---

[15] I think I shall not be violating any confidence if I say that Professor Bridgman once checked a portion of his own unpublished manuscript in which the word " concept " appeared fifty-three times, and found that without any sense of loss he could omit it in all but four cases; in two of these four, the casual word " notion " did service, leaving only two resistant cases out of the fifty-three. Professor Dewey has written me that he has made sufficient examinations to convince him that " the word is useless at least four-fifths of the time — my own writings included."

with organism and environment entering not as eternal verities or achieved basic knowledges but as themselves subjects of progressing inquiry. Note the sharp difference between this and the philosophical approach which makes knowledge be concerned with something it calls " relation," where " relation " is a primitive form of placeless naming for phenomena one senses as present but which one is unable to trace down as facts in space and time. " Knowledge " itself in this philosophical process comes to appear as a sort of relation between relations, possessing placelessness, and in a comparably discreditable sense timelessness (and so non-factuality) in a sort of second degree. Under the modern approach " relation " disappears entirely from the reckoning,[16] and full event and process is spread out for inquiry. Knowledge is now recognized not as a kind of spaceless " being " but as phenomenon that is present there and there only where knower-known activity is under way. " Knower " and " known " are now constrained — despite their Neanderthal footings and their colloquial universality — to submit at last to examination in system. " Knowing " and " knowledge " no longer differ as though the former were a process and the latter its product, but show themselves as manners of stress in description. In the biological regions in which behaviors occur, organisms are central — " nuclear," if one will. Knowing, knowledge, the knower, the known, are all forms of description of the biological region examined when it is in action in a highly specialized way. They involve no limitation to any spot or to any type of spot, nuclear or other, within the region, and no necessary prescript as powers, capacities, qualities, or properties of any spot.

In another paper (P, v. 48) dealing with the localization of behaviors generally, I have used the name " behavioral superfice " for the boundaries of any area in which organism-environment adjustments of the behavioral type are in progress. Just as " skin " bounds the narrowly physiological activity of the organism, not geometrically but functionally, so " superfice " bounds the broadly physiological adjustments as we see these in expansion from Pavlov's view. In the particular case of the Pavlov conditioning, superfice brings dog, food, bell, and signalization all in one " system " of inquiry. Anatomically, skin rates as spatial determination; physiologically, it involves durational ranges also. For be-

---

[16] Dewey retains the word " relation " for symbol-organization, matching it against " connection " for non-language organization, and against " reference " to designate word-to-thing behaviors (*Logic*, p. 55). His is the only intelligible use of the word " relation " with which I am acquainted, once the old spiritist scheme is superseded. Just as the word " relation " can be rehabilitated, so also can the word " concept." On Dewey's basis " concept " may appear as a forward-looking, possibility-realizing " idea," or " rule," or " habit " of behavior; or alternatively it may show itself as a name for certain intricate language behaviors.

havioral demarcations within superfice, and for knowledges above all else, the intimacy of durational-spatial involvement heightens; otherwise activity, event, could not be depicted within it.

In simple, casual, natural approach nothing interferes with our accepting a " knowledge " as present within a superfice any more than a living organism as present within a skin. The sole interference comes from overassertive " local " points of view. Not as an attempt at nature-faking but as casual rhetoric we may say that from the local point of view of some ill-educated gene the epidermis of its organism would seem a far-off fantasy, absurd to insist upon. Chromosome, cell, gland would doubtless — if they could blurt it out — be just as solipsistically self-centered as is any human " self " enjoying power of assertive speech. A bullet, incidentally, like the captain in the Civil War jingle, would be " worst of all," as the self-assertiveness went round. Since Darwin a certain modesty toward the universe, which the bullet lacks, has become common among men, though not in nearly high enough degree so long as the single man regards himself as aloof from the universe in the skin-protected pretense that " he " is something bullet-like " inside," uniquely looking out. Superfice is just one way of exhibiting the single man as literally component of his universe; the great argument in favor of its use is that its technical position is in line with other technical procedures of modern science.

A knowledge may be viewed as located " within " a superfice as simply as may electricity " within " a battery or an electron " within " an atom — much more simply, in all probability, after a little practice is had. The interference, the obstacle, is mostly in a pattern of speech — a " patter " — to the effect that " nothing but spirit can know " which curiously survives among many men long after they have agreed that " no spirit exists." It is ultra-curious that our logicians today more than any others seem to regard this as logical. Of the three courses open when describing behaviors — to go magic, to go fleshly, or to go situationally [17] systemic — the present approach deliberately selects the last.

When one adopts the superfice as one's aid and examines descriptions within it in supplement to descriptions within skin, one finds that the position of anatomy with respect to physiology in narrowly organic in-

[17] The word " situational," in much the sense that I use it (J, v. 47, p. 311), was suggested thirty years ago as an improvement on " social " by Addison W. Moore in his book *Pragmatism and Its Critics* (p. viii, p. 230). He saw pragmatism as evolutionary and non-solipsistic, and by illustrating upon the work of Royce and Baldwin he drove home the point (p. 221) that no mere special pleading in the name of " evolution " or of the " social " would suffice, but that thorough basic development was needed. He thus forecast the main characteristics of the present paper, though his early death left his work without further development.

quiry is matched by that of ecology to psychology in broader environmental inquiry. Anatomy was once viewed as a study of structure in contrast with physiology's study of function, but it stands now rather as offering a spatial abstraction preliminary to physiology's full durational-extensional study. Passing to regions within the superfice where organisms and environments are seen in action together, ecology employs in the main the static, structural, spatial approach, while psychology or, if one prefers, the wider Pavlov physiology, undertakes the full durational-functional study. Psychology stands thus toward ecology within a superfice as physiology stands toward anatomy within a skin. Knowledge processes are the most intricate which psychology has to investigate. Whether they are to be regarded as within the domain of psychology proper, or as running beyond it in. much the way that the psychological in general runs beyond the more narrowly physiological, is unimportant. What is important is the opportunity we now have for their technical investigation by procedures expanded directly from those of physics, physiology, and the less intricate psychology, under the steady maintenance of directly durational-spatial observation.

To assign knowledges and other behaviors to regions within superfices is a step much like that which mathematicians took when they introduced continuity. Mathematicians were restlessly exploring, and the natural numbers did not suffice for all the realms they wanted to explore. So they took on negatives, infinites, irrationals, imaginaries, transcendentals — all sorts of queer gentry. They felt like sinners, but they went ahead and sinned — and thank God for that. Only very recently have they been losing their sense of guilt through finally becoming aware that after all the " naturals " are no sacred temple of " reality," and that it is only right and proper that every operator should have its day. The superfice enters as hypothesis; it enters to meet the needs of accumulating fact. The experience of the mathematicians justifies us in trying anything not only once but often enough to satisfy ourselves how it goes.

The only test of hypothesis is in the results that frequent patient efforts secure. In the present case two important forms of inquiry are under way that in the end will yield tests.

The first of these is an advance toward a consistent terminology of sign and symbol to cover all behavioral purposes, not in supplement to, but as complete substitute for, the old psychological terminology of faculty, quality, property, and power. Locke, Berkeley, and Reid started one line of approach. Peirce got a firm hold upon the most essential requirements, though the linguistic limitations of his day blocked all his efforts at positive advance. Jennings secured a sound initial expression in his study of the lower organisms. Pavlov and Dewey have made by far the largest contributions. In recent literature consider Hunter's vicarious functioning, Brunswik's cue-family, Bühler's attempt to apply signs to the behavioral study of language, and Tolman's various terminological applications of the word "sign." Klüver, Hull, Skinner, and doubtless many others with whose work I am not acquainted are furnishing building materials.[18] Almost all this emerging terminology, however, comes still trailing tatters of the old mental glory. Not till *all* the mentalist implications are stripped off, and the sign process is permitted to proceed under hypothesis within its own proper biological region, can a clear test of its efficiency be secured.

The second form of inquiry is that leading toward a general theory of language as human behavior. Skeletonized linguistics, mechanistic fragments, psychic oddities, Freudian trifles, are scattered around, but all together they do not add up to any coherent presentation of speech as a functioning phase of human behaviors. A full situational development within the region of a superfice is indicated as a simple and promising procedure.

The development of this paper rests upon the work of Charles Sanders Peirce, his pragmatism, his fallibilism, and his long search for a living, as opposed to a static, logic.[19] It rests not upon results he immediately obtained but upon his vision and upon his endeavor; and upon these, indeed, in the form which John Dewey has independently paralleled or definitely advanced.

Of our coupled subject-matters, skin and philosophy, most attention has been given, perhaps unwisely, to the latter. We may sum up with respect to skin. 1. Anatomically, as a separator, skin dominates philosophy. 2. Physiologically studied, it displays transition processes of organism-environment. 3. *Sensation-perception* problems can be surveyed in close correlation with such physiological inquiry; nevertheless, physiology has thus far yielded no continuous descriptive development even of this region of the behavioral. 4. As for *knowledge* problems,

[18] Any citations I might make to the work of the psychologists mentioned would require so much in the way of qualification and interpretation as to be impracticable here. The best guide I know of to the impending development, although it barely mentions the word "sign," and ends at the problem-setting with which the present examination begins, is the paper by Professor Fritz Heider, "Environmental Determinants in Psychological Theories" (*Psychol. Rev.*, 46, 1939, pp. 383-410). If the reader will take Heider's terms "proximal" and "distal" for variations in the focus of inquiry as he establishes them, without pigeonholing them in terms of conventional analogues, he will, I believe, find the discussion extremely profitable.

[19] For Peirce's non-mentalism, see E. Nagel, "Charles S. Peirce, Pioneer of Modern Empiricism," *Phil. Sci.*, 7, 1940, esp. pp. 73, 76, 79.

when the physiologist leaps to them at a single bound by way of the cortex, he employs skin like the philosopher as a separator rather than as a connector. 5. Further appraisals of the transitional status of skin in this region are essential. 6. In the meantime, a type of superfice-bounded area has been displayed within which " a knowledge " can be located if it is to be viewed in skin-traversing rather than in skin-dismembered form.

Under the old approach — the philosophical — the pint-pot dreams of the ocean. Under the new approach — the scientific — the pint-pot begins to get the measure of a pint, and epistemology goes to join alchemy and astrology in the limbo of man's crude endeavors.

Postscript

Since the completion of this paper a report has been made public upon the physiological status of pain [20] which is of high significance for the differentiation within science of physiological and behavioral inquiries. The work was done at the Russell Sage Institute of Pathology. The primary purpose of the inquiry was to establish how far " experienced distress " depends upon the pain threshold, and how far it is different in reaction. A technique having been developed for independent determination of the threshold, and results having been secured for single subjects, a test was made upon a group of 150 subjects differing in age and sex. The pain threshold in man is reported as " relatively stable and uniform " (0.206 ± 0.03 gm.cals./sec./cm^2). The standard deviation for the group was ± 1 per cent, the same as previously observed for individual subjects. This threshold cannot be correlated with subjects' reactions. Nor can it be correlated with subjects' estimates. It is independent of sex, uniform throughout the twenty-four-hour day, and not affected by feelings of lethargy, tension, or overirritability, nor by lack of sleep in the twenty-four-hour period. The investigators conclude that " individual reactions to pain are not the results of individual variations in the pain threshold." We may regard the variation they have shown as falling reasonably well within an ordinary anatomical range.

The importance of this work, if it is adequately confirmed, is that it enables us to give much wider appeal to the case in favor of the " situational " localization of behaviors, by eliminating a factor which in the eyes of many has been implicitly or explicitly a serious stumbling block. The

---

[20] Schumacher, Goodell, Hardy, and Wolff, "Uniformity of the Pain Threshold in Man," *Science*, 92 (1940), pp. 110–112. See also Hardy, Wolff and Goodell, *J. Clin. Invest.*, 19 (1940), p. 649; Wolff, Hardy, and Goodell, *ibid.*, p. 659.

full effect is secured where the sciences are regarded as "levels of description," even if not where they are still regarded as the portraiture of "realms of reality."[21] When so inspected, the "pain" factors (including all "raw" feeling factors, although without attempt here at further specification) are readily assigned to the organism. To assign them to the organism, however, if we come clean, is to withdraw them from any lingering psychic or pseudo-psychic base. Already we find concretely specialized behaviors observed and talked about as directly cultural or social phenomena, no matter what official creed of a psychic substratum is retained by observer or talker. And we everywhere recognize (unless we are logicians) that the extreme hypostatization of an "ego" on the basis of a grammatical "I" is semantically false. However, the foggy spook-person of ordinary conversation, of practically all sociological theory, and of most psychological theory, is a crude mixture of "feel" person, "actual behavior" person, and "fictive ego" person. With the "pain" element withdrawn for physiological specialization (which is simple and easy on a basis of descriptions, however repugnant it may be on a basis of "conventional reals"), there is nothing of this "spook-person" left for scientific consideration. The way is wide open for full "situational" procedure such as we have described above.

"Person" does indeed retain a very important status in sociological and psychological work, although no longer with "spook" values. It reduces to a specialized description — to a partial or limited description for special purposes and from a special point of view — of the "behaviors" which, more adequately reported, are seen to have situational localization in areas wider than those within skins. The scientist's "person" ceases to reside "in" the organism, and becomes a local description of an organic-environmental process from the behaviorally organic viewpoint.

Essential to these statements, if they are to have any meaning at all, is that they are to be taken *literally*. In the full subjective-objective fusion (except as linguistically dissected with careful semantic anesthetic and antiseptic) the behaviors *are* (for scientific observation) in the situation; and they *are not* in any sense whatever (except as the asserter gives nonintelligent meaning to his "are") in the spook.

[21] *Cf.* footnote No. 4, preceding.

CHAPTER ELEVEN

Some Logical Considerations Concerning Professor Lewis's "Mind"*

In a recent paper, " Some Logical Considerations Concerning the Mental," [1] Professor C. I. Lewis expresses himself thus:

1. " Minds are private "; each person is " directly acquainted " with his " own mind "; these existential allegations about mind are " essential," even though they may contain " irremovable unclarity " or " implicit inconsistency "; if we have " any such possible doubts " they " can be removed."

2. Mind includes all the " content of consciousness "; these contents are phenomenal " datum " or " appearance "; they possess " identity and character impossible to mistake — though admittedly any language used to name them may be inappropriate or inadequate and fail to express just what is intended."

3. "Whoever would deny that there are directly inspectable facts of the content of consciousness, would deny that which alone makes a theory of mind desirable and significant, and that which supplies the only final test of such a theory."

We have here the flavor of edict and excommunication. Much more serious, however, is the default in the simplest pre-logical candor. Professor Lewis demands that we accept as the inevitable technical control of research a handful of opinions which he himself, though a true believer, can only formulate with hesitation and tremor. These opinions start with a proclamation of the isolation of mind from world, proceed by admitting world into mind via the metamorphosis of " outer " into " inner," and end by requiring from us a blind allegiance to the " inner " thus mystically or magically produced, even though no de-

* From *Journal of Philosophy,* Vol. XXXVIII, No. 23 (November 6, 1941), pp. 634-35.
[1] *Journal of Philosophy,* Vol. XXXVIII (1941), pp. 225-33. The citations will be found on pages 225-29.

pendable naming for its phenomena can be found, whether " inner," or " outer," or on the fence between.

Professor Lewis would perform a great service if he would reduce his opinions to propositions and submit these propositions to logical control. If he can give them thereby any successful logical system or other form of organization, I shall gladly alter my present view.

CHAPTER TWELVE

The Factual Space and Time of Behavior[*]

I

I wish to make a report on the space-time of behavioral fact. In alternative phrasing, one may understand this to mean behavioral space-time, the spatial and temporal forms of behaviors, or its factual extensions and durations. The phrasing itself makes little difference in our present stage of ignorance in this field of research, providing one does not let his chosen words glitter so brightly as to blind him to the issues involved. I shall limit myself to a summary in the simplest form I can command.

Our consideration will be confined to "facts" in the sense of "scientific facts," where these latter are taken to be the content of the best technical observation and report of our time. By explicit postulation, behavioral facts will be included among scientific facts in this sense. This means that other manners of attributing factuality, actuality, or reality to behavioral facts are here irrelevant.

Ethnologists report much variety of space apprehension in different parts of the world. For Western Europe and America, from early Greece to the generation preceding our own, we find a three-dimensional space serving alike for practical life and for science. This space secured a successfully dogmatic statement from Euclid, was provided with improved technical tools by Descartes, and in Newton's hands became a formal space which, along with its companion, formal time, established itself as the "absolute" background of all physical inquiry.

The scientific authority of the Newtonian formalization held unchallenged until the present generation. Even psychologists, as candidates for reputable scientific status, found no alternative to fitting all their inquiry into the frame it offered. Nevertheless in their direct study of their own peculiar behavioral facts, psychologists could never technically hold them within the Newtonian form. Experimentation could achieve a little measurement with a yardstick and a little registration of time with a clock, but never more than enough to skirt the fringe of the be-

[*] From *Journal of Philosophy*, Vol. XXXVIII, No. 18 (August 28, 1941), pp. 477-85.

havioral facts. Purposings, as behavioral facts, remained far out of reach of such manipulation. The established attitude of the psychologist came to be that his facts were " in " the Newtonian universe but not technically " of " it. This attitude allotted the behavioral facts locations in the world, but not such locations as Cartesian co-ordinates could establish. The locations were quasi-locations, asserting the presence, not definitely but indefinitely, " in " or " at " an organism. The whole group of problems arising from this lack of definiteness was turned over to philosophy, which was assumed to possess special equipment for its examination. By some strange quirk the psychologist hoped to remain a scientist even while deliberately evading a most essential characteristic of his own observation. This may well have been the best he could do, since whenever any brash adventurer attempted to force psychological fact into mechanistic forms, a lifeless residue was all he obtained.

What could not be accomplished while Newtonian space and time were " absolute " for science can easily be done today. Today, looking backward, we can see that if psychologists had attended strictly to the extensions and durations of their own facts, without attempting either to force these facts into Newtonian forms or to expel them radically from it, the status of their present knowledge would be very different from what it is. They would themselves have attained a space-time form for their own research, and one notably closer to the newer physics of our time than it ever could be to the old.

It is, of course, Einstein's work that has opened new vistas of freedom to psychologies of the future. The present prevailing construction of physical relativity is not what counts, for if this has any direct authority over psychology today I am not aware of it. Freedom for research is what counts. The moment that Newtonian space was shown to be not absolutely precise in physics, that very moment its dictatorial authority over other sciences was ended. If the physicists could construct a space and a time to fit the facts of their research, so also could the psychologists for theirs. Space and time had become themselves factual; and if for one, then for all.

The status of psychological observation and description within science today may be summarized as follows:

1. Psychology has always concerned itself with facts which do not tolerate technical description in technical Newtonian space and time.
2. These facts, nevertheless, have their own manifest extensions and durations.
3. Psychology is now at last free to describe them as it finds and observes them.
4. Such observation and description becomes practicable within the frame of a full naturalism for organic and environmental facts.

II

Further comment on the last of these four assertions is desirable. In current research the words "organism" and "environment" stand for scientific facts in the natural universe as we know it. This natural universe is understood as itself in evolution. The whole universe-fact system is one of knowledge in evolution. Scientifically, factually, we have to do not with nature-absolute, but with nature-known. Only through evolution in the knowing is evolution exhibited in the known.

The facts of nature-known are investigated in part by physical methods and in further part by physiological methods. But beyond these we have a large group of facts not directly and technically studied by either of these methods. A most general name for such facts is "adaptations." Some of these adaptions, those, namely, for the most part which cover wide areas and age-long durations, are investigated in the evolutionary studies of biology. Others, mostly flashlike and involving limited areas, are investigated by psychologists under the name of behaviors. If this manner of characterization is unfamiliar, the reader may easily satisfy himself by stripping off his ordinary verbal scaffoldings and appraising all the events of organisms and environments, long-time and short-time, directly as natural.

Adaptions are events, not of organism alone, nor of environment alone, but of complex organic-environmental situations. If the organism is in the world physically, if it "lives" physiologically, it should in a similar sense proceed in adaptation and evolution naturally. If the organism enters naturally, it should be *kept* natural; if it is kept natural, it and its environment are phases of a common event. The biologist, it is true, most often speaks of an adaptation *of* the organism *to* the environment. The psychologist most often speaks of an *act* of the organism, of *its* action upon the environment. Though in the first case the organism seems to enter in the main as passive, and in the second mostly as active, both cases agree in throwing a sentimental spotlight upon the organism as if it enjoyed a higher order of reality than the environment. Such a spotlight falsifies. No organism-alone exists for the biologist. For that matter no environment-alone exists, although a very large amount of research, the physical, is able to proceed under such a simplified hypothesis. Biologists, talking of organism-alone, must keep the qualifying conditions in mind with almost every sentence they write. Adaptations are jointly of organism-environment. Behavioral adaptations require continual stress upon the organic-environmental extension of the event, if they are to be held within the full naturalistic procedure. To hold them so is equivalent to asserting that the behavioral event takes place in a natural behavioral space-time. Adequate description, freely made, eventuates in a construction of behavioral space-time, and behavioral space-time is a generalized report on such description. This is the length and breadth of the story.

III

A few illustrations of behavioral extensions and durations will now be given, accompanied by a hint at construction. Lengthy statement is not needed. If a reader insists on employing the Newtonian standardization of space and time, no words will influence him. If he can look freely, a simple suggestion will doubtless be enough.

Behaviors in the indicated sense of speedy adaptations comprise all the psychological facts that psychologists now investigate as directly within their own province. Purposive behavior is typical in such instances as cat wandering toward catnip, boy planning for college, or crusader striving for better city government. The word " experience " will cover the ground fairly well if it is taken to indicate characteristic behavioral adaptations, rather than as a dubious appendage to a falsely isolated organism.

In all purposing there is a " look before and after," perhaps likewise a dream " of what is not." Avoid distortion of the words " look " and " dream," hold them to the organic-environmental situation, and you have a fair exhibit of behavioral durations. This " behavioral time " is different from any of the physical types of duration, different also from " physiological time " as physiologists are beginning to recognize it in intra-organic events. It is to be found all the way from a simple perceptive or sub-perceptive behavior up to and including the most complex symbolic organization of word and world.

Take the case of boy-planning-college. Behavioral duration is *present*. It is " present," even though not in the manner of this instant's tick of the clock. The span " high school into college " has, indeed, a much fuller and richer factuality than the " instant " that any clock records, or than any series of instances. No adding of instances ever displays fully the purposing. The behavior spans the long period of clock ticks, and spans it *now*. The dilemma, so far as there is one, is overcome by the good old method, that of recognizing facts. Achilles *does* in fact catch the tortoise. Behavior does, in fact, what for clocks is impossible;

it spans the duration. Organic-boy-living is thus durationally much more complex than infinitely ticking clocks, or for that matter than infinitely extended parallels in three dimensions.

If an organism's behavior is durational in this way, it is also extensional. In a naturalistic world no duration is a timeless instant. Nor can any duration be observed except as involved in that which is extensional. No phase of behavior occurs either durationally or extensionally except as organic-environmental adaptation.

When once we have stated a behavior in its own extensional-durational form, we proceed to state other behaviors similarly. Then our report on their factual durational-extensional organization becomes directly a report on a factual behavioral space-time itself.

In the *Journal of Philosophy* two years ago [1] I examined the case of simple visual perception directly in the form of a " sight-seen," treating the " seer " and the " seen " not as separate ingredients that entered into a psychological broth, but as phases of the situational " sight-seen " behavior, with respect to which " seer " and " seen " themselves must be defined. In a more recent paper [2] I have used the name " behavioral superfice " to mark off the boundaries of any event of organism-environment across space and time in which a specific instance of behavior could be identified for research. When I examine the studies in color-constancy, most of them by Gestalt psychologists, I am left strongly with the impression that the descriptions in this field which are direct, full, and vivid are those which disregard for the moment all thought of posited organism (or ego) and of posited object, in posited detachment from each other, and report instead the color events as they come. Efforts to interpret the color events in terms of organisms and objects taken in radical separation from each other are always chaotic. The reverse process, namely, derivation of the organism and object as themselves *specifications within knowledge,* should promise good results whenever an adequate space-time construction is secured.

The simplest form of behavioral space-time enters, of course, at whatever point physical and physiological descriptions cease to be adequate, and by that very test. If the word " tropism " is used, as is customary, in the sense of direct physical-physiological effect, we have only to mark the point at which Jennings found it necessary to use the word " represent " [3] to describe facts of unicellular organic stimulation, in order to

---

[1] Vol. XXXVI (1939), pp. 169–181.
[2] " The Behavioral Superfice," *Psychological Review,* Vol. XLVIII (1941), pp. 39–59.
[3] H. S. Jennings, *The Behavior of the Lower Organisms,* 1906, p. 297: " In all these cases the reaction to the change cannot be considered due to any direct injurious or beneficial effect of the actual change itself. The actual change merely *represents* a possible

pass to the new space-time form. All " cue " behavior, whether described as bodily activities or as perceptions, has this form. So has language from naming through its elaborations of description up to its most complex symbolic development. All through this series the physical and physiological descriptions are present; they are, however, not adequate, and that is the whole point at issue.

To use a behavioral space-time means to employ a system which permits direct organization of the full range of behaviors, which is in harmony naturalistically with the space and time of physics and physiology, but which above all rests in its own direct simple observation of behavioral extensions and durations for its space-time construction.

IV

As the background against which to display the possibility of constructing behavioral space-time, we chose the situation of the older psychology which saw its facts as " in " but not " of " Newtonian space, or which in desperate alternative tried to force the facts into a mechanistic pattern. Further to orient the display, we may next consider various recent efforts to make superficial use of current forms of mathematical and physical expression as a sort of protective coloration for the old " psychic." The instances come from Gestalt psychologists and are offered in full recognition of the fine work these experimenters have accomplished. Criticism enters only at the point at which their construction falls short.

Lewin [4] and Brown [5] use the topological space of mathematics as a device for organizing their facts. Brown has made much valuable contribution on the " social " side but otherwise both he and Lewin take their " psychic," so to speak, in the raw — in other words, in the form of non-material but nevertheless quasi-mechanistic particles or " forces." Thus their topology comes to appear less as an implement of research than as a trick of description.

Koffka's " behavior space " [6] is widely discussed, but it is frankly " phenomenal " in the Gestalt sense, an element of " experience," remain-

---

change behind it, which *is* injurious or *beneficial*. The organism reacts as if to something else than the change actually occurring; the change has the function of a *sign*. We may appropriately call stimuli of this sort *representative* stimuli." My attention was first attracted to the high significance of this passage for psychological construction by Dr. Merrill Roff.

[4] K. Lewin, *Principles of Topological Psychology*, 1936.
[5] J. F. Brown, *Psychology and the Social Order*, 1936.
[6] K. Koffka, *Principles of Gestalt Psychology*, 1935.

ing always "psychic" in the sense that it is not physical. He uses behavior as an aid to establishing behavioral environment, and then employs behavioral environment to give a "definition" of behavior. His procedure does not satisfy him until it provides for the emergence of an "ego," as a non-natural concentrate. He can doubtless study a cow without postulating a detachable cow-ity, but not a human organism without introducing an ego-ity.

Be these comments as they may, a striking exhibit of the way some of the spatial locutions of modern physics can be used to dress up the ancient scheme of non-spatial experience is furnished by R. D. Williams in a paper written with a close eye on Koffka, under the title "What Is Behavior Space?"[7] Williams tells us that space is "*a set of terms and relations,*" without telling us what we are to understand by such words as "set," "terms," and "relations," although these three words are all loose and vague apart from certain mathematical uses, and are at their worst when used by psychologists. Similarly of "behavior space" he writes: "In so far as it is a space, there is only one thing to say — it is a set of terms and relations." Shifting his metaphor, if metaphor is what he is using, into the shop talk of the physical laboratory, he declares space to be "a distribution of probe-body testings," and behavior space to be the same except that now a living organism serves as the probe-body. Passing next to a still more vague terminology with a strong "psychic" stress, he tells us that behavior space is "constituted of our experiences," and again, "is a name for our experiences together with their interrelations and modes of arrangement." Not pausing to tell us what the factual status of "interrelationships, modes, and arrangements" may be, he proceeds in a still further transmogrification to make any space "the set of elements and their relations of which one chooses to speak." Williams believes he can distinguish three types of space: first, the x, y, z space of Newton, which employs "the concept of force"; next, the x, y, z, t space of relativity in which "the concept of force is no longer needed"; last, a certain p, v type of space (he does not refer to it as phase space) in which force re-enters and Gestalt dynamics may flourish without any "call for the denial of experiences." In this third space type he presents "visual, auditory, tactual, memorial, imaginal," and other "experiences" as the direct analogues of "pressures, volumes, and associated relations."

The reader may judge for himself whether we have here a positive report on research into behavior or just an orgy of phrases. In physical science the spatial and temporal determinations possess maximum precision and maximum factuality as well. The requirement in any behavioral science of the future will be no less severe.

[7] *Journal of Psychology,* Vol. VI (1938), pp. 69–79.

V

The position taken in this paper may best be connected with the work of Peirce and Dewey. Peirce felt much more powerfully than any man of his generation — perhaps even than any man of later generations — the import of Darwin's work for the future interpretation of human knowledge. His pragmaticism was a first fruit. His efforts throughout his life toward the construction of a living logic were in line. Unfortunately the terminological and other technical facilities of his generation thwarted his intentions. I will suggest the following sentences from his earliest important publication as forecasting what is needed: " From the proposition that every thought is a sign it follows that every thought must address itself to some other, must determine some other, since that is the essence of a sign. . . . To say therefore, that thoughts cannot happen in an instant but require a time is but another way of saying that every thought must be interpreted in another or that all thought is in signs."[8]

John Dewey has made more progress than any other toward a naturalism of statement essentially extensional and durational. His specialized development has been in logic[9] rather than in the primary psychological construction. His early determination that behaviors were to be taken, neither as " mental " nor as " physiological," but as directly subjects of research in their own right, is known by title to all psychologists, but in purport to almost none.[10] Dewey has recently pointed out that if James had revised his psychology in accordance with his mature philosophical views, then the whole course of psychology in this century would have been altered.[11]

My own earliest demand for freedom in social and psychological inquiries to develop a behavioral space-time form comparable to the freedom physics has acquired under relativity was made in 1926.[12]

VI

In the first section of this paper, I summarized the present status of scientific observation and description in psychology. I will now resum-

---

[8] C. S. Peirce, " Questions Concerning Certain Faculties Claimed for Man," *Journal of Speculative Philosophy*, Vol. II (1868), pp. 103–114. (Also in *Collected Papers*, 5. 253.)
[9] J. Dewey, *Logic, The Theory of Inquiry*, 1938.
[10] " The Reflex Arc Concept in Psychology," *Psychological Review*, Vol. III (1896), pp. 357–370.
[11] " The Vanishing Subject in the Psychology of James," *Journal of Philosophy*, Vol. XXXVII (1940), pp. 589–599.
[12] *Relativity in Man and Society*, chaps. 26 and 27, especially sec. 99, p. 206.

marize, but this time with more direct attention to the problems and reconstruction.

1. Search for a specifically behavioral space-time is legitimate within the present framework of science.
2. Behavioral space-time will be that construction which most adequately sets forth the factual extensions and durations of the behaviors themselves.
3. The behaviors are present events conveying pasts into futures. They cannot be reduced to successions of instants nor to successions of locations. They themselves span extension and duration. The pasts and the futures are rather phases of behavior than its control.
4. The Newtonian construction, though in close approximation to the factual descriptions of physics, is radically defective for the portrayal of behavioral fact. The newer space-time construction of relativity yields forms of expression much less antagonistic to behavioral fact, but offers it, so far as yet appears, no direct contribution.

VII

What and where is behavior? The location of behavior is literally in naturally evolving life on earth. It is literally in organism-environment. These sentences are not verbal generalities about some generality of behavior. They are intended as literal report upon the specific instance of specific behavior.

The " what " of behavior corresponds precisely to the " where." For our purposes here, behavior is not to be taken as a mental concentrate; no more is it to be taken in mechanistic degradation.

In the older philosophical terminology of subject-object, behavior involves the full subject-object process, with either subject or object alone regarded as chimerical. In the newer scientific terminology of organism-environment, behavior involves the full organism-environment process; no fictive " phenomenal " intervention is needed to hold organism and object together in inquiry.

VIII

Behavioral space-time records the form of observation in social inquiry as well as in psychological. Social studies may be distinguished from psychological for minor purposes of convenience such as the academic, much as anatomy may be distinguished from physiology in a medical school. The distinction has no status in *knowledge*. Monstrosities such as that of a social environment to a psychic force do not present themselves in behavioral space-time.

CHAPTER THIRTEEN

Memoranda on a Program of Research into Language*

We desire a General Theory of Language.

This does not mean a specialized phonetics, linguistics, philology, or semantics, nor a specialized logical, aesthetic, or ethical discussion.

I assume that our inquiry will take place within the framework of the world, and within knowledge. I assert that I am justified in assuming this for any serious research today. Let us say that we are to confine ourselves within the ranges of a known world. This known world includes the operating systems of physics in a framework of sidereal and terrestrial space and time, within which organisms are viewed as being evolved. It includes men among these organisms; and among the behaviors of men it includes their various aesthetic, moral, and logical procedures, as well as their industry and politics.

For preliminary designation of the subjectmatter of our inquiry we may describe Language as a *manner of behavior of organisms in a known world*. I know no theory of Language that is constructed within this framework. I find it necessary to undertake to construct such a theory for my personal purposes. I believe it desirable that such a theory should be constructed for the most general purposes of knowledge.

The words I have used above for preliminary designation of the subjectmatter of inquiry will hardly carry the same implications to any two persons in this room. The terms " organism," " behavior," and " known world " will exhibit sharp differences of application as between any two of you. You can test this by carrying on a one-minute conversation in which you use them, and immediately thereafter writing down as carefully as possible what your respective intentions have been in the use of them. In such a background as this, successful research is impracticable

* MS essay, dated October 14, 1941. Introductory lecture before Seminar on Language in the Philosophy Department, Columbia University, as Visiting Lecturer in Philosophy, 1941-42.

because communicable observation, experiment, and description will all be in default.

What we need is to establish a framework of research, and stick to it while we use it. If we do not like the results, we can improve the framework, or we can throw it away and start afresh.

I shall attempt to set down what I understand by " organism " and " behavior " in the " known world " called " natural." This will provide a postulatory basis for research into language.

The world, as we inspect it today within knowledge, is something that is spread out, and changes, and evolves. Reports upon it no longer aim to establish " causes " or other types of initiative or of " power " at spots. Force, *vis viva,* energy *in situ,* have all in turn yielded to cosmically distributed energy. The electromagnetic spectrum offers [measurable] space as an unattainable at one end, and [measurable] time as an unattainable at the other. " Vital " force is not now needed to make an organism run, but physiological statement within a skin is not itself enough. An organism taken as if existing in isolation from the world is not credible. A behavior taken as if located inside an organism and as if capable of existing there apart from the rest of the world is no more credible than an organism or an electron in such isolation. It has no place in the present postulation. My opinion is that it will disappear more and more from future work. I make this assertion despite the fact that 99 per cent, and more probably 99.9 per cent, of all the output of our psychological laboratories assumes or implies such intra-organic location for what it calls behavior.

I hold a place among the many workers who are struggling toward a contextual, or interactional, or situational treatment of psychological materials. The main difference is that I stand farther to the left than most of the others when I insist upon a direct and immediate description of behaviors as having location in a fused organic-environmental region. I postulate this for observation, for preliminary statement, and for developed construction.

Behavior is a durational and extensional event. In this it corresponds with a physical and physiological event. It differs from these others in not being reducible, as our knowledge now stands, to the types of description which show themselves adequate in the physical and physiological regions.

Language, as a manner of behavior, is to be taken as event in this same sense: not as assignable magically to some fictive spot, but as spread out where its processes are — as itself " being " or " existing " across the space and time in which full observation of it can be made. Even gravitation, we may recall, has been compelled to drop its earlier special localizations, and take on wider description. This is what is asked also for Language, if a General Theory is to be secured.

We are to regard language as process covering the regions: Men, Thing, and World. It has to do with:

THINGS-IN-A-WORLD	talked about by men
MEN-IN-A-WORLD	talking about things
A MAN-AND-THING COMPLEX	composing the known world of Talk.

In this we postulate SYSTEM for our field of research. To postulate system settles nothing. The problem is to find out whether our postulation is sound. Fixation in the form of spatial or temporal instantaneity is always, of course, permissible, if one keeps constantly in mind that he is using snapshot procedure. Snapshots frequently give great temporary aid. They do not, however, establish the materials for the widest generalization.

" Meaning " as an Illustration

On our rough preliminary level of approach, how shall we treat the word " meaning " ? Let us simplify by limiting ourselves here to the phenomenon, process, event, or fact known as " the meaning of a word." We exclude thus not merely the modest meanings of an amoeba and the super-meanings of the symbol, but even our everyday ordinary sentence-meanings and theory-meanings.

The " meaning of a word " must be for us under our postulation an event of human behavior in the world. It must be something we can observe in such a sense that we have some kind of an idea as to what we are talking about when we talk about it. What are some of the possibilities for its factual observation?

The specification " meaning of a word " seems to imply the presence of two different phenomena: word and meaning. Under the older mentalist terminology the difference was definite. The word was physical, or bodily, or something of the kind; while the meaning was mental. We may pass this case by and confine ourselves to current naturalism.

Among the possibilities we shall find:

1. The meaning may be assigned to the " thing-meant " while the " word " is retained for the organism. Certain neo-realists tried this. The proposal has had no developments, and absurdities arise early in the attempt.

2. Word and meaning may be two separable forms of behavior. Factual presentation of the Meaning-Behavior in separation from the Word-

Behavior would then be necessary. I know of none. Apparently we would have a clumsy endeavor to retain a distinction of traditional form.

3. The Word-Behavior and the Meaning-of-the-word-Behavior may be taken as one behavior. Word and Meaning-of-word are taken as one in the sense that behaviorally what does not have word-meaning is not a word, and whatever has word-meaning is a word.

This third procedure is adequate for me, and I adopt it.

"Concept" as an Illustration

"Concept" historically is something that has a mental existence.

If you frankly retain the mental procedure and build honestly within it, I have no objection whatever to concept. You posit it. You use it. You stand or fall by it. Not I.

Abandoning the mental construction, I find concept and conceiving unobjectionable as casual descriptive words — loosely used like "the fields and the flowers," or "the birds and the bees."

Again, concept may be used as one uses "verb," or "noun," or "preposition" to designate a class of words, or a distinguishable verbal function. To do this you must be able practically to classify such words, and you must be prepared to stand or fall with the fate of the other names for language-forms. The present tendency is to abandon the old reliance on the technical justification for their use.

Finally, you may proceed as I do and say that conceiving is a form of language behavior, and concept is a word that names this behavior in the ordinary way in which processes of various kinds are named, with no heavy magic in its use.

The Locus of a Word or Sentence: Its Where, When, or What

We may now enlarge our statement about Language as follows:

Language is a specialized representative, or meaningful behavior, of Organisms-in-World.

This statement yields next to nothing positively, but it does emphasize what is not ordinarily stressed with regard to Language.

A theory that does not seek to establish the where, when, and what of its subjectmatter does not interest me.

The only way to determine such facts is by experimentation. You specify some spatial and temporal location for your word, and make the assumption that that is where you will find it. To experiment you do not go outside of language behaviors. You stay right on the printed page. You mark off an area of usage for the word, and see what the contexts will permit you to conclude about it. Such inquiries are laborious, and I am not going to consider them here. To anyone interested I suggest the word " rule " as it appears in Carnap's recent writing, or in a couple of recent essays by Felix Kaufmann. If you can determine factually what, where, and when a rule " is," you will give me great pleasure, for thus far I have not been successful myself.

At the present moment I shall confine myself to setting down some of the considerations which offer us useful guidance in any search we may make for the locus of a word. These considerations cover the technical background of research as it is commonly conducted in its more successful branches in our present generation. Most generally we may say that observation involves determining the locus of what is observed; and that the determination of location in any one field may properly be undertaken in harmony with the procedures of research in other fields.

I postulate:

1. That durational and extensional presentation is needed for fact.
2. That the Newtonian form no longer dominates.
3. That the behavioral form is something for behavioral research to establish.

If we start out in a Newtonian framework, the manifest possibilities for the location of an act or fact of speech are:

1. In some superorganic accompaniment of the organism. This yields a pseudo-localization of no value.
2. Inside the organism, as in a region of the cortex. This yields a pseudo-mentalism of no value for general theory. Speech becomes a secretion. So what?
3. In speech as comprised by three components: the Communicat*or*, the Communicat*ee,* and the Communicat*ed.*

This third procedure is a great advance. It does not, however, actually hold itself in the space-form chosen. It adds to mechanistic causation certain mentaloid imitations of causation. It cannot distinguish between individual and social contributions. It leads to numerous subtle distinctions of heavily over-verbalized type. In specifying what language in the end really *is,* it usually falls back upon some single component with which other inquirers are very apt to quarrel. In short, all three of the above procedures are deficient in their answers to the questions " where," " when," and " what."

The outcome of the third procedure impels us to seek better answers to this question of locus, even though in the process of getting the answers, the "where," "when," and "what" lose their old forms of determination and secure new behavioral forms very different indeed in appearance and technical employment from those of the specialized regions or coordinates. We are led to search for a durational-extensional form which will transcend the causational difficulties, which will permit complete direct description, and which by the very fact of such completeness will lead to a full descriptive interpretation on a much higher level than causational accounts in Newtonian frames have ever given us.

The only justification of any system is its efficiency. Survivals such as galvanically contracted frog's legs, Carrel chicken-hearts, spring foliage on a dead-root tree, or a talker isolated on a desert isle, offer no obstacle.

Conditioning and favoring the advance from a rigid physical to a free behavioral space and time are the following:

1. The disappearance of the "power" factors from physics, and the transition to wave formulations.

2. The disappearance of vital force from physiology, the increased stress on ecologies, the stringing of individual organisms together across long periods of time by way of the genes, and the radiational and other physiological processes which proceed across skins.

3. The heavy transfer of stresses in many sociological studies from individual to situational statement, even though generalization of this change is lacking.

4. The general trend of successful scientific report from causational to descriptive forms.

With these may be assembled as helpful indications:

5. The "sight-seen" observation by Woodbridge.

6. The increasing use of group pressures, deriving from Gumplowicz and Ratzenhofer, and still capable of much further generalization.

7. The outcome of every thorough appraisal of the subject-object presentation, as philosophy has dealt with it, or of the individual-social situation as sociology has failed to deal with it.

I proceed now to summarize:

I. The progress that has been made by the last two or three generations in establishing widened historical and social accounts of language phenomena has been accompanied by an increasing confusion of statement, until we have now pressing need for clarification and simplicity.

II. The nature of the steps that should be taken are indicated by the general status of technical research in the present age.

III. The primary step is the adoption of a spatial and temporal form which conforms to the behavioral fact. This simply means that if a man is found planning for a future, his present, pasts, and futures be held together in one event just as they factually come.

IV. Given this much start, a full cross-sectional statement of language and of all other behavioral phenomena should be practicable, in which organisms and things, knowings and talkings, are held together in system.

I repeat: I possess no general theory of language. I possess only aspiration and effort. The program, nevertheless, has something of the following form:

We start with man using names, sentences, and simple linguistic theories about things. We start, that is, right in the middle of a knowledge-stage which proffers men and things in sharp severance.

We let our inquiries run backward from name-signs to perceptive signs, and back of these to sub-perceptional action-cues. Again we let it run forward through mathematical and logical constructions to symbolic systems which operate with unquestionable reliability within their own chosen linguistic ranges, and which at times suddenly and most curiously bring about surprising transformations in the thing-knowledge from which we started.

We soon ascertain that no sharp dislocation of thing and organism is to be found at the lower stages of the behavioral series. There the processes merge into the physiological-physical. Similarly we observe, if we will permit ourselves to look, that no dislocation is to be found in the upper symbolic ranges. Not all the efforts of the logicians to force dislocations in have won them any success. Mathematical induction remains its own clean self, no matter how the logicians attempt to debase it.

Thus by looking down and then up, and working hard enough, we may hope to bring our word-thing behaviors into competent organization at the center.

CHAPTER FOURTEEN

The Jamesian Datum[*][1]

I

MISSTATEMENTS

Having listened to a number of James Centenary addresses, and having read several more, I have turned to such other characterizations as come readily to hand. I learn that:

1. James admitted the importance of the world of conscious awareness, but said it was no business of psychology (Dunlap, **14**,[†] p. 308, p. 313).

2. James's psychology was a thoroughgoing "*consciousness*-psychology" (Spoerl, **57**, p. 5).

3. James's life-work was definitely materialistic, when you get down to it, and what comes out of him and after him is physiological psychology, and rightfully nothing else (Holt).[2]

4. James employed an atomistic approach, and saw the larger integrations as a sort of mental chemistry (Skaggs, **56**).[3]

---

[*] From *Journal of Psychology*, Vol. XVI (July, 1943), pp. 35–79.

[1] In a correlated paper (2) I have examined the general status of "factuality" with respect to "truth" and "reality" as James came to view it in the course of his development. The reader will, I trust, note that in neither of these papers are citations introduced as if they were outpourings of a man's mind, or — in different figure of speech but to similar purport — as if they were pins to fix a specimen bug on a shelf, or racks, perhaps, of torture. Always the passages cited enter as human behaviors — linguistic behaviors — specific ways of man's reacting upon other reactions — phases of his on-going living, requiring localization and description in situations extensional and durational — to be understood thus always in full durational sweep, and to be "smoothed" in their successive manifestations as a statistician might smooth a curve or as a geographer might appraise a mountain slope disregarding ravines and ridges for his better view of the ascent. The difference between pin-point mental treatment of human affirmation or assertion, and a full durational-behavioral view, is radical — and in future prospect, enormous.

[†] Parenthetical boldface figures refer to References at end of chapter.

[2] From an address by Edwin B. Holt at the James Centenary meeting of the Conference on Methods in Philosophy and the Sciences, New York City, November, 1941. The published version of Holt's remarks (**60**, p. 46) is less vigorous, but elsewhere he has written: "Radical empiricism . . . means, and I believe that it so meant for William James, that conscious phenomena are to be explained entirely, without reserve or residue, in *physical* terms, and specially of course in the terms of physiology" (**16**, p. v). What James would have thought about this is adequately expressed by the "decidedly *not*" which he wrote marginally to Mach's suggestion that psychology take as its domain the dependence of sensations or elements on the nervous system (**48**, II, p. 389).

[3] "We doubt seriously if there ever was a thoroughgoing atomist among psychologists since the time of James and Wundt" (**56**, p. 347).

5. James's phrase "felt transition," giving the word "felt" the meaning he gave it in 1884, and forgetting everything he did after that, would enable us to summon him to Whitehead's support (Lowe, 43).[4]

6. James was a personalist who believed that "mind" is "the locus of ideas," and Dewey is in basic divergence (Wiggins, 59, p. 193 ff.).

7. For James and Dewey alike, and no matter what else they say, the "inner perception" is primary and the "outer" aspects are secondary. What James needs is an antecedent "feeler" or unifying "conator." Give him this, and the warfare between his "radical empiricism" and his "biological organism" will cease, and the two will come together again in a primordial philosophical paradise of parallelistic peace (Brotherston, 7, pp. 98, 100, 101, 102).

8. James held certain views that he never held; and these may be cited in support of a crude dualism which is the necessary frame for a future "sociology of knowledge" (Wirth, 44, p. xxii).[5]

The lack of coherence among the above statements is not the fault of James, but lies with readers who fail to take into account his long life of continuing progress toward better envisionment of fact, and who consider only their personal snapshots at his words of the moment about his problems of the day. The first seven content themselves with such glints of James as best suit their own prepossessions or needs. The trouble with the eighth is sheer ignorance.[6]

II

THE FACT-SEEKER

The following characterizations fall in a different class:

9. James replaced an inaccessible "consciousness" by a theory of "pure experience" to which "nature" could present itself as "accessible and familiar"; he thus made possible the use of "nature" as the context within which all distinctions are made (Lapan, 41, p. vi, p. 64).

---

[4] According to James's radical empiricism "the relatedness of the stream of human experience is achieved by *transitions* that are *felt* in the drops of experience" (43, p. 119). For analysis of this statement see Sec. XI of this paper.

[5] See comment in Note 16 following.

[6] Another striking exhibit of complete ignorance of James and of the problems he explored, will be found in a volume (46) issuing from the very halls in which James worked. The title is *Unconsciousness*, but we find nothing to show that the author is aware that James worked in the field of "consciousness," although it is with respect to "consciousness" that "unconsciousness" has to be identified and described. One finds three indexed references to James, one distorting him, one misquoting him, and a third quoting Boris Sidis. This is as against 58 indexed references to Freud. With a grossly pre-Jamesian naïveté the factual existence of a thing-like "conscious" is assumed, and along with it of a thing-like "unconscious." This heaping of fiction upon fiction proceeds in total disregard of the analyses of James, and apparently also of all other serious inquirers.

10. James went through a phenomenalistic phase with respect to "pure experience" intermediate between his psychological and metaphysical phases (Perry, 49, Chap. III).

11. James's psychology shows a double strain: a dualistic in terms of which he carried on most of his discussions in the *Principles*; a naturalistic which finally dominated him so completely that had he been able at the end of his life to rewrite the *Principles* to conform, the main line of American psychological research in the last generation might well have developed in a broadly interactional, adaptational naturalism, rather than in the narrowly facultative, physiological form that is now prevalent (Dewey, 13).

Characterization No. 9 directs attention upon what is unquestionably James's outstanding observation of fact: the very datum we are here to consider, the "neutral," "immediate," or "pure" experience. It does not, however, stress this factual presentation for its own sake, but instead treats James's view of "experience" as a preparatory phase for further philosophical speculation. Perry, in Characterization No. 10, stresses fact in James, and he stresses it much more heavily than he has ever done in any of his earlier publications, but he still falls short of full, positive presentation (see 2; also Sec. XI of this chapter).

The last of this set of characterizations, that of John Dewey, operates on a very different level. By skilled analysis, in marked contrast to the others, Dewey disentangles and identifies two main approaches to research and exposition which James employed. We shall accept Dewey's analysis 100 per cent as an analysis without which we could have made no progress here. We shall then concentrate upon the factual core of James's report, and endeavor to indicate the basis upon which it can secure thorough organization with the factual core which Dewey himself presents, and which he has brought to its highest development in his *Logic, The Theory of Inquiry* (12).

One additional characterization which came to hand after this essay had been otherwise finished may be inserted here, although it neither falls among the first group of happy-go-lucky misstatements, nor among the second group of recognitions, partial or complete, of James's factual assertion. It displays, instead, at the very point at which James stressed fact, an inversion of his radical procedure.

12. "As the years went by he [James] shifted his emphasis more and more from the positivistic empiricism to which he himself had given such impulse, and defended that special form of subjectivism which he chose to call ' radical empiricism ' " (Allport, 1, pp. 100–101).[7]

---

[7] Allport's paper is one of eight under the general heading "The Centenary of William James" in the *Psychological Review*, January, 1943. Close scrutiny of these papers re-

In turning James's progress toward neutral affirmation into a lapse backward into subjectivism Allport rests largely on some of Perry's incidental remarks, and fancies he can attribute this deterioration to James's excitement over the varieties of religious experience about which he lectured to a British audience (32). He ignores entirely the long, slow growth and deep roots of James's observation, and sees in the outcome only the makings of a " somewhat synthetic psychophenomenology " akin to certain recently popular evasions of factuality; thereby achieving what may very probably rank as the ultimate insult to James's memory.

Despite James's fame as educator, philosopher, lecturer, and intellectual adventurer in many regions, we have a sound right to undertake our present inquiry from a strictly " factual " point of view. Above all James was empiricist among empiricists, a fact-lover and fact-finder. Recall what Peirce said of him after watching his " intellectual side " for half a century: " I believe him to be and always to have been . . . about as perfect a lover of truth as it is possible for a man to be " (52, VI, Sec. 183; 48, I, p. 540). James is entitled to distinctive consideration on this basis alone with a definite presumption, greater than in the case of most workers in the field, that when he reported a *fact,* something was there to report. He took his empirical stand in 1884 (20; 31, Chap. XII) and held it. Again and again he asserted free hypothesis and the open mind as against self-assurance and dogma (25, pp. vii–viii; 29, p. xii; 31, pp. vi–vii, pp. 41–44). The wide range of his interests, the openness of his approach in all of them, his practice of talking to college students in words they attached meaning to,[8] and to all sorts of audiences from dumb to giddy in words they took pride in thinking they understood: all these explain, although they do not necessarily excuse, the great variety of interpretations we see given him.

Concentrating on the fact-finder, and leaving all biographical and other personal considerations aside, we may assert that one basic observation, slowly and steadily developed across three decades, dominated James's

---

veals no recognition by any of them that James had ever stressed " neutral " experience as basic behavioral fact. Similarly with sixteen papers *In Commemoration of William James, 1842–1942* (60), among which I notice only two approximating attention to experiential " fact." D. C. Williams (p. 118) sees only " introspective descriptions," and G. S. Brett (p. 83), while saying that James's energetic labors had " arrived at experience in its original uncontaminated purity," has in mind only part of the field and that for limited philosophical purposes.

[8] The heavy use of dualistic language in the *Principles* which Dewey has exhibited (13) may have been due largely to pedagogical needs, as well as to James's habit of giving each branch of psychological inquiry a thorough workout in its own terms. A dualistic language is often, of course, a useful convenience in minor problems of research. No objection need be raised to it so long as it is localized and kept from spreading; it is only malignant when sanitary control defaults.

career. Why this basic observation, this datum, this fact, has received so little attention *qua* fact since James's death is an issue which in due course we will consider. Primarily it will be necessary to specify the datum, show its gradual growth in range and in firmness of statement, present the supplementary evidence James assembled to back it up, and exhibit its characteristic presence in his work even where he most loosely popularized his phrasings. We shall connect his work with that of Darwin, Peirce, and Dewey, examine briefly the manner in which his presentation can be organized with Dewey's, and give a hint of the importance of the datum for future research. To go further would involve broad issues of formulation for psychological and sociological, and indeed even for physical, research: a task far beyond us here.

III

The Jamesian Datum

Taking his stand in observation, and choosing as his goal the establishment of fact, James reported it as his observation that the first-hand facts which philosophers and psychologists primarily observe are neither conscious phenomena nor non-conscious, neither non-physical mentals nor non-mental physicals, neither the subjectives and objectives of sophisticated discourse nor the inners and outers of vulgar speech. Instead he saw them as actually, literally, and factually " neutral " to such characterizations, and as " immediate " or " pure " in their own " concrete " right. He recognized fully, of course, the standardized differentiations of current report and description — he like everyone else started out and grew up with them thus — but he found them late in their time of appearance (31, p. 219) and false in their wider claims. He denied flatly their phenomenal primacy for research and scientific report. The early years of his life of research were given to specific factual determinations. In his middle years he secured a broad naturalistic setting for his observations under the name of pragmatism. His last years were devoted to a wide-ranging probing of all the philosophical speculation and construction he could find affecting his discovery: so elaborate that ever since men have thought of him more as philosopher than as psychologist or scientist. But never for a moment did the core of his interest cease to be fact — fact that he could observe. " The one condition," he wrote late in life, " is to become inductive-minded oneself; . . . it means a real change of heart; . . . reality is the vaguest term of all; . . . the whole subject is inductive and sharp logic is hardly yet in order " (29, p. 56, p. 57, p. 60, p. 100). His final " radical empiricism " was " empirical " because it was based in observation, and it was "radical"[9] because he had extended his observation to new and wider fields — fields which stretched beyond observable sensations and perceptions to include relations which were themselves similarly observable (31, p. x).

Everyone engaged in psychological or philosophical research knows that James used language of the above import. To gain a hearing — and indeed even to satisfy himself about his own course — it was necessary for him to slice through the linguistic tangles of the sophisticates of metaphysics. Admirable as his machete work was in the verbal jungle, it is a side issue for us here. Our point is that *he meant what he said about fact*. He meant it literally. Here was no verbal titillation of philosophers' ears, and no philosophical intrusion into the psychological bailiwick. Here was for James the hardest kind of common sense, the most direct observation, and the truest report. As he finally attained it, his datum was to him primary *fact*; as fact it was *observable*; as observation it was *verifiable* by any and every observer who could free himself from ancient verbal habit long enough to open his eyes to look. He built his work around it — more and more as his life went on — no matter what everyday language he used to everyday audiences in the effort to open up a glimpse of what he himself was seeing.

Was James's observation true? Was his report sound? If not, it is just a curiosity which will have no place in future science. Our purpose in this paper does not run to answers in terms of "true" or "false" any more than to speculations in terms of "reality" (2). It centers attention instead upon the datum as "fact" capable of future experimental test.

---

[9] James's critical terms grew in meaning as he advanced. To avoid the confusion that often arises from reading a "dated" term out of its proper range, and at the same time to indicate the lines of growth, the following hints are given:

Radical: Used in 1896 to mark a free empiricism in which the current monistic dogmatism was itself reduced to hypothesis (25, p. vii; 31, p. vii); later used for the broadest empirical postulation (31, pp. 41-44) with a reliance on relational immediacy (in sharp contrast with "mental atoms") which carries it well beyond the range of the earlier pragmatism (31, p. x, p. 42; 28, pp. 279-80).

Pure: An early use was for the simplest attainable or available item capable of isolation, as in "pure elementary feelings" (19, p. 10); later applied to neutral perceptional experience, and finally to similar relational experience; in specialized application it could stand for "the immediate flux of life" or for "proportional amount of unverbalized sensation" (31, pp. 93-4). Most broadly as "the principle of pure experience" it is equated with "radical" (31, p. ix, p. x, p. 159, p. 241).

Immediate: James remarks that this word commonly stood in philosophy for the "simply perceived" in contrast with conceivings as "mediated" (30, p. 48); he used it in this way as late as 1910 to help out beginners, long after his developed construction had made relations matters of "direct particular experience" (29, p. xii), and "immediate" itself a synonym of neutral and pure.

Neutral: I have happened on no uses prior to 1904.

Concrete: (31, p. 10, p. 96, p. 198; see also 48, II, p. 385, and occasional phrases such as 28, p. 326).

Indication that James's report is more than a curiosity — sufficient evidence to justify further investigation, even if James's standing as an empiricist is not enough — may perhaps be found by comparing the two following sentences:

James (1909) asserted his factual base as follows in his definitive statement in the preface to *The Meaning of Truth:* " The statement of fact is that the relations between things . . . are just as much matters of direct particular experience . . . as the things themselves " (29, p. xii; 31, p. x).

Lashley (1938) appraised experiments with rats born and brought up in darkness, and suddenly confronted with objects in light, thus: " This demands the immediate perception of relational properties " (40, p. 450).

Lashley's phrasing is much less precise than James's. While his observation is much more closely centered, his framework of report is diffuse. His word " immediate " is not James's " neutral," though Lashley has now and then shown certain tendencies in its direction. So far as his comment goes, however, it expresses an advance in knowledge, and if we cannot claim that it brings James into full view, it at least does something toward bringing present research, factually speaking, into touch with James.

James himself used the word " datum," sometimes casually, sometimes in emphatic passages in which he made it flatly equivalent to the word " experience." Thus: " The paper seen and the seeing of it are only two names for one indivisible fact which, properly named, is *the datum, the phenomenon, or the experience* " (29, p. 49).[10] To restate James's datum by injecting, however craftily, some form of subjective into its veins is to falsify your report on James. To assign it physiologically a research home in a brain or neural system is to abandon James's full field of behavioral inquiry for a narrow specialty — no less narrow though noisy. Speak of " awareness " in connection with James's final results and you *must* mean its status with respect to *his* datum, not some subjectivity which you assume lies behind the datum so as to possess or produce it. Speak of " consciousness " or " the conscious " for James, and you will be dealing with an aspect of the datum under certain manners of observation, not with any substance or separate factor, perhaps not even with a leading color or quality. Speak of " experience " and you must mean " *pure* experience " if you want to talk about James in his own sense;

---

[10] *Datum:* For later uses of this word by James see 31, p. 10, p. 145; for a variant, see 30, p. 145. The citation in the text is the affirmative part of a conditional sentence written in 1895. The " condition " represents an intermediate stage of James's progress to be noted in Sec. VII below.

you cannot imply that "experience" exists by that name, with the "pure" form as one of its varieties; you are obligated in James's texts to understand the full "double-barreled"[11] phenomenon of the "experiencing" and "the experienced" equally and together — the "subjective and objective both at once" (31, p. 10) — unsevered except as in later inquiry you may trace and appraise any differentiation that may show itself.

In our account we shall omit the word "experience" and substitute "datum," which we may hope is a word that can be read as James meant it, where the word "experience" would have no chance.

The first of the following citations shows James's trend toward the organization of knowledge long before he had established his datum. The second reports partial observation in preliminary phrasing. The next five stress the neutral character of the primary perceptual datum. Then come three citations, one of which has already been given in part, which announce the final establishment of the relational-conceptual observation along with the perceptual in full harmonious organization.

(1885) "Knowledge as *acquaintance*" is "in the origin . . . more . . . phenomenal." Knowledge "about . . . is in its origin the more intellectual. . . . There is no reason, however, why we should not express our knowledge, whatever its kind, in either manner" (21; 29, pp. 11-12).

(1895) "To know immediately . . . or intuitively is for mental content and object to be identical" (24; 29, p. 50).

(1904) "Experience . . . has no . . . inner duplicity. . . . A given undivided portion of experience" is "subjective and objective both at once" (31, pp. 9-10).

(1904) "The instant field of the present is . . . only virtually or potentially either object or subject as yet. For the time being, it is plain, unqualified actuality, or existence, a simple *that*" (31, p. 23).

(1905) "*Cette réalité sensible et la sensation que nous en avons sont, au moment où la sensation se produit, absolument identiques l'une à l'autre*" (31, p. 211).

(1905) "*Le partage du subjectif et de l'objectif est le fait d'une réflexion très avancée*" (31, p. 219).

(1906) "'Pure' experience for me antedates the distinction [of subjective and objective]. It is my name for your ambiguous reality from which . . . the two sets of data come" (Letter to Warner Fite) (48, II, p. 392).

(1909) "The statement of facts is that the relations between things, conjunctive as well as disjunctive, are just as much matters of direct particular experience, neither more so nor less so, than the things themselves" (29, p. xii).

(1909) "Relations . . . are just as integral members of the sensational flux as terms are. This is . . . the 'radically empiricist' doctrine. All real units of experience *overlap*" (28, pp. 279, 280, 287).

(1910) "In a continuously developing experiential series our concrete perception of causality is found in operation. . . . Almost no philosopher has admitted that perception can give us relations immediately" (30, p. 211, p. 219).

[11] See footnote No. 24.

In seeming conflict with the above but, when contextually read, in harmony, are the following sentences which are inserted here expressly to highlight the variations of phraseology that at times accompany variations in the specialization of attention:

(1909) "I now treat concepts as a co-ordinate realm [of reality]" (29, p. 42).
(1909) "It seems incredible" to charge that we ... "deny the existence *within the realm of experience* of objects external to the ideas that declare their presence there" (29, p. xvii).

In the first of these sentences concepts are co-ordinated with percepts, and the immediate context places these latter with respect to the truth-relation and to the variance of subject and object "inside of the continuities of concrete experience." In the second sentence James's italicized phrase establishes the characteristic of "being external," at its very introduction as falling "within experience," and as in no way to be regarded as a prior condition of existential affirmation.

In such assertions we find: (a) acceptance, as such, of the preliminary common-sense distinction between ideas and objects; (b) report of deepened observation; (c) expectation, scientific in type, that the deeper observation will improve the shallower primitive report.

IV

WHY THE NEGLECT?

Before filling in the picture of James's progress toward clear observation, it will be profitable to note the reasons why his final factual report has so long and so completely been neglected as a basis for further research. The background is that of Darwinian evolution. Later (Sec. XII) we shall consider James's position in the line Darwin-Peirce-James-Dewey which represents direct presentation of behaviors adaptationally in environments (13). The issue here is not merely one of corporeal evolution, nor one of superficial cultural description, but strikes much deeper. The psychologists of the last generation have, of course, regarded the organism as anatomically a product of evolution, and have recognized behaviors as organic manifestations, but they have not themselves seriously pursued behavioral research in the direct adaptational form. Kantor is the outstanding exception in that he constructs his psychology by expressly offsetting and jointly including organisms and objects as "functional" to each other in a naturalistic world (36, 37). The pattern that psychologists have made their standard is one of emergent thing-like behaviors in ganglionic, cerebral, or cortically centered locations. This is a *quasi-*

Darwinian (indeed, rather, a *pseudo*-Darwinian) approach. However great an improvement is may be over *pre*-Darwinian procedures, it is so alien to the advances that have been made by James and Dewey that those of their readers who are controlled by it in unsophisticated acceptance find their eyes blinded to the factual import of the "radical" Jamesian datum and to the Dewey naturalism as well.[12]

This can be stated in another way without reference to the Darwinian background, and perhaps even more effectively. For both James and Dewey human "knowings" are open to behavioral inquiry, free from any epistemological veto. In contrast, the standardized type of current psychological research treats "knowings" only in the narrowest and most superficial ways.[13] The procedure is as if a "knower" on the outside of the science, and not itself in need of investigation, was in charge, rather than as if his own "knowings" along with all others were themselves components of the field of research. This can hardly be more than a contemporary evasion, already in sight of the time when it will be listed and "dated" as the mannerism of a past generation.

These two ways of characterizing the neglect come, however, to much the same. Psychologists before James specialized heavily on a cognitive "faculty." James dropped all the "faculties," including the cognitive, and went ahead unhampered with empirical research into knowings. The *quasi*-Darwinians camouflaged the faculties physiologically and thus retained them. The "cognitive faculty" was, naturally enough, highly resistant to their device. Hence their "flight from reality" and their proffer of an epistemological excuse for a default in empirical research.

V

Type and Limitation of Inquiry

In the preceding section and elsewhere in this paper the following use of terms should be noted:

Darwinian: applied to an era of research in which an evolving universe is accepted to include organisms, among them human beings with *all* their behavioral activity.

---

[12] Recent analyses of two instances of the misapprehension and distortion of Dewey's construction in his *Logic* were made in the endeavor to locate the source of the trouble (5d, 5e).

[13] This is well evidenced by the vagueness of the use of the word "concept" in the titles to many papers in psychological and other scientific journals, and further by chaotic use of the word in laboratory reports undertaking to deal with problems in regions in which the name is found in use, though without examination of its precise factual reference (5b, p. 233).

Behavior: (apart from technically physiological and ecological uses) applied to the full range of adaptation-adjustment of the organism in its full evolving durational and extensional environment; not limited or hampered by any pre-Darwinian mentalistic or mechanistic, nor by any *pseudo*-Darwinian physiological, requirement of " inners," " outers," or any of their substitutes.

Datum: applied to fact-of-research, nuclear in further research, itself the outcome of research, untampered with by either externalizing or internalizing verbalisms.

James used the word " datum " in this way. He could easily have used the word " behavior " as above, had the word been current in his time for anything other than overt or ethically appraised action. His use of the word " Darwinian " was, however, always in a limited zoological sense, and he nowhere employed it, so far as I have noted, to characterize atmospherically the new era in which he himself was working. In one passage, however, he did identify pragmatism with naturalism, writing: " Naturalism, or (as I will now call it) pragmatism " (31, p. 100). That " Darwinism without materialism " is the " keynote of James's psychology " was, however, long ago stressed by a British interpreter of James's pragmatic viewpoint in a discussion, excellent in so far as it went, but nevertheless falling far short of envisaging James's neutral datum in full naturalistic terms (39, p. 23).

Our assertion has been that the datum is *there,* and *significantly* there, in James's work; or, in more detail (a) that we can isolate in James his fact-finding activity; (b) that the datum was his great " find "; (c) that the " radical " in it explains its neglect during the past generation in favor of duller tools, less difficult to use.

James was slow and cautious in progress toward his final factual report. We shall be cautious in the presentation. We shall exhibit his emphatic outcome in *fact,* but we shall not say that he had become wholly familiar with it, nor that he had more than hinted at its wide application in research, nor even that he would have been pleased in his final years at the picture we are here to give of it. With attention to his philosophizings reduced to a minimum, with his threshings to get rid of them but lightly touched upon, and with the many distracting patterns of life he suggested wholly omitted, the richest colorings of his career are absent. But we have the advantage that we can hold our technical examination closely to our objective.

VI

JAMES'S RESEARCH EQUIPMENT IN 1884

About 1884–5, when the account of James's development as outstanding observer of behaviors may properly begin, he had the following specialized adaptation to his inquiry: (a) a working equipment of little " states " of consciousness which he chose to call " feelings " (21; 29, Chap. I); (b) a brilliant figure of speech about the flow, current, flux, or stream of consciousness (19); (c) a strong interest psychologically in the phenomena of human " knowings " with no one around to fuss, grumble, or complain that this business of " knowings " was no proper business for psychology or for him; (d) a strongly asserted liking for matters he could examine directly such as the *functions* of knowing, combined with a total lack of respect for things he couldn't, such as souls, minds, " brains," or " faculties " when they claimed to be creators, producers, or operators of the functions (29, pp. 1–2).

In broad generalities — we mention them merely to sweep the verbal trash off the floor — James began with an official " monism " which in later life looked to him like a set of chains. He came out with a " pluralism," the meaning of which was that the chains had been thrown off and that plenty of room was open for the free and the new (30, p. 114, pp. 140–146). Employing a practical " dualism " in his earlier presentation, he thrust it steadily behind him and subordinated it as he proceeded (13). He was " realist " always, but never fetish-worshiper, and epistemologically he rid himself of realisms and idealisms alike, and of the " gulf " between them, immediately he had a good start (29, p. xvii; 29, p. 41, Items 1 and 6; p. 50; 31, p. 16, p. 76, p. 100).[14]

His growth as observer must be inspected from two sides: the positive and the negative. These should be appraised with respect to each other. The positive outcome is the datum. The negative is the factual rejection of " consciousness " — the " denial " of its " existence," in the terminology of James's day. The negative had spectacular acclaim in its time, while the positive has never yet come into the clear light of laboratory and library workshop. The old idol was easily tried, convicted, and sentenced to public shattering. But the success of a negation without accompanying positive affirmation is not enough. Many a man today still

---

[14] It was the " epistemological gulf " James got rid of, not research in the field the epistemologist claimed. At the same time that he eliminated the " gulf " he declared it to be one of the merits of his system that it was so " purely epistemological " (29, p. 215), meaning thereby so little metaphysical. For a provisional and temporary expression on the idealistic side, see 33, p. 373.

frolics over the shattering, while he continues to make shift with the shards much as in earlier days he would have had intimate relations with the idol itself.

The following citations on the negative side, introduced merely to recall the vigor with which James asserted himself, may supplement the citations already given on the positive:

(1904) "Consciousness ... is on the point of disappearing altogether. It is the name of a nonentity. ... The hour is ripe for it to be openly and universally discarded" (31, pp. 2-3).

(1904) "The word 'I' is primarily a noun of position, just like 'this' and 'here'" (31, p. 170; 28, p. 380).

(1905) "*L'acte de penser ... la conscience ... sont-ce au fond autre chose que des manières rétrospectives de nommer le contenu lui-même*" (31, p. 214).

(1905) "*Je crois que la conscience ... soit comme entité, soit comme activité pure ... est une ... chimère*" (31, p. 222).

We can greatly simplify presentation by asking the reader to keep in mind that James never dealt with myopic fragments, but always saw behavioral life in *full* flow, and that this manifested itself (a) in his use interchangeably of the words "consciousness," "thought," "feeling," and "knowing," along with various occasional substitutes such as "subjective life," "being aware," or "reporting"; [15] and (b) in his free, elastic application of his central terminology of "knowledge by acquaintance" and "knowledge about" (which represented primarily perceptions and conceptions) "downward" from perceptions to sensations, forward from actuals to possibles, and "backward" in time to include "previous truths." [16]

[15] Of course in specialized studies of "aspects" of the process he would temporarily differentiate the terms, but never so as to split the facts. It is interesting to note that Dewey has recently made a vigorous defense of his own similar employment of an abundance of overlapping terms in empirical inquiry in the field of knowing (9, p. 295).

[16] James promptly greeted Dewey's first logical studies as a sound development along lines similar to his own, and in highly characteristic phrasing he observed that in this matter of "knowledge of the truth of general propositions," "the SP in combination" was "the 'terminus' that verifies and fulfils" (31, p. 53 n., 33, p. 445 ff.). For extension toward sensation see 22, II, p. 2, p. 77; where the change in application of terms is one of phrasing only, not of factual coherence. For the possibles, see 31, p. 53, p. 60; for "previous truths" see 34, p. 245. The reason that misrepresentation Number 8 (44) in the first section of this paper is so flagrant is that it presents James's distinction of "knowledge of acquaintance" and "knowledge about" as if it gave authority for the severance of "outer" observation from "inner," and of "objective facts" from "subjective," and more generally for the construction of two distinctive "modes of knowing." The slightest glance, however, at James, if unbiased, will show that these terms were introduced as part of James's effort to bring system into the study of knowings, and get rid of conventionalized splittings. In his very first use of the terms (29, p. 41) he writes of the conceptual: "Woe to her if she return not home to [feeling's] acquaintance." In the *Principles* (22, I, p. 221) he writes: "The two kinds of knowledge are ... relative

VII

Positive Development of the Datum

We begin with the positive datum, since it is this observation of fact that gives vigor to the decree against consciousness rather than the other way around, even though attention to the decree may later on help clear the way for further observation. James addressed the Aristotelian Society in 1884 on " The Function of Cognition " (21; 29, Chap. I). Taking his little " feelings " (one could call them " thoughts," or " ideas " in the " old broad Lockian sense," or just " states," if one wished) he proposed an interpretative mechanism whereby perceptions, cognitions, and the known world could be brought into a single intimately organized system. Perceptions were organized directly to " realities " as known. Then perceptions and cognitions were so organized to each other that in normal, sound functioning the latter came to " terminate " on the former. Here for the first time he gave prominence to Grote's distinction between " knowledge by acquaintance " and " knowledge about " (29, p. 11). In " acquaintance " the feeling *was* the knowledge; all one needed to do was to couple a " reality " with it and go ahead. In " knowledge about " the feelings were in " contexts " with each other, so that a " knowing " about any " it " was just that " it " with a context added (29, p. 15). Little awarenesses were aware of each other, and validities lay in the efficiency of their organization. Looking back at the end of his life on his position at this time he commented that he used a reality, a knower, and a connecting environment yielding relations, but with all phases of the knowing falling " inside of the continuities of concrete experience," and with the " epistemological gulf " eliminated (29, p. 41). Just how thoroughly " inside " James was at the time is a question. The most we can safely say is that he had here the " makings " of his later observation — initial glimpses of it, and a pathway to it — but that is all.

Most of James's papers around this date were written for and incorporated in the *Principles,* but this Aristotelian Society address was not reproduced there, nor was any heavy use made of the mechanism it set up (*Cf.* 22, I, pp. 549–463). Dewey has remarked upon one of James's acute observations in this period which may have entered significantly into

---

terms," and later on introduces a " principle of constancy in the mind's meanings " (22, I, p. 459) to cover them. In the *Briefer Course* (23, p. 167) he says the difference is reducible almost entirely to fringes or overtones. It would seem that a " sociology of knowledge " undertaken in profound ignorance of everything about Peirce, James, and Dewey except their names, and using a procedure in terms of " concept " and " thought " without any effort whatever to find out what such words mean is — well, just what it is. Some recent constructions under the label " sociology of knowledge " are examined by Lavine (42).

his later factual development (13, p. 595): the case of infant sensation, "neutral" (in the sense of "indifferent") to both inners and outers (22, II, p. 8). James's presidential address of 1894 on "The Knowing of Things Together" (24; 29, Chap. II; 33, p. 371 ff.), which he later (29, p. 42) mentioned as offering a "broader grasp," used transitional phrasings; "immediately or intuitively" was the phrase for the lower level, and "conceptually or representatively" for the higher (29, p. 43). At the lower level he defined "mental content and object to be identical" (29, p. 50), while at the higher he saw objects as led "through a context which the world supplies" (29, p. 46). He noted that these two definitions were "very different," but remarked that they harmonized in the main point, the elimination of certain "mysterious notions." While his first-level definition is categorically offered, the full context of his paper (see two citations of this date in Sec. III above) would indicate that his own view at that time was confined to cases of "our own private vision . . . considered in abstraction" (29, p. 48). Emphatic as he made his assertion, it thus still had as late as 1895 a string attached to it, even in the perceptual case, by which it could be pulled back if necessary. That he did not pull it back, but continued to strengthen his observation year after year, is the factual point of our story.

James was very active during the following decade, not only in orienting himself to other men's views, but in experimentation and research of all kinds; ever more detail of observation is found in the pages of his papers; but he offered comparatively little fresh formulation of his own, except for his proclamation of pragmatism by that name in 1898 (26; 33, pp. 406–37). Even in 1902 "pragmatic description" still placed conceptual "transition" in contrast with perceptual "identity" (48, II, p. 746). Then suddenly in 1904–5 came the important series of papers which were assembled and published in book form after his death, but following a plan he himself had drawn up, as *Essays in Radical Empiricism* (31). Perry remarks on his "new tone of intellectual self-confidence" (48, II, p. 391).[17] We find here the full observation and report described earlier in this paper, including a new sharp assertion of the immediacy and neutrality of the perceptual datum; a strong assertion of comparable immediacy for the re-

[17] Perry finds the relational immediacy — the newly enriched "radical" — adding strength to the older perceptual immediacy (31, pp. x–xi). It would be a difficult and thankless but very valuable inquiry into the technique of the growth of knowledge to identify fully the precise stages by which James's "pure" passed to "neutral" in the perceptual field, and by which his relational became "pure" in association with the perceptual. Perry's prefaces to the *Collected Essays* (33) and to the *Essays in Radical Empiricism* (31) are the required starting-point. His books on James (47, 48, 49) are essential; but a positive shift from Perry's metaphysical envisionment to a factual envisionment must be adopted and maintained.

lational datum; and the recognition and adoption of Dewey's inference theory as a further range of knowings. Finally, in 1909-10, the last months of his life, he takes one more forward step in formulation, as he advances a " perceptual view " of causation and of the infinite (30, Chaps. XI and XIII).[18]

James's stages of observation thus covered: first, the establishment of system between feelings and facts (acquaintance), along with further system between feelings of things and of relations (knowledge-about), 1884; second, a strong, though specialized, assertion of the immediacy of acquaintance (canceling fully the old distinction of content and object) accompanied by retention of contextual formulation for knowledge-about, 1895; third, the final generalization of perceptual immediacy, accompanied by a similar generalization for " relational feelings," now advanced to a full immediacy of their own, 1905.

VIII

Negative Development as to Consciousness

Turn now to the reverse of the picture: the status of " consciousness." Had James been a philosopher proper he would have made up his mind and then arranged the facts to suit. Since he was thoroughly empiricist, his view remained open until decision forced itself upon him. Nothing is more illuminating than his frank and full report, stage by stage, of the way non-observability led him to postulation, and postulation led him to fact. To begin with, as we have noted, he eschewed " souls " and " brains " (29, p. 1) simply because he could not examine them direct in their knowing functions.[19] Although it was " function " he was after, he was willing to introduce his little feelings " subjectively," i.e., " without respect to their possible function " (29, p. 2), but it is easy to see that he tolerated them solely because they were inoffensive, and he could proceed free from interference by them. His Aristotelian Society address is probably the most " atomistic " statement he ever made. His figure of speech

---

[18] For the great possibilities James's position offered for the behavioral discussion of mathematics along modern lines, see 30, pp. 172 ff., 48, II, p. 540 ff., pp. 664-5, and also Peirce's appraisal, 52, VI, sections 182 ff.

[19] James lost much caste among close-hauled empiricists later in life because of the amount of interested consideration he could give to " souls," in their various purported manifestations. But this was different business from letting the souls interfere with his direct inquiries into knowings. It was not James who came out the fool from these adventures. I suspect that he was equally the empiricist in both cases: giving the souls a chance to perform if they could where claims were made for them; on the other hand, keeping them thoroughly outside his own primary business in which, so far as he could discover, they did not and could not perform.

about the "stream" had appeared a year earlier (19).[20] Though he had played brilliantly with it, it was still in the main a lively metaphor. Its "continuity" meant an "absence of *separate* parts in it" (19, p. 6), but he failed to use this characteristic in his Aristotelian Society address the following year, where the word "context" was as far stream-ward as he went, not even such an expression as "overlapping," common enough in later years, being found in this paper.[21]

In the famous Chapter IX of the *Principles* (1890), entitled "The Stream of Thought," what had started as a figure of speech became a vigorous assertion of fact. About half of the detail of the old essay reappears, but all the strongest affirmations of the stream are new matter. James's position in this chapter and in its companion chapter on the "Self" had as leading features: the characterization and classification of a number of "selves" in each human organism; the rejection of all substantively proffered selves — egos, minds, and consciousnesses — along with the previously rejected substantive souls and brains; the adoption of the "stream" as psychology's primary fact or datum, and its vigorous presentation; a personalization of this stream as "activity," with a good deal of the flavor of "actor," and thus with a sort of existence which could still be talked about to a considerable extent in the old "mentalist" terms. Typical of this phase of James's factual growth is the well-known sentence: "The passing Thought then seems to be the Thinker" (22, I, p. 342). It was, indeed, not till 1905 that James expelled this personalized "activity" along with the earlier "substances." When he did it, his way of recalling the sentence just quoted was that "we need no knower other then the 'passing thought'" (31, p. 4. note). Even in recollection an affirmation with caps had changed to a negation without.

Dewey in his recent analysis remarks the *verbally* the chapter on the stream is "probably the most subjectivistic part" of the *Principles,* but adds that this is true verbally only since it is "quite possible to translate 'stream of consciousness' into 'course of experience' and retain the substance of the chapter" (13, p. 589, p. 597). A transitional stage in inquiry such as this results, of course, in fumbling efforts at formulation. Philosophical fumblings on minor issues often extend over generations or centuries. The wonder is not that James had two decades of it, but that he advanced through it as strongly as he did. He could set "real" rela-

---

[20] This paper "On Some Omissions of Introspective Psychology" (19), says Perry in his *Annotated Bibliography* (47, p. 14), contains "the earliest statement of many of James's characteristic doctrines," including "his provision for feelings of relation."

[21] Of course the whole background of observation is common to both papers, as when in the first one he writes: "As a matter of fact *every* segment of the stream is cognitive" (19, p. 10). It is merely the technical use of the "stream" that is missing in the second of the two papers.

tions over against the " feelings " of relation to which the " reals " were known; then in almost the same breath he could transpose the realistic distinction into one resting on point of view, or manner of talking; " if we *speak* objectively," he said, we have relations, while " if we *speak* subjectively " we have feeling (22, I, p. 245; italics mine). Similarly in the *Briefer Course,* published two years later, he proceeded in the most matter-of-fact way in terms of " consciousness " all through the book, only to wind up vividly in an " epilogue " by announcing that so far as he was concerned states of consciousness were not verifiable facts — they were postulates, about which he himself was not at all sure, even though he kept on using them in his descriptions (23, p. 467). It was here also that he advocated " sciousness " as a safer name to use for the phenomena than " consciousness."

In this we have a striking illustration of the maturation of thought in speech.[22] The advance from a traditional hypostatization was made through a vivid word-picture, which proved workable in practice, to a factual assertion which in turn was found to involve excess hypostatization; and thence into other wordings which yielded a new and better factual assertion ready for test. The process had beginnings as far back as 1884, when James demanded " a concrete and total manner of regarding the mind's changes " (19, p. 12). Now in 1890 he was specifying that the " entire thought " was the minimum that must be considered on the mental side, never its separated fragments (22, p. 177; 23, p. 464). This " entire thought " stands out as the precursor of the *entire event,* the " pure " or " neutral " phenomenon, which later became its developed replacement. But ever the trial and error of language adapting itself to the circumstance of purpose and audience went forward, feeling its way along. In 1895 James could still talk freely (to his fellow psychologists) of the " mental image " as one phenomenal event, and the " tiger " as another (29, p. 45). The proclamation of pragmatism in 1898 transferred the whole " subjectivistic " activity into the broader behavioral world of Darwinian naturalism that Peirce had caught sight of. Yet in 1902 in the Gifford Lectures (though we must allow much here for his popularization) James could still write: " The world of our experience consists at all times of two parts, an objective and a subjective part, of which the former may be incalculably more extensive than the latter, and yet the latter can never

---

[22] Late in life James remarked on the ways the words "run out of my pen," and added: " these words I write even now surprise me, yet I adopt them as effects of my scriptorial causality " (30, p. 211, p. 213). Cassirer (8) has discussed the work of language in object-determinations with interesting illustrations from Kleist's essay on the ripening of thought in speech. It, of course, does not follow that anybody's pitter-patter will turn into fact. James, as fact-seeker, was ruthless in destroying his own phrases, when practice showed they did not " work."

be omitted or suppressed" (32, p. 498). Here the "subjective" was put down as the "inner state" where "the thinking comes to pass," and "inner state is our very experience itself — its reality and that of our experience are one." (No wonder the casual reader of James can go wrong, when so many possibilities of wrongness can open up in so few sentences.) Finally, in 1904–5, the pragmatic viewpoint, along with steady deepening of factual observation, and strong backing from the contemporary work of Bergson[23] and Dewey, brought about the formal and final elimination of "consciousness" down to its last shreds of personalized "activity" (27; 31, p. 3 note, p. 160 ff., p. 169 ff., p. 222). The "stream" was now the flow of the neutral datum in a natural world of organism-environment; "*simon-pure* activity," regarded as something "that does, and doesn't merely appear to us to do," was "specious sham" (*ibid.*, p. 170). James had achieved the "functional" understanding he had so long sought. He had achieved it positively in the datum, and negatively in the final extermination of the ancestral claimant "consciousness." But — and this is the meat of James's life-career — the full behavioral factuality remains in the datum richer by far than puny mentalistic report had ever shown it; richer also than — if the experience of the last thirty years is enough evidence — the mechanistic or physiological solvents are likely to produce.

In summary as to consciousness, in correlation with the summary as to the datum above, we find: first, James's acceptance of subjective "feelings," which nevertheless could be kept in limbo while their "functions" underwent illumination and examination in research; next, stress on the "stream" as activity, though always, when inquiry paused to take account of its doings, with a question mark as to actual existence in that form; finally, through an interminable variety of experimental formulations, to the dropping of all the double-talk and to the simple straightforward factual statement of 1904, with the claimant "consciousness" out of the way for good.

IX

COLLATERAL EVIDENCE

In reporting his datum James relied primarily on his own ripe observation. Call him trifler, if you will: call him even unbalanced; but do not

---

[23] "Reading his works," said James of Bergson, "is what has made me bold" (28, p. 214). Dewey has remarked that James got something out of Bergson the latter did not know was there in the way of perceptual immediacy, and that, when he had this, his older "feelings of relation" would transform themselves similarly, since the very use of the word "feeling" in his early phrase, instead of "thought" or "association," contained the beginnings of immediacy as he later developed it.

The Jamesian Datum

pretend he was not intent on fact as he could see it, and honest in his report. In his formal statement of relational immediacy in 1909 he was so sure of his earlier perceptual datum, and even of his readers' acceptance of it, that he made no express assertion of it, but took it casually for granted as he wrote that " the relations . . . are just as much [particular] . . . as the things " (29, p. xii). Far from protesting too much, he saw no need to protest at all. One finds little in his texts to show that he met direct contradiction as to fact. He had plenty of controversy, but not on the direct factual issue. Nevertheless he gradually accumulated, and offered, much factual evidence, scattering it around in his essays. We may list his main points, some inferential, some illustrative, despite the relics of ancient talk-ways they contain. What James was doing was not to fuss over old dilemmas, but to clear the ground by exhibiting some of the simpler facts of behavioral life.

1. Primarily, James *pointed* to the observable fact. Thus: " If the reader will take his own experiences he will see what I mean " (31, p. 11) ; or " Let the reader arrest himself in the act of reading . . . ' Reading ' simply is, is there " (31, p. 145).

2. He noted that all our ordinary namings in the region of " experience " are " double-barreled " and that there is no getting rid of it; we might as well accept the situation for what it is — a linguistic reflection of *fact*. Our words fluctuate back and forth in ordinary practical use from subjective to objective and then to subjective again; they cannot hold firmly on either side. If one attempts to force them into single-barreled forms they get beyond the reach of profitable inquiry (31, p. 10).[24]

---

[24] " Single-barreled " terms, in James's figure of speech, are such as " thought " and " thing," hypostatized beyond any possibility of getting at them to probe them empirically. James continued to use double-barreled terms, specifying them explicitly as such, and hoping (erroneously) that his specification would be heeded. Dewey has used much of this old terminology in default of anything better, accompanying it with a running fire of cautions (as in the case of the word " belief " in the *Logic* and the word " desire " there and elsewhere) against subjectivizing it. He has used the word " experience " very liberally, especially in *Experience and Nature* (11), and always in the " pure " sense, but what he has got from it is unlimited disputation and little else. His tendency is to replace it, and in the *Logic* (12), while it still occurs, it is slightly stressed, and more specific expressions are seen taking its place. My own practice, from a point of view closely in line with theirs, has been to deny the factuality of " concepts," " percepts," and " relations " in all thing-like identifications (though, of course, not the indicated behavioral processes as subject matters of inquiry), and to reject the nouns entirely. As an efficient means of communication this has seemed equally unsuccessful. Anyone who can devise a form of speech in this matter which will reach eardrums will perform a great service. I may perhaps with propriety add that not only have I followed James in this matter of double-barreled terms without recalling his leadership, but in several other matters as well I have reworked his ground without recalling him at the time as the pioneer. One of these is my effort to justify widened observation (3, Chaps. XX–XXII) which could have been explicitly based in James's relational immediacy. Another is the use of Woodbridge's phrase " sight-seen " in place of the much stronger " neutral " of

3. He found it significant that Locke in his fresh search for facts about human understanding held his word "idea" to reality by deliberately making it two-faced. This, he said, was a soundly "pragmatic" attitude and Locke was the first to employ it (31, pp. 10–11). The Berkeleyan common-sense view was founded here, and the *esse est percipi* was an early philosophical application (31, p. 10, p. 212).

4. In the case of external perception it is difficult — indeed impossible — ever to tell what is contributed by sense-organs and what part comes "out of one's own head" (31, pp. 29–30, p. 216).

5. Consider qualities, attributes, and adjectives. Where does beauty reside, in the statue or in the spirit? We say agreeable heat or agreeable sensation indifferently. We call the diamond precious, a storm frightful, a man hateful, an action unworthy, a road painful, a heaven sad, or a sunset superb. Santayana arrived at the term "pleasure objectified." Such linguistic insolvables are everywhere. Do they not point straight at true factuality in its full form? (31, pp. 34–6; pp. 142–6; pp. 217–22).

6. Much that is objective to common sense is subjective to the physicist. Whether heat, sound, or light are in the thing or in the person is a problem our standard language will not handle (31, p. 219).

7. Even pain is "local" and can be spoken of in objective as well as in subjective terms (31, p. 142).

8. Consider the "primary" qualities. They are already going the way the "secondaries" have gone, taking up a certain subjectivity along with their ancient objectivity. (James wrote this in 1905 while Newtonian physics still stood unchallenged; 31, pp. 146–8.)

9. Philosophers commonly take the reality for a crudity, and fashion themselves a fiction to call real. They construct an entity from their "breath moving outward" (31, p. 37). Of this James proceeded to exhibit specimens "on the hoof."

10. Take a philosopher who starts out with the admission that whenever he tries to fix his attention distinctly upon consciousness it "seems to vanish," and that when he tries to "introspect" the sensation of blue, for example, all he can see is the blue. Next thing you know you find this very philosopher (G. E. Moore) saying: "Yet it *can* be distinguished, if we look attentively enough, and know that there is something to look for" (31, pp. 6–7). Knowing what he wants, such a philosopher proceeds to get it in a way that James would doubtless have styled, if a

---

James (5a). A third is the permissible extension of the duration of "an event" to any desirable degree as soon as the durational characteristic is recognized in it at all (3, pp. 254–5). To these procedures I have added a comparable "social immediacy" under direct factual observation (3; 4).

The Jamesian Datum

phrasing current in his day had occurred to him, "by main force and awkwardness."

11. Take another philosopher who proceeds by the most delicate and refined analysis to produce a "necessary" form of consciousness. When he settles down to study the outcome of his analysis we find him admitting that what he (in this case, P. Natorp) has secured is something that "can neither be defined nor deduced from anything but itself" (31, pp. 7-8).

12. It is of these two exhibits that James remarks in a much mulled-over passage that "the separation . . . into consciousness and content comes, not by way of subtraction, but by way of addition" (31, p. 9). His word "addition" was perhaps unfortunate, but his context is perfectly clear. There is no subtraction as of pigment from oil, but no more is there addition as of pigment to oil. The "addition" James presents is that of differentiation, upbuilding, development, growth. The garblers of James would do well to consider this passage, not as a play of word against word, but for its conveyance of meaning in the full.

13. Establish your split, stick to it doggedly, and proceed. What happens? There's a gap. You *must* get across it some way. You insert a "third" something. And then? You find that now you have two gaps to deal with in place of one. The harder you try — if you work honestly — the worse off you get. You land plump in some transcendental as the only agent you can find to handle the job for you.[25]

14. Why such violence, why such force, when all you need to do is to recognize where the trouble lies, and orient this "duality" with respect

[25] James's antipathy to the unnecessary intervention of a non-factual third runs back to his early work. In 1884 he pointed out that the more strongly the opposition between a feeling and a fact is stressed, the more surely "a third psychic entity will intervene to interpret" (19, pp. 7-9); also that if we start with isolated data, no matter how we struggle or what we do, in every case "the datum we start with remains just what it was" (21; reprinted 29, pp. 16-17). In later life he called attention to the way in which representative theories "put a mental 'representation,' 'image,' or 'content' into the gap as a sort of intermediary" (31, p. 52); he spoke of the "intervening mental image" as unknown to our "sense of life" and violating it (31, p. 12); discussing concepts, he spoke of the "intrusion of *percepts* that third group of associates" (31, p. 17). The discussions (31, pp. 11-15, pp. 150-2, and pp. 212-16) are all pertinent; and compare 48, II, p. 760, where "on the level of analysis" (as distinct from "the level of history") "the percept is not the *effect* of the object; it *is* the object." James's continued use of "percept" or "concept" as a name for a differentiated process "within" experience, as in his wise-cracking interchange with Chapman on the subject (35, II, p. 321; 5c, p. 132) leads to confusion only if the reading of his words is casual. A striking illustration of the verbal phantasms that arise from ignorance of James's discussion and from blindness to his point of view may be found in a recent essay undertaking to construct an epistemology for pragmatism despite the fact that the very thing all pragmatists have agreed on is their getting rid of the old dialectical epistemologies and their covering the ground in their own way. This particular undertaking (15) starts off with *four* pre-existents: thing, thinker, connecting medium, and space-time co-ordinates; it winds up with an exhibit of much-prized concepts and percepts "emergent within the perspective," which is philosophese for "rabbits out of the hat."

to the factual datum, in terms of which it "can always be particularized and defined" (31, p. 10)?

15. Not in James's formal assertion, but in his practice, and in a way thoroughly in accord with his datum, we find him more and more as he went along treating subjectives and objectives as ways of talking. An instance from the *Principles* (22, I, p. 245) has already been cited (Sec. VIII above). Phrases such as "get reported," "are known" (31, p. 4, p. 132); "taken, i.e., talked-of" (31, p. 23); "'outer' and 'inner' are names" (31, p. 139); and "retrospective manners of naming" (31, p. 214) are common. Again: "Concepts are . . . notes taken by ourselves" (28, p. 253), and "Their names . . . cut them into separate conceptual entities" (28, p. 285).[26]

X

CONFLICTING PHRASEOLOGIES

James's steady advance in observation, his attainment of the datum as his basic report, and his extension of it toward causation and the infinite in his last years have been exhibited as the structure of his lifework. The incidental reasons for his variety of specialized terminologies and for the consequent superficial appearance of incompatibilities among them have been mentioned, and a half-dozen illustrations given in passing.[27] He had to maintain the full behavioral values of the "mental" in all phases while at the same time eradicating the spectral entitative nouns, and this was no easy task. We may illustrate the communicative difficulties a little further with respect to the words "concept" and "relation." "Concept" was no entity, and as an "intervening third" was, like "percept," out of the reckoning as soon as relational immediacy had been secured. Nevertheless, in order to prevent other distortions of his position, James had to insist continuously on the behavioral actuality of the process. In his posthumously published volume for beginners (30), in order to differentiate concepts from percepts he gave heavy presentation to both of them as named phenomena, with the result that many of his sentences taken in isolation seem to conflict with his fuller statement. The full context is necessary for their understanding, and in this particular book much of the context could never be supplied. Then as for "relation," although it was itself a form of knowing, he could find

---

[26] For other phrasings approximating the above, see 31, p. 1, p. 5, p. 10, p. 12, p. 13, p. 94, p. 129, p. 222; 28, p. 217, p. 253; 30, p. 9, p. 48, p. 65; 48, II, p. 761. Earlier hints may perhaps be found in 29, p. 13, p. 14, p. 49. The references in Footnote 22 above also have interest in this connection.

[27] See the end of Sec. III, and the last part of Sec. VIII; also Footnotes 8, 16.

himself at a convenient time and place telling his hearers that knowledge itself was " a relation " (31, p. 4, p.25); and indeed so effectively that Perry could even report James's view to be that " consciousness is a relation " (47, p. 47), or again that James held " that reality and the field of consciousness were one and the same " (48, II, p. 589). Here what we must always understand in James's affirmation is his insistent " inside the tissue of experience," or " within the realm of experience " (31, p. 57; 29, p. XVII).

Even when full allowance is made for the varieties of presentation, some critic may inspect James's preoccupations in his last years in such an instance as the " Miller-Bode Objections " (48, Appendix X), or perhaps take up an earlier case such as the " Syllabus of Philosophy 3 " (48, Appendix IX), and point out that the factual stress is slight. He may then argue that James's real interest was manifestly metaphysical. The answer must be made in terms of James's intellectual integrity and acuity, and of the fact that he had to force his route of observation through a dense linguistic smoke screen, the clarification of which had for centuries upon centuries rested in the hands of men whose creed had been: clarification if possible, but preservation at all events, clarified or not. When James finally decided " *to give up the logic,* fairly, squarely, and irrevocably " he did it on the somewhat emotionally philosophical ground that " reality, life, experience, concreteness, immediacy, use what word you will, exceeds our logic, overflows and surrounds it " (28, p. 212). But Perry's compact phrase gives a better ground than this. James, says Perry, " resolved to renounce his scruples and to accept *what experience teaches* (my italics) even if it be at variance with what logic proves " (48, II, p. 589). Instead of " what logic proves " write " what ancestral language habits demand," and we get an accurate statement of the battle and triumph of James's later years.

Persons whose viewpoints lead them to read James in a way sharply at variance with our account may perhaps accept the following statement, which avoids specialization either from " philosophical " or " factual " points of view: (a) The " subjective " of James's attention was from the start " functional "; (b) As time went on he reported this " functional " in settings wider than those of his original description; (c) His " pragmatic " must be recognized as one great phase of widening, no matter how desperately its opponents tried to make it appear " solipsistic "; (d) The " radical " was another great widening, and a firmer and fuller report. Put flesh on these bones, and James's datum is what you have.

Many of these who are willing to recognize the datum as " fact for

James " will nevertheless variously evade or belittle it. One critic says: the datum is true enough, but a trifle; or, unless a man had a " mind " he could never know about it, true or not, trifle or not; or, it is a by-product of the neural. Another says: subject and object are " implicit " in it, and thus implicitness is what really counts; or, after subject and object have " emerged," the datum is husks that fall away. However, it is just barely possible that, if the datum *is* fact, someone someday may come to say — particularly in an era when there is little agreement on psychological formulation, and no decent sociological formulation at all — that it may be worth while taking account of the *fact itself*.

A reasonable question might be: How *real* did James regard " subjects " and " objects " once they had become differentiated *via* the advance of datum-processes? This is a biographical question in the sense that it has personal interest, though lying apart from the main issue. The answer in general, I take it, would be for almost any date, that he did not question the " reals " at all where he found them and as he found them. Philosophically speaking, he was always a realist " inside of the continuities of experience." [28] His remark that differentiation marks an " advanced stage of reflection " (29, p. 63; 31, p. 75, p. 219) is highly significant. What " advanced stage " indicates to an empiricist is a great opening for inquiry and for determination of " reality " in terms of temporal stage itself. To a question as to what future generations would say about the " reals," James's whole cautious approach in research would be answer enough — he was one man who refrained from settling the world's intellectual future in advance. To a question, yes or no, as to how to specify these " reals," he would probably have answered: In any way that enables you to communicate with others, provided you know a little what you are talking about, and have sufficient sense of the limitations of your knowing.

XI

What Philosophers Do to James — and How

Among the misstatements of James listed in the first section of this paper were several originating among philosophers. We have given no direct attention to these, but it is worth pausing now to illustrate what philosophers get out of James, and to show how they get it.

In a separate paper (2) I have analyzed Perry's recent exhibit of a " phenomenalistic " phase in James's career (49, Chap. III) and have

---

[28] See Footnote 14 above.

shown in detail that Perry weakens James's wordings, and falls far short of recognizing the full strength of his factual assertion. Perry represents, and has steadily represented — and this in the very best sense — James's philosophical setting. In his great work on James — the *Thought and Character* — he summarized the many striking ways in which James anticipated our present generation (48, II, pp. 668-9), but he did not there mention the neutral fact, unless his putting the word " experience " in quotation marks may be taken as hinting at it. Consequently his later recognition of a " phenomenalistic " phase in James's career marks a definite, even if partial, forward step.

Among the psychologists whose squints at James were listed in Section I is Edwin B. Holt. Holt once underwent a metaphysical attack (17) — he later disavowed it — in which he gazed upon " neutral entities " and " concept stuff," and then more intently still upon their verbal fusion as " neutral stuff." This book was published in 1914, which was two years after the posthumous publication of James's *Essays in Radical Empiricism,* and ten years after James had played with such words as " primal," " aboriginal," " neutral," and " stuff " in literary contact. Holt had studied at Harvard under James, and taught there later, and it is significant that he did not refer his " neutral stuff " to James, nor unload upon him any of the responsibility for it. Instead he named Sheffer as having suggested the word " neutral " to him for such use.

Bertrand Russell, however, was not so fortunate — or perhaps not so well informed. Among the books he published in 1927 were two in which he committed himself to " neutral monism." In one of these (54, p. 10) he referred to Holt and Sheffer, but in the much wider development of the other (55, p. 210) he brought James heavily into the foreground. James, he said, had startled the world in 1904 by setting out " the view that ' there is only one primal stuff or material in the world,' and that the word ' consciousness ' stands for a function, not an entity." To James he attributed the theory " that there are ' thoughts ' which perform the function of ' knowing,' but that the ' thoughts ' are not made of any different ' stuff ' from that of which material objects are made." Thus, he said, James " laid the foundations for what is called ' neutral monism,' a view advocated by most American realists." In a third book, of earlier date (53, p. 22), Russell had mentioned " realists who retain only the object," and had said that " their views . . . are in large measure derived from William James."

Now Russell's eleven-word citation from James as given above is verbally accurate (31, p. 4), but what Russell does not mention is that later in the same essay (p. 26) James said of the word " stuff " that it had only been used by him "for fluency's sake," and that there is "no *general* stuff of which experience at large is made." Further than this, in a subsequent essay James denied emphatically that subjectivity and objectivity were "affairs of what an experience is aboriginally made of" (p. 141). Russell's account of James does violence to him in many ways. It makes him (a) primarily interested in "stuff," when actually James disavowed the term. (b) It makes him out a "monist," when actually he struggled much of his life against the prevailing monism and ended in a vigorous anti-monism he called pluralism. (c) It was not in 1904, as Russell says, that James set forth the view that consciousness was a function; he started out with that attitude in 1884, and had tossed out all of the main "substances" by 1890 in the *Principles;* what he reached in 1904 being his final conclusion that even as "an activity" — as a named and specialized "function" — he could not give consciousness existential status. (d) James was no more a realist "retaining only the object" than a realist or idealist retaining only "the subject," nor was he a progenitor of any such view. (e) If the proof of the pudding is in the eating, then Russell's life-long retention of a primitive individualistic mentalism, with paradox its sole fruit, is evidence that he never properly comprehended or used James's views, but quite the reverse. The distortion in such a case as the above lies, of course, in picking up a few phrases from a book, taking them literally without examination of context, adapting them to alien uses (such as Russell's passion for "stuff"), and then making the other fellow responsible.

A quite similar procedure is evident in a recent attempt by Lowe (No. 5 in Section I above) to attach James to the chariot wheels of Russell's old-time associate, Whitehead, who still, much like Russell, reeks with antiquated mentalisms and is philosophically adored therefor. Lowe runs across the phrase "felt transition" in one of James's texts and seizes upon it, though without citing the passage in which it occurs. The sole occasion on which James used this phrase, so far as I can discover, was in his 1904 essay "The World of Pure Experience" (31, p. 56).[29] The way he came to use it gives an excellent illustration of his method of

---

[29] In a later paper (60, p. 171) Lowe mentions "felt transition" with a footnote to say that "E. R. E., pp. 41–51 is the basic text here." "Felt transition" does not occur in the eleven pages cited. "Feel" occurs three times in the sense of "experience" or "occur," but never stressed for itself. With this goes heavy warning by James against the correction of incoherencies by the addition of agencies, substances, powers, or selves (31, p. 43). In other words, Lowe is the victim of an illusion. This comment seems true also of his assertion (60, p. 173) of "the absence of 'pure experience' from *A Pluralistic Universe,*" an assertion hardly possible to anyone who has noticed the last 122 pages of that book.

discourse in general. He had employed the words "feel" and "felt" quite casually in the preceding paragraph and then, finding them usefully expressive, he firmed them up a little as he went on. "Denoting definitely felt transitions" was one phrase he wrote, and "wherever such transitions are felt" was a second. In neither of these cases (and this is the whole collection) was he positively stressing the "felt" as characteristic of the event. In both he was talking about a process of knowledge in which "transitions" are important and, in order to show that he was talking not of dead wood but of going events in the behavioral life, he called them "felt transitions." Had he let the phrasing stand in this way he might easily be held responsible, by carelessness at least, for false interpretation such as Lowe gives. But he did *not* let it stand this way. He at once pointed out that the whole process "comes to life inside the tissue of experience," and what he understood by "experience" he had reiterated so often in the accompanying text that there is no excuse whatever for ignoring it. Beyond this he warned his reader before closing the paragraph that to speak of an object's "being in mind" meant the presence of "transitional experiences," and that is all it meant, since "of any deeper more real way of being in mind we have no positive conception, and we have no right to discredit our actual experience by talking of such a way at all" (31, p. 58).

There is certainly no stress on "feel" in this last passage. What Lowe does is this: He starts out with his personal predilection that if Whitehead "can convince you that you actually felt your experience ... growing ..." then you will become enthusiastic for him. With Whitehead he proposes to assimilate James, to whom, as protagonist of the "feeling," a bit of the enthusiasm will be allowed to pass. Toward this objective he transfers the stress in James's work to the world "felt," oblivious of the fact that in so doing he adopts just such a "deeper conception" as James refused to tolerate in his maturity, however he may have had remnants of it operative in him in his youth. James's "radical empiricism," Lowe tells us, rests on "*transitions* that are *felt*" (the italics are Lowe's). Where James had written that "parts ... hold together ... by relations that are parts ..." and where James's whole development proceeds in this pure or neutral sense, Lowe calmly announces that "the correct expansion" of James's view is in terms of "transitions that are felt." He gives four or five pages (43, pp. 114–119) to his exhibit of this "expansion," always incorporating the heavily stressed "felt" which is not in James at all. He supports his attitude incidentally by citing Perry to the effect that James chose "feeling" as the best term for use, but he neglects to say that this had been James's choice in 1884, at which date James used "feeling" synonymously with "consciousness," "thought," and three or four other words; nor does he say that by 1904 James had subordinated this whole cluster of terms, "feeling" still being one of them, to his "neutral," "concrete" presentation. Lowe remarks that the "evidence" for "felt transition" is in the *Principles* (1890), which would be a perfectly sound remark if coupled with the further statement that the overwhelming evidence against it is in *Essays in Radical Empiricism* (1904–6): that evidence, namely, which we have already summarized in Section IX above.

It is by procedures such as Russell and Lowe employ that James is made out to be a "philosopher" instead of a fact-seeking scientist, which was what he continued to be, even if his route led him into ground over which philosophers claim sovereignty. James was no serf bound to that soil. To clear his memory not only must his own free action be observed, but likewise the spurious nature of the bonds assigned him.

XII

Darwin-Peirce-James-Dewey

No attempt will be made here at adequate orientation of Peirce, James, and Dewey to each other and to Darwin. The material is too extensive, the range of appraisal too wide, and our present generation not yet sufficiently mature for clear vision. It is necessary, nevertheless, to sketch the naturalistic characteristics of the work of the three Americans. As stated before (Sections V and VI), all three have struggled steadily to envisage the full behaviors of human beings in that world of evolving adaptations which Darwin demonstrated to be scientifically valid as hypothesis or frame for research. All three will be thus in contrast with the prevalent *pseudo*-Darwinians who see neural systems naturally evolved up to and including the cortex, and then proceed to treat the cortex as an emergent "thing" entitled to perform with all the tricks, abuses, and disabilities of the ancient "mind."

Peirce led off in 1869 by asserting that every thought "requires a time ... must be interpreted in another ... is in signs" (50; 52, V, Sec. 253). The first part of this declaration is basic to all three men, and alien to the mentalists and *pseudo*-Darwinians alike; it will be touched on further in a moment. The middle part might almost have been taken by James as a text for his papers of 1884 and 1885. The last part has nowhere in the world begun to be developed as yet in a sense consonant with Peirce's procedural background, and with the great forward strides of James and Dewey.[30]

Peirce's pragmatic approach of 1878 which made "the conception of the effects" be "the whole of our conception of the object" (51; 52, V, Sec. 402) is an empirical report on the evolved human organism "knowing things" in an evolving biological nature of Darwinian type. His fallibilism and common-sensism, fully shared, whatever the form of expression, by both James and Dewey (and it is to be hoped by everyone not chronically suffering from epistemological paranoia) fall within the new approach; so also his late-life efforts at a functional logic designed to surmount the effects of his own virtuosity in his earlier studies. A recent complaint by one of the editors of his collected works that "Peirce never gave sufficient weight to the fact of individual existence and undoubtedly exaggerated the place that signs occupied in men and things" (58, p. 259) gives evidence that no one ever suffered more than Peirce from his editors, and indicates to what extent his contribution to the advance of knowledge remains in neglect.

Peirce, James, and Dewey all survey human behaviors in durations; they agree that thought "requires a time"; they agree in holding knowings among the durational behaviors; they agree in rejecting the spaceless-timeless pattern of Molière's *vis dormativa* — the pattern typical of pre-Darwinian and *pseudo*-Darwinian inquiry, which insists on having a "doer," knows such a doer only from his "doings," defines him, nevertheless, as an entity apart from his doings, and endows the entity (which is to say, the definition) with powers of *fiat* — the pattern which, when once embraced, seems to make a full durational inspection (in other words, modern science) eternally incomprehensible to the embracer. What most hampered Peirce was the traditional mentalistic terminology with its "intervening thirds." James and Dewey surmounted this, but Peirce remained caught in the verbal mire of triadic iteration.

James's concentration on "knowings" and his steadfast maintenance of the empirical approach were unbroken. You cannot take a verbal flash at some hypothetical, instantaneous "true William James," and get a description of him at all. You cannot state his datum this way; you

---

[30] Recent activities with the word "sign" by some of Peirce's obtusely incoherent camp-followers do not rate as development. Peirce used every device he could find in the psychological setting of his day to develop the organization he sensed, but terminology defaulted, and he failed. To pick up the worst of his discarded efforts, transport them into a later generation, and parade them Punch and Judy style is not what Peirce would have called progress. What James would probably have thought of it appears in his comment on the "doctrine of signatures," and upon all the "mancies" and "mantics" in which "witchcraft and incipient science are indistinguishably mixed" (30, p. 18).

cannot even locate it in his work in this way. Full durational inspection is required to attain his observational advance. His " stream " was itself manifestly durational. His " datum " formed itself in the stream, and stream and datum transformed themselves together into clearly recognized fact. The datum is straight factual report of what is empirically observed when trained examination of durational organism-in-nature is made in the special region of the phenomena called " conscious." In his earlier work James had asserted that " the unit of composition of our perception of time is a duration " (22, I, p. 609) and had coined the phrase " specious present " (*ibid.*, p. 631). " Collateral contemporaneity " was a phrase of his transitional period (25, p. 119). In his later work he expressly established " experience as a whole " as " a process in time " (31, p. 62), insisted on seeing " the distance-interval concretely " (*ibid.*, p. 198), talked of " simultaneous characters " in terms of continuity and overlapping (28, pp. 278–8), and went so far as to assert that " a pure experience can be postulated with any amount whatever of span or field " even up to millions of years (31, p. 135).[31]

Dewey entered the Peirce-James continuity in the eighteen-nineties, bringing a psychological formulation of stimulus-response in full circuit, rather than in partial " arc " (10), and developing a pragmatism which James saw as offering a " wider panorama " than his own (29, p. xix). No one has known better than Peirce or felt more strongly how deeply social our knowings are. No one has made a more brilliant raid into the social field than James in his analysis of the " selves " (22, Chap. X). Either of them was, in basic envisionment, far ahead of the academic sociologies of today, but neither followed this lead in systematic development. It was Dewey who broadened the study of knowings into a full cultural form. " Transaction," for Dewey, underlies " action," and the " indeterminate " underlies the " determinate " in a way similar to that in which, for James, the factual datum underlies the purportedly independent subjectives and objectives. In each of these cases a view in full system is offered as a vastly richer approach to knowledge than any the dualistically split views have ever yielded. Where James expelled the " conscious " pretender by name, Dewey has made development with the pretender already expelled. In the *Logic* the " belief " of a " believer " does not enter as a significant element; and belief and believer together are shoved back to whatever minor descriptional status continued

---

[31] Cecil Miller (45) has recently examined James's theory of time in terms of his pragmatic method. He regards it as " comparable to a non-Euclidean geometry neglected by the Euclideans," has asked why it has " remained a cipher," and has used it as a text for remarks upon the " restraint of free speculation " which certain academic habits in America seem to have imposed on James and other workers.

future inquiry may show them entitled to. Where James gives a static snapshot of the stream, Dewey gives a free, broad account in historic-geographic setting, not puttering around in the current pedagogical style about the this and that of time, place, and circumstance, but showing the process in full sweep. Dewey has repeatedly proclaimed Peirce's leadership in the treatment of logic as a " theory of inquiry," and in stress upon the continuities which underlie its study (12, pp. 9, 12, 14, 156, 490 *et al.*). It is significant that Dewey, and Dewey alone, has realized Peirce's logical ambition, though in a manner very different from what Peirce could have attempted.

Where Darwin places nature beneath organism and environment to bring them into system, Peirce by a great vision extrapolates this approach across the full field of knowings, and identifies durational " sign " as the procedural unit. James, placing his microscopic observation upon the phenomena called " conscious," and holding doggedly to his task, brings the datum naturalistically to view. Dewey maps the wide cultural procedures of knowing — the prospectings, the testings, and the stabilizings of warranted assertion — with never a break away from the natural universe. For all four there is a common denominator of formulation — indicated, if not yet advanced in use. The immediacy of Darwin, literally present in the treatment of organism-environment as system, is the frame of the behavioral immediacy which James identified by name, which Dewey has organized and established for inquiry, and to which Peirce supplied the key.[32]

XIII

What Difference Does the Dictum Make?

The question: "*What's the use?*" so commonly asked by outsiders to lines of research in which striking new knowledge is being reported, is today rarely asked by insiders, since these latter know very well that the practical results are sure to come along in due time, wherever facts

[32] Surveying this finished report, I become increasingly aware that Herbert Spencer should have been taken expressly into account. Around 1880 James wrote several papers and reviews based on Spencer's work, one of which (18) is said by Perry (47, p. 7) to contain the " germinal idea " of much of James's later development. In 1884 (19, pp. 4-5) James credited Spencer with first identifying the " feelings of relation." Most significant, however, is Spencer's treatment of " mind " as the " adjustment of inner to outer relations " (see James's comment, 22, I, p. 6), this being definitely adaptational in the sense of our present account, although retaining " internal " and " external " as separate realms. Spencer is unfashionable and out-of-date, and his intricate system of linguistic cog-wheels is wholly unattractive; his schematism is appalling, but his psychological initiative in the Darwinian setting, though lacking the importance of Peirce's, is none the less directly pertinent here.

are faithfully reported as they are. We cannot, of course, expect the Jamesian datum to be *finally* adopted as fact until it has proved itself in long research. On the other hand, we cannot expect workers occupied with minor problems which they can handle approximately well in terms of consciousness to put themselves to the trouble to try out research in terms of this richer and more highly perfected formulation. One thing we can do, however, is to ask the question " What's the use? " in the modified form: "*Assuming* that the Jamesian neutral datum is *fact*, then what *immediate* uses may it have for research?"

The first step to be taken before sketching an answer is to make sure that issues of " fact " are severed in inspection from those of the " real " and the " true " (2). No dispute as to the " real " existence or the " real " nature of a human " being " or " person " need be involved in research. The " being " may be " soul," mortal or immortal, or he may not, and yet technical research may be compelled to get along without either dogmatic assertion of his being or his not being. Similarly as to " truth," it is unimportant whether our asserted observations are " true " in any absolute sense; the important question is whether they are true in action, that is, as hypotheses at a given stage of inquiry, and whether progress can be promoted by maintaining and extending them, leaving the ultimate " reals " and " trues " for the future to determine. James made this plain enough for his own procedure by the parenthetic sentence he placed immediately after his " postulate " in the preface to *The Meaning of Truth:* " Things of an unexperienceable nature may exist *ad libitum*, but they form no part of the material for philosophic debate " (29, p. xii; 31, p. ix). Much less, James elsewhere argued, do they form material for scientific inquiry.

The great technical characteristic of the Jamesian datum is that it brings together the leading phases of behavioral event in closer system than they otherwise appear. The *system* is what is important. Separation and opposition of subject and object and of mental and material is replaced by inquiry into differentiation of report out of joint process. From the beginning of his work James had viewed " sensings " and " reasonings " in organization, and his later work laid the foundations for holding stimulus and reaction in intelligible system in psychological construction. Carry through these two improvements of " system," and the whole scheme of formulation for psychology and sociology will be transformed. Dewey's *Reflex Arc Concept* paper of 1896 (10) set up part of the necessary stimulus-reaction reorganization, and it is significant that even though this construction has been only partially utilized by psychology to date (and that mainly in a temporary " school " derived from it), it is still regarded as so valuable by American psychologists that upon the occasion of a recent vote to estimate the most important paper published in the fifty years' history of the *Psychological Review*, it was given Number One position.[33]

Setting generalities of the future aside, the question as to the immediate usefulness of the Jamesian datum in research may receive a twofold answer: first, with respect to waste labor avoided; second, with respect to stagnant fields of research that open up afresh.

With respect to the elimination of useless labor, consider the history of I.Q. in the last twenty-five or thirty years. The incentive to intelligence tests came from minor practical needs, flowering out wonderfully at the time of the First World War. A technique able to tell whether a man could sell ribbons better than handle mules led, however, under the old viewpoints to a theoretical presentation in terms of facultative ribbon-selling and mule-hustling " capacities," and that led to endless futile discussion and trivial experiment, with the net result that only recently have workers in this field begun to realize that they are reporting in terms of behavioral event at specified times, places, and circumstances, and that the " mental realities " are irrelevant. A few grains of James's common sense would have taken care of that long, long ago. Consider Pavlov's direct, simple extension of physiology into animal behavior in specific environmental settings. Degradation into reflexological and behavioristic renderings has resulted in endless experiments designed to improve Pavlov by adding some factor that he himself had embodied in the work from its start. All this is wastage, since Pavlov fits directly into the main line of advance from James, and the path of continuation is clear. Consider the current excesses of physiological psychologists who do good physiology, but never stop to appraise the terminology of report; " consciousness " gets a new home every now and then, perhaps in an artery, and all this is waste labor both going and coming. Consider the general run of psychological experimentation; so far as it is physiology it is good; so far as it is not physiology, it is apt to be pretty poor, and this is not because it is not physiology, but because it is still incomplete in its psychological approach. A recent volume mentioned elsewhere in this paper (46) is almost wholly made up of statements which are defective, not merely because of ignorance of James, but because of ignorance of the simplest of the difficulties which James as a young man undertook to face, and over which he worked all his life. James had his own troubles due to surviving remnants of the older formulations, as in the problem of " unity," where he wasted much time in wondering whether a " state "

[33] *Psychol. Rev.*, Jan., 1943.

built up out of other "unit" states could itself be "unitary" or whether it must be seen as a "compound." It took a great effort for even his own innovations to get him past this difficulty, which is one that other sciences have now resolved in their own fields, so that it no longer echoes annoyingly in psychological regions. Finally, consider the absurdity "social environment" as it is taken for granted in almost all forms of current psychological and sociological presentation. This is a construction which assumes for the most general purposes of theory that "a man" is an individual environed by "other men" who are mass-effects, ignoring the "individual" in the other men, and the mass-effect participation in the "a man," and destroying thus the significance both of individual and of social without admitting it on either side. James did better than this when he made his start, and it is very easy today from James's point of approach to see the individual-social phenomenon directly and simply.

Turn now to specific fields of fresh construction. The way the word "meaning" is neglected or abused in the psychological texts ought to suggest so much by itself that the question as to new important openings for research could be regarded as already adequately answered. Consider, however, in particular two specializations of "meanings" — "knowings" and "speakings" — both phenomena falling among human "behavings." In the field of "knowings" there were in the first decade of this century several extended sets of experiments with something called "concept," all in heavily mentalist terminology, and all fruitless. A decade or so ago a series of papers on concept-behavior in animals appeared, but all used the word "concept" so loosely that no significance could be read into it. More recent work with animals by aid of the word "sign" is doing better, and will be adaptable to James's manner of approach if full durational treatment is secured. On the whole, however, it can be said that psychology in the past generation, whether using mentalist or non-mentalist terminologies, has accomplished nothing whatever in the way of investigating human "knowings" as behaviors of organisms in the world, and has in general rejected the whole sphere of inquiry as lying beyond its range.

Whatever may be the case with a theory of behavioral knowing, the need for a general theory of language on a behavioral base is very great, and is growing. Dewey, in the preface to his *Logic,* says that no such general theory exists, and that until it does appear certain regions of logic are useless to cultivate. Apart from trivial mechanistic or Freudian toying with linguistic details, we have none but mentalist construction.[34]

[34] Exception may be made for Leonard Bloomfield, his latest presentation of his theoretical construction being in his monograph, *Linguistic Aspects of Science* (6). He is

All that these last involve is that, given an "external" account of speech and writing — an account, namely, in which "meanings" are set to one side — then the meanings are added in terms of "mental" process; and all that results is double-talk; a restatement of a partially analyzed event in terms of a wholly unanalyzed "doer" of the event. James's procedure as he established it at the end of his life gave factual opening for construction in this field, in which event and meaning are not separated but appear in single fused presentation.

Why did not James himself make progress in these fields? For the same reason that he did not rewrite his *Principles of Psychology*. He was too old, in too poor health, and had too much else to do. He did not live enough more years after he was ready and, as has been said, he gave most of his little remaining time to the appraisal of philosophical and metaphysical linguistic presentation to see whether his asserted "pure experience" could maintain itself in the face of all the discussion that had been carried on about the region of life and fact in which he observed it. Whether he chose wisely or not in this final activity is a question, but not one of great importance. No man can do everything, and each of these things must at some time be done, if not by one man, then by some other man. But as to what James's own opinion was as to the outcome of his final metaphysical appraisal there can be but little doubt. On the flyleaf of one of his more intricate notebooks he wrote: "The writhing serpent of philosophy, to use a phrase of Blood's, is one gigantic string of mares' nests" (48, II, p. 393).

REFERENCES

1. ALLPORT, G. W. The productive paradoxes of William James. Psychol. Rev., 1943, 50, 95–120.
2. BENTLEY, A. F. Truth, reality, and behavioral fact. *J. Phil.*, 1943, 40, 169–187.
3. ———. Behavior, Knowledge, Fact. Bloomington, Ind.: Principia Press, 1935. Pp. xii+391.
4. ———. The Process of Government: A Study of Social Pressures. Chicago: Univ. Chicago Press, 1908. Pp. xv+501.
5a. ———. Sights-seen as materials of knowledge. *J. Phil.*, 1939, 36, 169–181.
5b. ———. Observable behaviors. *Psychol. Rev.*, 1940, 47, 230–253.

---

thoroughgoing in his expulsion of the old mentalist terminology, and in his requirement of a behavioral approach to linguistic phenomena. But he narrows his behavioral approach to the mechanistic, or technically "behavioristic," and on that ground decides that vocal speech alone (and not written) *is* language. The objection to this is that he is unable to adhere to his position in his development, and repeatedly discusses linguistic activities in writing as beyond what vocal linguistic activities can accomplish. He sees Dewey as subjectivistic and would doubtless regard James as even worse, and thus cuts himself off from the most important lines of factual development. Kantor's *Objective Psychology of Grammar* (38) has examined at length the confusions of the old mentalist terminologies in this field.

5c. ———. Physicists and fairies. *Phil. Sci.*, 1938, **5**, 132–165.
5d. ———. Decrassifying Dewey. *Phil. Sci.*, 1941, **8**, 147–156.
5e. ———. As through a glass darkly. *J. Phil.*, 1942, **39**, 432–439.
6. BLOOMFIELD, L. Linguistic Aspects of Science. Chicago: Univ. Chicago Press, 1939. 50, 95–120.
7. BROTHERSTON, B. W. The wider setting of "Felt Transition." *J. Phil.*, 1942, **39**, 97–104.
8. CASSIRER, E. *Le langage et la construction du monde des objets. J. Psychol. Nor. & Pathol.*, 1933, Nos. 1–4 (*Psychologie de langage*).
9. DEWEY, J. Inquiry and indeterminateness of situation. *J. Phil.*, 1942, **39**, 290–296.
10. ———. The reflex arc concept in psychology. *Psychol. Rev.*, 1896, **4**, 357–370.
11. ———. Experience and Nature. Chicago: Open Court, 1925. Pp. xi+443.
12. ———. Logic, The Theory of Inquiry. New York: Holt, 1938. Pp. x+546.
13. ———. The vanishing subject in the psychology of James. *J. Phil.*, 1940, **37**, 589–599.
14. DUNLAP, K. The postulate of common content. *Psychol. Rev.*, 1940, **47**, 306–321.
15. FITCH, R. E. An experimental perspectival epistemology. *J. Phil.*, 1941, **38**, 589–600.
16. HOLT, E. B. Animal Drive and the Learning Process: An Essay toward Radical Empiricism. New York: Holt, 1931. Pp. xii+307.
17. ———. The Concept of Consciousness. London: Allen, 1914. Pp. xvi+343.
18. JAMES, W. Remarks on Spencer's " Definition of Mind as Correspondence." *J. Spec. Phil.*, 1878, **12**, 1–8. (Reprinted in 33).
19. ———. On some omissions of introspective psychology. *Mind*, 1884, **9**, 1–26.
20. ———. Absolutism and empiricism. *Mind*, 1884, **9**, 281–286. (Reprinted in 31).
21. ———. The function of cognition. *Mind*, 1885, **10**, 27–44. (Reprinted in 29).
22. ———. The Principles of Psychology. New York: Holt, 1890. (2 vol.) Pp. xii+689; vi+704.
23. ———. Psychology (Briefer Course). New York: Holt, 1892. Pp. xiii+478.
24. ———. The knowing of things together. *Psychol. Rev.*, 1895, **2**, 105–124. (Reprinted in 33; also in part in 29).
25. ———. The Will to Believe, and Other Essays in Popular Philosophy. New York: Longmans, Green, 1897. Pp. xviii+332.
26. ———. Philosophical conceptions and practical results. *Univ. Calif. Chronicle*, 1898. Pp. 24. (Reprinted in 33).
27. ———. Does "consciousness" exist? *J. Phil., Psychol., & Sci. Meth.*, 1904, **1**, 477–491. (Reprinted in 31).
28. ———. A Pluralistic Universe. Hibbert Lectures at Manchester College on the Present Situation in Philosophy. New York: Longmans, Green, 1909. Pp. xvi+297.
29. ———. The Meaning of Truth: A Sequel to Pragmatism. New York: Longmans, Green, 1909. Pp. 404.
30. ———. Some Problems of Philosophy: A Beginning of an Introduction to Philosophy. New York: Longmans, Green, 1911. Pp. xi+236.
31. ———. Essays in Radical Empiricism. New York: Longmans, Green, 1912. Pp. xiii+283.
32. ———. The Varieties of Religious Experience: A Study in Human Nature. (Gifford Lectures). New York: Longmans, Green, 1902. Pp. xii+538.
33. ———. Collected Essays and Reviews. New York: Longmans, Green, 1920. Pp. x+516.
34. ———. Pragmatism: A New Name for Some Old Ways of Thinking. Popular Lectures in Philosophy. New York: Longmans, Green, 1907. Pp. xii+308.
35. ———. The Letters of William James. Edited by his son, Henry James. Boston: Little, Brown, 1920. (2 vols.) Pp. xxviii+348, 384.
36. KANTOR, J. R. Principles of Psychology. New York: Knopf. Vol. I, 1924, pp. xix+473; Vol. II, 1926. Pp. xii+524.
37. ———. A Survey of the Science of Psychology. Bloomington, Ind.: Principia Press, 1933. Pp. xvii+564.
38. ———. An Objective Psychology of Grammar. Blomington, Ind.: Indiana Univ. Publ., 1936. Pp. xvi+344.

39. KNOX, H. V. The Philosophy of William James. London: Constable, 1914. Pp. 112.
40. LASHLEY, K. S. Experimental analysis of instinctive behavior. *Psychol. Rev.*, 1938, **45**, 445–471.
41. LAPAN, A. The Significance of James' Essay. New York: Law, 1936. Pp. vii+69.
42. LAVINE, T. Z. Sociological analysis of cognitive norms. *J. Phil.*, 1942, **39**, 342–356.
43. LOWE, V. William James and Whitehead's doctrine of prehensions. *J. Phil.*, 1941, **38**, 113–126.
44. MANNHEIM, K. Ideology and Utopia: An Introduction to the Sociology of Knowledge. With a Preface by Louis Wirth. New York: Harcourt, Brace, 1936. Pp. xxi+318.
45. MILLER, C. H. The limits of freedom in philosophy. *Phil. Sci.*, 1942, **9**, 19–29.
46. MILLER, J. G. Unconsciousness. New York: Wiley, 1942. Pp. x+329.
47. PERRY, R. B. Annotated Bibliography of the Writings of William James. New York: Longmans, Green, 1920. Pp. 69.
48. ———. The Thought and Character of William James. Boston: Little, Brown, 1936 (2 vols.) Pp. xxxviii+826; xxiv+786.
49. ———. In the Spirit of William James. New Haven: Yale Univ. Press, 1938. Pp. xii+211.
50. PEIRCE, C. S. Questions concerning certain faculties claimed for man. *J. Spec. Phil.*, 1868, **2**, 103–114.
51. ———. How to make our ideas clear. *Pop. Sci. Mo.*, 1878, **12**, 286–302.
52. ———. Collected Papers of Charles Sanders Peirce. Cambridge: Harvard Univ. Press, 1931–1935. (6 vols.)
53. RUSSELL, B. The Analysis of Mind. London: Allen & Unwin, 1921. Pp. 310.
54. ———. The Analysis of Matter. London: Paul, Trench, Trübner, 1927. Pp. viii+408.
55. ———. Philosophy. New York: Norton, 1927. Pp. viii+307.
56. SKAGGS, E. B. Atomism versus Gestaltism in perception. *Psychol. Rev.*, 1940, **47**, 347–354.
57. SPOERL, H. D. Abnormal and social psychology in the life and work of William James. *J. Abn. & Soc. Psychol.*, 1942, **37**, 3–19.
58. WEISS, P. The essence of Peirce's system. *J. Phil.*, 1940, **37**, 253–264.
59. WIGGINS, F. O. William James and John Dewey. *Personalist*, 1942, **23**, 182–198.
60. In Commemoration of William James, 1842–1942. New York: Columbia Univ. Press, 1942. Pp. xii+234. (A collection of sixteen addresses.)

CHAPTER FIFTEEN

The Fiction of "Retinal Image"*

For three hundred years and more it has been an established belief in optics, physiology, and psychology that images in the form of pictures of outer objects are present upon the retina of the eye during vision. Except for the most recent laboratory work on the physiology of vision, where very little mention is made of them, the presence of such images is regarded as the critical feature of the visual process. Its assumption seems to conform to the unquestionably valid procedures of geometrical optics. It is a sound guide for the designer and manufacturer of optical instruments. For the ophthalmologist the name labels usefully the situations which he has to appraise in the most characteristic portions of his work. In psychology perhaps no text has ever been written without belief in such an image, nor without its use both in interpreting vision and as a model for other sense processes. Likewise many a weary and bored high school student has brightened visibly on being told about the image and its upside-downness; while the " Who-done-it? " writer has profited frequently from the superstition of the image remaining printed on the victim's eye in death to bring the murderer to justice.

Nevertheless the assumption is false, not merely as a survival after death, but as a fact of life. Examination shows it to be a confused mixture of analogies. By no pictorial test can the pictorial characteristics be established. The belief in the image, casually useful or indifferent in some fields, is positively hurtful in others such as the psychological. What was brilliant insight when Kepler transformed the guesswork of earlier dioptrics into a demonstrated system — what was a sound practical orientation for Descartes and Newton as they continued optical research — what has been a convenient catchword for many other workers in later years — is today an antiquated device much in the sense that a Ptolemaic sun or a Newtonian absolute space is antiquated. There *is* a

* Unpublished Ms. essay dated August 21, 1943. This early draft was never revised or put in final form, but is published by the editor because it opens up new perspectives. It should be read as of its preliminary status as well as date.

The Fiction of "Retinal Image"

sun, but not Ptolemy's circulating pygmy. There *is* spatial extension, but not Newton's divine rigidity. There *is* vision of form, size, distance, and color, but not vision which contains as a component a half-physical, half-mental hermaphrodite, stuck physically upon some indeterminate portion of a ten-layered retina, and from that precarious perch mentally " imaging " and " being an image." Mr. Facing-both-ways has been secure enough so long as nobody has had reason to look closely into his makeup, but the time has now come for him to face the court of fact.

No matter how much attention we give to the *word* " image," our attention will never be away from the *facts* it is supposed to name. We must no more be dogmatic about facts than about names, merely on the basis of what we have been accustomed to accept. For our present purposes we shall take fact to be *the best determination and report we are today capable of obtaining* about the phenomena we are engaged in studying. We shall require the *determination* of fact to be by way of experimental operations, direct and indirect, ranging from foot-rules and scales to cloud chambers and electron microscopes; and we shall require the *report* on fact to be made by verbal operations, similarly experimental — which is to say that it shall be in words that state the fact in ways compatible not merely with the needs of some limited field of inquiry, but with the broadest procedures [and varying theoretical structures] in the full complex of inquiry we call science (see *infra,* p. 277 f., point 20).

Understanding " fact " in this way, we shall proceed to examine the various facts that have been accumulated about the neural tissue called " retinal "; and equally the many types of fact assembled linguistically under the word " image." We shall seek to find what compatibility there can be among such facts, and in what sense retinal image may be image. Of such a retinal image we shall ask in especial: Just *where* is it? Just *what* is it? *How good,* as image, could it be? *What good* service as image could it perform in the modern physiology of vision?

To eliminate at once certain possible misunderstandings, the following preliminary statements are made with maximum emphasis:

(a) We are to deal with living vision, not with the dead materials of the enucleated eye.

(b) Geometrical optics, as it is fully developed in projective spaces, is not only accepted in full validity, but is basic to our procedure.

(c) The location of the image plane for the dioptrics of the eye in the approximate region of the retina is unquestioned.

(d) The use of the name " retinal image " by ophthalmologists and other technicians for their professional convenience is in no way criticized — as, for example, in the recent studies of aniseikonia in which " corresponding points" are minutely dealt with. Only where "image" is taken as "picture," and then only where further procedure of formulation becomes distorted under that rendering, will criticism sharply be applied.

The retina was not recognized as a distinctive structure of the eye till about 1270, when it entered as just another "tunic" alongside of sclera and choroid. Not till three hundred years later was it identified as the region of the eye at which light waves are focused. The early Greeks had sometimes explained "seeing" as due to effluvia from the object which entered the eye, and sometimes as the achievement of the eye which sent out its "fire" to waylay the object and bring impressions of it back. These are the great "push" and "grab" theories of vision which we still have active among us, in whatever rarefied forms. Aristotle, here as so often, did much better, from today's scientific point of view, by suggesting the presence of an intervening medium as the basis of vision. The Arabs, transporting Greek lore to modern times, developed the scheme of the eye as a dark chamber, or *camera obscura,* with a picture on its wall. The location of this wall that carried the picture, thought of sometimes as out in front at the cornea, and sometimes as in the lens or vitreous humor, was gradually agreed to be at the retina, with Maurolycus and Platter toward the end of the sixteenth century most active in making the identification. Finally Kepler, great astronomer and mathematician, took the matter in hand, and in 1604 established dioptrics firmly and permanently. He lacked little in completeness except the precision of the law of sines which Snell added a few years later. For the optical image proper Kepler used the word *imago.* For whatever screen received such an image he used the word *papyrus.* For retinal use he substituted by definition the word *pictura.*[1] Descartes followed, using the word *peinture.*[2] Newton surpassed them both in vividness, describing "the Pictures of Objects lively painted . . . upon that Skin (called the Tunica Retina) with which the Bottom of the Eye is covered."[3] The accompanying psychological view, in Newton's words, was that "these Pictures, propagated by Motion among the Fibres of the Optick Nerves into the Brain, are the cause of Vision."

So much for a great theoretical construction with a little guesswork on the side. As for demonstration and proof, it was Father Christophorus Scheiner in 1625 who first devised an experiment by which he took the

---

[1] *Ad Vitel. Paralip.* (1604), V. 3, Prop. XVII.
[2] *Dioptrique* (1637).
[3] *Opticks* (1704, 1730), Axiom VII.

The Fiction of "Retinal Image"

enucleated eye of an ox, scraped off the rear coatings, properly illuminated an object in front, looked through the eye-preparation, and "saw the image" upon its retina. Descartes, a little later, suggested scraping off the retina as well as the two other "tunics" and substituting a bit of transparent paper or eggshell upon which to "see" the image. Today it is common in medical schools for the instructor in physiology to take an albino eye, such as a rabbit's, scrape it, mount it in a tube, and let his students see things through it. All of which is interesting, but except for showing that the eyeball contains an optical system, reckoned at 58.64 diopters for a schematic eye, it has next to nothing to do with the process of vision in a living organism.

Interrupting this brief historical account for a moment, consider the enormous difference structurally between the retina in life and the retina in death. "During life," says Duke-Elder, the retina "is transparent, but 5 to 10 minutes after death it takes on a mat-white, translucent appearance."[4] "During life," says Polyak, "the retina is almost perfectly transparent, becoming opaque within a few minutes after death."[5] Now while there are well-known uses of the word "image" in which we identify an image as a "fact" located "at" a translucent screen, there is no sense (except a highly technical one of geometrical optics)[6] in which we locate such an image as a "fact" assignable for its location to the transparent medium through which we see it. Looking through the window we report that we see the object, not the image of it; so also when we use our spectacles or a simple microscope.

Inference from the enucleated eye to the living eye is therefore on the face of it unwarranted. This does not, of course, destroy the possibility

---

[4] *Textbook of Ophthalmology* (London, 1932), I, 85.

[5] *The Retina* (Chicago, 1941), p. 3. Shortly following the quoted sentence Polyak proceeds to say that "Physically, the eye may be compared with a dark chamber (*camera obscura*) or a photographic camera, where the screen or the sensitive plate is represented by the retina." Now Polyak is firmly of the opinion (p. 139) that the retina is the locus of the "image . . . formed in the eye" by means of which "external objects" come to "produce subjective reactions." Since, before we are done, "retinal image" will turn out to be just a careless use of words, it is illuminating to see how extremely careless Polyak is, not only in this, but in other respects, in the passages just cited. If the enucleated retina were really "opaque," as he says, then it could yield no image to observers behind it; however this, being merely a slip in phrasing, not in factual intent, needs no criticism. But when he tells us that the retina in life is both transparent and usable as a screen, the matter is serious. Nor does he stop here, for he makes it comparable at one and the same time both to the light-diffusing screen of the *camera obscura* and to the sensitive plate of the photographic camera. Neither the "either . . . or" nor the "both" construction is permissible for the retina we know.

[6] If the glass is normal to the axis of vision, geometry asserts only a "distance" variation of image from object, not one of size or direction; and even here the image is not located "at" the glass. So no help for retinal image comes from this case.

of the factual presence of "retinal image" in life. It does, however, eliminate an analogy — we might say, a rhetorical "image" — and transfer the burden of proof into the field of living vision where it belongs, and where we will direct our further attention.

Many varieties of experiment have been made since Scheiner's time to display or test the image in the enucleated eye. These include Kühne's optograms, Hidano's photographic technique, and recent work by Lashley.[7] The translucent retina may be stained with 4% aluminum potassium sulphate which acts upon the visual purple, or it may be used as a screen for photographs. In most experimentation, however, in order to get good results, the retina is removed and replaced by other substances better for the purpose. All these experiments are made with materials which, we may say, are dug out of the dead body much as raw materials in general are dug out of the ground. They deal with the optical system of the eye — cornea, lens, and humors — and show its action; but they do not deal with the processes of living vision, nor with living retinal tissue at all.

In the early years of the nineteenth century there was a sizable flurry over the retina and various speculations about it were made.[8] Only one single man appears, either then or at any other time so far as my search has been able to go[9], who notes the significant difference between the living and the dead eye as applied to retinal image. This is John Campbell of Carbury.[10] He asserted that it was improper to apply the word "picture" to a collection of rays passing through a transparent medium and asked his readers to say whether they were prepared to see an "image" upon a black screen, when focused light struck it. Campbell drew some fire, but no real attention from his contemporaries or from men since his time. Polyak lists the essay in his bibliography as one he has examined but without remarking on the distinction between life and death. Fifty years later Helmholtz was so sure of the retinal image that he reported on someone else's authority that, under proper lighting arrangements, one could, with the naked eye, sometimes see the image on "the inner side of the retina" of a patient, and "through the sclerotica." On his own authority he said that by use of the ophthalmoscope one could "see clearly not only the retina itself and its blood

---

[7] For Lashley's pictures see *J. Comp. Psychol.*, XIII, 1932, p. 173; and for full references to other experiments, see Polyak, *The Retina*, p. 138.

[8] For references see Polyak, *op. cit.*, p. 138. Full reports are to be found in Gehler's *Physikalisches Wörterbuch*, 1828, iv., pt. 2, p. 1364.

[9] The author of the article in Gehler, *op. cit.*, mentions a certain Mühlbach who wrote a book denying the existence of retinal image, but only to sneer at him without stating his grounds; the book itself has not been available.

[10] *Annals of Philosophy*, X, 1817, p. 17 ff.

vessels but the optical images that are projected on it." In this latter case he put the image " on the surface of the retina." [11]

In recent years a case of momentary hesitation occasionally appears as when Bragg in *The Universe of Light* [12] says that when we say a picture is formed on the retina, " we must not take the statement too literally," and then goes ahead and talks literally about it throughout his book. Occasionally some writer lists a few defects of the retina and then forgets them. Polyak, a true believer, has one of the strongest statements of this kind, for he says that in the vertebrate retina much greater defects than those of the dioptric media and accommodation occur, these being " chiefly the consequence of the peculiar structure of the retina itself." [13]

Recent physiological experimentation has many developments unfavorable to pictorial image, of which a few will be brought together at the close of this paper. Even the word " image " tends to disappear from such work. In examining the symposium *Visual Mechanisms* [14] (though not with attention to this particular point) the word " image " was noted only once, and then in quotation marks. Elsewhere positive optical or physiological terms were used. Bartley indexes " image " only three times, though seven other cases of the use of the word were remarked.[15] A fair idea of a similar changing attitude in optics may be given by early and late citations from Southall, a writer exceptionally careful in expression in this field. In 1918: " The . . . image . . . on the retina . . . is more and more finely executed in towards the center, until at the *fovea centralis* itself the details are exquisitely finished." [16] In 1937: " The eye has all the faults that instruments have in quite a

[11] *Helmholtz's Treatise on Physiological Optics*. Edited by James P. C. Southall (3 v., Menasha, Wis., 1924–25), I, pp. 91–92. The naked eye may have seen Purkinje-Sanson images. Having just invented the ophthalmoscope, Helmholtz appears to have been led away by his enthusiasm. Joseph Le Conte, *Sight* (3d ed., New York, 1895) pp. 25, 29, possibly on Helmholtz's authority says that " the image may be seen in the living eye by means of the ophthalmoscope," and also " If there is no image, no object will be visible . . . therefore the image *must be* a facsimile of the *real* object, for the *apparent* object *will be* a facsimile of the image " (his italics). Reports of observation are extremely rare in the texts, considering how notorious the fact itself is.

[12] (New York, 1933), p. 39.

[13] *Op. cit.*, p. 176. Other indexed remarks on retinal image are on pp. 3, 131, 422–3.

[14] Heinrich Klüver, ed. (Lancaster, Pa., 1942), Vol. VII of *Biological Symposia*, edited by Jacques Cattell.

[15] S. Howard Bartley: *Vision: A Study of its Basis* (Toronto, New York, London, 1941). Many instances of the use of the word undoubtedly escaped notice, but all of those noted could have been replaced by positive optical or physiological expression except one (p. 99) in which he said that the illumination pattern on the retina is a fair copy of the environment. Even this, when closely read, implies no pictorial image, and as against it, he says (p. 333) that the whole system of copy is in doubt.

[16] *Mirrors, Prisms, and Lenses* (New York, 1918). The quotation is from the third edition, 1933, p. 430.

high degree, only, so far from interfering with the keenness of vision it would seem that on the whole these very irregularities are perhaps conducive to that very end." [17]

The discussion thus far yields the following situation:

1. Physiology reports the retina in life to be transparent, and after death translucent.

2. Transparent media do not offer images of the picture type.

3. The translucent post-mortem retina gives information about the optical system of the eyeball, but none as to the living process of the transparent retina.

4. Physiological research into vision has no direct dealings with a picture-image. Even the name "retinal image" as a popular convenience tends to be dropped.

We are now ready for detailed consideration of the *where*, the *what*, the *how good*, and the *good for what* of retinal image. A first group of facts (No. 5–17 *infra*) has to do with the anatomical retina as a locus for image. A second group (No. 19–24) examines the various types of image, and asks which type might find a home on the retina. A third group (No. 25–35) stresses certain of the broader observations of recent physiology.

5. The retina, except at the central fovea, is covered by a network of blood vessels enough to make it look like the red-ink picture of the circulatory system in the old physiology charts; it has a blind spot at the optic disc making a sizable hole in any picture it could produce; it is affected by lachrymal lubrication and much blinking. All this without mentioning astigmatisms, aberrations, accommodation difficulties and phorias. How *good* a picture could be imaged on it? What would you do to your kodak, if you found it working like this? [18]

6. The old upside-downness puzzled inquirers for centuries, until finally they agreed to allow the geniculo-striate system to have a hand in procedure. The points in No. 5 are harder on the retinal image-copy view than upside-downness, and put more work on the cortex (see No. 31 *infra*), thus reducing the presumed independence of the retina in its contribution.

7. Ordinary reference as to retinal image is made to the retina as a

---

[17] *Introduction to Physiological Optics* (London, New York, Toronto, 1937), pp. 25–6.
[18] "The retinal image is blurred," writes Bartley, *op. cit.*, p. 334, "and shall we expect that this 'accident' be compensated for and that by some process the succeeding parts of the optic pathway reform the pattern so that it turns out to be a copy of the object viewed? Shall we not expect such an outcome in the physiological system? This question also has not been answered, although a great many of us assume that there must be a mechanism to resharpen what became blurred."

The Fiction of "Retinal Image"

sort of "entity" with little distinction between fovea and the rest of the retina. Fovea is the area of sharpest vision. It is about 1.5 mm. diameter, subtending an angle at the node of about 1 degree, and recording impressions thus from a very small section indeed of the field of vision. Incidentally, it is thick with cones which are commonly stressed as color-discriminators in current theory. When light is reflected from the area of its cup-shaped depression it is as a small bright spot, not as an "image."[19]

8. The retina has ten layers. We certainly ought to know which contains the image.

9. Rods and cones are at the "back" of the retina as light approaches. To reach them light must pass through the other transparent layers.

10. Rods and cones absorb light; they do not reflect or refract. "Latent" or fixated image (No. 23) might be the result. But who advocates this?

It should be added that no ideally perfect transparency or reflecting is known to physics; that latest researches show a slightly higher transparency for the red wave lengths than for the blue-green, and that the concavity of the fovea can return enough light to look like a white spot, though not like an "image" of something even though the fovea is the high-precision region of the eye.

11. The other layers of the retina contain nuclei, ganglia, radial fibers, and sustaining membranes. Will these give a seat to the "image"? Or will the nerve fibers running laterally toward the disc yield an image? In their full presence at the disc what they yield is the blind spot.

12. If image rests in such regions (No. 11), how will it get to rods and cones, or into the visual system at all?

13. Rod receptivity, so far as our best knowledge goes,[20] is by single quanta of energy to single rods. Similar action seems probable as to cones. This corresponds as neatly to the punctate patterns of geometrical optics as does "image" — indeed, much more neatly. Assume an appreciable amount of unabsorbed light available for reflection or re-

---

[19] This report on reflection is not inconsistent with points #1 and #2, nor with the remark as to absorption in #10. "Perfect" or 100% reflection, refraction, or absorption is unknown to inquiry, but only dominant quantities of one or the other. Scattered light from the most strongly illuminated portion of the retina has been studied at length by Bartley (*op. cit.*, pp. 58 ff.). Whether reflection and scattering is from retina proper or mainly from the *retina-choroid* region I have not seen stated. Hecht finds that only about 10% of the energy that enters at the cornea reaches the rods and cones for absorption. *Visual Mechanisms*, 13.

[20] This is for low visibility only, according to Hecht. If the ratio of combined rods and cones to ganglion cells is 1 to 130 (Polyak), this might give small picture set-ups "within retina."

fraction, yielding a sort of residual image, what sort of picture would these independently punctate light impacts form, just as they occur at the retina?

14. Polyak's remark, previously cited, as to the structural inadequacy of the retina [21] should be kept in mind in appraising these questions, and likewise Bartley's conclusion that the retinal image is not a perfect copy but a blur, and that the whole copy system is breaking down.[22]

15. Image plane is normal to the axis of vision, but the retina curves like the inner surface of a hollow sphere. The geometer can operate with small tangential areas, but what price image in the copy sense with small image-bits spread around like eyes in a fly?

16. Three-dimensional objects are represented in the presumptive retinal image as two-dimensional projections, which means that retinal image at its best falls one dimension short of being the pure copy it pretends to be.[23]

17. Granting, despite all the above difficulties, a worth-while picture on the rods and cones, what happens to it in the many types of cells within the retina itself? Could spatial coherence in the form of image be retained in the nerve fibers as they go along? How would the case stand at the switchtrack of the optical chiasma, where right and left cars are brought together for passage to right and left lobes of the brain? How about the double dealings in the cortex?

So much for examination of the *where, what,* and *how good* of a putative retinal image, carried on from the point of view of retinal structure. Certain of these points seem sufficient, each by itself, to dispose of retinal image as a possible fact. Others make such a heavy case against its assumed efficiency in its own right that to the geniculo-striate regions fall heavy burdens in making vision come true — far heavier than " retinal image " can reputably allow. The whole situation is one of such confusion that we are justified in pausing long enough to insert a simple scientific norm to which all inquiry subscribes:

18. Basic terms in research demand sharp specification if they are to remain basic. Vague terms mean uncertain facts. So vague is the term " retinal image " that it is little more than a linguistic blur-circle, and it is high time that a sharply focused terminology should be introduced to replace it.

Let us now transfer our inquiry from the point of view of the anatomi-

[21] *Op. cit.*, p. 176.
[22] *Op. cit.*, p. 333.
[23] True believers have endeavored every now and then to work out a three-dimensional image in the eye. They, like their literal-minded friends who try to plot the image at chiasma or brain, are famed only for failure.

cal retina to that of the various types of image-facts all stitched together by the word "image." We may begin by listing the main types of application of the word. We may be sure that retinal image should belong to one of these types, unless either (a) it can establish itself as a type of its own, or (b) someone can exhibit a type which is overlooked in the list to follow.

19. The pertinent types of image (omitting topological, electrical, rhetorical, and sundry others) are:[24]

A. The image of geometrical optics

B. Physical image; focused light at plane

C. Image or after-image as physiologically established in electro-chemical waves through the retino-cortical system

D. "Latent" image in the sense of chemical fixation

E. Enscreenments: images visible on screens as in the pin-hole camera, *camera obscura,* movie projector, or ground-glass plate in a photographic camera

F. Sharp reflections: as the image from a plane mirror

G. Embodiments: physically durable images such as sculpture, painting, or photograph

H. Images in the subjective-mental sense of psychology, such as percepts, eidetic images, memory images, or concepts.

RI. The *presumptive* retinal image may be added here, and spoken of as RI to shorten phrasing in the comparisons to follow.

The make-up of RI involves implication or application of all the forms A to H at one stage or another of its confused presentation. It itself, however, is none of them. Certain of them can be discarded at a moment's inspection, while others require closer examination. For completeness we will run over them all. Vital to the whole issue is the status of Image "A." Here is involved the relationship of mathematics to fact, one of the most complexly difficult of modern inquiries.[25] We shall not here indulge in "philosophy," nor in any of the logicians' subtleties, but shall put the immediate case of the two types of images, the geometrical A and the retinal RI, as concretely as we can on the table in front of us.

20. The image of geometrical optics, A, is a "symbol" of a particular

---

[24] For consideration of related issues, enlargement and justification of this classification see my collateral paper "Image Terminology in Optics," yet to be published.

[25] Consider Whitehead and Russell, *Principia Mathematica,* the many rival "logics" of mathematics, the various recent "non-Aristotelian" logics, the syntactics of Carnap and his group of logical positivists, and the semantics of Korzybski. In contrast with all of these, as substituting a firm behavioral naturalistic foundation in place of the old superficial psychologies, stands John Dewey's *Logic, The Theory of Inquiry* (New York, 1938) with which the present writer's *Linguistic Analysis of Mathematics* (Bloomington, Ind., 1932), and his more recent linguistic essays, may be associated.

status within a symbolic system of "rays." It is an "object of" or a "formulation of" such a system. It is *not* the "name" of a "fact" outside that system, nor does it in any way guarantee that the retinal facts, which it so powerfully helps us to understand, are of the form RI.

In illustration of the relationship of symbol to fact consider the natural numbers, 1, 2, 3 . . . in full inductive system as symbols. We could not get along without them, yet in our daily use they do not name facts such as one-ness, two-ness, three-ness. The most powerful effort to use such symbols for names collapsed when infinitesimals were abandoned as intelligible features of the calculus. Compare with them the status of image A. Geometrical optics has adopted a simple form of projective geometry, that of collineal optical spaces, to secure dependable development. Full reversibility as between object-space and image-space is asserted, and this means that neither a factual object nor a factual image is a component of it but that it is fully symbolical. It employs, always symbolically, rays, direction indicators, position letters, indices of refraction, light sources, and images, under an elaborate postulation (if one works it out in full) adapting it to certain uses in dealing with light phenomena, but notably excluding diffraction. When geometrical optics was first built up in terms of "rays," the light-ray was assumed to be factual. Today the word "ray" is a specification for three or four essential elements of the postulation employed. Nobody thinks of calling it itself a "fact." Most often it is spoken of as a "path" of light, but it is not even that; it is a symbol for a path — a symbol for a characteristic form of energy-transfer. Now image A is built up in terms of "rays." If rays are not facts, how can images be facts in their own right, or guarantors of other facts in any one specific form? Consider it more concretely still. Images do not require screens to receive them; they do not require eyes to see them; they do not even require the lines drawn on paper for their demonstration to be factually true to them; symbolic precision, not factual, is what they present; they are, in short, in no sense pictorial; their operative value is of a different, and much more efficient, character.

Let the reader whose main reliance for RI's factual existence rests in Image A ask himself: Does A guarantee image in the factual sense, if the light whose course it symbolizes falls on a black screen? or on transparent glass? or on the eye of a blind man? or if its energy is subliminal? Not even physical image B, which optical image A symbolizes, can do this. Whatever happens on the retina must be factually investigated as it factually is.

If this much is clear — if we can get it firmly into our heads that facts are what we are seeking — we can then go ahead to consider the remaining image-types, B to H, with respect to their possible use as patterns or models for RI.

21. The physical image, B, will not serve as a model (1) because we know almost nothing as to what light itself factually " is "; (2) because it is not itself pictorial, and if that characteristic is allotted to it, this can only be by inference from other image-types; (3) because for all present optical purposes it is represented by A; (4) because it involves diffraction, and the possibilities of diffraction-images are sometimes startlingly different from those of geometrical images; finally (5) because its status as predecessor in time of RI can assure the actual status of RI only when proof is given.

22. Physiology is developing a type of image, C (if it should be called image at all — see No. 31) which is definitely not of the pictorial RI type. It is in terms of electric waves, chemically initiated through visual purple reception of light quanta. After-image, which formerly was a sort of small brother of the more pretentious subjective images, H, is entering physiologically, but still uncertainly, whether retinal, cortical, or in part each. After-image may move as the head turns but that does not make it of the H-type; it is rather after-effect, and how far retinal remains to be demonstrated. The topic cannot be gone into here, but the indications are that current retino-cortical researches in wave form will break down entirely both the H and the RI forms of image. (See No. 26 to No. 36.)

23. The " latent " image (D) of photography seems plausible at first sight as a model for RI, but not on examination. Vision process on the retina is swift; photography relatively slow. The former is in electrical waves, the latter is chemical; the former is transitory, the latter seeks fixation. Vision corrects itself; a plate falsely affected is ruined. No prints can be taken from the living retina. The analogy, such as it is, is again with dead materials, not with living vision.

24. Enscreenments (E), pictures on the wall, are what, in the great majority of cases, the believer in retinal image has most vividly in mind. They are, however, impossible analogies. An enscreenment requires basically three items: a light-giving object, a light-receiving screen, and a seeing-eye, all in operation together.[26] It requires, indeed, two other components, the light-energy in transit, and the selection of " the " image out of the entire field of retinal stimulation (see No. 30). Giving atten-

[26] No philosophical subtlety is involved here, and no issues of reality. The remark is matter-of-fact that the imaged object, the imaging object, and the eye to receive the reflected light are all involved in the screen-image fact.

tion at this point only to the screen and the seeing eye, and assuming the possibility of some sort of effect of retina as screen upon a seeing eye, despite its transparency (No. 1-2-3 and footnote No. 5), we may consider the two cases of viewing from behind and viewing from in front. Diffuse reflection from a screen is required in the latter case, and what may be called translucent diffusion in the former.

The only observer from behind is the person, mind, or brain of the organism. In older days it was common to speak of the mind (or the brain) as actually seeing the image on the organism's own retina. But seeing is a process accomplished with retinal activity. Set the retinal image aside as the thing to be seen; then, if it is located *on* the retina, the retina is set aside at the same time. This requires a retina-less eye to see the image — a statement so absurd from a factual point of view that it is today rarely made explicitly, though something of the kind is still often implied. We have the further absurdity that if the mind or brain saw its own retina it would manifestly see nothing else in the world, unless some magic power were in use, to see or see through at will, and to see a central selected image or not at will.

As for observation from in front by some other person, we have a very few old reports that it can be done, and for the rest blank silence despite this being the one evidence that would effectively count. We know that the *macula lutea* is seen by the observer with a slightly yellowish cast, and that the fovea gathers enough reflected light to appear a white spot. Purkinje-Sanson reflections are found from several spots, but they are not retinal. Even if a retinal image could be seen, it would apparently be an irrelevant by-product to the vision of its owner-eye (No. 12). The whole question of what we see and where we see it in the cases of images and objects is complex (consider spectacles, simple microscopes, compound microscopes, and a variety of telescopes, as well as different kinds of screens) but need not be gone into here, as the next point, in regard to mirrors, will give sufficient illustration.

25. The mirror-image (F) will not serve as a model. " Seeing an image in a mirror " is a convention of speech much like " bowels of mercy," " my heart aches," " I'm on fire with joy." It is nothing more. Popular speech says the image is " in " the mirror. Geometrical optics determines a technical optical image at assigned distance and angle " behind " the mirror. *What* one sees via the mirror is, however, the object *just as truly as* when one looks straight at it. The sharp bending of the rays at the reflecting surface of the mirror is not an act of creation by which a new " thing " (such as an " image ") is created. If the mirror shows someone coming from behind to tickle you while shaving, you don't

dodge the image; you dodge "someone." Which is the proof of that pudding. Decisive factually is the direct energy-transfer from object to eye via mirror surface. This is "fact." The so-called "image," whether at or behind a mirror, transfers no energy, and would be of no service in vision, even if an image of such a type could properly be said actually to "exist" in the eye.

25a. Physical embodiments, G, are out of the question, unless one thinks of little particles of matter entering the eye, in place of light.

25b. The subjective image, H, is equally out of question. It is a sort of fixation at one end of the traditional visual scheme as items like G are at the other. Anyway it is excluded because, as the putative successor of RI, it cannot be allowed to read its own characteristics back into the very RI which it then turns around and uses as a main element in the explanation of its own presence. Even in its crudest form RI is too respectable to admit anything like that.

We have now accumulated evidence against presumptive retinal image (RI) both with respect to "retina" and with respect to "image." No one has ever tried to be precise as to *where* on the retina the image could have a place. Living retinas lack the characteristics of image-housing substances. Among the many types of phenomena covered by the word "image" none has the characteristics of what an RI must be. And if, by any chance, some type of image *sui generis* has a home on the retina, the evidence is that it would be as inefficient compared with actual living vision as a broken-down juke box in a dive is in comparison with the Philharmonic Orchestra at tops. RI remains with about the same status with respect to the physiology of vision that signs of the Zodiac have for astronomy — an interesting relic of the fumbling-feeling of the past — nothing to make maps of or write books about today.

Let us next list certain newer viewpoints which enable us to get a broader view of what "image in vision" in real life must be. After this a word about the psychological status of image, and a mention of a few confirmatory details in recent laboratory research, must suffice to close an essay already too long.

26. The field of vision is wide. The retina receives light impact from all of it, or it would not be the field of vision. If there is "image" in a direct object-image sense, then "image" is the whole field of vision.[27]

27. RI, as we have examined it, presents something very different from this. It presents a central picture. When "boy sees girl" the RI is of "girl." How is one to explain this?

28. If RI is *basic* to vision, is it girl that makes RI? Or is it RI that

[27] Bartley, *op. cit.*, pp. 57, 99, suggests this.

makes girl — interesting? Either answer is kindergarten talk, or rather as a mess of verbal pottage, it is as much worse than kindergarten talk as domestic, political, or economic treachery in war is worse than the enemy.

(I am putting each little point here separately so that it can be examined, and approved or rejected, for itself alone; and not stewed to nothing in a witch's caldron of words.)

29. Science often, and almost as a rule, gets names that cover too much territory. "Cosmic rays" enter; they are sought even; they may be this, that, or the other; or a little of each. Science finds out. RI is a primitive naming. It names a region of phenomena to be inquired into; and not a reality to be guarded to the death. (Cf. No. 18).

30. What all this comes to is that *selection* goes on in the process of vision. Vision is focused on centers of attention.[28] What kind of selection works (even if one wants to speak of "a selector") is something to be established in fact.

31. Is it not, on this showing, the full retino-cortical system — not only retina but geniculo-striate as well — that is the locus of this process of selective seeing — and hence, if we still use the name, *the locus of image as well?* The retina, all the authorities agree, is peculiarly a brain component, embryologically and in adult structure too.[29]

32. The retinal receptivity of specific light-points is retained in this view; the manners and extents of organization in the visual paths and in the cortex are open to free investigation, no longer as a scheme of picture-transportation, but of living organic process.

33. Here retino-cortical system is not picked out and severed from organism. If we wish "image" it locates it; but only insofar as the retino-cortical system is a component of a behavioral-environmental process.

34. Is not the actuality of the processes listed in No. 26 to No. 33 the reason for the rapid disappearance of the word "image" from laboratory reports (see No. 4)?

35. Do not the observations of the full field of vision (No. 26) and of the full retino-cortical system (No. 31) belong coherently together in construction?[30]

36. The answer to our fourth query about RI is contained in these last points. It not only has no *where* and no *what*, and if it had them could have no *good* quality, but it is *no good* for research.

[28] Sharp differences of intensity of light may reduce portions of the field and give promise to others just as too great intensity may destroy them.
[29] Polyak, *The Retina*, p. 3; Bartley, *Vision*, p. 81.
[30] From the present point of view by far the best discussion of visual organization the writer has found is that of Lashley in *Visual Mechanisms*, pp. 301–22.

The Fiction of "Retinal Image"

A word now on the psychological status of RI.

37. The presumptive retinal image (RI) is a survival from the behavioral mythology of the past; this being akin to, but not the same as, the cosmic mythologies, which are now departed into the realm of curiosities. The myth of mental substance is gone; but the myth of little fragments of mental substance, each supported by a little fragment of brain or ganglion, remains. The inner image, mental or neural, still opposes the outer object as of a different realm, as the subjective does the objective. To handle this procedure a fictitious construction of something that sits on the skin (or nerve-tips — the construction is vaguely either or both) intervenes and has been historically dominant. Descartes knew better and said so (although he accepted RI in vision), but the modern researcher, in many cases, does not yet know better. Dewey, however, distinguished the construct in 1896.[31] The procedure indicated in No. 35 permits visual process to be isolated as a whole from diffuse reflection (at the "object") through light-energy-transfer, into retina-cortical resonances as one complete functional presentation. "Image" and "object" and "mind" as separate existences cancel out, and we have the great factual determination of William James — his neutral datum — directly before us for research.[32] This bare mention of the newer point of view must suffice here, its development to be made elsewhere.[33]

The following details of recent inquiry that have come to attention may be suggestive to persons who may desire to assemble such developments and appraise them connectedly.

38. Much less use of the "subjective" as a name for phenomena is found in recent reports. It is no longer structural, but a verbal resort for mentioning uninvestigated phases. In Bartley's *Vision* I note expression of doubt about the "copy" system, recognition that sensation itself is dependent to some extent on central system, and is patterned by the nervous system. Objects are not dependent on contours (the sharp stationary tending to lose contour). (This is emphatic against the retinal image theory.) The stray light in the eyeball from central retinal illumination has gained significance, also the non-focused alongside the focused.

Consider the many studies on the revamping of first retinal stimula-

---

[31] "The Reflex Arc Concept in Psychology," *Psychological Review*, III, July, 1896, pp. 357-70.
[32] See Chapter 14 above.
[33] [See John Dewey and Arthur F. Bentley, *Knowing and the Known* (Boston, 1949), p. 103 ff.]

tion, in bipolars, ganglia, and along the rest of the optic pathway. Some of these are becoming definite, as with respect to flicker. Inquiry is advancing as to initial independence at rods and cones, and as to possible point-to-point correlations between retina and cortex. Marshall and Talbot stress the expanding cylinder effect from retina to cortex as 1:10,000 in area ratio, and assert that rigidities between retina and cortex are impossible. Lashley stresses very strongly the resonance of multiple connections in the cortex, abandons " stimulus equivalence " for a more efficient phrase " equivalent nervous connections," says nothing is known of topographic projection upon cortex, and (very important) develops an analysis of the sensory and motor interplay. [See H. Klüver, ed., *Visual Mechanisms.*]

The study of retinal after-effects in part interpreted as after-images, still leaving some after-image phenomena as central in sense memory-image, is very significant. Another point is alternations of response in cells with recovery and renewed participation. The whole business of interactions and isolation at retina is under examination and the very question-raising is unfavorable to " image."

(*The above to be checked and limited to matter which can be definitely shown to be applicable.*)

SUMMARY AND TENTATIVE CONCLUSIONS

Another listing of points of approach, made at a later date than the above, follows:

1. No image on the retina can be observed, and none can be justified as assumption.

2. A sharp differentiation between physical and physiological components on the sentimental basis of inanimate and animate is (on the basis of wave-trains) no longer justified.

3. Where should one draw the distinction between organism and environment? At the cornea or at the retina?

4. The physical-physiological train runs from the light-source through the retino-cortical system, with small energy.

5. Many other physical-physiological trains run with cortical, spinal, and ganglionic routings.

6. Destroy the image-isolation and we have left the cortical psychological-mental image versus the outer thing.

7. But we do not start with thing — we start with light-source. We should not wind up with thing at far end (mental or cortical) but with light-events.

The Fiction of "Retinal Image" 285

8. The physical-neural (more specific for physical-physiological) should not be laid off against the image, but against the light-event all the way through as one train.

9. What we get is not a seeing, plus a percept, plus an object, but the seeing-effect; and this not as sensation but as thing-seen, seeing-experience, this-seeing-effect.

10. This is substantially in the vision field the Jamesian Datum.

11. For further study we differentiate between organism and environment, taking them in mutual interaction.

12. We do not, however, take the organism and environment as if we could know about them separately in advance of our special inquiry,[34] but we take their interaction itself as subjectmatter of study. We name this *transaction* to differentiate it from interaction. We inspect the thing-seen not as the operation of an organism upon an environment nor as the operation of an environment upon organism, but as itself an event.

13. To get object and organism separately, we must combine not merely the visual transaction, but also all other relevant transactions (smell, sense, hearing, touch are typical names). Handling and moving operations are most significant; the on-going-organism-in-environment (a) as a build-up out of our physical-physiological trains, and (b) as a complex with respect to which we can orient the single train (whole organism, in the vernacular). Also a specialized handling operation, the verbal, enters, which *must* be taken into account as a phase of the on-going-living process.

[34] This being J. R. Kantor's way.

CHAPTER SIXTEEN

Logic and Logical Behavior[*]

POSTSCRIPT AS PREFACE

This essay was commenced under a three-word title, *Nature and Logic*, which, in the expanded phrasing given it toward the end of Section I, posed a query as to " the status of the processes of logic themselves as facts in life and in nature." It proceeded with successive changes yielding more specific forms of headings, and ended with one directing attention upon a manner of differentiation between Logic as Inquiry, and logical behaviors as the subjectmatters inquired into. There was, in other words, an increase in definiteness. Since even a slight change in definiteness is of value in the regions in which the background problems of logic, the sciences, and mathematics are considered together, I mention it. This outcome, if it proves to be a step in the right direction, should be credited to the postulation in use, within the range of which I have attempted to hold steady the treatment of all logical fact.

Far from giving factual denial to contrasting views, these postulates do not even assert *themselves* as having factual values. They enter simply as working tools with which we may experiment, and which will be appraised in the end solely in accord with whatever service or disservice they may render. Among them we may stress:

1. The living of organisms on earth is found under way as activity or process within a setting of physical processes such that, however vast may be the hopes we nourish for increased future learning about living, we have no need today to look outside of the ranges of this physical setting for interpretive constructions.

2. All of men's knowings are found as activities among the other activities of the living organism, and this in a way such that, however vast may be the hopes we nourish for increased future learning about know-

[*] Ms. essay, dated June 27, 1949. This essay remains about three-quarters finished. It states the problem and indicates the answer, but does not attain the necessary development which would give the maximum precision to the author's ideas. But this essay is regarded by the editor as being so important in carrying forward the central insights of Bentley and Dewey that he deems it worth publishing even in this imperfect state.

ings, we have no need today to look for interpretive constructions outside of the ranges of the physical, physiological, and ecological.

3. All of our knowns, including the physical, physiological, and behavioral facts, together with all our knowings as themselves facts known to us, are established by way of the processes of their being known, and as aspects or phases of the processes of knowings and knowns, and are not to be treated as if possessing or guaranteeing to possess some manner of " existing " in independence of these processes. Our knowns are thus always before us " as known to us men of today," and with the knowings themselves components of the system of the knowns.

4. More generally: What we know as fact, or by way of oncoming or departing fact, we know subject to its being known. Our knowing as itself fact is itself so subject. The cosmos of our knowing reports our knowings themselves as among its knowns.

5. To take these postulates as in any way involving metaphysical, cosmological, or epistemological issues would be to destroy them before using them.

I

THE SITUATION OF INQUIRY

For several years I have been privileged to work in co-operation with John Dewey in an examination of certain issues involved in that ancient region of verbal entanglement known as " the problem of knowledge." Upon this work we have recently made report in a book, *Knowing and the Known*. Our approach departed from both the philosophical-epistemological viewpoint and from the viewpoint of the behaviorists. It was made, instead, with special attention to the scientific research of the last generation as this has remodeled the status of its identification of " fact," or, more accurately let us say, of " fact for science." We were influenced not so much by any of the specific discoveries the sciences have made in their more favored fields, the physical and the physiological, as by the possibilities for employing the newer standards secured through exploration in these favored fields toward securing an increased efficiency of factual determination within our own.

Characteristic of the scientific advance of the past generation in physical fields has been the dethronement of the " particle," with its interplay of actions and reactions, from the basically unchallenged status it had held in Newtonian procedure for over two hundred years. Characteristic also, and much more sensational in running discussion, though perhaps less radical for future construction, has been the displacement of the authoritarian Newtonian " formal " or " absolute " space and time, and the insistence that these ancient dictators shall now enter democratically into the observation and system of things-known, where their status is comparable with that of other subjectmatters of open inquiry. The new powers of observation, their widened ranges, and the abandonment of the rigidities of the traditionally accepted namings of components such as particle, space, and time, after they had outlived their day of usefulness in their ancient forms — these are the characteristics of method and appraisal in modern science which are taken as significant by us here. They are, likewise, though not so prominently, characteristic in the great forward swing of the most recent physiological inquiries.

It is just these characteristics that are deficient in most current inquiries into the problems of knowledge. The field here is dominated by authoritarian standards and verbal survivals from the past — and often from an ancient past. It is rarely treated as if open to direct inquiry under factual observation approximating the scientific type. What is true of the theory of knowledge, including its regnant manifestations in the logics, is true also in great measure for all those psychological and cultural inquiries within the range of which research into knowledge proceeds. The unquestioned use of ancient namings, the easygoing display of purported observations in terms of such namings, and the great difficulties faced in every attempt to break through the verbal crust to more adequate identifications, are all well known, though their effect in deflecting the attention to irrelevant and obstructive procedures does not seem so well understood.

The strongest evidence of this is the lack of any dependable terminology, even in the most intensively cultivated portions of the field — those varied inquiries currently known as psychology. Except in the most backward regions where the old traditions in the use of the specialized terminology of an actively dominating " self " survive, a terminology of stimulus-response is at the forefront, with the word " stimulus " having pretenses to as prominent a place in psychology as the word " particle " once held in Newtonian mechanics. Yet whether the " stimulus " is to be regarded as an object, as a " property " of an object, or as an " energy " capable of detached envisionment, is everywhere unclear. Whether the stimulus is to be described in terms of sense-impingement upon bodily integument, or to be developed with respect to the higher neural centers; and what gradations of structure it is assumed to present in correspondence with levels of neural organization and with variations of environmental participation — for no part of this whatever is firm phrasing available in psychological description and construction today.

Indeed, only one group of workers, those of "Gestalt," may be said to make determined effort.[1] A huge waste of manpower results from this lack of firm terminology in communication between individuals, and between the various "schools," "sects," and "isms" that still appear in these branches of inquiry.

One of the surprising features of the situation is that psychologists commonly refuse to have anything of significance to do with the theories of knowledge. Epistemologists and metaphysicians dislike modern psychology, and psychologists return the dislike with interest. Certainly, nevertheless, the processes of knowings and those of stimulations are deeply connected in the life of the organism. On the one hand, psychology, like any other science, is a branch of knowledge; no more than any other science can it free itself from the implications of this fact. Knowledge processes, on the other hand, have their locus among those very forms of animal life, human and other, whose behaviors are psychology's own primary subjectmatter. Yet if one attempts to consider the connections of these two inquiries, or to appraise the possible contributions of either to the other, it quickly appears that the psychologist insists on tossing all his problems of this sort, as fast as they appear, to the metaphysician or epistemologist like scraps from his table, and, at that, with pronounced expressions of disrespect; while specialists in the theory of knowledge much prefer the use of their own familiar psychological reference points, verbalisms though they are for the most part, to any that psychology as a would-be science is bringing them today. Neither helps the other. Either wishes from the other only the boon of non-interference.

The result of this for Logic — if logic is in any proper sense to rank as a form of guidance for and within knowledge — is to leave it in worse position than is either psychology or knowledge theory. Its atmosphere becomes so rarefied that it is apt to regard itself as living a rarefied life of its own. It comes to feel itself as distinct and superior to that world of nature about which nevertheless it hopes to affirm and even to guarantee perfect "truth"; while the logical "entities" it produces often seem to it far superior to either the "physical" or the "mental" "entities" it accepts as if ready-made.

It is in the face of such a situation, both with respect to the new status of inquiry in other fields, and to the strange dismemberment of inquiry in the case of knowledge, that I propound the question as to the status

---

[1] The extreme vagueness of "stimulus" is best displayed in the argument between Lashley and Hull over what Pavlov was talking about (*Psychological Review*, Vol. 53, p. 72; Vol. 54, p. 120).

of the process of logic itself as a fact in life and nature. In asking this question I shall consider logic as a report upon the most efficient procedure the world, through the men in it, has yet developed for appraisal and maintenance of balance in its more complex inquiries, such as are found in the recent rapid upward spiraling called "scientific," of all our knowings.

The issue here in no way involves a question as to the precedence of logic over psychology, nor one as to the precedence of psychology over logic. Upon this point I desire to take most emphatic personal stand, since the issues lie in a region of luxuriously thriving misinterpretation. I would no more permit my own work to toss logic into a psychologist's den, whether he be a behaviorist or any other kind of programist, than I would tolerate a task force of logicians striving to enmesh psychology in a verbal net of their own handiwork, with no matter what logical guarantees attached. The problem, as I see it, is one of forward work, not one of backward-looking, or currently conventional, enchainment.

II

The Postulation of Knower in Nature

Since logic is to be taken as process of knowledge, it is wise to open the way, before closing in upon the issues of *Logic* and nature, by considering the broader processes of *knowledge* and nature. We begin by posing the questions: "In inquiries into knowledge can we assume that man as the knower is a part of the world as it is known? Can we hold steadily to such an assumption throughout our inquiry? Can we make it cover *all* of man's knowings along with his lesser behaviors and his physiological and physical processes? Can we employ it as assumption free from prejudicial beliefs pro or con? Can we, that is, so establish this assumption that we can extract its possible usefulness, and let its maintenance, apart from this particular place in inquiry, stand or fall with the value of the results it brings us?"

A comparable assumption has become normal, when it is offered as basis for inquiry into the *organism* physically and physiologically, ever since the days of Darwin and Wallace. There is, further, little obstacle offered to it when made for the study of behaviors of organisms in their lower ranges, nor even to carrying it so high as the processes of human speech, including namings and everyday factual determinations. Beyond this, however, runs the question: "Will the assumption prove usable when one undertakes to bring under it all the outgrowths of linguistic and interpreting behavior — all our knowings, all our knowns, and all their linkages?" Not speculation but inquiry is what is here involved; and manifestly those issues which since Kant's time have been appraised under use of the names " *a priori* " and " analytic " are at the heart of the problem.

The wording of this question as provisionally set down above, namely, whether man may be taken as " part of his world as it is known," is full of obscurities. The word " inquiries," " knowledge," " assume," " world," and " man," so far as our present application of them goes, suggest merely a general region of inquiry, without stress on any particular issue of construction. Since not so stressed, they may here be given provisional tolerance as not definitely and immediately treacherous, and with them the six or eight connectives employed in the sentences. All these words must be understood, however, as leaving the way open for anyone who finds them harmful as here used to put forth his accusation and gain for it a hearing. The active spots of danger in the question as formulated lie in the " knower " and " part." If the " knower " is taken in traditional psychic detachment, or if the " part " is taken to apply to the " knower," even when he is naturalistically viewed, in a way that makes him a detachable component (perhaps as individualized " emergent ") under some form of mechanistic or other inter-actional procedure, then the question posed is judged in advance, and adjudged unfavorably. For present purposes the words " knower " and " part " are to be so taken that the answer remains open in either direction, and that neither of the imposed treatments is dragged in by the wording alone.

Given this much preliminary clarification of the phrasing, our question may now be changed to read: " In inquiries into human knowledge, may we, under an assumption deemed useful as a guide to our further investigation, and solely as assumption, bring the man as knowing, together with his known world, into a common system of observation, description, and interpretation, with the understanding that the word ' system ' here introduces no restriction on the investigation, but that instead the characteristics of such system, if indeed any system at all is found to be present, are exactly what is to be investigated? "

I shall make this assumption, and shall proceed to outline certain steps which, I believe, are indicative of the progress that may be secured through its use. If a favorable answer is given for knowings generally, then the status of logic as a phase of knowing can more readily be appraised.

Let us take the word Nature as a name for the world in course of being known. Cosmos and Fact will be synonymous with it.[2] Let us take the word Logic as a name for certain critical procedures of appraisal in the upper reaches of the knowings. If full natural system for the inquiry is assumed, then the knowing man is studied as present — or, let us say, as himself under way as a " knower," or locus of knowing — in the system of nature, while at the same time nature is to be studied as it is found under way of being to him known. The study in both ranges — both as respects the knowing and the being known — is taken as in process. Moreover, both the study and the studied are taken as in growth. No " ulterior reality " is predicted as to our knowledge here and now involved in these expressions, either on the side of the knowing or on that of the known. Presence as timelessly instantaneous, rather than in durations, is not implied in any of them. Durations and extensions alike are taken as involved both in knowings and in knowns. " Existence " when studied is existence in and to the system, and not outside or beyond it.

This is the postulation. It is the " system " concerning which our question is asked. It is presented as one particular possible guide to experimentation and research, and that is all. " Things " are themselves events, and events, under this assumption, enter full-bodied in time as well as in space. They are not regarded as capable of introduction into research as spaceless; no more are they regarded as capable of introduction as timeless. These remarks neither apply in support, nor toward the rejection, of the proposed postulation; they merely set it out more fully — describe it a little better — but leave it as postulation still. More particularly the postulation no more denies than it asserts the existent unitary person, whether he is offered as spirit, soul, classic mind, emergent mentality, or cortical actor-manager. The question is simply one as to the type of procedure that may be expected to be most productive in a search for soundly usable knowledge about knowledge.

III

Indicated Scientific Justification

The scientific justification for experimental construction on these lines — justification in terms of the methods and of the appraisal of scientific outcomes as mentioned in the opening paragraphs of this paper — needs only the briefest further statement, since it should be fully known already to probably every reader, and especially since, for our purposes, we treat

[2] Any apparent obscurity in the terminology here employed can be checked through the index of the book mentioned in the opening paragraph of Part I of this paper.

it as *permissive only,* with no claim whatever that from it we secure positive support. The nineteenth century marked the disappearance of belief in created " kinds " of animals in fixed Linnaean species, and this was followed by the quick abandonment of the old imagined gap between man and the other animals. The living organism had thus been brought, for purposes of research, basically within nature. Einstein's work, resting in Maxwell's, brought, as was said before, space and time alike into system with other facts of nature, and opened them up to new methods of observation. Most vividly " nature " now became framed in man's behavioral activity, and this as comprehensively as man in the two preceding generations had come to be framed in nature. Wave presentations developed usefulness in ever-fresh respects running beyond particle presentation. Gravitation became *describable,* instead of being viewed as a forceful power behind the scenes. Uncertainties found their places alongside the older presumptive certainties. A universe under expansion or other evolving became as reasonable to the physicist — or tentatively so — as a universe in fixation with merely minor alterations permitted. Milne's alternative time-scales now give fascinating suggestions as to the possible variety of aspects of such a universe in growth.

The bare reference to these facts of development would seem to be enough to justify us in saying that if all of man but his knowings is already under inquiry in one great system along with the facts he knows, then his knowings themselves should have fair reason to be studied in that same system. Even if the appearance of man in the world as its knower, with the world at the same time entering as his known, should be a bit startling at first glimpse, the familiarity we now permit ourselves with the transformed appearance of the physical world should encourage us in anticipating that it would not take us long to settle down on a changed basis in our view of our own sphere of inquiry — provided, of course, always and emphatically, that the fruit of this particular tree of knowledge turns out to be sound.

For such a system of man in nature, with all of the knowings and the knowns included, we may say of the full subjectmatter: (1) that it permits *concrete* approach and development; (2) that it is presumptively throughout *observable* (whether or not we can achieve adequate observation at as early a stage in inquiry as we might wish), and (3) that as observable it is open to *description* in connected development throughout. These three statements are neither outgrowth nor supports of the chosen assumption; they are again merely phases of its presentation. The particulate " physical " and the particulate " psychical," where construed in radical contrast, are here pushed firmly to one side and held there, while we proceed to discover whether the amount of organization we know to be present between them, under whatever point of view they have been examined in the past, is now sufficient to justify inquiry into them under assumption of full system between them as they are now becoming better known.

IV

THE SUNDERED AND THE CONJOINED

Our concern is with Logic. But let us repeat: If logic is a phase of knowledge, it is wise to know what it is that we are taking to be knowledge or, perhaps, that we take knowledge to be, before going too far. And if our treatment of knowledge is to be under express postulation, it is wise to make that postulation as clear as possible, as early in our procedure as possible, which is what we are endeavoring to do.

Consider now a concrete case of a knowing and an accompanying known, first stripping away as best we can all the looser generalities which the word " knowledge " commonly drags in its train. Consider (a) a star — the kind that twinkles not with its toes but overhead — taken as an existence apart from any and all of our knowings of it; (b) take the " star " as seen, named, studied, described, and assigned factual status in company with other seeings and describings; (c) take the man-organism's active seeing, naming, studying, describing, with pens and paper, telescopes and spectroscopes at work, as well as with eyes, ears, hands, and voices; (d) take the " person who knows " — the " knower " — considered as an existent individual in particulate separateness from all his knowings, and perhaps even from all other knowers. We at once see that the separations (a) and (d) under our postulation have little claim, and no right, to entry. They are not introduced under any of the characterizations: duration, extension, concreteness, observability, and describability. They lie, indeed, in their own sense " beyond " all of these. Is there anything at all in the range of actual knowings and knowns that we miss by omitting them? Centering on describability as standing for this full group of characteristics, can we find anything in the way of description in (a) or (d) that is not already covered in (b) and (c)? Blunt assertion in endless repetition is all that (a) and (d) seem to add. However the case may seem to stand in terms of the romanticisms of " knowledge," all the thousands of years of study and report upon the manifest subjectmatter of our inquiry, the regions of the knowing and the known, have never yet exhibited to us a knower that knows with naught that is known, nor a known that is known with naught that knows it. In none of this are we going out of our way to renounce, deny, or denounce any man's desire for or interest in any such separable " realities " as (a) and (d); it is simply that such separable realities are none of our business unless and until they contribute to our study. For us a " what " that is declared to be " real " makes no addition by this mere declaration to the full collection of the " whats " in the direct knowings (b) and (c); it is reduplicative, adding nothing to what is otherwise present. Nor is a declaration of reality for (d) as independent power either a necessity or an aid. No shotgun marriage of the (a) and (d) with the (b) and (c) is required. The (b) and (c) face the world in as full legitimacy as they may wish; while the (a) and (d) are allowed to flourish (or, as the case may be, wither) on their vines. The static world of " substance " may crave these latter; the active world of knowings and knowns, under our assumption, needs them not at all.

Our procedure, please never forget, is always under postulation, assumption, hypothesis — not under assertion. Nevertheless the moment this postulation is in working order, interesting things begin to happen. In illustration, with (a) and (d) disregarded, our attention becomes sharply focused on the *togetherness*[3] of (b) and (c). We begin to see that the two entitative name-fixations (a) and (d) have been just the factors that have heretofore made (b) and (c) appear as if sundered and non-joinable rather than one close union. The ranges of the knowings in (c) and that of the knowns in (b) is one range. The knowings in (c) are matched with the knowns in (b) all along the line; though always, of course, with the " hazes " of marginal growth, such as Bridgman reported to us in his *Logic of Modern Physics,* but never at any time in the universal authoritarianism of the logical atomisms, such as Russell's, which strive for the purities of (a) and (d), though the living world of (b) and (c) be wholly lost.

V

Memoranda for Orientation

Much further orientation is desirable before proceeding, but development becomes too extensive. Brief mention of outstanding points is alone practicable.

1. The word " knowledge " is dropped altogether. To do this is vital. The word is vague as to its " where " and its " what "; so vague that it blocks the path of all careful inquiry. No one can say just what it denotes, and its conventionally honorific status blinds men to the need.

---

[3] Whitehead's " togetherness " (*Process and Reality,* New York, 1929, p. 288) may be compared with the type indicated here.

Hereafter we shall speak of " knowings " and " knowns," always with concretely describable cases of *a* knowing and *a* known in view.

2. The words " existence " and " fact " are comparably deficient, and will remain so until definite specification is provided for their employment under postulation. Accuracy, as distinguished from exactness, is what is required for them.

3. The word " mind," for hypostatized power or product, is of course, dropped, but the conversational use of the word, and likewise of the word " mental," in free casual reference, is not harmful unless specialized stress makes it so.

4. The word " consciousness " is today so rarely heard where pertinent inquiry is under way that it hardly needs mention. The central hypostatization offered by the word, together with all euphemisms for it, and all modifications by way of prefixes such as " self- " or " un-," are rejected.

5. Careful specification under transactional or other expressly indicated form of observation is needed for all such words as the specimens above mentioned, if they are to become sufficiently dependable to hold place in research. Where specification is resisted or evaded, there replacement, temporary or permanent, will be required. The words " aspect " and " phase " will be employed at times (see Sec. X) as technically indicative of transaction.

6. *Trans*action is to be understood as involving observation of organism and environment in common direct system, in contrast with *inter*actional interpretations along lines patterned upon Newtonian physical constructions into which " mental particles " have been introduced in supplement to the physical particles. The word " transaction," as here specified, is never to be applied in situations in which organism and environment are viewed in sharp severance from each other.

7. The " togetherness " which appeared for (b) and (c) in the preceding section (IV) shows itself with advancing familiarity as an instance of transaction. Concreteness is here gained for the knowings with no loss of it for the knowns.

8. The word " behavior " is taken to cover transactionally all ranges of factual report to which psychological, sociological, logical, and kindred studies extend. Behaviors are represented as organic-environmental events of natural occurrence, never as possessing presumptively internal organic location in presumptively separate organisms.

9. Surveying the full field of inquiry as a preliminary to determining the place of Logic within it, we start from the current acceptance of physical and physiological events as prior to behavioral events in stage of evolutional entry and as underlying them in all living action. We take

Logic and Logical Behavior

them, however, not as external "reals" or independent "actuals," but always with the status of factual "knowns" under "factual" knowing. Upon and within this setting we place the behavioral region — that region within which knowing-knowns themselves make their entry. Among behavioral events, as their lowest level and stage, we find all sensori-manipulative-perceptive events, and we style them Signalings in transactional presentation, to distinguish them from all forms of presentation as internal to the organism, or as in any definite way located "inside" its skin. The level of behaviors above Signalings is that of Designations (namings), and is differentiated into three levels; Cue, Characterization, and Specification. Last behavioral level to reach is that of Symbolings, with Mathematics its present chief representative.

10. Inquiry into behavioral knowings does not proceed directly with physical or physiological processes, nor are its reports convertible into terms of such processes. It deals with events which — no matter how fully we may stress the completeness of the physical and physiological setting — nevertheless are not today examinable and describable themselves through the use of physical and physiological techniques and vocabularies.

11. The word "subjectmatter" is employed with technical application in place of words indicating materials or matter as "existing" apart from its being under inquiry or being known. It corresponds to the procedures (b) and (c) in Section IV. Matters and subjects, with these latter both in their "subjective" and their "objective" renderings, are thus presented as "together" in inquiry.

12. The word "knowing" may be taken so broadly that it applies to processes all along the behavioral line, from the most comprehensive down to the earliest and most primitive signalings. It is *not* so applied here: first, because that range of application runs far beyond our immediate undertaking; and secondly, because name-selection as distinguished from selections of the to-be-named through the aid of namings lies also far outside our immediate purposes. We shall say instead that all behavior, when transactionally viewed, may be described as *sign-process* from its earliest appearance onward, and that the levels of signaling, naming, and symboling are all characteristically sign-process. "Knowings," then, are inspected by us as located in the upper reaches of sign-process with signs as typically characteristic of behaviors as waves, charges, and gravitational effects are of physical, and as proteins, hormones, and genes are of physiological processes.

13. The factual basis for the differentiation of symboling from naming should be recognized as such, apart from all specialized interpreta-

tions, whether one on the lines here offered, or any alternative. During the past century many branches of mathematics have established definitely beyond all question that efficiency for themselves is best secured by withdrawing their symbols from the designational level — by depriving them, that is, of all service as names. To make this discovery by the mathematicians the basis for one of the main distinctions of an inquiry into knowings may seem strange, particularly since the total quantity of mathematical activity in the cosmos as we know it seems minute under ordinary spatial and temporal determinations. But this form of quantity is not everything. Proteins are small in quantity compared with the masses of inorganic matter; neural tissues small compared with all the organic; and cortical small compared with all the neural; yet the significance of the differences is great. Mathematical activity is small in quantity compared with all linguistic, and linguistic small compared with all sign-activity, but the two distinctions, the one of naming from perceivings, and the other of symbolings from namings, may nevertheless each have its special significance.

14. Behavioral subjectmatter covers individuals and social descriptions alike, the differentiation being reduced from one of opposed components to one stressing rather the manner of observation. Interpretation of what is called individual in terms of what is called social appears more efficient than the reverse line from individual to social, if anyone feels impelled to make a choice. The distinction thus is of value only for minor inquiries, and otherwise is apt to be positively harmful.

15. The distinctions analytic-synthetic, rational-empirical, universal-particular, take on new appearance in transactional construction. So also does that of class-property. The distinction semantic-syntactic, with or without an annexed pragmatic, is too weak on its own ground to enter definite comparison, while the words "interpretation" and "foundation," so often given heavy stress, collapse altogether for the uses intended.

VI

Positions under Postulation

Accepting nature as known and knowings as natural; securing release under postulation from obstructive hypostatizations, whether "physical" or "mental"; developing direct observation of knowings and knowns as transactions in common process; we are able to arrive at certain Positions which we offer contingently as factual report, by the aid of which to make further studies. The word "position," derived from *pono,* was common in the older logic, where it was used both for position-taking and for position-taken. It has a further advantage in that its comparatively slight recent use has saved it from the terminological insecurity which has come about for many important logical terms, including such even as " proposition " and " definition." Always it must be understood as positing under way — as activity, not as fixation.

These positions can be stated even now, I believe, so that they may gain working comprehension, although they will require much further refinement of expression through careful development and adjustment of terminology before one can hope to be able to say that they are adequately presented. They are as follows:

Position A. *Words and Meanings*

A, a. Word-body and word-meaning enter together as a phase of behavioral transaction.[4] Rejected is all severance of word as " physical " from meaning as " mental." Asserted is behavioral process in which the full activity of the living organism is brought under view instead of *disjecta membra*.

A, b. More broadly, naming and knowing, in the region of knowing by way of language-using, form together a common phase of a single behavioral transaction, the phase of naming-as-knowing. Rejected is all severance of presumptively separable names — physical from presumptively separable knowings-mental, with the dignity of knowledge-in-person claimed for the latter. Asserted in companionate expression are knowing-in-naming and naming-as-knowing, with either phrasal stress permissible according as the needs of inquiry may suggest; provided that the full transactional observation retains methodological precedence over specialized formulations.

Position B. *Knowings and Knowns*

B, a. The knowing and the known form together one behavioral transaction in a common activity of organism-in-environment or environment-embracing-organism. Rejected under postulation is all attempted inter-

---

[4] This position was taken by John Dewey as early as 1929. (See " Context and Thought," *University of California Publications in Philosophy*, XII, 1931, pp. 203–224.) The general trend of all the positions is observable also in his identification of " object " as the outcome of inquiry (*Logic, The Theory of Inquiry*, New York, 1938, p. 119). Peirce contributed through his early attitude toward thought, time, and sign (*Collected Papers*, 6 vols., Cambridge, Mass., 1931–35, 5. 253), which he partly developed later, and through his treatment of continuity (*ibid.*, 5. 313 ff.; see also Dewey, *op. cit.*, pp. 9, 9 n, 19). James's observation of the double-barreled terminologies belongs in this development (*Essays in Radical Empiricism*, New York, 1912, p. 10). See also the index to the book mentioned in the text, *Knowing and the Known* (Boston, 1949), especially the entries for " word."

pretation by imposition of presumptive separates, one upon another, under whatever power-claims for either may be set forth. Asserted is a behavioral process of organism and environment in full action together.

B, b. The naming and the named, developing as a specialized region of the knowings and the known, form similarly a transaction. The differentiation between them is aspectual and not, as in the older manner, "entitative," with the "named" as "entity" coming first, and the "naming" aping this status as the logical effort to secure coherent construction became more desperately pushed.

Position C. *Signalings and Symbolings*

C, a. Perceivings (along with manipulations and sensory activities) enter under full transactional presentation, and, to hold this status, are styled Signalings. No "percept" as itself a "thing" is recognized, and no activity of perceiving as a "power" of the organism within its own skin and of its own right. Percept-things and perceiving-powers alike are rejected as needless fixations. The locus of a perceiving, transactionally viewed as signaling, is the full space and time of the activity of the organism and environment together in the given event. Legitimate, as always, are specialized studies from either the organic or the environmental approach, provided that full transactional observation re-enters in the completed report on the specialized results.

C, b. Symbolings represented primarily by mathematics of the type called "pure" do not themselves act as namings beyond their own symbolic ranges of activity; while even within those ranges such appearances of namings as they seem to employ are reduced to the status of temporary expedients, abbreviations, or other technical conveniences.

Position D. *The Named and the Known*

D, a. Differentiating the phase of the named and known within the complete transactional naming-knowing-named-known procedure, we identify transactional signalings as the "that" which is primarily named and known-in-naming. These signalings are transactions prior to their entry as nameds, and as such they participate in more complex transaction when they become the nameds. Rejected as dependably known and named are all "things," as they appear under the old terminologies projected either as "external" to man's behavioral living or as "internal" to it. Accepted as known and named in the naming-knowing levels of behavioral activity is always that which enters as already organic-environmental event.

D, b. As behavioral evolution progresses namings themselves come to take place, in addition to signalings, among the nameds and the knowns in naming-knowing process. In still later stages symbolings become thus differentiated as nameds and knowns. In both cases, whether that of namings or of symbolings, these nameds and knowns, like the perceivings before them, enter as themselves already transactional into the further transactional procedure.

At points within the above statements, the name " organism-as-a-whole " could have been used, given an understanding that no " mental-as-a-whole " was implied. The full organic activity, in contrast with presumed action by organic components separately on each other, is acceptable. This conventional expression is, however, too limited for present purposes since, in addition to what it might provide, our heaviest stress is throughout demanded upon the joint system of organism-environment in action as one system as it opens itself to view under adequately trained observation.

Transfer of the above Positions into free expression is not too difficult. Position A holds that sounds from throats and marks on paper are *not words at all* unless they are " human," and " living " human at that, borne always in human action and life. Nor are disembodied word-meanings words at all; no pretense will suffice; the meaning must be living human meaning. Summon word-meanings from some vasty deep as you will: they rise word-embodied, if they rise at all. So also if one segregates any part of knowing as knowing through naming, then that knowing is not knowing without the naming, nor is the naming naming unless the knowing is coupled with it. This seems the simplest common sense, and clearly apparent after the slightest analysis of the situation, provided that this analysis is held directly to its own courses and is not controlled by alien considerations. Position B recombines the artificially split organism and environment much as Position A recombined word-body and word-meaning, name-knowing and known-named. A knowing that knows with nothing it knows, and a known that is known with nothing to know it, are wraiths from nowhere. Position C posits the full transactional naming-knowing in organization with perceivings and symbolings, these running the full range of behavioral process. Position D specifically brings all that is known as named within the scheme of human living by way of the knowing and the naming.

These positions are offered in words to be taken literally as presenting observations that are practicable and renewable, in a manner of description for which the possibility of further expansion seems well assured. They bring the meaning and the word, the knowing and the naming, the named and the known, together in a system which is as directly observable as that of any human living in progress. The obstacle to such envisionment lies neither in deficiency of man's skills nor in other facts of man's present knowing. It lies, we believe, wholly in the crippling verbal traditions of a pre-scientific age, which in so many fields of living succeed in dominating what one may, and what one may not, see or do. Surely, as a straight matter of observation under modern standards it should be easier to *see* the knowing and its known, the known and its knowing, in common system, than to profess to see " meanings as such," " meanings *qua* meanings," in existence of their own apart from all embodiment. Such unembodied meanings are of the style of unseeing believings, along with which unbelieving seeing is fairly sure to go wherever verbal habit is rigidly fixed.

VII

What Is Logic?

The questions " What is Logic? " and " What is Logic about; just what is its subjectmatter? " should mutually determine each other in the answering.[5] They are too important and too pressing to be shoved aside. Catchwords and slogans are not answers. A logician who evades such questions is apt some day to discover himself in a painful state of uncertainty as to what, actually, he is doing. So great, however, are present confusions of attitude that these questions, no matter how simple they may seem at first glance, are extremely difficult to answer in a way that permits adequately developed description. The great need today seems to be to become able to follow the advice Bacon gave and Jevons stressed after him: *ipsis consuescere rebus* — to accustom ourselves to things themselves; or, with still further modernization of expression, just simply to try to get hold of the facts.

By way of a factual answer as to what Logic and its subjectmatters are, we find in current discussion almost nothing that is phrased up to modern requirements for competent expression. The historical quirks of report as exhibited by the dictionaries, the encyclopedias, and the histories of logic are numerous. Divisions into abstract and concrete; *docens* and *utens;* theory and art; metaphysical, empirical, and formal; cognitional, formal, and conjoint; and presentations as analysis, whether of words, of entities, or of concepts — with many slippery variations of each — are scattered around. Older makeshift answers, such as the

---

[5] As a convenient device for definite reference, I shall in what follows capitalize the words Logic, Physics, Mathematics, etc., when standing for the differentiated inquiry as science; and shall leave uncapitalized all references to the subjectmatters of Inquiry, such as physical fact, logical behavior, or scientific fact generally.

one in terms of "the laws of thought," seem today so non-informative that they rarely appear in print except, perhaps, in casual conformity to old routine. Expansion from this answer to one that makes Logic "the science of the necessary laws of thought," leans, despite the use of the word "Science," far over to the practical side where only that which is correct, or thought so, is approved. To speak of "rules of language" is no improvement, so long as the word "language" is, if anything, more cavalierly treated by logicians than is the word "thought." The word "rules," moreover, is merely an evasive modernization of the older word "laws," with a side-thought for the logician as rule-giver, and with no attention whatever paid to the observer's inevitable question as to where, factually, such rules are to be found. To speak of "a general science of order" was exhilarating once upon a time, but this likewise has remained wholly indefinite as to the "it," the "what," and the "where."

Quine says, both of the older formal and the newer mathematical logic, that while "they both have, vaguely speaking, the same subjectmatter," and while "they are both 'logic' in the strictest sense of the word," nevertheless "just what that subjectmatter is, is not very easy to say."[6] Logician A stalks his quarry circuitously by setting up Semiotic as the science of language, Semantics as a part of Semiotic, and "Logic, in the sense of the theory of logical deduction" as "a part of Semantics," though logical deduction, he tells us, may also be found operative in a different region, that, namely, of Syntax. Concerning language, which he takes as the basic *fact* or point of reference for all of this, he has nothing specific to say, its problems, like all other factual problems, being in his development sent away to a separate and presumably unimportant region, to be dealt with by other workers under a procedure called Pragmatics. Logician B makes Logic include broadly (a) "deductive reasoning in the strict sense," and (b) "Methodology." Methodology, however, does not speak "about" science, nor can it be "strictly separated" from Science, since it is "the logic of science," "the theory of correct scientific decisions," i.e., a process of clarification under an ideal *inherent* in all science. Such a Methodology we may probably best envisage as primarily a scientific "analysis of scientific procedure," developed later in Logic into "logical analysis of the rules of scientific procedure." For Logician C, Methodology becomes the widest name out of which he believes he can see developing "a Science of logic and mathematics," probably best to be styled "Meta-logic and Meta-mathematics," and capable of dealing with "deductive theories as wholes" in

---

[6] *Mathematical Logic* (New York, 1940), 1. See John Dewey and Arthur F. Bentley, *Knowing and the Known*, pp. 205-32.

addition to their components separately. Logic here takes a subordinated place, though still with powers and authority sufficient to enable it to "analyze the meaning of the concepts common to all the sciences, and establish the general laws governing concepts."

There is little nutriment in any of these expressions, and the descriptions developed around them fail in every case to hold together coherently. In marked contrast with all this is John Dewey's proffer of "a Logic based inclusively and exclusively upon the operations of inquiry"; a Logic in which "control" is developed by inquiry within its own activities, and is neither brought from without, nor allotted intuitive status, and in which a procedure which separates logic and scientific method from one another and places them in "external relation" to each other has "no valid meaning." What Dewey presents is the thoroughgoing development of a "logic without ontology." He has never, so far as I have noted, given his work that label, but at least half a hundred demonstrations of this status will be found in his *Logic, The Theory of Inquiry*, in which the "ontological" is shed like a useless husk from problem after problem as the development in terms of inquiry proceeds. Despite which, discussions of the possibility of a "logic without ontology" are elaborately carried on without mention of his work, and the common attitude seems often still to be that of the friendly acquaintance when the book first appeared: "A fine book, very; but, of course, you know, it's not Logic at all." What Dewey does is to see men in natural action, which other Logics do not; he sees them in problematic situations, developing solutions which in due course open up new problems leading to further and newer solutions. His procedure throughout is open-ended in correspondence with the manifest scientific characteristics of "nature" so far as we have yet become acquainted with them.

Inquiry, then, is the factual exhibit of the very processes of knowing, and of the appraisal of knowings called logical. Where, in the traditional Logics, its seat was far below the salt, in Dewey's Logic it is at the head of the table to the displacement of those older operators, the "minds," and the "reals," and often even the "transcendentals."

VIII

Logical Behaviors

Accepting Logic as a branch of organized inquiry, but without further commitment, let us turn now to consideration of the subjectmatters it investigates. Under the approach called *natural*, these subjectmatters enter inquiry as *activities* of living men. They enter, this is to say, factually. As *facts* they are, under our postulation, *transactional* facts; they make no claim to independence of their own, neither do they rely for backing on descriptions deriving from primitive days, but traditionally boasting themselves as basic. *Behavioral* activities form one great group of life activities, being differentiated from physiological activities by new complexities and by outstanding differences in the technical methods needed for their inquiry. The activities investigated by Logic form a distinctive species within the behavioral group. They are the *logical behaviors,* viewed as living activities taking place in the world-system, the cosmos, as it is known to us. Logical behaviors are *logical facts*. As such they are comparable as Logic investigates them in the logical field with physical facts as Physics investigates its facts in the physical field. In what follows we shall speak freely either of logical behavior, or of logical fact, letting the expression adapt itself to the context in whatever way may be simplest.

Adequate presentation of the differentiation of Logic from the facts that form its subjectmatter is of high importance. The types of subject-object organization that are involved must be understood, if we are to secure descriptions of the processes under our consideration that lend themselves to coherent expansion. The current Logics lack such understanding, as was remarked by Quine in a passage already cited. The hotbed of this deficiency is probably to be located in the long-established convention of referring all logical activity to the " mind " as actor, either in direct allegation (as if that were ample interpretation), or else indirectly by the way of the " thoughts " it is supposed to have produced. For any actor so taken, distinctions in terms of the factual cannot readily be drawn, while more often no hint ever arises that such distinctions have place.

The differentiation can be made — and here will be — in a manner factually comparable to that which is now being increasingly made between Physics as inquiry and " the physical " as the subjectmatter Physics inquires into, whenever the inquiries taken into account are those of the developed physical knowings of the last two generations. The older physicist found himself confronting Fact-Compulsive, toward which it was required that he approach with bended knee as true " existence " delivered, and perhaps even guaranteed to him, by powers outside his own research and limiting the range and manner of that research. Recent Physics, however, deriving from Clerk Maxwell and Einstein, and possessing a rich new world of discovery within the atom, has a changed eye for the physical fact it deals with. Alleged guarantees from without have lost their influences; and so completely have they been shattered that today Physics feels no longer even a conventional need to accept a preformed World-Physical as " real " basis of its research, no matter how busily the old-time talkers keep on talking in the old-time ways. Instead, and sharply in contrast, Physics today accepts as physical fact whatever it can learn — whatever becomes known to it — under its own physical techniques of inquiry, regardless of all " ideas-primeval." Physical fact remains, even though the old " reality " stresses on the word " fact " are gone. Physical fact becomes that which Physics is now knowing and on the way to better knowing, under the qualification always that even the " existence " of the " fact " offers itself in terms of " its being known." Physics, the Science, over against the physical fact it examines, is, then, the best and most fully developed presentation of the physical which men have yet secured, with the securing and the presenting both transactionally behavioral.

In contrast with the older physicist, the older logician — and he is still active among us — far from approaching his facts on bended knee, is mostly found demanding that it is to him, as their arbiter and judge, that the facts themselves must show their deep respect. It is not with past Logic that comparison with the present " Physics and the physical " should be drawn, but rather with Logic as it will appear in a natural setting. Logic should here show itself as the differentiated inquiry and report upon its own type of behavioral facts much as Physics shows itself as the differentiated inquiry and report upon the physical facts. The logical facts and the Logic, the physical facts and the Physics, will in each case be in factual growth, with, in each respectively, the facts under inquiry as the knowns in the joint process of the knowings-knowns. In whichever case, logical or physical, any allotment of precedence to Science over fact, or to fact over Science, is to be regarded merely as the outcome of short-span observation and incomplete attention. Under wider observation, both phases, the knowings and the knowns, the namings and the nameds, should be, alike for Logic as for Physics, found in advance together.

We are here proceeding manifestly under the acceptance of (b) for the knowns and (c) for the knowings as illustrated in Section IV above, and under complete rejection of the older pattern represented by the primitive pseudo-realities, (a) and (d). Both logical behaviors and Logic are viewed as evolving within the great system of knowings and knowns in freedom from the conventional compartmental separations engineered by misplaced definitional rigidities deriving from the past. Here Logic has the aspect (c) among knowings as over against the aspect (b) of the knowns, these knowns being just the logical behaviors that Logic inquires into.

We are now ready to locate the areas of the known in which logical behaviors may be looked for. Brief indication of the range was given in item 9 of Section V. We first eliminate as locus for such behaviors all physical and physiological knowns. We are not concerned with sermons in stones, divinities that shape our ends, or the imminent logics of " nature-in-person " or of any of its euphemistic substitutes. The field of behaviors remains alone under consideration, as, indeed, the terminology here in use certifies, so far as its ability goes. The position here taken cannot, however, be too often reiterated, wherever there remains any danger of its being overlooked. The behavioral knowns are before us in a setting of the physical and physiological knowns. These latter may, indeed, be viewed as the stem of the tree of behavioral knowings and knowns. Nevertheless today, no matter how smartly a physical reading of physiology is advancing, there is nowhere any direct expansion of the behavioral out of the physiological in the range of the knowings and knowns. No behavioral without physiological, true enough; no knowing-knowns without the neural, true enough; no complexly existential knowings and knowns without cortical process, again true enough. But at the same time, no expansion of a behavioral report out of a physical or physiological report — no reading of the language expressions of the one straight through into the other, no " interpretation " — to use a much weaker phrasing — of the behavioral knowing out of its physical-physiological setting. Wave and color vision may lie in parallel channels in inquiry, but the renderings of neither cross the channel walls. There is no seeing of far nebulae without the eyepiece in the telescope, yet the eyepiece does not do the seeing, nor is it so spoken of in any form of talk. The two forms of report do not translate into one another, whatever may be our future expectations. The experimentalists of Gestalt, seeking system, but seeking it under retention of a severed " mental," have most clearly faced this issue, and most completely failed to advance with respect to it. The key-word of advance, " stimulus," is still wholly unclear to all, as was stressed before (Section I). " Milking a cow " may be given elaborate physical and physiological description in various respects, but neither form of report, no matter how far developed, extends directly into statements of knowings and knowns, either as of the cow, or as of the dairyman. Much less does it extend to regions where the problems of " better milking of better cows " fill the field of attention.

Among the behaviors the lowest level has been styled that of Signalings, this including all sensori-manipulative-perceptive process transactionally observed. Logical behaviors will not be sought by us in the region of Signalings, though we still find many a logician, incredible as it may seem, striving to force a plainly sub-linguistic perceptional activity, that called "ostensive," into Logic as if itself directly and immediately a form of logical "definition."

The next level of behaviors, that of namings or designations, comprises, still in the ascending order, cue-namings, characterizations, and specifications. The cue-namings, themselves hardly yet in full parturition from signalings, and largely ejaculatory in form, will not be here examined for possible logical aspects. One can hardly at today's stage of inquiry seek with profit logical behavior in a typically ejaculatory distinction, such as that of the words "cat" and "dog" in a toddler's mouthing. Bertrand Russell's atomistically logical strivings do, indeed, seem aimed at highly refined specimens from this region of cues; but we may leave the field free to him and his recruits for such victories within it as they may still hope to secure.

We have now left for logical appraisal the two higher levels of designational behavior, those of characterization and of specification, with still beyond these a third great region of behaviors: that, namely, of symbolings.

Consideration of these last, the symbolings, will come later, and the problem they offer will not be entangled with that of namings until the latter have been surveyed. It will be well, however, to indicate something of their status at once in a preliminary way. Their central core is found in Mathematics, taken as freed from the primitive swaddling clothes of its practical linguistic evolution, and now at last running free in its own precision. The region to observe is that of the modern enterprise of attempted conversion of mathematics into a derivative naming procedure under the control of a Logic of namings. It is characteristic of symboling as contrasted with designatings that if it is to attain maximum efficiency in its own field it must strip itself of all pretense of power to name (see item 13, Section V). It is comparably characteristic, under our postulation, for the designatings that for maximum efficiency they must strip themselves of all claims to the type of precision that Mathematics achieves, and establish their own differentiated standard of accuracy in its place. Perhaps we shall be able to say in the outcome, or at least experiment in saying, that Mathematics and Symbolic Logic taken together, with the latter finally clarified in its own range, as Mathematics now has been in its, can be shown as a region of highly specialized behavioral activities. In this it would be seen rising above the older attempted designational linkages of symbols to "things" taken as other than symbols, and making its advance upon the cosmic problem in which the older designational procedures are in collapse. The designational value here would be concentrated in the symbolic system as a whole rather than spread out in detailed namings.

Putting this intricate situation before us in the much more general form of language, or, let us say, looking at it from the point of view furnished by the coverage of the word "language," we may say that our treatment divides the field of language, most widely taken, into two regions, one of mathematics (in the sense of mathematics as language) and the other of language in the ordinary sense not including mathematics. The earlier in development is from crown to toe a business of namings; the later in development proceeds so differently from naming procedure that even the phrasing " crown to toe " should be omitted in mentioning it. Whether language is used in the broad sense to cover mathematics, or in the narrower sense without it, is indifferent here. The factual rather than the verbal differentiation is what is here under attention.

Taking up designations, we have two levels: that of characterizations corresponding fairly well with the common-sense activities of everyday living; and that of specifications which reach up into the activities of modern science, advancing therein at full pace. In considering them we shall use throughout literally and without hesitancy or qualification, the position numbered A in Section VI, wherein word-body and word-meaning are presented as a single transactional event, such that, if the full event is examined by the use of physical techniques alone, no live word of language at all is found — only the lifeless husks; whereas if search is made for word-meaning, for itself, whether as "mental" or otherwise, no techniques are known which will produce anything but emptiness.[7]

---

[7] P. W. Bridgman, who holds the "mental" and the "physical" sharply apart, and regards "thought" as "closer to experience" and "infinitely richer" than language, and as capable of accomplishing unnumbered results that language can never reach, nevertheless gives substantially the same description of both. Language, he says "separates out from the living matrix" of experience "little bundles and freezes them"; while "the fundamental device of practically all thought" is "analyzing experience into static bits with static meanings." Further, he says that the "structure" of thought is "very close to the structure of language" (*The Nature of Physical Theory*, Princeton, 1936, pp. 24, 58, 26). Bridgman's *observation* thus goes far in the direction I have taken in the text, even though his personal *choice of belief* puts him near to an opposite pole. Examination of his heavy use of the word "concept" in his texts further supports this view. It is easy to show that his texts will permit the flat elimination of the word "concept" 90% or 95% of the time, while very simple variations of phrasing will suffice to get rid of it in the remaining cases. Word-meaning-in-action is sufficient, however various aspects for various purposes may be variously studied. The added "mentalist" component then becomes pleonastic.

We may go back with Characterizations to the common nouns of everyday life and talk in early Greece for the first signs of what we are calling logical behavior. This is, of course, no venture at an historical account, but merely an impressionistic use of eras for a sketch of variations. The early cues advanced to Characterizations through developing descriptions. Namings name descriptions, while descriptions are made up of names (no basic split between the naming and the named, each with its separate power plant, being permitted here to interfere with observation). When descriptions come to be checked against each other, this specialized linguistic checking, contrasted with the more primitive language behaviors, may be regarded as the earliest of logical behaviors. It is living language, of course, and not dead, with which we are concerned both in the original expressions and in their proto-logical checking. The logical behavior is language developing in guidance of itself. In Dewey's phrase it is the "control of inquiry" developing "from within inquiry itself." The Sophists in time seeded wide fields of argumentation. Socrates concentrated on forms and tools. Aristotle formulated outcomes. Logic had now arrived as an established branch of learning. Developed out of logical behaviors, it is, of course, a form of logical behavior in the very broadest envisionment, but more strictly viewed it rates as a specialized branch of inquiry taking logical behaviors as its subjectmatter.

What was then established remained without significant change till the advent of modern mathematics and modern science. It endured thus through the terminological turmoil of the Schoolmen, through Bacon's effort to bring the world more widely into the account, and through Kant's great factual discrimination of the analytic from the synthetic. It kept the worse along with the better. It retained the Schoolmen's fiction of a "concept" existing in some mental realm; it developed bombinating chimeras known as logical entities; it handled Kant's factual observation all too often in theaters of word-juggling exhibitionism. What Boole started to do a century ago was, at least he so at the time imagined, not to put Logic in control of Mathematics, but to gain help for a sadly confused Logic from its much more powerful neighbor, Mathematics. What Frege and Whitehead and Russell and their followers accomplished was to engineer a deformation of Boole's original program into a program for the domination of Mathematics by Logic, an enterprise which has some interesting fruit in odd corners of its field, as any diligent and long-continued research may do, but as itself a creed is still keeping life in bits of ancient witchcraft as it travels its path through the Valley of the Shadow of Antinomy.

Specifications, the soundest scientific namings of our day, have introduced a great change from the older namings under the aegis of the medievally degenerate Aristotelian syllogism and its descendants to this hour. These latter were themselves developed from common-sense characterizations, and it is with this older form of logical development, not with the earlier characterizations themselves, that specifications are in conflict. The signs of change date from Galileo, but the change itself can hardly be reckoned as dating further back than Darwin and Wallace. The Linnaean terminology dwelt within the old framework of names. The newer terminologies are namings developed with a keen eye to growth. The gene is already past its youthful period of strident hypostatization. Chemical terminologies look rigid to the bystander, but as a group are fluid for whatever need may arise. The Newtonian particle, which was anything one might need to impound so as to deal with it as a unit, was a great advance, but proved in the end to be too highly specialized. For Physics or for any other Science, or for the Sciences all together, we may say that the total system of specifications *is* precisely that which *is* the differentiated science itself. Full scientific activity takes in of course the scientist with hands, eyes, feet, ears, body in action as well as with names and symbols, and all the physical processes in progress through the laboratory. Specialized as the Science of (c) form, as over against its scientific facts of form (b), is the full knowing-naming equipment of its specifications in use in the field. The whole is life-in-process on an earth-in-cosmos, with all the old rigid particle-like components, whether called " physical " or " mental," loosened up into action.

In none of this have we spoken of characterizations and specifications as themselves technically logical behaviors. They are before us primarily as linguistic behavioral facts, which, when examined by further specialized linguistic processes, have certain of their aspects brought to view which in due time are called logical. The process is transactional throughout. Sentence-events pass before logicians for study, just as chemical events pass before chemists, and logicians and chemists alike ride herd on their respective facts-in-action.

We have now before us, as determined by techniques of inquiry, physiological process rising in a physically known world; the organisms, so processed, widening their ranges of activity through signalings; language processes, that is to say, namings, adding extension to the signalings, and within the language ranges, specialized language processes carrying immensely further the ranges of effective linguistic action. Beyond these lies the region of the symbolings differentiated in a new process of advance, the inquiry into which is one of the outposts of knowings in our era, where the symbolings can be seen running step for step alongside "expanding universe" and perhaps "collapsing universe" as well if such there be, and less advanced in comprehension as the knowing, than such hardy universes are as the knowns. In all of which statement the words "advance" and "rising" and "widening" are employed in lines of what is measurable, but beyond that without claim to honor or value.

A characteristic is in sight which it is of the utmost importance to glimpse, but which it is of equal importance to let lie as glimpsed, without further pretense to make use of it till much further knowing, perhaps that of some far future, is achieved. It is no concern of ours here beyond such glimpse. In all stages of behavioral activity new processes are seen developing out of old, and turning back upon the old for their further strengthening. This *turning back* is what needs to be glimpsed. If something comparable lies below the behavioral, that is not our concern here, and need in no way concern us here. Whether or not it is in the class of "lifting oneself by one's bootstraps" is likewise none of our concern. The symboling helps the naming, the naming helps the perceiving, and the perceiving is the survival agency of the organism that achieves it. There is no novelty in such a statement. In radically different approaches to this region of inquiry, the intellect is supposed to guide the senses, and the senses to guide the body after their fashion. The "self-conscious" is supposed to do things for the "conscious," and in some regions of surviving superstition, a "sub-conscious" is constructed to fight back, imp against imp. The mechanist even stores his helpful hints in a population of particles ready to accomplish all things for all time, if given only time enough. Speculative constructions lie around by the dozen. All that needs mention here is that the same kind of situation shows itself practically in the detail of our study. Enough of it is seen to make sure that the "nature" in the case is not merely one that kicks from behind, any more than one that lures us on with far-off starry gleam. We are not hampered by it. No more are we prejudiced against it. If it is *natura naturans* it is this for us only in the way its small track can be traced and verified. If spoken of as emergence, it is the emergent process in its small corners, and not Creature Emergent, that holds the eye.

Symbolic Logic makes use of this turn-back procedure, but in a highly artificial way — the way of the stuffed specimen in the museum. This is seen in the case of the "meta-language" through which some other "language" is to be interpreted. The museum curator in the case of such languages seems to make no effort at all to find out how his specimens acted when alive. He says: "Pry and prod this specimen as we will, we cannot make it do all the tricks we are told it claims to do. It just hasn't got it in itself to do it. So what to do?" And he continues: "Put another dead specimen on the shelf above, and make happen what you wish by mirror or by wire." So enters the meta-language. It is fairly well known that for each "meta" a "super-meta" is needed to handle *it*. One meta alone looks plausible. Many metas in serried ranks do not. It was De Morgan who expanded Swift to read:

And the great fleas themselves, in turn, have greater fleas to go on;
While these again have greater still, and greater still, and so on.

IX

SCIENCE OR DISCIPLINE

In the two preceding sections we have endeavored to secure at least the beginnings of a dependable identification of the logical fact — the fact which Logic investigates — finding it in the logical behaviors of men, themselves a definitely characterizable outgrowth of linguistic behaviors generally. We have herein treated Logic as a Science, or rather it is that phase of Logic dealing with operations with namings that we have so treated. By "science" is here understood a developed system of specifications, i.e., of the best perfected technical namings of the age, free from the inclusion of purported ultimate certainties as among the specified and named, and free thus always for growth of the system of knowings and knowns as one system.

Such a commitment as the above to the scientific dealing with facts ought to be adequate without further elaboration in almost any other branch of inquiry. But in the case of Logic it is not sufficient. The reason is that what is involved in this case is not just issues of method and materials of construction, but instead a deep-seated attitude among workers — something in the manner of a constitutional defect in their behavior if our present method of approach is a proper one. I am opposing the name "Discipline" to the name "science" to characterize the manner of Logic developed under this attitude. It is a Logic of the *should be* rather than of the *is*. It represents the approach of priest, prophet, and mentor, of the well-wisher and uplifter, even at times that of the do-gooder, taking this latter label as a current superlative for a variety of evils found at times in the other namings. It is the approach of medicine and of pathology, including probably all psychiatry, but it is not the approach of physiology. Not that a sharp cleavage between the *is* and the *should be* is intended. Far from it. We no more expect to find the crystallized pure than to find the purely applied in any range of knowing. Heavy attitudinal distortions are what is here involved. The discipline uses "logical" for what is proper and correct, or for what it may intend to show is such, and sets an illogical over against its logical, with no attention to the environing field of the nonlogical. The science in contrast sees logical and illogical companion phases of a single process, neither identifiable except in terms of the other (and certainly neither God-given prescriptions, Topsy absolutes, nor mental creations); and it also sees the setting of the logical in the nonlogical as an essential subject of preliminary inquiry, much as any other science of evolving fact finds questions of this kind, and with all the interesting possibilities of inquiry that the advance in physiology from the days of vital principles to those of viruses involved.

Consider a few sample illustrations from the field of Logic as Discipline. Consider a proclamation that all science is to be unified by the stroke of the logician's pencil on paper in his regal room in his lofty tower on Mental Heights. The Cosmos is on leash to a lead pencil; and no man laughs. You can find announcement that now at last the truly "positive" has been established, itself positively guaranteed to last "as is" for thousands of years. Much contemporary logical activity, probably most of it, is directed toward little pin-points of contemporary fixation, as assumed "realities." Basketsful (and not wastepaper baskets either) of medieval posers can be found, still hopeful that some lightning stroke of genius will some day declare their solutions, antique crudities of formulation and all, at one stroke. Ultimate certainties are so strongly demanded that when they are omitted from a Logic, the very name of Logic is denied to all the work. Factual orientations are no sooner suggested than they are tossed through the window into a garbage bucket called "pragmatics," within the dirty ranges of which no logician is expected, nor indeed even permitted, to soil his clean fingers or break his well-trimmed nails. "Pragmatic," the word from Peirce — for whom it was to be a guiding light to future advance — after seventy years has come down to this. Perhaps worse than anything else, linguistic components, words, descendants of the Logos, are inserted into Logic as "thirds" — "intervening thirds" was James's phrase — between the lips of the man who utters them and the "things" they are about (with no taking into account of the ears to hear) like eternal jigsaws between a boy and a stick of wood.

Comes the high-power calculating machine. The headlines say: Look, it can *do* logic; it *is* logic. It is not hard to note that what the new devices show is not that the machine is logical, but that the logic brought in question is mechanical. No wonder the Transposed Heads suggest themselves. One may better trust in the human behaviors in developed human society that are behind them both — behaviors perceptive, linguistic, logical, mathematical — all en route.

X

Aspect and Phase

Some events can be handily dealt with in footrule space and clocktick time. Other events cannot; for them the rules and the clocks are too crude. For the events that can be so dealt with, the word " thing " is commonly used with fixational stress even though, like most comparable namings, its own origin lay more in the field of action than of fixation, and even though, at one time or another, it is apt to be used for almost anything and everything else mentionable in the universe. The entitative stress on the word is often so heavy that its " properties " or " qualities " are severed from it, and turned into separate " things " under separate examination. Consider how " thing-ing " is from time to time marked out for attack as a detriment to " think-ing." Consider the strangely chaotic incidental expression that results in symbolic logic when " property " as itself a " thing " enters the account.

Under our present postulation we rid ourselves of this complex of separable components by securing full system for the full event. The noun " aspect " becomes technically applicable to events observed. The verb " to aspect," emphasizing the last syllable, may be rescued from the past for " to observe in system." The word " phase " becomes available for events reported with stress on their enduring in time. Footrules and clockticks are assumed as applicable everywhere, but not as profitably used everywhere. Much greater delicacy of attention for the spaces and times that will be adequate to hold observation, must be developed in the inquiry — here as they have been in physics. Namings, when treated as processes in progress, are among the foremost aids to observation. We do not use " aspect " and " phase " in the way that " property " and " quality " are most commonly set up as if independently identifiable apart from the things to which they appertain. They enter as descriptions developed in inquiry, and profitable for use in further inquiry, of a type such that any " full " description will be the full " naming," while a full naming in a form convertible into description will be a full knowing of the form (b) and (c) of Section IV, where the word " full " as itself a naming must itself be aspectually taken, and therefore neither for a fixation nor asymptotically, but as a process involving progress, with "progress" again in turn entering as aspectual report of observation upon observation.

"Aspect" and "phase" are thus introduced not as developed rivals to older methods of naming, but as preliminary approaches to what is needed, in a form of inquiry which is still in a preliminary stage. Consider them in the instance of our immediate inquiry: that of Logic and logical behaviors. A book on Logic is a "thing" dimensional in M, L, and T. Put it in a room overnight, lock the door, and leave it. You have it "in a pumpkin shell," and there you "keep it very well," or so you think. The "thing" you have there, if fully shut off from the outer human world, is a thing in physical dimensional description only; it is not even a weapon to hurl or an article to sell, if there is no world of living men to go with it. To be a book in the sense of writing or printing, a long physiological and manipulative history is needed, with generations of the future as well as of the past involved. Such a history is not something separate and apart from the book. History and handling must be involved for it to be a book at all. For the book to be a Logic, much more highly specialized human behavior is needed in the pasts and futures of all the inquiries, the writings, and the readings. If we try to take it as a Logic in language crudely borrowed from other fields of inquiry, and as a "thing" which has been "caused" by another "thing" or "things," we fail to get through to the Logic itself. Cancel all future readings and writings and ponderings of the book and its lines of activity, and no Logic is left. Pressure in the pipes must be steadily held to maintain such a knowing and a known. Analogy with blood pressure in the veins, if life is to be maintained, is not strained.

Taking our background as heretofore laid out, we have physiological process channeling (organizing, engineering, manipulating, if one sees fit so to put it — all such words needing cautious use) the physical processes; we have behaviors becoming, so to speak, "service departments" of the organisms; we have language behaviors servicing the perceptional behaviors; and we have Logic as inquiry becoming the formulated presentation of the logical aspects of the language behaviors. We may take this Logic as a phase of linguistic behaviors, just as we would certainly take linguistic behaviors as a phase of the wider behavioral evolution. Taking Logic and the logical behaviors in one, we may describe the former as the knowing aspect and the latter as the known aspect of the full ongoing process. We, of course, do not yet have the symboling in the reckoning at all. We may therefore see at each stage, within the regions of designation generally, the logical behavior as itself a language behavior turning back on preceding language behaviors to give them a bit of housecleaning. At a very early stage a caveman, while narrating, may have hesitated, appraising his speaking, and yielding thus a trace of logical effect. Later on a speaker may much more carefully study how he is saying what he has to say, either while he is saying it, or afterward or before, yielding thus other logical aspects. Again the listener, whether himself at times speaker or not, may turn on the speakings of others to praise, appraise, or rend. Also he may do this from the garden or he may do it from the chair. The ways are endless. In time we come, as briefly sketched before, to Sophists, Socrates, and Aristotle, with Euclid in years not far removed, securing a more powerful tool still, one concealed in his direct development, its presence hardly noted, its power not at all, till very many centuries had gone by.

In each stage and at each step, the logical behavior is an aspect of the linguistic behavior. It is itself a linguistic aspect, but one which in more advanced specialization is distinguished by specialized naming. There is nothing bizarre about this treatment of the subjectmatter. Other inquiries have similar procedures. What would be bizarre for logic would be not to have such procedures, or in the end to refuse to recognize them. Take a simple matter of eating a meal. You can look up and see the man eat. But it is not a thing in a locked room, and still the thing, any more than the book on Logic is. " Eating " is not an independent in space and time. The whole life process, the organism built up in environment, the environment at work in organism, the digestive system under way, are the process. The man sitting at table with knife and fork in action would not be furnishing an instance of eating at all, except in such a setting. It is a case of aspects. (The word " abstract," incidentally, is not here used, because of the great variety of its philosophical uses, and because so many of these are " oriented toward a mind " in a way which makes the surrounding implications of their use difficult to determine for precautionary purposes.)

Comprehensively: all behaviors are seen as aspectual to the knowing organism, and to whatever to it is the known. The nameds are aspectual to the namings, and the namings to the nameds; or more carefully speaking, both aspects pertain to the full transactional event. Growth is from the body of the past, and to be seen as aspectual to it. Always the word " aspect " is to be taken as indicating differentiations in the activity of the joint knowings-known — never is it to be taken for detachables as " things " in separation — always the naming and the description are taken in organization such that the named — except in the streamers of indication for immediate futures — does not go outside the ranges of the fullest description.

Postscript *

The aim of this paper, so far as it has here been advanced, is to establish the locus or field of operations of Logic and logical fact with respect to their status in a factual cosmos. Only preliminary outlines of such location are here secured. The difficulties of communication with other workers form the most serious obstacle. Indeed I know not a single specialized word in the indicated regions of inquiry upon which I can safely rely to convey to a hearer just what I say it stands for to me in the present undertaking.

All procedure of this research is transactional in the sense in which the word transaction is established in the book *Knowing and the Known,* written with John Dewey. By this it is to be understood that the knower and the known are of joint significance in the general transactional case, much as are the entomologist and his bug in a particular case. The procedure is not by way of an attempt to pinch logic down to physical size, but, on the contrary, to build Physics and other Sciences alike along with Logic into comparable status for the task.

If we inspect Physics and the physical the former represents the Inquiry or Science of Physics; the latter represents the differentiation of fact. Similarly for Physiology and the physiological; and again for Behavioral Science and the behavioral (where Psychology and Sociology, today academically separated, are taken together under the name Behavior, as a third major region of inquiry). We locate Logic and the logical in the behavioral range of inquiry, the Logic being aspectually the Inquiry, and the logical fact being aspectually the subjectmatter inquired into. Within behaviors we inspect linguistic behaviors as operating upon the perceptual subjectmatter to increase its effectiveness. We inspect these linguistic behaviors on three levels of advance, styled respectively cue, characterization, and specification. Specifications become the best factual statements of today, or of any particular day, that are available. Here logical behaviors are found as advanced language turning back upon earlier language to improve its efficiency, much as the earlier language had in its time turned back upon the perceivings. Logic, we may say (without stressing the classification) is the Inquiry which examines this control of earlier language by later language.

* Written February 1954.

We have one further factual advance in this evolutionary procedure which is not reached for study in the portion of text here before us. It is that of Symbolic procedure, by which let us understand the " pure " mathematics of the present century, taken in coupling with Symbolic Logic so far as this latter seeks " purity " itself through the stripping off of ontological illusions. The issue, to be stressed further at another time, would be the application of a full symbolic system, whether mathematical or logical, to any sufficiently developed factual system; as, for example, let us say the nature of the application of mathematics symbolically viewed, to the most advanced range of physical specifications.

To repeat: we have physical, and then physiological, operations leading to behavioral operations primarily of the perceptual form. We have next linguistic stages of advance, first to improve perceivings, then in higher efficiency to improve the earlier language forms in their development step by step. We find Logic in its old traditional form attempting to deal with the most advanced linguistic specifications, again as program of improvement. Thus Logic appears as handled in a way akin to any one of these sciences that advance in linguistic form. We find this system of specifications being supplemented by another which, namely, we have called the symbolic and which is marked by its ceasing to hope to secure successes by supplying names to factual presentations outside of its own system along the lines of the ontological program of the older Logic. The difference in the attitude of the student at this point is that he no longer expects one form of linguistic-logical procedure to solve directly the hardest problems of another form; but lets each procedure do its own work factually in its own factual field.

CHAPTER SEVENTEEN

An Aid to Puzzled Critics*

Church and Smullyan undertake their reports [1] from a specialized point of view: namely, that logic and psychology offer radically different inquiries into radically different subjectmatters. They treat this point of view as if it were commonly known and everywhere accepted, but nevertheless as a fact which Dewey and Bentley overlook (Smullyan), or as one which by its very neglect permits these writers to regard themselves as investigating logic though actually working in different territory (Church). They thus allege a manifest deficiency in the constructions they review. Church's attitude is that " these papers take us outside the field of pure logic and into those of biology and sociology." Smullyan holds that there is " no evidence . . . that Dewey and Bentley have a clearer conception of the distinction between logic and the behavioral theory of inquiry than " has a certain psychologist he names, to whose work, he fancies, the writers give their " manifest approval "; and he adds that " it is only by confusing the two subjectmatters that they could have been led to affirm that ' modern logic ' is undependable without a developed theory of behavior." Under this approach both reviews seem to us to make defective reports upon the positions we occupy. In addition, neither review so much as mentions any of the half-dozen leading characteristics of our construction. We recognize fully that reports on scattered papers cannot be as accurate as those on organized books, and it is not at all by way of complaint, but rather as precaution for the future,

---

* The following is a communication prepared in 1948, revised in 1949, given approval by Dewey in April, 1949, and sent to the editor of *The Journal of Symbolic Logic* in September, 1949. It was originally intended to be offered for publication as a reply to criticisms by Church and Smullyan. We held it out, however, until shortly before the *Knowing and the Known* (Boston, 1949) book appeared, and then sent the communication to the editor as a memorandum, not for publication, but for the information of any reviewer of that book. The *Journal* did not put it to use in that way.

[1] Alonzo Church, review of four papers by John Dewey and Arthur F. Bentley, *The Journal of Symbolic Logic*, Vol. X (1945), pp. 132–33. Arthur Francis Smullyan, review of a paper, " Definition," by John Dewey and Arthur F. Bentley, *ibid.*, Vol. XII (1947), p. 99.

that we desire to reply. We shall not take space to develop, nor to discuss in any way, the merits of the main issues; nor shall we take space to examine specific charges of error against us, since debatable postulatory oppositions are involved in nearly all such cases. We aim to limit ourselves to the correction of statements about our position which seem to us to be misapprehensions.

There can be no possible objection — rather only strong endorsement — when Church and Smullyan employ the postulatory positions they occupy as the basis for their criticisms. For them, however, to treat the failure of other men to employ these positions as evidence that those other men have overlooked them, or are perhaps unaware of them altogether, is something different. Before all of us alike is the distinction between logic and psychology. We regard this distinction as primarily academic, or perhaps even in a more special sense as pedagogical. Church and Smullyan put a much higher valuation on it than this, however, when they take it to represent a basic differentiation of fact. As pedagogical it has been thoroughly well known both to Dewey and to Bentley since their college days. As a positive presentation of fact it has long since been opened up to persistent inquiry. Dewey's first publication in book form on this subject was forty-five years ago (1903), and this was followed by his treatises of 1916 and 1938. Bentley has approached the subject in books from the linguistic side in 1932 and 1935, and in sundry papers since then. If psychology is taken as inquiry into the psychological facts of human living, then beyond it one still finds human living involved when one turns to logic taken as dealing with logical facts. No matter how " pure " one makes his logic, it is still by and of men on earth; or, if it is not, then its isolation therefrom should be explicitly set down and described, and not merely taken for granted as adequate basis for construction at one time and for criticism at another. On our side, for us to assert such a common behavioral setting for both logic and psychology is not to attempt to absorb one into the other any more than it is to fail to notice the academic distinction involved. Instead — and this is a quite different matter — it is to endeavor to bring together into observation and inquiry much that today commonly enters as severed, and to seek to develop in human union certain phases of the system of human living in which both occur. It is just this that the recent joint studies of Dewey and Bentley have undertaken: to carry forward further research into the logical and the psychological as alike human. In it they no more seek to reduce logic to psychology than they seek to reduce psychology to logic. They face the split as they find it, in its various aspects. On the one side is logic, employing basically a terminology of a traditionally psychological character which involves or implies a "division" of men's "faculties" in a form which psychologists have today almost wholly abandoned; and demanding rigid fixations both of the elements out of which to build, and of the operations to be used in building. On the other side is psychology, which has lost its old confidence in the terms which it still uses as basic for its more comprehensive dealings with the main phases of the environed living of organisms: terms such as stimulus, action, reaction, and response. Here lies a region in which research is much needed, one that has no more bias on the psychological side than on the logical, one with no bent whatever for the reduction of the latter into the former. In such a situation an allegation of deficient acquaintances fails to do justice to the facts. Such an allegation, indeed, comes much as if one should object to biophysical research on the ground that the would-be biophysicist is ignoring the distinction between living and non-living matter, and should know better.

Closely akin to the above failure to give adequate statement is another comment in the Church review. This is to the effect that if one seeks firm names (such a search being the specified primary objective of the papers under review) then "the objective of exactness . . . ultimately requires that firm names be embedded in a firm language," while any language, to be firm, must rest upon "explicit listing of the primitive words or symbols, and explicit statement of the formation rules and rules of inference." This comment does not at all meet the distinction presented in our work. In one of the earlier of the papers under review, we forecast the position further developed later on: namely, that accuracy and exactness should be theoretically differentiated on the basis of a differentiation of name from symbol. We used "firm" with respect to naming in the sense of accuracy of naming. The "primitive" in the reviewer's sense lies in our region of exactness. We accept his "primitive," not as a hoped-for absolute control over naming, but as one of the verbal instruments for the technical formulation of a special theory of exactness. For our reviewer to say that firm naming cannot be achieved without initial foundation in "primitives" is adequate expression of his own position. For him to use this statement, however, as a criticism of our work is for him to leave our work itself wholly out of the situation. Here is no question of right or wrong between two procedures, but a preliminary question of correctness or incorrectness in setting down what one of the procedures is. The development of the use of primitives as the initial step in the fixation of namings is one program (theirs). The differentiation of symbols from names in such a way that a full symbolic system can be applied to a naming system to guide and aid it under a wide presentation of both symbols and namings as the activity of human beings is a contrasted program (namely, ours).

A further comparable misapprehension in the first review is assuredly its inference from a condensed phrasing in an early paper, taken apart from further development, that our position (or perhaps more narrowly directed, Bentley's position) " seems to be intended as a verdict against the step of abstraction . . . in pure semantics . . . hence presumably likewise against that involved in treating pure geometry in abstraction. . . ." Abstracting, however, is a process which we regard as characteristic in one way or another of all behavior, and not merely of the logical, so that its rejection thumbs down by what the reviewer calls a " bare dictum " would seem inconceivable to us as an attitude or expression of our own. We trust the constructive element may, in further readings, be found in recent work. It certainly is present in Dewey's treatment of proposition as proposal, and in his discussions of generals and abstracts of various kinds in his *Logic, The Theory of Inquiry*.

The second of the two reviews, except for the point mentioned in the opening paragraph above, seems to have nothing to do with any phase of our work, and certainly little or nothing to do with the subjectmatter of the paper on " definition." We dropped the word " definition " provisionally in our own work with regret, but it was not the word " definition," as Smullyan writes, but instead " the jumble of references " attached to the word in present logics, which we believed, and said, could not be brought into order without " a fair construction of human behavior across the field." This reviewer's attention is almost wholly given to the psychologist he mentions, instead of to us, and while we did, indeed, offer a citation from the psychologist with " manifest approval," we did it, not for his theoretical construction, of which little has yet been published or become known to us, but for his lively attention to facts as compared with some other workers, and for a certain remark he made from the psychological point of view, which we were pleased to find closely paralleling a remark of Ernest Nagel's from the logical point of view. Our position on the relation of logic and psychology would seem to us to be unmistakably set down in such passages as that at the end of a paper on " Definition " which Smullyan reviews, in footnote No. 13 of a paper on " Logicians' Underlying Postulations " in *Philosophy of Science*, 1946, and in repeated comments on the applications of the words " behavior " and " nature " throughout all the series of papers.

We appreciate the close analysis and counter-criticism given by Church to some of our criticisms of the often incoherent use of terminology in many current logical discussions. We expect to find faults in our own examination comparable to those in the texts we examined, and we believe also that somewhat comparable faults can be pointed out in Church's further treatment. We are not interested in particular defects, but in the status of our common linguistic background which permits so many confusions in the procedures of keen workers in the field. Better knowledge in this respect should, we feel, greatly benefit us all.

CHAPTER EIGHTEEN

Carnap's "Truth" *vs.* Kaufmann's "True"*

The renewed discussion[1] by Felix Kaufmann and Rudolf Carnap of the technical status of " truth " in logical construction brings the issues closer home than we commonly have them. The two logicians are in agreement that logical implication is not involved in the immediate argument and that it can be set to one side. Kaufmann finds Carnap still making use of " notions of absolute certainty or perfect knowledge or unalterable factual truth " (total coherence) and still treating these as constitutive rather than as regulative principles. Carnap, replying, gives his assurance that he can get along without employing the absolute viewpoint in any of these forms (except that he seems to have said nothing about " alterability ") but nevertheless still maintains the need and the factual presence of " truth " as a logical component, distinct both from " fact " and from " knowledge," in all logical inquiry and construction. In Kaufmann's view, however, there is here left only a shadowy wraith of truth, which should be as fully rejected as is the " absolute " truth of which it is remainder and reminder; and his proposal is to restrict " truth " — now reduced in effect, one may feel, to the word " true " — to the region of warranted assertibility as this may be developed on the basic of Dewey's construction of logic as inquiry. Kaufmann thus locates truth within the finding processes, against which Carnap holds that truth, while it may be found or known, is something for itself which has nothing to do with the processes of its finding or its knowing. Or, in still another phrasing, Carnap assigns to " semantic " truth in his system an essential

---

* This manuscript essay, written in January 1949, was not put in finished form, or intended for publication. The reader should consider the substance, not the wording, of this essay, which is published because of the editor's belief in its value for critical analysis of the issues discussed.

[1] Felix Kaufmann, " Rudolf Carnap's Analysis of ' Truth ' "; Rudolf Carnap, " Reply to Felix Kaufmann ": *Philosophy and Phenomenological Research,* Vol. IX (Dec. 1948), pp. 294-299; 300-304.

and necessary position over and above, and apart from, any " truth by warranty," by " high confirmation," or by " being known to be true," which Kaufmann's program can produce.

The discussion as it is before us includes on both sides much débris from past strategies and incursions. I shall confine myself to the central argument, though this must include an exhibit of the background of beliefs and verbal attitudes which underlie it, and I shall employ everyday phrasings so far as I can approximate them. The ordinary language is troublesome enough because of the various overlappings of all the more important of its pertinent terms, but logical phrasings regress at times into impactions even more destructive of understanding. At any rate, whichever form of expression is used, an occasional check from one to the other has its merits.

On Carnap's side the discussion is in terms of " sentences," and although Kaufmann finds that Carnap's distinction of sentences from propositions is an improvement in clarity, he himself employs in the main the propositional form. I shall assume that the two manners of statement approximate each other sufficiently well to permit issues to be joined for our present examination, even though it may be held that a further clarification in this respect would quickly do away with the present theoretical incompatibilities altogether.

I

Carnap continues discussion, under Kaufmann's citation, of four sentences he had previously employed as bases of development. They are of the following types:

(1) (. . . is . . .)
(2) (. . . " is " is " true " . . .)
(3) (. . . X, at the present moment, knows " is " . . .)
(4) (. . . X knows " ' is ' is ' true ' " . . .)

Carnap's established background, his controlling attitude in all his procedure (it is also controlling in most present logic, though this point is not significant for the moment), is the particulate differentiation, or rather the particulate stress in the differentiation, of the names, mostly nouns and verbs or replacements for them, in his sentence presentation. (Status of other verbal components may be set to one side during the present inquiry.) When he writes " it is " he fixates both the " it " and the " is." For " knows " he puts the form " X-knows." When he writes " true " the indicated sentential " is " is given stressed status in advance as particulate " truth." (" Entails," " leads," " follows," etc., in the present text under examination have particulate adaptation, but this also can be set aside in the immediate task.)

Using his sentential device as a sort of culture medium in which to breed specimens adapted to his purpose for study, Carnap asserts that (1) and (2) entail each other, and are thus equivalent, other allied phrasings being that they have " the same factual content," and " convey the same information." More definitely put, the assertion is that, for all purposes, to say " it is " is to say that " ' saying it is ' is ' true,' " and *vice versa*. Derived from this equivalence, another equivalence, one between (3) and (4), is asserted. Within these equivalences, sentences (1) and (3) are held apart from (2) and (4) respectively by placing the two former in the " object " language and the two latter in a " meta " language (this being apparently not a form of sentence classification proper, but rather a current device *ad hoc* to deal with certain types of difficulties), though without employing this distinction further in this particular discussion. Somewhat surprisingly, this distinction does not interfere with the equivalence between (1) and (2), i.e., between " is " and " true "; and still more surprisingly, the equivalence of the " is " and the " true " does not interfere with the further maintenance of " true " in the self-existential and self-evidential manner in which it is primarily introduced, as will appear in the several citations to follow which set forth Carnap's central and essential opposition to Kaufmann in this matter. As for (1) and (3), Carnap reports that it is obvious that they do not say the same. By an inference from this, (2) and (3) do not say the same, this being in Carnap's phrasing " rather obvious." By further inference (2) and (4) do not say the same; still further we may presume that in the somewhat bizarre case of (1) and (4) these do not " say the same."

Rephrasing in the hope at once of increased vividness and increased precision, we may report Carnap thus far holding that an expressed " is " and an expressed " is true " are the same in content. Likewise (and continuing to understand sentential embodiment) are a " know-is " and a " know-is-true." But an " is " and a " know-is " are not; nor are an " is-true " and a " know-is "; nor an " is-true " and a " know-is-true," nor an " is " and a " know-is-true." In other words, for practical purposes of sentential procedure, and subject to one very great reservation, Carnap incorporates being-true with being, and knowing-being-true with knowing-being; while at the same time he rejects as " obviously " false all suggestions that knowing is involved in either being or being-true after the manner in which being is involved in being-true, or after the manner in which the two knowing forms are involved in each other. By inference from this, he rejects all suggestions that being-known-as-true is so involved. Of this a portion is called "obvious"; a portion is said to be inferrable and also "rather obvious" (by which an ought-to-be-obvious is perhaps intended); while the remainder is variously inferrable.

What is here actually "obviously" — if I also may be permitted to use the word — is (i) that "be," "true," and "know" are deliberately introduced in particulate separations; (ii) that "be" and "true" are specially organized by what one might call "tacit dictum" in a situation in which further description would be welcome and in which, without it, the equivalence asserted may cause eyebrows to rise as high as my juncture of "tacit" and "dictum" in a single appellation is apt to do; (iii) that the "X-knows" which is introduced is a closely limited particularization of "knows"; and (iv) that "true" and "know" are forcefully held apart by a procedure based on the "obvious" and backed up by an "implies." By uniting "be" and "true" sententially Carnap gives "body" to his sentence-constructions which otherwise they would grievously lack. By severing "true" from "know" he gives to "true" precisely that separateness, that maintenance of the particulate, which marks in the outcome the difference between him and Kaufmann in their treatment of this word. So far as the set-up goes, what comes out at the end is what went in at the start. What went in as judged by this outcome was apparently an already fortified "true" and an already despoiled "know."

II

Kaufmann, appraising Carnap's sentential exhibit, proposes the replacement of the "X-knows" by "it is known." Making this change, he quickly shows, through a simple verbal manipulation, a certain redundancy and a certain contradiction. Carnap rejects the change to the form "it is known," though not contesting the point as to the redundancy and the contradiction, but insists nevertheless that his "main point" — what he was really after — in his exhibit continues to hold good despite this: the point, namely, that (2) does not imply (4), that is, that "to be true" does not imply that an "X knows it to be true." This, however, as we have seen, merely means that if one starts by cutting down the knowing to a trivial individual X, at a trivial moment, one winds up in that way also. While Carnap's position in his reply to Kaufmann cannot be contested — and I doubt if we could find many in everyday life who would want to contest it — that for any "it is known" there must be *some* person as a knower, i.e., as a knowing organism, it does not follow that this makes a statement in the form "X-knows" the most significant and useful manner of statement available for logical purposes. Kaufmann's " it is known " is not merely an impersonal phrasing for a personal fact; it is a positive assertion that by " knowing," for logical objectives, he understands, establishes, and employs the *acceptance* of a proposition on the basis of *evidence* in accord with adopted *rules of verification*.

It is here that the radical distinction lies. If Carnap's case is merely that of " this little man knows or does not know it's true," then the " truth " for logic will at once be seen as " big " and as " far beyond the little man's private range." If, on the other hand, the case is the sweeping one of the full cultural growth and presence of truth, there is much more involved than " little man, here and now." Every reference to food requires a reference to an X-that-eats, but physiologists do not cast their main statements in the form of X-eating, nor do they erect a special realm of digestivity somewhere in between a presumptively absolute life-force and an observable human nature's daily food. There are physical, physiological, special pathological, ecological, and cultural inquiries to be made; and this remark applies as much to inquiry into knowings as to inquiry into feedings. This situation is much more significant for logic than is such a verbal slippage of inference as that to which Kaufmann called attention, and which both Kaufmann and Carnap treated as an incidental defect, and not by its very presence at all as crucial. Summarizing background for Kaufmann, we find he retains the particulate structure, and does not alter the status of " is," unless the difference between his " proposition " and Carnap's " sentence " has this effect; but that by broadening " know " he gets a marked simplification (or " error," if one takes that view of it) in his account of " true."

One further comment suggested by Carnap's treatment of " truth " should be made before comparing his construction in more detail with Kaufmann's; although the comment for that matter applies as much to Kaufmann's work and to that of any other logician. That is, if the logician's determinations are held to be correct, they are to be so regarded *strictly within the framework of his assumptions:* these being in the Carnap case, namely, that sentences can be made the subject of study with an eye glancing sideways at what they stand for; that the components of sentences enter as particulate, and as standing for particulate facts; and that the particulate " is," " true," and " a man knows at the present moment " are adequately logical presentations of the being, truth, and knowledge that is under inquiry.

III

So much for backgrounds, without acquaintance with which the appraisal of the specific characterizations of truth, on the one side or the other, would be futile. Kaufmann's exhibit is simple. He strips off logical implication, and after that everything in the nature of the absolute, the timeless, or the unchangeable, and for true accepts what is left plainly before the eyes, namely, those assertions that are verified, highly confirmed or warranted. Carnap's case is more difficult, for he strips off not only what Kaufmann stripped off, but also what Kaufmann retained, and declares the actual " semantic " truth to be different from all three. In addition to Kaufmann's " true," Carnap posits " truth." One might say that it is the " warranty " itself, the process of warranty, that Carnap rejects. However, this *process* of warranty is not that which Kaufmann calls true, but the " warranted assertion," or assertibility, while it is something over and above even this warranted assertibility that Carnap must exhibit as specialized " semantical truth." I shall exhibit the difference mainly in citations, despite the additional space this takes, because of the greater safeguards it gives against the shifting implications of words.

" Factual truth," says Kaufmann, " is synonymous with warranted assertibility . . . for the logic of science " (though of course other ways of applying the words exist). " We can always replace ' true ' by ' verified,' " etc. " Degrees of certainty " can be handled " without any reference to the notions of absolute certainty or perfect knowledge." To say that what " is at present warranted . . . need not be true " is merely to say that what " is at present warranted, need not be *permanently* warranted." " Truth . . . as unalterable (timeless) " is a residue of old beliefs under which empirical knowledge was inevitably *im*perfect. " The assignment of unalterable *truth-values* . . . is bound to lead us astray." So little actual use is made of " the notion of truth as an unalterable property " of synthetic propositions, as to strengthen " the suspicion that there is none." Purported " truth-functions " are nothing but meaning-relations. " The regulative principle (ideal) of factual truth " should not be mistaken for " a constitutive principle of inquiry."

In contrast with Kaufmann, consider Carnap's equally, or perhaps even more, confident affirmations. " The truth of a sentence means simply that the facts are as described in the sentence, whether anybody knows it or not." " The question as to how we are to find out whether the facts are as described is a different matter." It is this latter question which " is to be answered by stating criteria of confirmation." " We *must* " (my italics) " distinguish between ' true ' on the one hand and ' known to be true, . . .' ' warranted as assertible,' etc., on the other." " This is what I maintain against the conceptions of Kaufmann, Dewey, Neurath and others." Truth in the semantical sense " has nothing to do with . . . perfect knowledge or absolute certainty." " I . . . state emphatically that the semantical concept of truth does not encompass any one of [Kaufmann's] three concepts "; i.e., logical implication, warranted assertibility, or total coherence.

I have given these citations instead of using a swifter paraphrase to make sure there will be no slippage in understanding of the words on either side. I do not hesitate to assert that both men must be taken to mean literally what they say, and that reinterpretations are not here in order. Compare verification as process, warranted assertion, and semantical process. Kaufmann does not say that the process is the truth, or true, but rather the warranted assertion. Carnap requires a further step: semantical truth, truth *per se,* even though not truth *in excelsis.* Kaufmann's " known to be true," broadly taken, *is* what " true " is. Carnap's " known to be true " is linked with " verified "; " warranted," etc., is seen as a stage on the way to " truth." More concisely still, Kaufmann's goal is the *true;* Carnap's the (semantical) *truth.*

Ostensively speaking, Kaufmann makes his exhibit. But at what does Carnap point the finger? That is still for him to show us, or for his sympathetic reader to locate on his own account. For myself, I have gone over his text repeatedly and I have found only a single sentence which purports to exhibit semantical truth in operation or operationally. This is in terms of the equivalence of sentences (2) and (1), which, he says, " simply refutes " Kaufmann if the latter " means to say that the concept of truth is meaningless because no procedure for its application is specified, in other words, no operational definition is given." Carnap's development of this is that if we possess sentence (1) " which none of us regards as meaningless," it follows then that sentence (2) cannot be meaningless. However, under the examination of these sentences in section I of the present essay, such an argument lacks conviction.

In place of *pointing* at instances of semantical truth, Carnap shifts to a question of " the usefulness of the concept of truth," which, he thinks, may be the problem which Kaufmann really has in mind. To appraise his procedure here we must differentiate his " concept of truth " in a way he himself does not expressly do, into (a) the use of the word " truth," (b) Kaufmann's warranty concept, and (c) Carnap's semantical concept, referring to these as (a) the word, (b) K-true, and (c) C-truth. Thus differentiated I find in his assertions and illustrations (a) and (b) and (c) rejected for certain cases, and (a) and (b) in certain acceptances but nowhere an indicated case of (c) in asserted use — this, of course, assuming my reading of his text is adequate. The points Carnap makes are as follows: (i) The word is not needed in either inductive or deductive logic. (ii) C-truth is not needed in either; (iii) the word is convenient in deductive logic; (iv) it would be overly ascetic to exclude the word from deductive logic, merely " to preserve the conceptual purity " of such logic; (v) " in other fields " . . . " the concept of truth " (a?, b?, c?) " is indispensable "; (vi) while in these other fields the simpler statements require neither word nor C-truth. (vi) For the more complex statements, the word (here called " the term ' true ' ") in general is not eliminable; (vii) a statement of the form (2) such as " the sentence uttered by X at 10 A.M. this morning is true " cannot be transformed into a sentence of the form (1) eliminating " the term ' true.' " (viii) A comment on the relative frequency of " true statements " in statistics cannot be transformed so as to eliminate the " term," nor can in general any statement about other people's statements which do not repeat the statements themselves (though analogous, but not equivalent, statements are in some cases practicable). (ix) Finally we are told that with respect to " empirical investigations concerning human behavior " (those from psychological, sociological, legal, and historical points of view being particularly mentioned) " when the concept of truth appears within contexts of this kind it is not, in general, eliminable."

As to the first eight illustrations, if there is anything of C-truth positively indicated in the various uses of " term " and " concept " I have failed to detect it. There's nothing there but what men force in. A casual " correct " would serve most needs. As for the last case, that of the social sciences, it seems certain that no experienced worker in any of its fields would dream today of attaining by his own efforts, no matter how strenuous, any trace whatever of C-truth. A K-true would be a wild ambition in anything but the most trivial cases. The exhibit of an instance of C-truth still remains to be made.

Excursus

The whole scheme of Carnap's postulation is badly in need of assembly, arrangement, and appraisal. He assumes the " sentence " as an adequate tool for dealing with contents or referents of sentences and words. He tries to lift himself by his bootstraps.

Probably " is " and " know " are unalterable properties of sentences as much as " true " is assumed to be. " Carnap " is a property of a sentence too. If my memory is right, Fritz Mauthner stated this decades ago in his *Kritik der Sprache*.

"True," "is," and "know" all enter in particulation. Carnap should show in what sense this is dependable. "X-knows" falls far short of the "know" that involves or is involved in, or may need study, as involving or being involved in "is" and "true." "K-knows-now" is still worse.

A form of "knowing," namely, inferring, is used to establish the distinction between knowing and true. One might say out of a wider union a minor cut is engineered. One should not forget that the severance is partly "obvious," or somewhat so.

Without the declared union of true and is, the sentence for "is" (1) would lose what appearance it has of being of this world in any respect.

The retention of particulate separates in "is" and "true" despite the "equivalence" (though the only backing for the separation is in the distinction of object- and meta-language) is all that keeps "know" from tangling with a clotted "is-true." Even an "X-knows" would be in for the kill like a wolf on the fold. A genuine "know" would merely need to sit and grin.

Holding conclusions within range of assumptions might be suggested. Ultimately the background study of Perception, Naming, and Symbol using will be required. Carnap never dreams of such knowledge.

Some Additional Comments

Carnap deals with verbal building blocks, not with men in an actually investigatable world, and insists that logical inquiries be pursued on his basis.

Carnap's form of "X-knows" is what makes him need a C-truth beyond the K-true. Kaufmann's wider "knows" is what connects with true.

Carnap should examine his continual listing "knows to be true" as if synonymous with verifying, confirming. Carnap starts with a fortified truth and a despoiled know. And he ends so also.

Pedigree of C-truth is out of Absolute by Sentence.

The leap from K-true to C-true is a bigger leap than that from the denumerable Aleph (Aleph-zero) to the upper Alephs. The denumerable infinity is needed. The continuity is needed as long as verbal formulation remains defective as now. But C-truth has no need at all. It is the faint shadow of ejected Pretense.

This study is worth while to me because it shows vividly how trivial is a logic separated from life.

It will be argued from Carnap's point of view that his " X " is a free variable and not a limited particularization. The " X " would then be read " someone knows at any time " and not " a certain individual knows at a certain moment." My attention will also be called firmly to the " is true " as dealing only with sentences. Given such appraisal my examination may then be taken directly as treating such distinctions and limitations as untenable.

CHAPTER NINETEEN

Muscle-Structured Psychology*

I find today that almost all behavior subjected to psychological inquiry is still approached and studied as if programmed by a Patterner, Maker or Decider, which (or who) is taken as present as an inhabitant or associate of the active human organism. No doubt a fair half of the research workers do not profess belief in such an actor, nor do they introduce one *officially* in their studies. My point is that, belief or no belief, acknowledgment or no acknowledgment, these companionate actors are still distinctively at work inside the terminology through which behavioral research is developed, and that they are still used as border-markers between an alleged physical and an alleged psychological in this subjectmatter. A half century ago mechanistic attempts to replace the human actor gained prominence but proved themselves to be as meager and inadequate as have been the conventional mentalist's attempts to hold the fort permanently and irrevocably for himself. Bowels of mercy, splenetic dispositions, kind hearts, and big brains were no more organically developed than were similar qualities and quantities put in mentalistic terms. The current material and psychical "particulars" are equally non-constructive and disintegrative for modern inquiry. And when the organic process is handled as if within a skin, and not as technically a transaction of the organism and environment jointly, the effect is all the worse.

The human body, anatomists tell us, is about 80 per cent muscle. Inquiries into habit are inquiries directly into muscular patterning, and do not need assignment to powers and capacities developed in other than muscular terminologies. I do not mean this statement to interfere with anyone's belief, or customary method of talk — I am considering only workmanship in research and its needs. But it is just as reasonable, if not as conventional, to refer all the behaviors, so far as they are studied as actions within a skin, to muscular locus as to refer them to neurocephalic locus. The value of "intentionality," if one wishes to adopt

* From sketches for a paper on Behavioral Locus (1950).

a strong phrasing for marking off the psychological from the physical, may be assigned to muscle as reasonably as to a mind, a brain, a brain escort, or, for that matter, to an escorted brain. By a turn of a wrist the mental and the mechanistic phrasings alike become unnecessary and the disturbing influences running between individual and social in pompously fictitious terms are on their way toward disappearance.

CHAPTER TWENTY

Kennetic Inquiry*

Kennetic inquiry is a name proposed for organized investigation into the problem of human knowings and knowns, where this is so conducted that the full range of subjectmatters — all the knowings and all the knowns — form a common field. Such inquiry is to be undertaken under express postulation, and without specific allegation or assurance of ultimate factual status. The postulation deals with concrete instances of knowings and knowns instead of with purported faculties, powers, or realities; and under it every specific instance of a knowing is taken along with its specific known as a single *transaction* in the field. It abandons, root, branch, and fruit, the conventional severance of detachable knowers from detachable knowns. To it the word " epistemological " rates as a historical curiosity, stripped of all pretense to authority in research, and ripe only for the museum. The words " philosophical " and " metaphysical " become similarly irrelevant to our inquiry: as irrelevant as they are in physical laboratories today when actual research is in progress. Even the word " knowledge " itself is, at least for the time being, discarded, since it is steeped in vagueness, and unable to qualify technically as purveyor of determinable fact. The words " knowing " and " known " remain, however, usable, if properly provided with plural forms, and thus made able to stand for concrete instances of organic-environmental action in behavioral space and time.

Thus organized, knowings and knowns together become events in process in a cosmos, system, or field of fact, such as postulation projects and anticipates. The inquiry is then on the way, or believes itself on the way, toward becoming science. It is science in the making, if by " science " is understood a procedure of observation and postulation, with all observation recognizing that it takes place under postulation, and with all postulation recognizing that it arises out of observation; and if freedom for inquiry is secured through the smashing of the old blockades so long

* From *Science,* Vol. CXII, No. 2922 (December 29, 1950), pp. 775-83.

maintained under the dominance of inadequate speech forms of barbaric origin and overripe habituation, peculiarly those proclaiming purportedly particulate sense-data.

Although the name " kennetic " has not heretofore been in use, inquiry along these suggested lines has already been undertaken, and report thereon has been made, in a book *Knowing and the Known* (22)† by John Dewey and the present writer. To form the name " kennetic," the Scottish " ken " or " kenning " has been preferred to any word in the groups centering around " cognition," " gnosis," or " epistemology," since the latter have long since become fixated beyond recall in implications hostile to present purposes. " Ken " has a further advantage over these other roots in recalling the early Teutonic " can," which signified the activity of knowing, inclusive of " know-how " and of " be able." Using " kennetic," we may, with minimum risk of distortion, deal with active knowings as found among men who are known phases of a cosmos, which is itself in process of being known.

We here proceed to take men as in nature, to take their behaviors of whatever kind as " natural," and to take all their knowings as naturally behavioral, along with their other activities. We then strive to discover what observation may yield under the employment of such new namings as we may attain when freed from the interference of the old hostile terminologies.

The Kennetic Procedure

Kennetic inquiry, as already indicated, omits from its proceedings all facultative action of " mind " or otherwise individuated " knowers " on the side of the knowings, and all dogmatically proclaimed or otherwise individuated " ultimate reals " on the side of the knowns. I have never myself made observation of any such " pure knowers " or " pure reals "; I know no one who has; and I believe no claim to such observation has ever yet been made in a way to conform with modern scientific standards free from linguistic hypnosis. I assert that *it is easier literally to observe — to see — man-in-process with environs,* and to see this full process as one transaction, than *it can possibly be literally to observe a " soul," a " spirit," or a psychic " mind "* (this last, a lineal descendant from the two others), or to see a " thing " as a " real " substratum apart from all our knowing and from conditioning thereby. What we find to observe under our postulation is the organism and its environs in natural presence and

† Parenthetical boldface figures refer to References at end of chapter.

process together, linguistically still unfractured or otherwise schizophrenic. Permitting observation to run free within its framework of postulation, and putting all the concentrated attention we can behind it, we secure reports on the unfractured knowing-known events. All such observation and such reports and such events-reported we style *trans*actional, in contrast with the *inter*actional reports obtained under mechanistic inquiry, and with the *self*-actional reports under conventionally " psychic " presumptions. In so doing we require the " selves " and the " mechanisms," equally with the " transactions," to present themselves in postulatory form, free from pretense to underlying authoritative status. We shall adopt the word " behavioral "[1] to apply to those events involving organisms and environs which, as events, are not technically physiological or physical, nor directly covered in physiological or physical inquiry. To repeat: All behavioral events are by postulation transactions; all knowings and knowns as subjectmatters of inquiry belong among transactional behaviors.

Before undertaking to locate the knowings and the knowns definitely among the behaviors, let us briefly characterize the setting of the behaviors themselves as *naturally* viewed within the vastly wider field of all that is " known-to-modern-science."[2] Many differences in viewpoints as to the range of scientific inquiry are still offered us, and many different classifications of the sciences are given. We need here give attention solely to the three great technical fields recognized as basic under all classifications, and perhaps best styled Physical, Physiological, and Behavioral (where Psychological may be used as a possible alternative for the third, if strongly preferred). We treat the distinctions as those of subjectmatters of inquiry-in-growth (i.e., of science) and not in the older way as marking off, or resting on any assured differences in the

---

[1] Anyone who prefers " psychological " may substitute it for " behavioral," provided he holds it to the given postulation, and adequately rejects the introduction of every form of disconnected " psyche." Those who prefer the word " cultural " would find it necessary to make that word expressly include the full range of the " psychological."

[2] An appraisal of the organization of scientific knowing with common-sense knowing will be found in Chapter X of the book referred to (22). Other recent papers by John Dewey make further development. A recent comment by E. U. Condon, in which he notes " the doubtful speculation which has characterized most of the philosophic absorptions of modern science," speaks of Dewey in the following terms: " One of the rare exceptions, one who has in a significant and profound way understood and used both science and the scientific method is John Dewey. He points out clearly that the growth of rational thought processes may be considered as a response to the biological necessity of adaptation to the environment. Its ultimate function, he says, is that of ' prospective control of the conditions of the environment.' It follows then that ' the function of intelligence is not that of copying the objects of the environment, but rather of taking account of the way in which more effective and more profitable relations with these objects may be established in the future ' " (19).

" kinds " of " materials " that " exist." [3] It is indeed true that " physiological " and " behavioral " belong alike under " biological " when this is brought into contrast with the " physical," since they both have to do with the organic. But under present-day observation, and in the status of current inquiry and for it only, the *differentiation* of *techniques* between physiological and behavioral research cuts as deep as that between physical and physiological, and this should be technically recognized in all appraisal as of today.[4] Physical research cannot adequately advance its own technical form of description and report across the full physiological field, nor can technical physiological research in the general case be advanced to portray the behavioral field. The " languages " of report remain for the present noninterchangeable. No examination of brain or nerves or of muscle or viscera can report that " an election was held," nor even that " a cow was seen." The central cores of the three great regions are natural; the bands of transitional vagueness between them are to be taken as natural; the inquiry into them is natural. But for present-day guidance with respect to the knowings of the knowns and to the knowns as undergoing knowing, the technical differentiation as above set forth remains in effect.

The Behavioral Background

As between physiological and behavioral subjectmatters, the differentiation can be stated in terms of a comparative directness of process in the former, which shows itself in contrast with a certain typical indirectness in the latter (22, Chap. VI). Soon after Jacques Loeb at the beginning of this century published his — at that time world-exciting — reports on dominant physical processes within and across the skins of organisms (28), H. S. Jennings (26) noted a characteristic in low organisms different from that of any immediate direct physical or chemical excitation and reaction. This was found in the sea urchin, for example, when an enemy cast a shadow, and the organism moved to evade, not the shadow itself, but the oncoming, hostile shadow-caster. The present investigators, reporting in *Knowing and the Known* (22), have employed the word " sign " to name this technically characteristic " indirect-

---

[3] The word " exist " occurs in two other passages in this paper but there, as here, it is set off by quotation marks so as not to involve the writer in any claims conventionally made with respect to its range of application. If here brought into the discussion, the word would be treated transactionally within the range of designational behaviors. Signalings are too immediate, vivid, and hard-hitting to pause for existential reference, whereas symbolings have passed beyond the need for it and are even beginning to overcome the desire. (For this terminology, see the section on " Specific Positions Attained.")

[4] For a strong warning against " biologism," see Bertalanffy (10).

ness," as it is found across the entire behavioral field. They chose this word, not so much despite its enormous variety of current applications, as perhaps on account of them, and because none of these applications has succeeded in ruling the field in which dozens of applications are needed to work in harness. The range of "sign," understood *always* as *trans*actional sign-process, was made coincident with the range most generally of behavior itself. This was to make, in effect, sign-actings (which include sign-knowings) the characteristic technical process in the behavioral field, as distinct from the physiological and, of course, also from the physical processes.

Within the range of sign, the word "signal" was chosen to name the underlying sensori-perceptive level; the word "designation" for the next higher evolutionary level — namely, that of linguistic sign operation; and the word "symboling" for a still higher range in the evolutionary sense, to which specific differentiation was given — namely, that of mathematics, inclusive of a comparatively small, but very important, part of modern symbolic logic that is itself rigorously mathematical, rather than a still-confused survival from the older logical attitudes.[5]

The words "know" and "known" are applied in current writing at almost any point across this range of behavior, from protozoa to the purest of pure mathematics. An insect is said to know its way around, and a mathematician (it is said), his technical business. Without objecting to other uses or attempting to set up a program of naming for others, attention here will be centered closely on the range of knowings that occur in the central regions, those of designation. This knowing is by naming,[6] and its implications are of the general type "knowing-to-exist." Common procedures in these regions are of the type that seem all the more dogmatically satisfied as to *what* they assert to "exist," the less

---

[5] Fifty years ago a typical classification of the behavioral (psychological) was into sense, intellect, and will — all "faculties." Josiah Royce's sensitivity, docility, and initiative, covering physical contacts, social setting, and individual going-power, might have brought a great advance, if factually developed (33). Present-day psychologists' organizations are all, or almost all, "capacitative" — that is to say, merely weakened forms of the "facultative." Our proposed distribution into signaling, designating, and symboling is, we hope, fully freed of the capacitative. In the ordinary conventional organization of behavioral subject-object, where "subject" appears we are to understand "environed organism," and, where "object" appears, "known-named-environs." Lacking, however, in the present exhibit is treatment of emotional events, which, from the crudest to the most refined, are handled by assigning all direct pain components and comparably direct "liking" components to physiological inquiry, stripping out the blurred knowing-naming effects for transactional study, and thus readying oneself for further inquiry into the unclear physiological-behavioral marginal regions.

[6] For a single instance of temporarily widened application of the word "know," see part (g) of the section on "Specific Positions Attained." For the word "exist," see footnote 3.

assured they are as to what is meant by the *exist* portion of their assertion.

The word "signal" was adopted for the lowest stratum of behaviors largely because of Pavlov's increasing employment of it as his skill and breadth of vision increased (24, 31, 32). It is used to cover the entire complex of perceivings, inclusive of the sensory, the locomotive, and the manipulative. It covers them as action in living organisms. It covers them — and this must be continually reiterated — transactionally and not otherwise. It presents organisms and environs in process in system. It does not have to do with something organic or superorganic taken on its own. It permits no such fictional "third" item as a "percept" of the kind one finds still accepted in many current texts, despite William James's brilliant identification and rejection of such "intervening thirds" fifty years ago (25). If a dog's bark scares a rabbit, the signal as here viewed is neither a bark in a world of its own, nor is it a dog as such, nor is it a specialized process of rabbit's nerve and brain, but always an aspect or phase of the situation seen in full.

The word "designation" is used as the name for the next higher level of behaviors. It would be better if we could speak always, as is here done occasionally, of "name" directly. "Designation" is substituted only because "name" is still so desperately involved conventionally with presumptive, external, static "things named" — the kind out of which word magic grows — that almost inevitably conveyance of meaning is distorted or destroyed. Designations are subdivided into cue, characterization, and specification, as stages in evolutionary growth; the first of these still in process of emerging from signal behavior; the second, comprising ordinary common-sense naming; the third, demanding ever-increased accuracy and, at its highest level, representing modern science itself — not as static, but as living growth, and with the old expectant certainties gone for good. This great expansion of designation not only arises out of signal, but operates, no matter what slips and falls it has by the wayside, to increase the efficiency of signal. This can be vividly shown under transactional postulation, although under the traditional constructions it is only partially and crudely apparent. In the old form observation breaks into fragments that cannot well be patched together again. In the new form, organisms-environs, knowings-knowns, namings-nameds, can be seen in operation and studied without putative know*ers* or putative *reals* behind them as guarantors or guarantees.

Symbolings evolve out of designatings and operate to increase the efficiency of designatings, much as the latter evolve out of signalings and work to increase the efficiency of signalings. The symbolings have learned in long experience that, for best results, they must forfeit the right to use their own components as names. This forfeiture is no loss; it strips the symbolings down for action. The surviving logics of the past and their reconstructions of today, including most of symbolic logic, still operate under a confusion of symbolings with designatings and even with signalings as well. The struggle, dating mainly from Frege and Russell, to put "logical foundations" under mathematics without seeking any foundations for the reliability of the "logic" relied upon, makes the confusion all the worse. Under the transactional approach a great simplification occurs, with exactness of symbol coming definitely and explicitly to the aid of accuracy of specification.

A Reminder

Let us summarize with respect to observation of behaviors in a scientifically transactional background, within which background, in turn, definite examination of knowings and knowns may proceed. We accept the cosmos as before us in knowings, and at the same time we accept all our knowings as its outgrowth. We regard this cosmos as no better assured in our knowings of it than our knowings are assured by reference to it. We are satisfied with this basis for our research. The cosmos is our realm of fact, where "fact" requires both knowings and knowns, but makes no claim to be either of them by itself, whether today or in extrapolation into the future. Darwin brought first animal life, and then human life, under evolution called natural. Driblets of behavioral interpretation have followed his course, but little more. Efforts are here being made to bring knowings-knowns, as themselves behaviors, into system with the rest of fact in a factual cosmos. They are not in system now. The psychologists toss all such issues to the "dogs of epistemology" they seem to find whining under their banquet table. The epistemologists officiate proudly at a high altar of their own persuasion.

Specific Positions Attained

Kennetic inquiry is still regrettably compelled to spend a good part of its time in delivering itself from old philosophical-linguistic bondage. It has, however, already acquired positively a number of footholds that it regards as safe for future use. However bizarre at first sight some of the reports thereby secured may seem, they will as a body, we believe, establish their reasonableness as acquaintance grows.

For this outcome, however, free development of the extensions and durations of behavioral events must be permitted in behavioral, rather than in Newtonian, forms. To postulate events outside spatial and temporal characteristics altogether, as was the older " mentalist " procedure, would be absurd today. Newtonian clock ticks and foot rules, however, are far from sufficient. When physicists needed greater freedom in this respect, they took it; but even adjustments under Einsteinian relativity will not alone suffice for our needs, nor are the various suggestions of recent physiologies adequate to reach across the behavioral field (8). Behavioral *pasts* and *futures* — histories and goals, habits and purposings — are before us descriptively in behavioral *presents*. Descriptively factual knowings-knowns hold fars and nears together under their own specializations of action. Without at least the beginnings of appreciation for this possible need in behavioral inquiry — without, at least, tolerance for experiment under it — grasp of the following positions will not be gained.

(a) Word-meaning and word-embodying are not separates but occur together as one behavioral transaction. No locus in the cosmos can be found either for verbal " meaning " by itself, or for verbal " embodiment " held in separation. On the one hand, word-meanings as severed from man's linguistic activity are not observable, nor are they attainable as subjectmatters of independent inquiry, despite all the reams that have been written purportedly about them. On the other hand, sounds and graphs apart from their meaningful appearance as man's living activity are not " words " at all for anything beyond a surface inquiry. Physics and physiology are, of course, justified in their special inquiries into their respective aspects of verbal activity, but as aspects only. To use the ancient academic labeling, what they offer is of the character of anatomy and is not an analysis of the full event. For adequate behavioral analysis a full and fair field must be open.

(b) More broadly inspected, no field of events identifiable as " language " can be accurately established and brought separately under inquiry in severance from another field alongside known as the " meanings " of language. Without life-in-process neither language nor linguistic meanings can survive any more than could other behavioral events, of whatever kind.

(c) In the region of designations the namings and the knowings are one process, not two. Where the naming is taken transactionally at its level of behavioral advance, it itself is the behavioral knowing. Knowing through naming is a phase of human organism-in-action. In organism-in-action the knowing is the naming; so postulated; so observed; so investigated.

(d) Once able to see word-meaning and naming-knowing as living processes of organism-in-environs, we may next advance to observation of the knowing and the known as transactionally comprised in common event. An organism, a rock, and a tree remain before us as heretofore, subject to such physical or physiological inquiry as we may wish. Insofar, the scientific situation remains unchanged. But when rock flies and dog dodges and tree is evaded in flight, the situation becomes one in which subjectmatters are on a further level of complexity. Here it is but crude and imperfect presentation, an affair of casual, practical report rather than of scientific procedure, when rock and dog and tree are taken as separates, and when independent initiatives or resistances are attributed to any or all of them separately in the style of the older days, when " actualities " were presumably certified to the scientist as " given " to him in advance of his inquiry. Physicists faced a *similar* transformation in the case of the electron. To say today that the electron is an " entity " known to be such on its own, outside of and apart from the processes of its being known, would be to misrepresent modern scientific report. The electron is " known " under specialized knowings, and in highly specialized technical manners. The electron accepted in physical research is one that " works," not one that claims " reality "; it is dealt with, this is to say, as fact within the frame of existing research, not as assured for eternity. The gene in physiology more and more comes to occupy a similar position (23).

(e) What is the case for the knowing-known is the case also for the naming-named. We have a single event such that without both phases — both the namings and the nameds — we would have no event at all. What here most seriously interferes with full technical observation is the old set of verbal fixations which sunder name, named, and namer. The evil of reliance upon severed name, out of organized contact with manner and named, is illustrated, perhaps at its historical worst, in many of the procedures of professional logics today.

(f) These steps lead to a radical outcome with respect to *what* it is that is *named* by a naming, and so *known* linguistically, within an event of naming-knowing. This " what " no longer enters as if it were a " thing " outside the range of behavioral activity. Instead, " the named " is, in the primary case, itself a behavioral transaction: a signaling or perceiving that requires the joint action of its two presumptive " ends " — roughly, the intradermal and the extradermal — if it is to have any " middle " of factuality at all. This " what " that is named, therefore, neither rests upon some demand made by a " thing " upon an " organism "; nor does it enter as the determination of an " outer " thing by an " organism acting *solo*." The designational processes of organism-environs grasp the underlying signaling processes and bring them into increased behavioral organization. We not only say that a knowing without its known, or a known without its knowing, is an incoherence, but that a knowing-in-naming that pretends to know and name something outside of, or beyond, all signaling — or other organic-environmental contact — is equally an incoherence. The known-in-naming is primarily what is already being perceived or is otherwise in transactional process.

(g) Even more radical may seem a further assertion, again one to be taken strictly under transactional postulation. It is that the characteristic behavioral process is the process of knowing. Knowing — the naturalistic knowing-contact between organism and environs — is that which must receive basic examination and expression the moment the effectiveness of physiological techniques has been left behind, and the behavioral field has been entered. Its study constitutes the primary behavioral science. Knowing is not some wonder perched on top of organic life; it happens as process in and of the world; it is to behavioral science what radiation and gravitation are to physics, and what blood circulation and neural transmission are to physiology.

In this statement we are temporarily changing our form of expression from the technical manner established above, where " sign " was made the general name for behavioral process, and in which " knowing," as a special form of " signing," was limited to the range of " knowings-by-naming." The present passage is the only one in this paper in which this deviation occurs.[7] The deviation is made deliberately: first, because current uses make the word " knowing " run loosely and irregularly, as previously indicated, over almost all phases of behavioral organic-environmental contact, from the most primitive to the most subtly mathematical; and, second, because these same current uses subordinate " knowing " in one way or another to almost every other manner of psychological inquiry. Given this conventional looseness of expression and neglect of fact, which is found as much in professional psychology as in common speech, we accept it for one moment in order to secure the impressionistic report that is lacking at first view under the technical statement in terms of " sign."

In this background of expression, then, the knowing contact is the typically behavioral process; it is what must be inquired into first, instead of being evaded and slurred. For such inquiry it must above all things be brought fully into the " natural " frame of scientific observation. Here it is that kennetic inquiry brings the situation out into

[7] See footnote 6.

the light, and literally lays it on the laboratory table for detailed examination. In curt expression we may say, if we wish: "World flows, Life grows, Behavior knows, yet with the knowings and the knowns always components of the flow and of the growth." Most generally, then, the behavioral contact points are know-points in differentiation from physical and physiological contact-points. In kennetic inquiry, under the terminology of "sign," the crude particulate reports are passed over, on the one hand, and the wide sweeping generalizations are passed over, on the other. Transactional presentation is secured as observation gains strength. Translations into "minds," whether of moron or of mage, cease to enter. Use of the techniques of other sciences can be made without forced subordination or pretense of dominance — all of which means that the prospect improves for inquiry and report of the type we today call scientific.

With respect to the above positions (a) to (g), we may recall the various freedoms insisted upon for inquiry at one or another stage of the discussion. These freedoms are indeed at times as much in demand by physiologists as they ever are by behavioral investigators, since the best physics may at times constrict physiological progress, just as the best physiology may at times constrict behavioral; though, of course, in the latter case, protection against the old "psychical" and "mentalist" fixations is the primary need. The freedoms required are: freedom of postulation; freedom of observation under postulation; freedom from conventional speech-forms insistently surviving from prehistoric cultures; freedom for linguistic, as well as for laboratory, experimentation; and, finally, freedom for the establishment of new systems of nomenclature in the open daylight of inquiry.

A general theory of language should become practicable in this framework, perhaps one such as John Dewey has forecast in the preface to his *Logic* (21). No such presentation exists. What we have, instead, is ever-renewed divagation about minds and things, all fictional, with a fictional "language" as hare to both hounds. Leonard Bloomfield's linguistic study (11) is probably the only work to be mentioned as differentiated from the old line, and his construction was hampered by his use of a comparatively early form of psychological behavior*ism*, something not here employed in any phase.

STATES WITH RESPECT TO SCIENCE

The above program of observation and interpretation is not one of speedy recent development, but instead one of slow growth. It is definitely not in favor with — often not even in the field of vision of — metaphysics or other standardizations of the traditional psychological-philosophical terminologies. John Dewey laid the foundation for it in his famous essay "The Reflex Arc Concept in Psychology" in 1896 (20)[8] and has carried it forward through studies in almost all lines of cultural development, culminating in his *Logic, The Theory of Inquiry* (21). The present writer approached it in his study of group pressures in *The Process of Government* in 1908 (4), an inquiry much wider in scope than any study of pressure groups, the "discovery" of which is occasionally attributed to, though emphatically not claimed by, him; and he followed it later with studies of cross-sectional process in society (5), types of linguistic coherence in society (6), and communicational psychology (7, 8). Probably the best sociological construction undertaken from this direction is that of George Lundberg (30). In psychology the earliest and most important effort to see perceptions in terms of interactions between organisms and environs was that of J. R. Kantor (27). The ecologies are well known in all biological lines. Specialized cultural inquiries have in many cases almost reached the transactional form, though without, in any case that I am aware of, having made the necessary generalized formulation.

The greatest strength of the transactional approach at the present time is given it by the advances of physics following the initiative of Einstein, as this rested upon the observation of Faraday and its mathematical presentation by Clerk Maxwell (22, Chap. IV). Newton had achieved the construction of the interactional in its region of greatest usefulness. In the last generation, in place of the interactional, physics has secured envisionments of particle as wave, of mass as energy, and of gravitation as conformation of space-time. All these changes involve widened observation and are transactional in their orientation in the sense of that term as here used. The present procedure falls into line, though at a proper respectful distance, with Einstein's long-concentrated effort to secure a unified field theory for physics.[9] Any physical field theory of most general scope will, we believe, when once soundly secured, show

---

[8] At the time of the celebration of the fiftieth anniversary of the *Psychological Review*, this paper was judged by a vote of several hundred leading American psychologists to be the most important paper ever published in that journal. Even yet its values are only partially realized.

[9] Although the word "field" has repeatedly appeared in this paper, its use has been casual, and it has nowhere been specifically adopted, despite its apparent superficial advantages. This is partly because certain problems as to its application are not yet standardized by physics, but more because the word has been so widely abused by overly optimistic appropriators in other than physical regions. On this point see a discussion by Ivan D. London (29).

itself to be a process of knowing, as clearly as it shows itself to be a system of the known. The impress of the physical knowing will be upon the physically known, and the status of each will depend upon that of the other. In this case the need of a kennetic theory on the knowing side, as correlate to the field theory on the side of the known, will make itself strongly felt. Einstein's personal attitude, as is well enough known, will not tolerate anything comparable to kennetic theory on the side of the knowing, but the observation of Bohr, and of others, is clearly in line for it. Einstein, amidst the efflorescence of German philosophical terminology — the most resplendent in the world — maintains, largely in the Kantian tradition, all the ancient self-actional treatments, inclusive of the wholly redundant, entitatively personalized know*er*, at the very time that he has been the greatest of all leaders in overcoming the rigidities of the old "knowns" by expelling that sort of reification from the physical range. Bridgman, who has been the world leader in interpreting Einstein's work as human progress (14), holds in his latest discussion that the traditional metaphysical bias in Einstein is now at work where it may be positively hurtful to the results Einstein secures. Bridgman's comment is that "in Einstein's yearning for absolute information and meaning it seems . . . that the ghosts of Newton's absolute space and time are walking again, ghosts which Einstein himself had apparently exorcised in his special theory of relativity" (15, p. 19); and again, more specifically, that Einstein "believes it possible to . . . sublimate . . . the point of view of the individual observer into something universal, 'public,' and 'real'" (16, pp. 349, 354).

Recent Transactional Approximations

Several papers have appeared in *Science* within the past year outlining scientific development on lines sympathetic to, and in some cases directly comparable with, kennetic treatment. Cantril, Ames, and their associates expressly accept transactional observation and construction under that name for psychology. Bertalanffy proposes regions comparably transactional for physiological inquiry. Bohr sharpens his long-maintained stress on physical complementarity as opposed to the epistemological type of "reality" toward which he, as well as Bridgman, sees Einstein still straining. Dobzansky's discussion of "basic concepts" in the genetic field sees openings for ever-greater observation and research into "system" free from patterns and methods, the enforcement of which earlier workers demand.

Bohr's paper (12) is supplemented by his extended contribution to the volume dealing with Einstein's philosophical cerements in the *Library of Living Philosophers* (13). Where Einstein still holds to man-the-predictor as the test of whatever "element of physical reality" there is to be found, Bohr asserts the rights of verified observations as they come (the issue of "indeterminacy" being central to this discussion); he permits the contrasts of observation to stand undisturbed within the system of the known, asserting that in them "we have to do with equally essential aspects of all well-defined knowledge about the objects"; he finds here growth, not confusion; and he insists that "causality" will not be lost, but will in the end be better understood. Outstanding is his demand for the clarification of the many ambiguous terms, ambiguously standard to all the philosophico-scientificoid rummagings. Above all, the word "phenomenon," he declares, should be confined to "observations obtained under specified circumstances including an account of the whole experiment." Such a demand runs side by side with Bridgman's requirement (14) that the "operations" involved in any naming be made known, and with our present insistence that "observation under postulation" should be companion to "postulation derived from observation." With strictly practical intent Bohr quotes the ancient saying that men are both actors and spectators in the drama of existence.

Bertalanffy (9, 10) appraises the intra-integumental organism taken as subjectmatter of general observation and description, and finds it inadequate as a system. He then considers a wider system of organism-plus-environment and develops its import. His attention is not directed to the specialized range of behaviors-in-environment, such as we have been discussing "transactionally" in the still more specialized case of knowings-knowns, but instead covers the underlying field of physiology in general, and covers it in such a manner that, if he so happens to wish, he could readily apply to it the word "transactional" in a sense not in conflict with that in which Clerk Maxwell employed the word three quarters of a century ago, or with that in which we have been using it here. Bertalanffy makes his main differentiation run between "closed" and "open" systems. Most physical systems are closed systems. The organism by itself is an open system. In the technically closed system no material enters or leaves, reversibility is in most cases practicable, and an equilibrium-state in which entropy is at a maximum must ultimately be attained. In the open system, in contrast, there is a continuous flow of components from without, their flow and ratio are maintained constant, irreversibility appears in great degree, growth is characteristic, a steady-state characterized by minimum entropy-production may be approached, and, finally, when disturbance occurs, "self-regulation" operates to restore balance. The status of Bertalanffy's distinction of the physiological from the physical is akin to our present distinction of the behavioral from the physiological in that in neither case are sharp borders set up; in neither case are " existential realities " pretended to; in each case future studies may reduce or eliminate unexplored border-areas; and, more important than all, in each the differentiation rests jointly upon the techniques of inquiry established and upon the main systems of the knowns that appear as the outcome of inquiry. Under this approach Bertalanffy anticipates that biology may advance toward being an exact science, and physics itself will have new pathways open to it. It might comparably be considered assured that, if a sound working basis for the differentiation of knowings and knowns in system is sometime attained, all branches of scientific inquiry will benefit thereby.

Dobzhansky's paper (23) is throughout an exhibit of advancing freedom in genetic research. A transactional attitude, though not in specific development, is seen replacing the earlier interactional stresses deriving from common speech and physical formulation. Priority of research for physics is, of course, maintained here as in the other papers mentioned, and in kennetic inquiry as well. Terminology is not developed, and interactional expression is still largely employed. But whatever components are introduced as particulate quickly reappear in broadened system. The chromosome is an organized system. The genotype (except for viruses) " is an integrated system of many kinds ('loci') of genes." The genotype is in system with the environment. The environment of the moment " is only a component of the environmental complex that determines the mutation." The development of the individual " is an orderly sequence . . . in which the genotype and the environment are involved." The geneticist's growing freedom from the patterns with which he began is manifest in all this; and it is manifest as widening interconnection of the factors, not as their mechanistic application, one to another.

In three papers under the general title " Psychology and Scientific Research" (18), Cantril, Ames, Hastorf, and Ittelson argue in favor of a transactional approach for psychology, adopting that name as it is established in the book *Knowing and the Known* (22) and believing that they are justified in anticipating revolutionary developments when psychology comes to be investigated from such a viewpoint. The solid strength behind their position lies in the work Professor Ames has carried on for more than twenty years in his laboratory at the Dartmouth Eye Institute, and as elaborated more recently in conjunction with psychologists at Princeton through the Institute for Associated Research. One of his exhibits, that of the distorted room, in viewing which ordinary perceptive processes default, has become well known through widely circulated accounts in newspapers and magazines a year or so ago. An even more startling exhibit, dealing with motion rather than with objects at rest, is that of the revolving windows, the report on which, at the present moment, is still in manuscript (2). A rectangular window of conventional appearance can be seen slowly revolving on its vertical axis. A trapezoidal window, comparable in size, and similarly revolving alongside, cannot be seen to revolve, and cannot even be plainly seen as a trapezoid. Persistent efforts by experimenters to see complete revolutions of the entire frame have failed. Even when a long rod touching the window is used as an aid by the observer, he makes little progress, and that little is lost by the following morning. Headaches and nausea may mark his disturbance. What the observer " sees " — or, perhaps, " seems to see," depending on what meaning one gives the word " see " — is an apparently rectangular window of changing length, oscillating at changing speeds to right and then to left in a total arc of about 100° (if degrees of arc can be injected at all in a case like this), and then returning to its starting point, just as the rectangular window completes its full observed revolution.

Professor Ames's workshops offer some fifty interrelated exhibits of persistent perceptions or, more properly, perceptual processes, that are out of agreement with the commonly accepted approaches to the physiological and behavioral interpretations of vision. We have here not simply illusion in the ordinary sense, but illusion so pronounced that doubt is cast on the apparent " actualities " or " realities " of ordinary visual report, and the need arises for an ever more rigorous inquiry into the conditions under which such observation takes place. This is closely akin to Bohr's requirement, quoted above, for the word " phenomenon ": that its use in physics should be confined to " observations obtained under specified circumstances including an account of the whole experiment " (12). Professor Ames would hardly make as radical a statement as this. Nevertheless, in summary, he holds that perceptions as they come cannot be referred flatly to outer objects, nor to inner capacities as producers; and no more to the latter when neurologically postulated than when taken in the old slipshod form of the " psychic " (2, 3). Perception, to him, tends to become frankly and openly a " transaction " involving organism and environment in union, in the presentation of which both what he styles " assumption " and what he styles " purpose " or " value " must be included; namely, the past history of individual and race, and the advancing objectives of living man and group. " Prognostic directive " is a name he favors as best characterizing this perceptual activity of the organism. He has sketched the organization of the neural processes involved, and has proceeded with patience, ingenuity, and steady attention to openings for further test. In an address to architects a few years ago (1) he summed up: " While in no way denying the existence of the ' external world ' our disclosures apparently show that the only aspects of it man can know anything about are those aspects which are either helpful or thwarting in carrying out his purposes."

In harmony with Ames's work is that of Hoyt Sherman at Ohio State University in which unexpected abilities have been aroused in students by a drawing technique that organizes the total visual field with the muscular requirements of the procedure under way (34).

REFERENCES

1. AMES, A., JR. Architectural Form and Visual Sensations. In T. H. Creighton (Ed.), *Building for Modern Man, A Symposium*, p. 82. Princeton, N. J.: Princeton Univ. Press (1949).
2. ———. *Psychol. Monogr.*, in press.
3. ———. *Am. J. Psychol.*, 59, 333 (1946).
4. BENTLEY, A. F. *The Process of Government*. Chicago: Univ. of Chicago Press (1908); Bloomington, Ind.: Principia Press (1935, 1949).
5. ———. *Relativity in Man and Society*. New York: Putnam (1926).
6. ———. *Linguistic Analysis of Mathematics*. Bloomington, Ind.: Principia Press (1932).
7. ———. *Behavior, Knowledge, Fact*. Bloomington, Ind.: Principia Press (1935).
8. ———. *J. Phil.*, 38, 477 (1941).
9. BERTALANFFY, L. VON. *Science*, 111, 23 (1950).
10. ———. *Brit. J. Philos. Sci.*, 1 (2), 134 (1950).
11. BLOOMFIELD, L. Linguistic Aspects of Science. In *International Encyclopedia of Unified Science*. Vol. I, No. 4 (1939).
12. BOHR, N. *Science*, 111, 51 (1950).
13. ———. Discussion with Einstein on Epistemological Problems in Atomic Physics. In P. A. Schilpp (Ed.), *Library of Living Philosophers*, Vol. VII, *Albert Einstein, Philosopher-Scientist*. Evanston, Ill.: Northwestern University (1949).
14. BRIDGMAN, P. W. *The Logic of Modern Physics*. New York: Macmillan (1927).
15. ———. *Rev. int. de phil.*, 3 (10), 479 (1949).
16. ———. Einstein's Theories and the Operational Point of View. In P. A. Schilpp (Ed.), *loc. cit.*
17. CANTRIL, H. *Sci. American*, 183, 79 (Sept. 1950).
18. CANTRIL, H., et al. *Science*, 110, 461, 491, 517 (1949).
19. CONDON, E. U. *New Republic*, 11. (February 13, 1950).
20. DEWEY, J. *Psychol. Rev.*, 3, 357 (1896).
21. ———. *Logic The Theory of Inquiry*. New York: Holt (1938).
22. DEWEY, J., and BENTLEY, A. F. *Knowing and the Known*. Boston: Beacon Press (1949).
23. DOBZHANSKY, Th. *Science*, 111, 161 (1950).
24. FROLOV, Y. P. *Pavlov and His School. The Theory of Conditioned Reflexes*. London: Kegan Paul, Trench, Trubner (1937).
25. JAMES, W. *Essays in Radical Empiricism*. New York: Longmans, Green (1938).
26. JENNINGS, H. S. *Behavior of the Lower Organisms*. New York: Columbia Univ. Press. (1906).

27. KANTOR, J. R. *Principles of Psychology*. New York: Knopf (1924, 1926).
28. LOEB, J. *Comparative Physiology of the Brain and Comparative Psychology*. New York: Putnam (1900).
29. LONDON, I. D. *Psychol. Rev.*, 51, 266 (1944).
30. LUNDBERG, G. A. *Foundations of Sociology*. New York: Macmillan (1939).
31. PAVLOV, I. P. *Conditioned Reflexes*. Trans. by G. V. Anrep. London: Oxford Univ. Press (1927).
32. ———. *Lectures on Conditioned Reflexes*. Trans. by W. H. Gantt. New York: International Publ. (1928).
33. ROYCE, J. *Outlines of Psychology*. New York: Macmillan (1903).
34. SHERMAN, H. L. *Drawing by Seeing*. New York: Hinds, Hayden & Eldredge (1947).

Epilogue

It is written: "In the beginning was the *Word!*"
I'm stopped already. Who will help me further?
I cannot possibly rate the *Word* so highly.
I must translate it otherwise,
If I am rightly enlightened by the spirit.
It is written: "In the beginning was the *Thought!*"
Consider the first line well,
Lest the pen write too hastily.
Is it the *Thought* that works and creates all?
Should it not be: "In the beginning was the *Power!*"
Yet, even as I write it down,
I feel I cannot let that stand.
The spirit helps me! Suddenly I have it,
And confidently write: "In the beginning was the *Deed!*"

Goethe's *Faust*, translation by MacIntyre

Arthur F. Bentley: A Bibliography

BOOKS

The Condition of the Western Farmer as Illustrated by the Economic History of a Nebraska Township, Johns Hopkins University Studies in Historical and Political Science, Eleventh Series, Nos. VII–VIII. Baltimore: Johns Hopkins Press, July–August, 1893. 92 pp.

The Process of Government: A Study of Social Pressures. Chicago: University of Chicago Press, 1908. 501 pp. Second Edition, Bloomington, Indiana: The Principia Press, 1935. Third Edition, Principia Press, 1949.

Relativity in Man and Society. New York, G. P. Putnam's Sons, 1926, 363 pp.

Linguistic Analysis of Mathematics. Bloomington, Indiana: The Principia Press, 1932. 315 pp.

Behavior, Knowledge, Fact. Bloomington, Indiana: The Principia Press, 1935. 391 pp.

(with John Dewey) *Knowing and the Known.* Boston: The Beacon Press, 1949. 334 pp.

Inquiry into Inquiries: Essays in Social Theory. Boston: The Beacon Press, 1954. 365 pp.

ARTICLES

" The Units of Investigation in the Social Sciences," *Publications of The American Academy of Political and Social Science,* No. 149, June 18, 1895, pp. 87–113.

" Remarks on Method in the Study of Society," *American Journal of Sociology,* Vol. 32, November 1926, pp. 456–60.

" A Sociological Critique of Behaviorism," *Archiv für systematische Philosphie und Soziologie,* Bd. 31, Heft 3/4, 1928, pp. 334–40.

" L'individuel et le social: les termes et les faits," *Revue Internationale de Sociologie,* Vol. 36, March–June 1929, pp. 243–70.

" New Ways and Old to Talk About Men," *The Sociological Review* (London), Vol. 26, October 1929, pp. 300–14.

" Sociology and Mathematics I & II," *The Sociological Review,* Vol. 23, July, October 1931, pp. 85–107, 149–72.

" The Linguistic Structure of Mathematical Consistency," *Psyche,* Vol. 12, January 1932, pp. 78–91.

" The Positive and the Logical," *Philosophy of Science,* Vol. 3, October 1936, pp. 472–85.

" Physicists and Fairies," *Philosophy of Science,* Vol. 5, April 1938, pp. 132–65.

" Situational vs. Psychological Theories of Behavior:
Sights-seen as Material of Knowledge
Situational Treatment of Behavior
Postulation for Behavioral Inquiry."

Journal of Philosophy, Vol. 36, March 30, June 8, July 20, 1939, pp. 169–81, 309–23, 405–13.

"Observable Behaviors," *Psychological Review*, Vol. 47, May 1940, pp. 230–53.

"The Behavioral Superfice," *Psychological Review*, Vol. 48, January 1941, pp. 39–59.

"The Human Skin: Philosophy's Last Line of Defense," *Philosophy of Science*, Vol. 8, January 1941, pp. 1–19.

"Decrassifying Dewey," *Philosophy of Science*, Vol. 8, April 1941, pp. 147–56.

"Some Logical Considerations Concerning Professor Lewis' 'Mind'," *Journal of Philosophy*, Vol. 38, November 6, 1941, pp. 634–35.

"The Factual Space and Time of Behavior," *Journal of Philosophy*, Vol. 38, August 28, 1941, pp. 477–85.

"As Through a Glass Darkly," *Journal of Philosophy*, Vol. 39, July 30, 1942, pp. 432–39.

"The Jamesian Datum," *Journal of Psychology*, Vol. 16, 1943, pp. 35–79.

"Truth, Reality and Behavioral Fact," *Journal of Philosophy*, Vol. 40, April 1943, pp. 169–87.

(with John Dewey) "A Search for Firm Names," *Journal of Philosophy*, Vol. 42, January 4, 1945, pp. 5–6.

"On a Certain Vagueness in Logic: I, II," *Journal of Philosophy*, January 4, 1945, pp. 6–27, 39–51.

(with John Dewey) "A Terminology for Knowings and Knowns," *Journal of Philosophy*, April 26, 1945, pp. 225–47.

(with John Dewey) "Postulations," *Journal of Philosophy*, November 22, 1945, pp. 645–62.

"Logicians' Underlying Postulations," *Philosophy of Science*, Vol. 13, January 1945, pp. 3–19.

(with John Dewey) "Interaction and Transaction," *Journal of Philosophy*, September 12, 1946, pp. 505–17.

(with John Dewey) "Transactions as Known and Named," *Journal of Philosophy*, Vol. 43, September 26, 1946, pp. 533–51.

(with John Dewey) "Specification," *Journal of Philosophy*, Vol. 43, November 21, 1946, pp. 645–63.

(with John Dewey) "Definition," *Journal of Philosophy*, Vol. 44, pp. 281–306.

(with John Dewey) "Concerning a Vocabulary for Inquiry into Knowledge," *Journal of Philosophy*, Vol. 44, July 31, 1947, pp. 421–34.

"The New 'Semiotic'," *Philosophy and Phenomenological Research*, Vol. 8, September 1947, pp. 107–31.

"Signs of Error," *Philosophy and Phenomenological Research*, Vol. 10, September 1949, pp. 99–104.

"Kennetic Inquiry," *Science*, Vol. 112, December 29, 1950, pp. 775–83.

N.B. Julius Altman has compiled a valuable chronological listing of the writings of Dr. Arthur F. Bentley, published and unpublished, which is available for consultation at the Manuscript Division of the Indiana University Library.

Index of Names

Compiled by Julius Altman

Abelard, 123
Allport, F., 232–233
Ames, A., Jr., 349, 351–353
Aristotle, 270, 310, 317

Bacon, F., 310
Baker, R. P., 19
Baldwin, J. M., 13f., 16–17, 19, 26, 207f.
Bartley, S. H., 273, 274f., 275, 281–283
Beard, C. A., xi
Bender, W., 117f.
Benjamin, A. C., 118f.
Bentley, A. F., *see listings under titles of his books in subject index*
Bentley, M., xiii, 187f.
Bergson, H., 16, 248
Berkeley, G., 208, 250
Bernard, C., 197
Bertelanffy, L., 340f., 349–351
Bloomfield, L., 264f., 347
Blumberg, A., 102, 107f., 110–112
Bohr, N., 349–350, 352
Boole, G., 310
Bragg, W., 273
Branford, V., 43
Brett, G. S., 233f.
Bridgman, P. W., xii, xiii, 82f., 108, 111f., 116–128, 131, 134–139, 150, 177, 205, 295, 309f., 349–350
Brotherston, B. W., 231
Brouwer, L. E. J., 54, 56f., 57, 98
Brown, J. F., 165f., 187f., 200f., 219
Brunswik, E., 165f., 209
Burrow, T., 201f.

Campbell, C. M., 159f.
Campbell, J., 272
Cantor, G., 35, 98
Cantril, H., 349, 351
Carnap, R., Chap. XVIII, 101–110, 118f., 165f., 227, 277f.
Carrel, A., 76f., 94f., 228
Cassirer, E., 247f.
Chapman, J. J., 113, 251f.
Chase, S., 149f.
Chistwek, L., xii
Church, A., Chap. XVII, 320–324
Coghill, G. F., 157f., 180
Commons, J. R., xv, 151–152

Comte, A., 40
Condon, E. U., 339f.

Darrow, K., 117f.
Darwin, C., xiv, xvi, 14, 192, 198, 207, 221, 234, 238–240, 258, 261, 290, 311, 343
Descartes, R., 67, 74f., 268, 270, 283
Dewey, J., ix, x, xii–xvi, 14f., 16–18, 20–26, 104–105, 107, 150f., 173–174, 191f., 199–201, 205–206, 209, 221, 231–234, 238–239, 242f., 243, 245–246, 248, 249f., 258–262, 264, 277f., 283, 286f., 287, 289f., 304, 310, 318, 320–321, 323, 325, 331, 338–339, 347–348
Dirac, P. A. M., 133
Dobzhansky, T., 349, 351
Dunlap, K., 230
Durkheim, E., x, 66, 149f.

Eddington, A., 175, 178
Einstein, A., xi, 67–69, 74, 82, 117, 122, 136, 144f., 215, 293, 305, 348–350
Ely, R. T., ix
Euclid, 91–93, 317
Evans, G. C., 53f., 99–100

Faraday, M., 348
Feigl, H., 102, 108f., 110–111, 118f.
Fermi, E., 133
Fisher, I., 53f.
Fite, W., 17
Fraenkel, A. A., 98
Frege, G. L. G., 310, 343
Freud, S., 152, 181, 190, 196, 209, 231f.
Frolov, Y. P., 157f.

Galileo, G., 179, 311
Geddes, P., 43–44, 58, 63f., 86–87
Gibbs, J. W., 93
Goethe, 355
Goldstein, K., 201f.
Goodell, H., 210f.
Grassmann, H. G., 93
Grote, G., 243
Gumplowicz, L., x, 228

Halstead, G. B., 15f.
Hamilton, W., 123
Hamilton, W. H., 152f.
Hardy, J. D., 210f.

Index of Names

Hastorf, A. H., 351
Hecht, S., 279f.
Heider, F., 209f.
Heisenberg, W., 134f.
Herring, P., xi
Hidano, K., 272
Hilbert, D., xii, 54, 56f., 57, 98
Hobbes, T., 123, 148
Holcombe, A. N., xi
Holt, E. B., 146f., 152, 230, 250
Hull, C., 165f., 209, 289f.
Hunter, W. S., 209

Ittelson, W. H., 351

James, W., Chap. XIV, ix, xiv, 16, 18, 113, 149-150, 154, 181, 221, 283, 285, 288, 299f., 314, 342
Jennings, H. S., 196, 204, 218, 340
Johnson, W. F., 130f.

Kant, I., 69, 130f., 192, 291, 310
Kantor, J. R., xiii, 78f., 113f., 157f., 160-163, 171, 173, 183, 185, 200f., 238, 265f., 285, 348
Kattsoff, L., 109f.
Kaufmann, F., Chap. XVIII, 227
Kepler, J., 268, 270
Kleist, H. von, 247f.
Klüver, H., 158-159, 209, 284
Koffka, K., 200f., 219
Korzybski, A., 149f., 277f.
Kronecker, L., 57
Kühne, W., 272

Lane, M. A., 11-12
Lashley, K. S., 140f., 159, 236, 272, 282f., 284, 289f.
Lavine, T. Z., 243f.
Leibnitz, G. W. von, 10, 197
Le Play, F., 40, 43
Lewes, G. H., 123-124
Lewin, K., 113f., 163, 183-184, 200f., 219
Lewis, C. I., Chap. XI, 212-213
Liddell, H. S., 122
Lindsay, R. B., 124f., 125-126, 134-137
Locke, J., 69, 123, 208, 250
Loeb, J., 340
London, I., 348f.
Lowe, V., 231, 256-258
Lundberg, G., xiii, 348

Maine, H., 40
Malisoff, W. M., 109f., 197, 198f.
Margenau, H., 124-134, 137
Marshall, W. H., 284
Maurolycus, F., 270
Mauthner, F., 333
Maxwell, J. C., xv, 74, 293, 305, 348, 350

McDougall, W., 43-44
McGilvery, E. B., 16
Menger, C., x
Meyer, A., 159-161, 172
Mill, J. S., 123
Miller, C. H., 260f.
Milne, E. A., 293
Mitchell, W. C., 152
Möbius, A. F., 93
Molière, 179
Moore, A. W., 207f.
Moore, G. E., 250
Morris, C., 172f.
Mukerjee, R., 86-87

Nagel, E., 209f., 323
Natorp, P., 251
Neurath, O., 331
Newcomb, S., 15
Newton, I., 68-69, 74, 82, 121, 179, 185, 186, 222, 268-270, 348
Norris, O. O., 69f.
Northrup, F. C., 117f.

Odegard, P., xi
Ogden, C. K., 30f., 149f.
Orbison, W. D., 187f.

Pavlov, I. P., 121-122, 155-158, 170-171, 173, 180, 182-183, 199-201, 206, 208-209, 263, 289f., 342
Pearson, K., 136
Peirce, C. S., xiv, 19, 192, 199, 208-209, 221, 233-234, 238, 243f., 245f., 247, 258-261, 299f.
Perry, R. B., 232-233, 244, 246f., 253-255, 257, 261f.
Pillsbury, W. B., 16-18, 22
Platter, F., 270
Poincaré, H., 57, 59
Polyak, S., 271-273, 275, 282f.

Quine, W. V., 303, 305

Ratzenhofer, G., 228
Reid, T., 123, 157, 208
Reiser, O., 118f., 175
Ribot, T., 13f.
Riemann, G. F. B., 93
Roff, M., 218f.
Romanes, G. J., 157
Royce, J., 18-19, 207f., 341
Russell, B., xii, 35, 54, 56f., 97f., 98, 152, 255-256, 258, 277f., 295, 308, 310, 343

Santayana, G., 250
Scheiner, C., 270, 272
Schiller, F. C. S., 16
Schilpp, P. A., 109f.

Index of Names

Schumacher, G. A., 210f.
Shakespeare, 13
Sheffer, H. M., 255
Sherman, H., 353
Simmel, G., x, 18, 85–86, 88
Singer, E. A., 145f., 168
Skaggs, E. B., 230
Skinner, B. F., 209
Smullyan, A., 320–323
Snell, W., 270
Socrates, 13, 310, 317
Southall, J. P. C., 273–274
Spencer, H., 261f.
Spoerl, H. D., 230
Stevens, S. S., 109f., 117f.
Stuart, H. W., 18

Talbot, S. A., 284
Thomson, J., 63f., 87–88
Titchener, E. B., 181
Tolman, E. C., 117f., 209

Urban, W. M., 19

Veblen, T., 151

Wallace, A. R., 290, 311
Watson, J. B., 31–32, 34
Weierstrass, K., 54
Weinberg, J., 109f.
Weiss, A. P., xiii, 165f.
Welby, V., 58
Wertheimer, M., 200f.
Weyl, H., 97f.
Whitehead, A. N., 54, 56f., 231, 256–257, 277f., 295f., 310
Wiese, L. von, 88
Wiggins, F. O., 231
Williams, D. C., 233f.
Williams, R. D., 220
Wirth, L., 231
Wittgenstein, L., 109f.
Wolff, H. G., 210f.
Woodbridge, F., 142–143, 157, 170–171, 173, 189, 228, 249f.

Zeno, 7, 24

Subject Index

Compiled by Julius Altman

absolutes, 15, 30
abstract, 55–56, 73, 75, 93–95, 317, 323
accuracy, 322
action, 22
activity, 167, 169
actor, *see* individual
adaptation, 216–217, 238, 240, 261f.; *see also* behavior
agent, *see* individual
analytic, 104f., 298
animal behavior, 158–159
anthropology, 190
aspects, 242f., 315–318; *see also* part

basic, *see* fundamental
behavior, Chap. VIII, Chap. IX, 78f., 140, 151, 153–154, 161–162, 164, 166–167, 172, 184–187, 198, 202, 214, 224, 230f., 240, 259, 262–263, 296–298, 305, 307, 312, 318, 335
Behavior, Knowledge, Fact, xii–xiii, xiv, 140f., 171f., 348
behavioral superfice, 206–210, 218, 339–341, 346–347
behaviorism, Chap. III, 78f., 181
belief, 176f.
biology, 180–182, 201, 350–351

characterization, 309–310
circularity, 63–64, 98, 100, 144–145, 193
cognition, 195, 197f., 200f., 338
coherence, *see* consistency
communication, xiii, 223–224
concept, Chap. VII, 102–103, 105, 108–112, 114f., 151, 172–173, 176, 178f., 205, 206f., 226, 238–239, 243f., 249f., 252, 264, 309f.; development of, 123–124, 139–140
concrete, 93–94
Condition of the Western Farmer, x
conditioned reflexes, 155, 158
connection, 175–176, 181, 184, 193
consciousness, x, 31–32, 39–40, 42, 45, 50, 69f., 103, 122, 142–145, 231f., 234, 236, 241–242, 245–246, 248–251, 296
consistency, 54, 57–58, 61, 65, 70, 90, 96, 104–110, 127, 142, 166, 177, 191, 209
construct, 178
continuity, 47–48, 52, 55, 208
cosmos, 25, 34–35

cross-sectional approach, xi, xii, 34
cruelty, 95
cue, 219, 229, 308, 310
cultural, 339f.

datum, 237, 240, 243–245, 248, 252–254, 260, 262, 283, 285
definition, 323
description, 177, 190
designation, 297, 309, 341–344
discipline, 313–315
double-barreled words, 237, 249
duration, *see* time

ecology, 202
economics, 79, 98–100, 190
ego, *see* self
electron, 175, 178
emergence, 135, 144
empiricism, 117–118, 146
environment, 5, 20, 51–52, 183–185, 197, 206, 216–218, 285, 350
epistemology, 195
ethics, 18
event, 146–147
everyday language, 5, 13, 61, 96, 187, 326
evolution, xvi, 14, 185, 189, 192, 203
exactness, 322
existence, 4, 12, 14, 23–25, 167–168, 296, 340f.
experience, 217, 236–237, 249f.
experiment, 178, 226, 269
extension, *see* space
external, *see* outer

fact, xii, 20–23, 31, 38–39, 41–43, 45, 60–61, 65, 70–72, 76–79, 82, 115–116, 119–120, 122, 141–142, 172, 190, 196–198, 202, 214, 217, 230f., 233, 235, 240, 248–249, 262, 269, 277–278, 281, 287, 290–294, 306, 325, 343
family, 92
field, 184, 187f., 348f.
firm, 322
form, 79f., 86
formal, 103–106, 109
freedom for inquiry, 347
full, 315

Subject Index

functional approach, 8–11, 25, 27, 50, 70–71, 83, 87–88
fundamental, 178, 191, 298

gestalt, 108–109, 158, 200f., 218–220, 289, 307
government, 83f.
group interests and pressures, xi, 228

habit, 22, 335
haze, 116–117
heteroplasm, 12
historical, 34
homoplasm, 12
hypothesis, 84

I.Q., *see* intelligence
idea, *see* theory
idealism, 15, 16
immortality, 4
indirectness, 340–341
individual, Chap. I, Chap. IV, xi–xii, 34, 36, 58, 81, 91–92, 107–109, 112, 159, 164, 202–203, 211, 264, 298, 335
inner, 78–79, 83–85, 157, 184, 196, 201–202, 212–213
inquiry, 304
instanteity, 44, 46, 49
instinct, 32, 44, 94, 181
institution, 40, 42–43, 45–46, 71, 79–80, 83f., 85, 92, 151–152
intelligence, 69f., 262
intention, *see* purpose
interactional approach, xiv, 6–7, 150f., 160–163, 173, 185, 187f., 224
internal, *see* inner
interpretation, 90, 148, 177, 298, 307
isms, 134, 192

kennetic, Chap. XX, 337, 339f., 343
knower, knowing, 15, 145, 195–196, 202–204, 239, 241, 264, 286–294, 297, 299–301, 306–307, 327–329, 333, 337, 341, 343, 345–346
Knowing and the Known, xiii–xvi, 283f., 287, 303f., 318, 338, 340, 351
knowledge, Chap. I, 63, 65f., 73–75, 78, 115, 144–145, 167, 169f., 191, 195–196, 203–209, 223, 288–289, 295–296, 325, 337; about, 243, 245; by acquaintance, 242f., 243, 245; evolution of, 14; persistency of, 15–16, 20–21; stages in biological, 180–182; stages in physical, 179–181; stages in psychological, 180–182; uniformity of, 167
known, 195–196, 202, 204, 216, 287–294, 299–301, 306–307, 337, 341, 343, 345–346

language, Chap. XIII, xiii, xiv–xv, 28, 41, 55f., 60, 137–138, 149, 171–172, 191–192, 209, 219, 223, 226–227, 247, 264–265, 303, 309, 316–319, 322, 340, 344, 347
leadership, 19
linguistic analysis, 127
Linguistic Analysis of Mathematics, xii–xiii, 57, 277f., 348
local point of view, 92–93, 207
localization, 143, 153–154, 175, 178, 187, 204–206, 215, 222, 226–228, 271, 274–275, 281; *see also* space
logic, Chap. XVI, xii–xiii, xv, 55f., 102, 104, 106–107, 212–213, 302–304, 318–319, 320–323, 325, 329, 333, 343
logical behavior, Chap. XVI, 304–313, 316–317
logical positivism, Chap. VI, xiii, 101, 119f.

Makers, Users, and Masters, xi
mathematics, Chap. V, xii, 29, 41, 47, 53–54, 55f., 58, 62–63, 73–76, 208, 245f., 277–278, 297, 308–310, 319, 341, 343; foundations of, 56–57, 97; in psychology, 163–165, 219; in social sciences, 89–100; *see also* symbol
meaningless, 139
meanings, 11, 103–105, 107–109, 112, 191, 219, 225–226, 229, 264–265, 299–304, 344–345
measurability, *see* space
mengenlehre, 98
mental, 122, 139–140, 145, 149–150, 166, 170, 179, 182, 219–220, 283, 335; *see also* consciousness
metalanguage, 312–313, 327, 333
metaphysics, 110–112
methodology, 303
mind, x, 4, 14, 25, 83, 103, 122, 181, 212–213, 296
monad, 10, 197
money, 79

naïveté, 37–38, 45
naming, 143, 167–168, 299–300, 308–312, 317, 322, 341, 344–345
nature, natural, 291–293
naturalistic, xiv, 177–178, 192–193, 200f., 207, 224–225, 240
nominalism, 24

object, 167, 169–170
objective, objectivity, 23, 34–35, 83
observation, Chap. IX, xi–xiii, 21, 28–31, 124, 143, 146–151, 165, 167–170, 186–188, 193, 200, 224–225, 234–238, 241–245, 249f., 260, 293, 301–302, 337–339, 342, 350
observation base, 179–183, 185–186, 193–194
ontology, 304

operation, operational, 35–36, 40–41, 44, 108, 118–121, 125–126, 130, 134–137, 139, 150, 350
ordinary language, see everyday language
organism, Chap. IV, 20, 32, 39, 41–42, 50, 143, 154, 159–162, 167, 169–170, 171, 184–185, 193–194, 197, 201, 206, 211, 216–218, 224, 238, 285–287, 289, 301, 350, 352–353
organization, 179, 188, 301
ostensive definition, 308
outer, 78–79, 83–85, 157, 184, 196–197, 201–202, 212–213

pain, 95, 210–211, 250
part, 86–87, 97–98
passivity, 167, 169
percept, perception, 176, 188, 300, 351–353; see also observation
personality, Chap. IV, 29
phase, 315–318; see also aspect
philosophy, 195–197, 203, 206
physics, physical, Chap. VII, 35, 38, 45, 62–63, 73–76, 115–116, 167–168, 169f., 172, 178–181, 305–306, 311, 318, 335–336, 339–340, 345, 348–350
physiology, 5–6, 69–70, 167, 172, 181–185, 198–200, 279, 307, 335–336, 339–340
political science, xi
position, 298–299
positive, Chap. VI, 102, 105
postulation, xii, xiv, 35, 53, 60, 68–69, 77, 91, 141–142, 154, 166, 227–228, 245–246, 286, 292, 294–295, 298–302, 321, 337–339, 346, 350
pragmatism, 14–16, 23, 221, 240, 244, 247–248, 250, 259–260, 314
primitive words, 322
process, 20, 73f., 144–145
Process of Government, xi, 24, 34, 171f., 348
product, 73f.
psyche, see mental
psychoanalysis, 32, 140
psychology, Chap. VIII, Chap. XIX, xiii, 27, 29, 69, 114, 153, 163–166, 169–170, 180–182, 186, 198–200, 215, 222, 283, 288–290, 320–323, 341, 351–352; faculty, 6, 239; organismic, 161–163; physiological, 182–185; topological, 163; see also reductionism, situational theories
pure, 313, 319, 321
purpose, 215, 217, 335–336

quality, 29, 93, 95, 105f., 250, 315
quantity, 29, 93, 97

radical empiricism, 234–235, 239, 244f.
reaction, see response

real, 93, 262
realism, 15–16, 23–25
reality, 55–56, 59, 65f., 141f., 235; physical, 350
reductionism, 151, 167, 172, 224, 297, 307, 340; see also physics, physiology
reference, 175f.
reflex-arc, 199
relation, 56–59, 175f., 206, 249f., 252–253
Relativity in Man and Society, xi–xii, 29f., 34, 221
response, 31–36, 199
retina, Chap. XV
rule, 227, 303

science, scientific, xii, xvi, 14, 24, 27, 34, 38, 40–41, 49–50, 52, 60, 72, 102, 141, 151, 166–167, 177–178, 187, 198, 214, 287, 290, 292–294, 303, 311, 313–315, 337, 339
self, 19
self-actional approach, xiv
semantic, 58–60, 86f., 92, 303
sights-seen, 142–152, 157–158, 189, 218, 228, 249f.
sign, 177, 208–209, 229, 297–298, 340
signal, 156–158, 297, 300, 307–308, 340–342
situation, 159–160, 216–217
situational theories, Chap. VIII, xiii, 32, 36, 143, 145, 155, 165–166, 170, 186, 188, 191–194, 207–211, 224
skin as boundary, Chap. X, 156–158, 171, 183–185, 196, 209–210
social, xii–xiv, 18–22, 27, 29–32, 35, 40–48, 62–63, 76–79, 88–100, 153, 298; as a limit, 19, 47, 55
social distance, 86
social environment, 155f., 264
social science, 28–29, 222
social will, 7–10, 42
society, Chap. I, xi, 58, 71, 88; logicians' approach to, 17–18
sociology, Chap. V, xi, 27, 33–35, 40–41, 46–47, 75, 153, 170–172
sociology of knowledge, 243f.
solipsism, 23, 148
Sophists, 310, 317
soul, 4, 6, 38–41
space, Chap. XII, xiii, 33–36, 44–45, 48–51, 59, 61–63, 67–69, 80, 140, 165, 167–168, 203–204, 207–208, 217–218, 288, 292, 344; mathematical, 62–63, 73–76; physical, 62–63, 73–76, 88; social, 62–63, 76, 88–100, 154; vulgar, 62, 64–72, 75, 96
specification, 143, 152, 186, 191, 296, 309–311, 319
stating, 168–169
stimulus, 31–36, 199, 201f., 288–289
subjective, 23, 34–35, 148, 247–250, 253
symbios, 11

Subject Index

symbiotaxiplasm, 12, 18–23
symbol, 177, 208, 229, 278, 297–298, 300–301, 308–312, 319, 322–323, 341–343; see also mathematics and symbolic logic
symbolic logic, xv, 196, 312–313, 319, 341, 343
syntax, 105–106, 112
synthetic, 104, 298
system, 179f., 181, 185–189, 192, 204–206, 213, 225, 262, 291, 315, 342
subjectmatter, 297, 302

temperament, 18
terminology, 55
terms, see words
theory, 80, 177
things, 27–28, 56–59, 76–78, 79f., 82, 123, 144, 161, 185–186, 300, 308, 315–316
thirds, 169–170, 251–252, 259, 314, 342; see also mental
thought, 137–138, 191–192, 247, 249f.
time, Chap. XII, xiii, 33–36, 44–49, 51, 148, 167–168, 203–204, 207–208, 227–228, 249f., 259, 288, 292, 315, 344
togetherness, 295–296

transactional approach, xiv–xvi, 143, 145, 147, 152, 163, 166, 168, 170, 188–189, 216–218, 222, 229, 260, 283, 285, 293, 296, 299–300, 318, 335, 337–339, 342, 346, 352; early formulations, 20, 46, 52
tropism, 189
true, Chap. XVIII, 262
truth, Chap. XVIII, xv, 23–24, 73, 141f., 235

unification of science, 314
uniformity of knowledge, 167

vagueness, 276, 288–289
values, 3, 23–24
verbal frames of reference, 29f., 83f.
verification, 148, 235–236, 331
visibility, see observation
vision, Chap. XV
vitalism, 39–40, 44, 69, 77–78, 165, 180, 183, 185, 190

whole, 86–87, 97–98
words, xiv, 32, 41, 52, 151, 191, 225–228, 247, 298, 301, 309, 344–345, 355